A History of Zimbabwe

There is currently no single-volume history of Zimbabwe that provides detailed coverage of the country's experience from precolonial times to the present. This book examines Zimbabwe's precolonial, colonial and postcolonial social, economic and political history and relates historical factors and trends to more recent developments in the country. Zimbabwe is a country with a rich history, dating from the early San hunter-gatherer societies. The arrival of British imperial rule in 1890 impacted the country tremendously, as the European rulers developed and exploited Zimbabwe's resources, which gave rise to a movement of African nationalism and demands for independence. This process culminated in the armed conflict of the 1960s and 1970s, a war of liberation that ended with Zimbabwe's independence in 1980. The 1990s were marked by economic decline and the rise of opposition politics. In 1999, Mugabe and his party embarked on a violent and chaotic land reform program that disrupted the country's prosperous agricultural sector and plunged the nation's economy into a downward spiral. Political violence and human rights violations made Zimbabwe an international pariah state, with struggles continuing to this day. This book is targeted primarily at students of Zimbabwean history, but will be useful to both scholars of Zimbabwean history and those unfamiliar with the country's past.

Alois S. Mlambo is Head of the Department of Historical and Heritage Studies at the University of Pretoria, South Africa. He has published numerous articles on Zimbabwe's social and economic history and has authored and edited several books on Zimbabwe. He is on the advisory board of the *Journal of Southern African Studies*.

A History of Zimbabwe

ALOIS S. MLAMBO

University of Pretoria

<CAMBRIDGE>
<UNIVERSITY>PRESS</UNIVERSITY>
</CAMBRIDGE>

CAMBRIDGE
UNIVERSITY PRESS

32 Avenue of the Americas, New York, NY 10013-2473, USA

Cambridge University Press is part of the University of Cambridge.

It furthers the University's mission by disseminating knowledge in the pursuit of education, learning and research at the highest international levels of excellence.

www.cambridge.org
Information on this title: www.cambridge.org/9781107684799

© Alois S. Mlambo 2014

First published 2014

Printed in the United States of America

A catalogue record for this publication is available from the British Library.

Library of Congress Cataloguing in Publication data
Mlambo, A. S.
A history of Zimbabwe / Alois S. Mlambo.
pages   cm
Includes bibliographical references and index.
ISBN 978-1-107-02170-9 (hardback) –
ISBN 978-1-107-68479-9 (paperback)
1. Zimbabwe – History. I. Title.
DT2925.M55   2014
968.91–dc23   2013049916

ISBN 978-1-107-02170-9 Hardback
ISBN 978-1-107-68479-9 Paperback

To my family, friends and the hundreds of students who have helped shape some of the ideas presented in this book through their searching questions, thought-provoking challenges and debates

Contents

Figures

Every effort has been made to trace and acknowledge copyright. The
author and publisher would be pleased to hear from copyright owners
they have been unable to trace.

Tables

Maps

Acknowledgements

I would like to thank all the colleagues and friends who contributed to this book directly and indirectly as well as the hundreds of students who have sharpened my understanding of the complex forces that shaped the Zimbabwean historical experience. I am also grateful to the various scholarly journals where portions of this book were originally published for allowing me to use the material here and, through them, the many faceless readers who evaluated and commented on these studies as part of the publishing process. Lastly, I wish to thank Cambridge University Press for publishing this work.

Timeline

850–1150 – The Leopard Kopje Tradition emerges in south-western Zimbabwe.

1100–1280 – The rise and decline of the Mapungubwe state on the Limpopo River in southern Zimbabwe.

1270–1550 – Rise and decline of the Great Zimbabwe state.

1450–1830 – Rise and decline of the Mutapa, Torwa and Rozvi states.

1830s – Ndebele people fleeing the Mfecane and Boer migration in present-day South Africa move north and settle in what becomes Matabeleland.

1888 – Lobengula, the ruler of the AmaNdebele, is tricked into signing the Rudd Concession, a document that virtually surrendered his powers to Cecil John Rhodes and his partners.

1889 – Cecil John Rhodes uses the Rudd Concession as the legal basis to secure a charter from the British Government for his newly established British South Africa Company (BSAC) to occupy Zimbabwe. The company was granted rights to occupy and administer land, raise its own police force and establish settlements within its own boundaries.

1890 – The Pioneer Column of white settlers funded by mining magnet Cecil John Rhodes arrived from the south at Fort Salisbury, the site of future capital Harare.

1893 – Ndebele uprising against BSA rule is crushed.

Timeline constructed from 'BBC News: Zimbabwe profile – Timeline' www.bbc.co.uk/news/world-africa-14113618 (accessed 10 September 2012); 'Timeline of Zimbabwe', http://www.history-timelines.org.uk/places-timelines/46-timeline-of-zimbabwe.htm (accessed 10 September 2012); 'Timeline Zimbabwe', http://timelines.ws/countries/ZIMBABWE.HTML (accessed 10 September 2012).

1902 – Cecil John Rhodes dies at age forty-eight.

1922 – The BSA Company administration ends and the white minority opts for self-government.

1923 – Southern Rhodesia becomes a self-governing British Colony following a whites-only referendum on the future status of the country in which the majority opt for self-government.

1930 – Land Apportionment Act allocates land according to race and restricts black access to land, forcing many into wage labour.

1930–1960s – Black opposition to colonial rule grows. Emergence in the 1960s of nationalist groups – the Zimbabwe African People's Union (ZAPU) and the Zimbabwe African National Union (ZANU).

1953 – Britain creates the Central African Federation, made up of Southern Rhodesia (Zimbabwe), Northern Rhodesia (Zambia) and Nyasaland (Malawi).

1963 – Federation breaks up when Zambia and Malawi gain independence.

1964 – Ian Smith of the Rhodesia Front (RF) becomes prime minister and tries to persuade Britain to grant independence.

1965 – Smith unilaterally declares independence under white minority rule, sparking international outrage and economic sanctions.

1966 – The United Nations imposes sanctions on Rhodesia.

1972 – Guerrilla war against white rule intensifies, with ZANU and ZAPU operating out of Mozambique and Zambia, respectively.

1978 – Smith and internal black leaders Bishop Abel Muzorewa, Ndabaningi Sithole and others sign the Internal Settlement Agreement creating Zimbabwe-Rhodesia and black participation in government. Subsequent general elections are boycotted by the Patriotic Front (PF) made up of ZANU and ZAPU. The new government of Zimbabwe Rhodesia, led by Bishop Abel Muzorewa, fails to gain international recognition. Civil war continues.

1979 – The British-brokered all-party talks at Lancaster House in London lead to a peace agreement and new constitution, which guarantees minority rights.

1980 – Robert Mugabe and his ZANU-PF party wins British-supervised independence elections and Mugabe becomes prime minister of independent Zimbabwe.

1982 – Mugabe sacks ZAPU leader Joshua Nkomo from Cabinet, accusing him of preparing to overthrow the government. North Korean–trained Fifth Brigade is deployed to crush rebellion by pro-Nkomo ex-guerrillas in Midlands and Matabeleland provinces. Government forces are accused of killing thousands of civilians over the next few years.

1982–1987 – The Matabeleland *Gukurahundi* atrocities perpetrated by Mugabe's North Korean–trained Fifth Brigade in these years only end with the 1987 Unity Agreement when Mugabe and Nkomo merge their parties to form ZANU-PF.

1987 – Zimbabwe amends the constitution to introduce an executive presidency, and Mugabe becomes executive president.

1997 – On November 14 in Zimbabwe the dollar, stock market and economy all crash over concerns about payoffs to former guerrillas. Zimbabwe's currency plunges a record 72 per cent.

1998 – In Harare, Zimbabweans riot over soaring food prices. The price of corn meal, the staple food, has risen 21 per cent, the third increase in four months. Army troops are deployed to quell two days of unrest. There are also numerous riots and strikes.

1998 – Zimbabwe sends 600 troops to support President Kabila in the Congo.

1999 – Opposition Movement for Democratic Change (MDC) is formed.

2000 – In February, President Mugabe suffers defeat in referendum on draft constitution. Squatters seize hundreds of white-owned farms in an ongoing and violent campaign to reclaim what they see as stolen by settlers.

2000 – In June parliamentary elections, Zanu-PF narrowly fights off a challenge from the opposition Movement for Democratic Change (MDC) led by Morgan Tsvangirai, but loses its power to change the constitution.

2002 – In March, Mugabe is re-elected in presidential elections condemned as seriously flawed by the opposition and foreign observers. The Commonwealth suspends Zimbabwe from its councils for a year after concluding that elections were marred by high levels of violence.

2003 – In December, Zimbabwe pulls out of the Commonwealth after organisation decides to extend suspension of the country indefinitely.

2005 – Between May and July, tens of thousands of shanty dwellings and illegal street stalls are destroyed as part of a 'clean-up' programme called Operation Murambatsvina. The UN estimates that the drive has left about 700,000 people homeless.

2006 – In May, year-on-year inflation exceeds 1,000 per cent.

2008 – In March, presidential and parliamentary elections are held. A month later, the country's electoral body says Tsvangirai won most votes in the presidential poll, but not enough to avoid a run-off against Mugabe.

2008 – In June, the run-off takes place. Mugabe is declared winner. Tsvangirai pulled out days before the poll, complaining of intimidation.

2008 – In September, Mugabe and Tsvangirai sign a power-sharing agreement.

2009 – In February, Tsvangirai is sworn in as prime minister, after protracted talks over formation of government.

Notable Figures in Zimbabwean History

Banana, Canaan (1936–2003) – a Methodist minister, Banana was the first (non-executive) president of Zimbabwe from 18 April 1980 to 31 December 1987, with Robert Mugabe as prime minister. He helped to broker the 1987 Unity Agreement which ended the Gukurahundi armed conflict of the early 1980s in Matebeleland and brought rival political parties, the Zimbabwe African Peoples' Union (ZAPU) and the Zimbabwe African National Union (ZANU), together into one party called the Zimbabwe African National Union–Patriotic Front (ZANU-PF). He died soon after release from a term in prison for sexual impropriety.

Burombo, Benjamin (1909–59) – founder and president of the British African National Voice Association (BANVA) of Rhodesia, a trade union association with strong political overtones. In 1948, he was involved in the national workers strike that led to an urgent examination of wages by the Native Labour Board. He campaigned strongly against the 1951 Native Land Husbandry Act.

Chikerema, James (1925–2006) – became active in African nationalist politics during his sojourn in South Africa as a young man before returning to Rhodesia to help to found the Southern Rhodesia National Youth League (NYL) of which he became president (1956–57). In 1956, the NYL led a successful African bus boycott to protest a recent fare raise. Later he helped to establish the Southern Rhodesia African National Congress (SRANC) of which he became vice president under Joshua Nkomo from 1957 to 1959. He was also a leading member of the next party, the National Democratic Party (NDP). When NDP was banned,

Chikerema became a founding member of the Zimbabwe African Peoples' Union (ZAPU) in 1960 and was voted into the party's executive even though he was in detention at the time of its formation. Following ZAPU's ban, Chikerema moved to Lusaka, Zambia, where he served as ZAPU's vice president. In 1971, he left ZAPU and established the Front for the Liberation of Zimbabwe (FROLIZI) with Nathan Shamuyarira. He became part of the African National Council (ANC) led by Bishop Abel Muzorewa in 1974, returned to Rhodesia in 1977 and became part of the Internal Settlement which Muzorewa signed with Ian Smith to set up the short-lived Zimbabwe-Rhodesia Government.

Chitepo, Herbert Wiltshire (1923–75) was chairman of the Zimbabwe African National Union (ZANU) until he was assassinated by unknown persons on 18 March 1975. In 1954, he became the first African barrister in Rhodesia. He served as a legal adviser to Joshua Nkomo and ZAPU at the 1961 Southern Rhodesia Constitutional Conference in London. When ZAPU was banned in May 1962, Chitepo went into exile to Tanganyika where he was appointed the country's first African Director of Public Prosecutions. He was elected chairman of ZANU from its foundation in 1963. In January 1966, Chitepo moved to Zambia to concentrate on the armed struggle. He was killed by a car bomb at his house in Lusaka, Zambia.

Coghlan, Charles (1863–1927) was the first prime minister of Southern Rhodesia from 1 October 1923 until his death on 28 August 1927. A lawyer by profession, he was elected to the Legislative Council in 1908 and was in the House for the next nineteen years. He was prime minister when Southern Rhodesia decided in favour of self-government rather than amalgamation with South Africa and became a self-governing territory in 1923.

Dabengwa, Dumiso (1939–) – nicknamed the 'Black Russian' by the Rhodesians against whom he was fighting during the liberation struggle years because he was trained in Russia, Dabengwa was the head of intelligence of ZAPU's armed wing the Zimbabwe Peoples' Revolutionary Army (ZIPRA). Two years after independence, he and General Lookout of ZIPRA were charged with treason by the Zimbabwe government following the discovery of arms on a number of ZAPU-owned farms and other properties. Upon release in 1983 for lack of evidence, he and Masuku were detained for four years. In 1987, he became a member of the joint ZANU-PF Party and served later as a member of the ZANU-PF

Politburo. From 1992 to 2000, he was the Zimbabwe Minister of Home Affairs. He later resigned from ZANU-PF and became the leader of the revived ZAPU-PF.

Huggins, Godfrey (1883–1971) – prime minister of Southern Rhodesia and prime minister of the Federation of Rhodesia and Nyasaland, leader of United Rhodesia Party, Huggins, 1st Viscount Malvern, was a Rhodesian politician and physician. He was Rhodesia's fourth prime minister between 1933 and 1953 and then became prime minister of the Federation until 1956. He was the longest-serving prime minister in the British Commonwealth. He was one of the staunch supporters of the establishment of the Federation of Rhodesia and Nyasaland hoping that this would pave the way for independence from Britain under white rule, and he was instrumental in its creation in 1953. He was succeeded as prime minister by Sir Raphael Roy Welensky.

Kaguvi (d. 1898) – also known as Gumboreshumba, he was a precolonial anti-colonial leader who was believed to be possessed by the spirit of Kaguvi, an earlier leader of the Rozvi Empire which had been destroyed in the mid-nineteenth century by the Ndebele under Mzilikazi. Together with other spirit mediums such as Nehanda and Mkwati, he is credited with helping to organise and coordinate the First Chimurenga of 1896–7. He was eventually captured by the settler forces and later tried and hanged in Salisbury in 1898.

Lobengula, Khumalo (1845–94) – the son of the Ndebele nation's founder, Mzilikazi, he was the second and last king of the Ndebele people. In October 1888, he was tricked by Cecil John Rhodes' envoys led by John Rudd into signing a document called the Rudd Concession that handed his territory and people over to Rhodes. Despite subsequent efforts to repudiate this document, Lobengula lost to Rhodes whose British South Africa Company (BSAC) used the document to obtain a royal charter authorising it to occupy the land that later became Southern Rhodesia. In 1893, Lobengula led his people in the Anglo-Ndebele War and was defeated. He and his court fled northward from his capital of Bulawayo to die under unknown circumstances thereafter. His burial place is unknown.

Mangena, Nikita (d. 1978) – born Alfred Mangena, he commanded the Zimbabwe People's Revolutionary Army (ZIPRA), the military branch of the Zimbabwe African People's Union, in the liberation war. Mangena led a ZIPRA uprising against ZAPU moderates in 1977, and with the support of hundreds of followers in camps in Zambia, he attacked ZAPU's headquarters in Lusaka. While Mangena did not intend to lead a coup against Joshua Nkomo, he wished to reassert his power over the organization's militant activities. Soon after the uprising he was assassinated by unknown persons.

Mnangagwa, Emmerson (1946–) – a leading member of ZANU-PF, he received military training in China and participated in the first armed guerrilla attacks on Rhodesia in the mid-1960s. He was arrested but was saved from the gallows by his youth. Upon release from prison, he went to Zambia where he obtained a law degree and participated in ZANU's anti-colonial struggle. At independence, he became the Minister of State for Security from 1980 to 1988 and, thereafter, Minister of Justice, Legal and Parliamentary Affairs (1989–2000). He held several other key ministerial positions thereafter, including the post of Minister of Defence from 2009. Within ZANU-PF he held the positions of Secretary of Administration from July 2000 to December 2004 and Secretary for Legal Affairs from December 2004.

Mugabe, Robert Gabriel (1924–) – educated at mission schools in Zimbabwe, he later attended the University at Fort Hare in South Africa where he met African National Congress activists such as Nelson Mandela, Govan Mbeki, and Oliver Tambo. In the late 1950s, he taught in Ghana, where he became interested in Marxism and African nationalism. After returning to Southern Rhodesia in 1960, he became publicity secretary for the National Democratic Party (NDP), a nationalist party led by Joshua Nkomo. After the NDP was banned in 1961, Mugabe became secretary general of the Zimbabwe African People's Union (ZAPU), which was also soon banned. Mugabe broke with Nkomo and ZAPU in 1963 and helped to form the Zimbabwe African National Union (ZANU) of which he became secretary general. In 1961, Mugabe married a fellow teacher, Ghanaian Sally Hayfron, whom he had met during his stay in her home country. She died in 1992. Meanwhile, in 1964, he had been arrested for his political activities and detained by the Rhodesian authorities for ten years. Studying law during his time in prison through distance education, Mugabe obtained degrees from the University of South Africa and the University of London. He displaced ZANU founding President Ndabaningi Sithole to become the party's leader while both of them were still in prison. After his release, he went to neighbouring Mozambique in 1974 and, subsequently, led ZANLA liberation forces in a protracted and bloody war against the Rhodesian Front government of Ian Smith.

Mugabe joined forces with Nkomo in the Patriotic Front to negotiate the transfer of power at the 1979 Lancaster House negotiations,
and he became the first black prime minister of Zimbabwe at independence in 1980. Soon afterwards, his government's North Korean–trained
Fifth Brigade wreaked terror in Matebeleland in the so-called dissident
war, killing thousands of civilians in the process. Following the Unity
Agreement of 1987, which ended the conflict in Matebeleland and saw
ZAPU being swallowed up by ZANU-PF, the position of prime minister
was abolished and Mugabe became Executive President of Zimbabwe.
As leader of ZANU, now known as the Zimbabwe African National
Union–Patriotic Front (ZANU-PF), he was re-elected in all subsequent
general elections.

One of the undoubted achievements of Mugabe's twenty-seven years in
power was the expansion of education. At 90 per cent of the population,
Zimbabwe has the highest literacy rate in Africa. However, in 1990, a
struggling economy forced Zimbabwe to adopt a World Bank Structural
Adjustment Program, which called for the Mugabe government to move
away from Marxism in favour of a freer economy. In 2000, a controversial land resettlement process began whereby 10 million hectares of white-
owned farmland were effectively seized by the state and turned over to
settlers who ranged from peasant farmers to members of the political elite.
In 2008, Zimbabwe held very controversial parliamentary and presidential elections which saw the MDC winning a majority in parliament and
MDC president Morgan Tsvangirai winning the presidential race marginally, thus necessitating a run-off. The violence that was unleashed by
ZANU-PF at this point was such that Tsvangirai withdrew from the race,
leaving Mugabe to claim victory. The political stalemate which followed
was only resolved when the Southern African Development Community
(SADC) brokered a power-sharing agreement between ZANU-PF and the
two MDC parties, which was meant to provide an opportunity for the
parties to negotiate and implement certain reforms that would enable the
country to hold peaceful and fair elections in the future.

Mujuru, Joyce (aka Teurayi Ropa Nhongo) (1960–) – she joined the liberation war as a teenage girl and rose through the ranks to become a
member of the ZANU Central Committee as the Secretary for Women's
Affairs in 1977. She was also Commander of ZANLA in a ZANU Camp
in Chimoio, Mozambique. At independence in 1980, Mujuru became
the youngest minister in Mugabe's cabinet. She later held the position of
Minister of Community Development and Women's Affairs from 1980 to

1985 before serving in other ministerial capacities until she rose to the positions of ZANU-PF and national vice-president in 2004. She was married to Solomon Mujuru until his death in 2011.

Mujuru, Solomon (aka Rex Nhongo) (1949–2011) – member of the Zimbabwe African People's Revolutionary Army (ZIPRA) in the 1960s, he joined the Zimbabwe National Liberation Army (ZANLA) in 1971 and rose to the position of acting Commander-in-Chief of ZANLA in 1975. Mujuru became a joint leader of Zimbabwe People' Army (ZIPA), a united force of ZIPRA and ZANLA in 1976, Deputy Secretary of Defence for Zimbabwe African National Union (ZANU) in 1977, Commander, Zimbabwe National Army in 1981, and was promoted to full general in 1992. He was a member of parliament from 1994 to 2000. Mujuru died in a fire at his farmhouse south of Harare on 15 August 2011.

Musodzi Ayema, Elizabeth Maria (Mai) (c. 1885–1952) – popularly known as Mai Musodzi or Mrs. Frank, she was a pioneer feminist and social worker in Salisbury who did much to advance the cause of women in colonial Rhodesia, particularly those in urban areas, and progressively challenged the traditional boundaries about women's place in society. She devoted much of her energy to the Harare African Women's Club which she helped to found in 1938 and led until her death. The Club was engaged in a variety of activities, including charity, community service, recreation and mutual aid, and offered sewing and knitting classes and Red Cross classes. It also helped women to secure marriage accommodation and lobbied successfully for a maternity clinic staffed by women trained in the Red Cross classes. The Harare African Women's Club and the many women's clubs that were established throughout the country and modelled after it did much to provide women with a sense of self-confidence and independence.

In addition, Mai Musodzi served on the African committee of the Native Welfare Society and on the Native Advisory Board, where she actively defended women's rights with regard to the arbitrary arrest of women in the city, their eviction from urban accommodation and their subjection to humiliating medical examinations for sexually transmitted diseases. She died on 21 July 1952 and had a recreational hall in then Harari (now Mbare) named after her.

Muzenda, Simon (1922–2003) – former vice-president of Zimbabwe under President Robert Mugabe, he was born of peasant parents in Gutu District and studied carpentry at Marianhill Mission in Natal,

South Africa. On his return to Rhodesia in 1950, he became involved with Benjamin Burombo in the fight against discriminatory laws. He later became Administrative Secretary of ZANU and was imprisoned for two years for his political activity. He was imprisoned two times after that, remaining in prison until 1971. Upon release, he went into exile to Zambia and later moved to Mozambique. Muzenda became deputy prime minister in 1980 and vice-president of the country in 1987, when the position of prime minister was abolished and replaced by an executive presidency.

Muzorewa, Abel Tendekayi (1925–2010) – Methodist bishop and a moderate leader of the anti-colonial struggle, Bishop Abel Tendekayi Muzorewa was prime minister of the short-lived coalition government called Zimbabwe-Rhodesia from June to December 1979, which failed in its attempt to create a biracial government to end the civil war in formerly white-controlled Rhodesia. He was elected the first African Bishop of the Methodist Church in Rhodesia in 1968 and soon came into conflict with the Smith regime, which banned him from 'Tribal Trust Lands', where most of the black Methodists lived, because of his criticism of the racist policies of the government. In 1971, he led the campaign against a British-Rhodesian government deal known as the Pearce Proposals, which the African majority opposed. In 1978, Muzorewa and Sithole (who had lost control of ZANU to Mugabe) signed an agreement with Smith to install a majority government within a year. He was voted prime minister of the renamed Zimbabwe-Rhodesia and took office in June, only to lose power to Robert Mugabe in the 1980 general elections. Muzorewa died on 8 April 2010 at age eighty-four.

Mzilikazi, Khumalo (c. 1790–1868) – founder of the Ndebele Kingdom in what became Rhodesia and is now Zimbabwe, he was born in Zululand, South Africa. He was the son of Matshobana of the Khumalo Clan and became the clan's chief after his father's death. A fearless warrior, he soon became one of Shaka's advisers, but had a falling-out with him when, in 1822, Mzilikazi did not hand over all the booty he had obtained from a military raid and had to flee from Shaka's wrath. He and his followers moved north and north-west, incorporating conquered people, such as the Sotho and Tswana, into his group as he went. After staying in various parts of present-day northern South Africa, and clashing with the Boer Trekkers in 1836, Mzilikazi led his group into south-western Zimbabwe in 1838 to establish the Ndebele state in Matebeleland.

Nehanda (c. 1840–1898) – Nehanda Charwe Nyakasikana was a *svikiro* or spirit medium of the Zezuru Shona people. She inspired the Hwata Dynasty of the Shona to revolt against British colonial rule in the 1896–7 Chimurenga uprisings and worked closely with other spirit mediums, including Kaguvi. She was arrested, tried and hanged by the colonial government in 1898 for her role in the Chimurenga uprisings.

Nkala, Enos (1932–) – he was secretary general of the National Democratic Party (NDP) in 1960, assistant to the Zimbabwe African Peoples' Union (ZAPU) President Joshua Nkomo in 1961, member of the Zimbabwe African National Union (ZANU) Central Committee in 1974 and minister of finance at independence in 1980. He later fell out with the party and resigned from government and the party. It was in his house in then Salisbury that ZANU was founded.

Nkomo, Joshua (aka 'Father of Zimbabwe') (1918–1999) – educated at Adams College and the Jan Hofmeyer School of Social Science in South Africa, he returned to Rhodesia in 1947 to work for the Rhodesia Railways as a social worker. In 1951, he became secretary of the Railway Workers' Union (later Railway African Workers' Union – RAWU). Nkomo was president of the African National Congress (ANC) from 1952 to 1959, of the National Democratic Party (NDP) in 1960–1, of the Zimbabwe African People's Union (ZAPU) in 1961–2, of the African National Congress in 1975 and of ZAPU–Patriotic Front from 1976 onwards. He was detained by the Rhodesian government from April 1964 to 1974. He lost the independence general elections of 1980 to Mugabe of ZANU and was appointed Minister of Home Affairs in the first independence government, but was later forced to resign and was hounded out of the country in the early 1980s. He went into exile to the United Kingdom after being accused of anti-government activities associated with the dissidents of Matebeleland at the time. Nkomo signed a peace agreement with ZANU in 1987, agreeing to his party, ZAPU, being swallowed up by the former in a unity government. Thereafter, he served as one of Zimbabwe's two vice-presidents until his death on 4 July 1999.

Nyagumbo, Maurice (1924–1989) – in his youth, he worked in South Africa where he was a member of the South African Communist Party until it was banned in 1948. On returning to Rhodesia, he became one of the founding members of the African National Youth League (ANYL) and, subsequently, a leading member of the African National Congress (ANC) between 1957 and 1959 and ZANU Organising Secretary in 1963.

He was detained and imprisoned for political activism for varying periods between 1959 and 1979. In 1980, he was elected ZANU-PF MP for Manicaland in the eastern part of the country and appointed Minister of Mines in the first independence government. He later committed suicide following his implication in a scandal known as the Willowgate Scandal, involving the buying and resale of new vehicles.

Nyandoro, George (1926–1994) – after training as a bookkeeper, he became involved in the trade union and independence movements. In the mid-1950s, he was secretary-general of the British African National Voice Association, founding vice-president of the African National Youth League and, later, secretary general of the Southern Rhodesian African National Congress (SRANC). Thereafter, he became the general secretary of Zimbabwe African People's Union (ZAPU). In February 1959, he was detained for his political activities and was released only in 1963. In 1964, he moved to Zambia, where he worked for the banned Zimbabwe African People's Union (ZAPU). Nyandoro later quit ZAPU to help to form the breakaway Front for the Liberation of Zimbabwe (FROLIZI) (1971). He returned home to take a ministerial post in Bishop Abel Muzorewa's transitional government of 1979. After independence, he retired from active politics and became a businessman.

Parirenyatwa, Tichafa (1927–1962) – Zimbabwe's first black medical doctor, Dr. Parirenyatwa graduated in medicine from the University of the Witwatersrand in 1957. He was appointed medical officer of Antelope Mine Hospital in Matabeleland but had to resign from government service when some whites complained about a black doctor attending to their wives. In 1961, he entered politics full time and was appointed deputy president of ZAPU in 1962. On 14 August of that year, he reportedly died in a car crash on the Gweru-Bulawayo road.

Rhodes, Cecil John (1853–1902) – Arch-imperialist, successful businessman and South African statesman, Rhodes moved to South Africa from his home country, Britain, for health reasons in 1870 and subsequently made his fortune in diamond mining in Kimberley. Together with C. D. Rudd and others, he established the De Beers Mining Company. In 1877, he was elected to the Cape House of Assembly and in 1890 became prime minister of the Cape Colony. In 1895, he supported an attack on the Transvaal led by his friend, the Administrator of Rhodesia, Leander Starr Jameson, which sought to overthrow the Boer government and to install a British colonial government which would support the interests of British mining capital. The attack was a flop. He also used his considerable wealth to expand British power and rule into the land north of the Limpopo River, which was eventually named after him as Southern and Northern Rhodesia (present-day Zimbabwe and Zambia). He established the British South African Chartered Company (BSAC) for this purpose.

Shamuyarira, Nathan (1929–) – former editor of the *African Daily News*, Shamuyarira later joined ZANU and became its secretary for external affairs between 1968 and 1971. He helped to form the Front for the Liberation of Zimbabwe (FROLIZI) and was its treasurer in 1972–3. Shamuyarira rejoined ZANU and became director of the Party's Department of Education and administrative secretary in 1977. In 1980, he was elected ZANU-PF MP for Mashonaland West and was appointed minister of information and tourism.

Sithole, Ndabaningi (1920–2000) – teacher, clergyman and politician, Ndabaningi Sithole played a critical role in the early nationalist movement in Zimbabwe. Educated at Dadaya Mission School which was run by the Reverend Garfield Todd, who was subsequently to become prime minister of Southern Rhodesia, Sithole later taught at the same school, while studying for a degree at the University of South Africa. In 1953, he went to the United States to study for the Ministry under the American Board Mission of Southern Rhodesia and was then ordained as a Minister of religion. In 1959, he published a book called *African Nationalism* about African grievances in white-ruled Southern Rhodesia. In August 1959, he was elected president of the African Teachers' Association and joined the National Democratic Party (NDP) led by Joshua Nkomo in 1960, rising quickly to become the party's treasurer. When NDP was banned, he helped to establish its successor, ZAPU, and later led a breakaway group to establish the Zimbabwe African National Union (ZANU) in July 1963. In 1964, he was placed under restriction following the ban of both ZANU and ZAPU. In February 1969, he was sentenced to six years imprisonment for allegedly plotting to assassinate Rhodesian Prime Minister Ian Smith and two of his ministers.

In defending himself against the charge, Sithole publicly renounced violence and thus angered his political associates in the process, since he seemed to undermine the armed struggle that was already underway and which he, as the president of ZANU, was supposed to be championing. Consequently, his associates deposed him as head of ZANU, while they were all still in prison. After his release from prison in 1974, Sithole lived in exile in Zambia with a section of the African National Council, but later withdrew his faction of ZANU from it. In 1976, he attended the Rhodesian Constitutional Conference and served as a member of the Transitional Executive Council in preparation for the long-sought transfer of power to the black majority in Zimbabwe-Rhodesia in 1978–9. After serving that year as an MP, he ceased to play a substantial role after his longtime rival Robert Mugabe became prime minister in 1980. In 1987, he went into exile in the United States, fearing that Mugabe was trying to kill him. He returned to Zimbabwe in 1991, when he occupied one of two opposition seats in a parliament overwhelmingly controlled by the ZANU-PF party. In 1997, he was arrested for an alleged plot to assassinate Mugabe. He died in a hospital in Pennsylvania on 12 December 2000 at the age of eighty.

Smith, Ian Douglass (1919–2007) – the last white prime minister of Rhodesia before it became the independent nation of Zimbabwe, he led his white government in a unilateral break with Great Britain (UDI) in 1965 and declared Rhodesia a republic in 1969. Educated in Rhodesian schools and at Rhodes University in Grahamstown, South Africa, he joined the Royal Air Force in 1941 and fought in the Second World War in North Africa and Italy. After the war, he completed his studies at Rhodes and then took up farming at his Selukwe (Shurugwi) farm in the Rhodesian Midlands. He served in the Legislative Assembly as a Rhodesian Party member from 1948 to 1953 and was then elected to the Federal Parliament as a member of the ruling United Federal Party in 1953. In 1961, he was prominent in opposing a constitutional change to give Africans representation in the Southern Rhodesia Legislative Assembly. He resigned from the United Federal Party and helped to found the Rhodesian Front Party of which he became leader in 1962. In 1964, he became prime minister of Southern Rhodesia. Smith wanted to negotiate the independence of Rhodesia under white rule. However, British Prime Minister Harold Wilson would not agree, insisting on the principle of No Independence before Majority Rule (NIBMAR). Consequently Smith declared unilateral independence in November 1965.

The Africans responded by taking up arms in a bid to get rid of colonial rule, and this plunged the country into a fratricidal war that was to last until the end of 1979 when the fighting ended after the Lancaster House Conference provided for peaceful elections the following year. In the meantime, in 1978, Smith had negotiated an agreement with moderate internally based African leaders led by Bishop Abel Muzorewa, producing the ill-fated Internal Settlement Agreement that saw Muzorewa elected to the position of prime minister in the renamed Zimbabwe-Rhodesia. In 1980, Zimbabwe achieved independence under Robert Mugabe as prime minister. Smith continued to serve in the parliament as leader of the white-only Republican Front. He relocated to Cape Town in 2005 and died there in 2007.

Tangwena, Rekai (1910–1984) – a traditional Chief of the Tangwena people of Eastern Zimbabwe, Chief Tangwena was well known for his courageous and determined resistance to having his people evicted from their ancestral lands to make way for white settlers. He and his people refused to move even after their homes had been bulldozed down by the Rhodesian settler forces. He is also known for having smuggled Robert Mugabe into Mozambique to join the liberation forces after Mugabe's release from political detention.

Todd, Judith (1943–) – Zimbabwean nationalist and writer and daughter of former Rhodesian Prime Minister Stephen Garfield Todd, Judith rose to prominence in the 1960s as a staunch campaigner against the illegal white regime of Ian Smith's government. She was an activist who used her many skills as a writer, journalist and public speaker in support of the anti-colonial cause in Rhodesia. Her two books, *An Act of Treason: Rhodesia 1965* (1966) and *The Right to Say NO*, were banned in Rhodesia because they were highly critical of the Smith regime, and she was periodically arrested and detained for her political activities. She was, successively, a member of the National Democratic Party (NDP) and ZAPU and its successor the People's Caretaker Council (PCC). In October 1964, she was tried, convicted and fined under the Law and Order (Maintenance) Act for leading a demonstration by University College of Rhodesia students outside parliament in response to the banning of the *Daily News*, a paper that was critical of government policies. She lived in London in the 1970s and returned to Zimbabwe in 1980. In 1998, she was stripped of her citizenship and subsequently moved to South Africa.

Todd, Sir Stephen Garfield (1908–2002) – born in New Zealand, Todd moved to Southern Rhodesia as a missionary working at Dadaya Mission Station. He entered politics in the late 1940s and was first elected to the Legislative Assembly in 1946 and represented the constituency of Shabani from 1946 to 1958. He served also as president of the United Rhodesia Party during the same years. Todd succeeded Godfrey Huggins as prime minister of Southern Rhodesia in 1953. In 1954, he harshly put down an African railway workers' strike in the mining town of Wankie in the north-west. Despite this, however, he increasingly gained the reputation of being too sympathetic to African progress among the white population. He was eventually forced to resign as prime minister in 1958 when he faced a revolt by his entire cabinet over his policies which they considered to be too pro-African. From 1972 to June 1976, Todd was restricted to his ranch by the Smith regime for being too sympathetic to the African struggle for freedom and his open criticism of the Smith regime.

Tongogara, Magama Josiah (1938–1979) – born on the farm that belonged to Ian Smith's parents in Shurugwi in the Midlands of Zimbabwe, Tongogara rose to become the commander of the ZANLA guerrilla army. He attended the Lancaster House Conference in London in 1979 and was reportedly in favour of unity between ZANU and ZAPU. He was killed in a car accident in Mozambique on 26 December 1979, only six days after returning from Lancaster House in order to inform liberation soldiers in Mozambique of the ceasefire.

Tsvangirai, Morgan (1952–) – Tsvangirai became the second prime minister of Zimbabwe on 11 February 2009. The first prime minister had been Robert Mugabe from 1980 until the office was abolished in 1987. At the age of twenty-eight, Tsvangirai had joined ZANU-PF at independence in 1980 and made his name as a trade unionist. In 1988, he became secretary general of the powerful Zimbabwe Congress of Trade Unions (ZCTU), an umbrella organisation for the country's trade unions. In January 1998, there were widespread public demonstrations and riots in protest against escalating food prices, which resulted in the arrest of a number of people, including Tsvangirai. In February 1999, he was part of a ZCTU-convened meeting of the National Working People's Convention (NWPC) of more than 350 delegates from the unions and various civic organisations to discuss ways of resolving the numerous economic problems facing the country. Out of the resolutions of the NWPC emerged the MDC, which was launched in September 1999. In 1997, Tsvangirai was elected founding chairman of the National Constitutional Assembly (NCA), a body established by a coalition of civic society organisations and workers to push for a new people-driven constitution for the country. In February 2000, he led the campaign against the government-sponsored constitution, succeeding in having it overwhelmingly rejected by a national referendum. On 11 March 2007, Tsvangirai was arrested, beaten and tortured. In 2008, he represented the MDC in the presidential elections and won the first round, but not with a sufficient margin to enable him to take office. In the run-off elections held in June that year, he was forced to withdraw due to the unprecedented violence meted against his party by ZANU-PF in a bid to discourage MDC supporters from voting. Mugabe then claimed victory, but the political situation was so tense that the regional organisation, Southern African Development Community, intervened and brokered an agreement setting up a government of national unity, with Mugabe as president and Tsvangirai as prime minister. The transitional government was expected to introduce various political reforms that would make it possible for the country to hold peaceful and fair elections in the future.

Tungamirai, Josiah (1948–2005) – born Thomas Mberikwazvo, he joined the ZANU Liberation struggle and rose to become a leader in ZANLA. At independence in 1980, he became a major general in the new Zimbabwe National Army and a member of the Zimbabwe Joint High Command. In 1962, he was transferred to the Air Force of Zimbabwe as chief of staff, later rising to the position of Air Vice-Marshall. In 2004, he became MP for Gutu North and a member of the Cabinet as Minister of State for Indigenisation and Empowerment. He died in August 2005.

Welensky, Sir Raphael Roy (1907–1991) – the second and last prime minister of the Federation of Rhodesia and Nyasaland, leader of United Federal Party, Sir Roy Welensky was a Northern Rhodesian politician. Born in Salisbury, Rhodesia, he became involved with the trade unions in Northern Rhodesia and entered the colonial legislative council in 1938. There, he unsuccessfully campaigned for the amalgamation of Northern and Southern Rhodesia but did manage to push for the formation of the Federation of Rhodesia and Nyasaland instead. He became prime minister of the Federation in 1957. He was opposed to black majority rule and used force to suppress political protests in the Federation. The Federation collapsed in 1963 following the independence of Northern Rhodesia (Zambia) and Nyasaland (Malawi). Welensky returned to Southern Rhodesia and re-entered politics and opposed UDI. At independence, Welensky moved to England, where he died in 1991.

Whitehead, Sir Edgar (1905–1971) – Sir Edgar Cuthbert Fremantle Whitehead became a member of the Southern Rhodesia legislative assembly in 1939. He was Acting High Commissioner for Southern Rhodesia in London from 1945 to 1946 and then became Rhodesia's Minister of Finance and Posts & Telegraphs. During the Federation, he served as Minister for Rhodesia & Nyasaland Affairs in the United States from

1957 to 1958. When Todd was forced to resign in 1958, Whitehead took over the country's leadership as the head of United Federal Party. He led the Rhodesian delegation to the 1961 constitutional negotiations which allowed for marginal increases in the black representation in the Southern Rhodesian parliament. This and some relaxation in the racial discrimination laws alarmed some of the whites who then formed the Rhodesian Front under Winston Field. The new party won the elections in 1962. Whitehead remained the leader of the opposition until 1964, when he lost his seat and all seats went to the Rhodesian Front. He retired to the United Kingdom where he died in 1971.

Zvobgo, Edison (1935–2004) – founding member of ZANU and a Harvard-trained lawyer, he was the Patriotic Front's spokesman at the Lancaster House in late 1979. In 1964, he was arrested and detained for political activism against white rule in Rhodesia, along with Robert Mugabe and Joshua Nkomo. He was freed in 1971, and he spent a period in exile in Canada. In the 1980 elections, he won a seat in parliament for Masvingo, which he continued to hold until his death. As Minister of Parliamentary and Constitutional Affairs, in 1987, he made several amendments to the constitution that concentrated power in the hands of the president and moved Zimbabwe toward a one-party state.

I

Introduction: Zimbabwe in Historical Perspective

The Land and the People

Zimbabwe, formerly a British colony known as Southern Rhodesia until 1965 and, thereafter up to 1980, as Rhodesia, is named after historical Great Zimbabwe monuments built of stone that are near the southern Zimbabwean town of Masvingo (formerly Fort Victoria). Built between AD 1270 and 1550, these structures, about which more will be said later, are the second-largest man-made structures from Africa's remote past next only to the pyramids of Egypt. The country obtained independence from Britain on 18 April 1980, following a protracted civil war that pitted a dominant small white population that governed the country against the African majority from the 1960s onwards. Zimbabwe's largest city is Harare, the capital. Other major urban centres are Bulawayo, the second largest, and Masvingo, Mutare, Gweru, Kwe Kwe and Kadoma. Zimbabwe is a landlocked country in south-central Africa covering a total of 390,580 square kilometres. Map 1.1 shows the geographical location of Zimbabwe and its major towns. It lies between the latitudes of 15.37 and 22.24 degrees south and longitudes of 25.14 and 33.04 degrees east. It borders the following countries: Mozambique to the east, South Africa to the south, Botswana to the south-west and Zambia to the north. Zimbabwe lies almost entirely more than 300 metres above sea level and is dominated by the Central Plateau (Highveld) watershed which runs through the middle of the country from the border with Botswana in the southwest to the east where Mt Nyangani is the highest point in the country at 2,592 metres. On each side of the Highveld towards the Zambezi River in the north and the Limpopo River in the south, the Highveld slopes into the Middleveld and then into the Lowveld, whose

I

MAP I.I. Zimbabwe (geography.about.com).

lowest point at 162 metres is the junction of the Save and Runde Rivers on the Mozambican border. Running along the Highveld for a distance of more than 500 kilometres is the Great Dyke containing a wide range of mineral deposits, including chromium ore, gold, nickel, copper, iron ore, and platinum. The country's economy is based mainly on mining, agriculture, and, until the recent crisis, on tourism and manufacturing.

Among Zimbabwe's main rivers are the Zambezi River in the north along the Zimbabwe-Zambia border, the Limpopo River in the south, which separates Zimbabwe from South Africa, and the Sabi River in the middle. Fed by a number of tributaries, all three rivers flow through Mozambique into the Indian Ocean. On the Zambezi River is Lake

Kariba built in the 1950s, as well as the Victoria Falls, a cataract 106 metres high. The country is predominantly savannah (tropical grassland), with patches of dense woodland in the evergreen forests of the eastern borderland and teak forests in the north-west, north of the city of Bulawayo. It has a tropical climate which is moderated by its high altitude, giving it average temperatures of 15 and 21 degrees in winter and summer, respectively, and has, essentially, two seasons, namely the dry winter period from May to September and the wet summer period from November to March.

At 2012, the country boasted a total population of just below 13 million, 70 per cent of whom were Africans living in rural areas. Those living in urban areas were concentrated in the towns and cities of Harare (approximately 1.5 million people), Bulawayo (approximately, 700 000 people), Mutare, Kwe Kwe, Kadoma and Masvingo, among others. By ethnic composition, the Shona accounted for 80 per cent of the African population, while the Ndebele and other groups represented 16 per cent and 4 per cent, respectively. Included in the Shona group were several subgroups, such as the Zezuru, Korekore, Manyika, Karanga, Ndau and Kalanga, which spoke closely related dialects. Included under the category 'other' are the Nyanja/Chewa, Tonga, Shangani, Barwe, Sotho, Venda, Chikunda, Xhosa, Sena, Hwesa and Nambya communities. Whites amounted to less than 1 per cent of the population, which was a much smaller percentage than at any time in the colonial period. This was the result of a large white exodus at Zimbabwe's independence in 1980 out of fear of black rule and, subsequently, in the wake of the acrimonious land reform programme of the early 2000s. The white population comprised mostly English-speaking immigrants from South Africa and Britain, most of who arrived after the Second World War; Afrikaners from South Africa, some of whom arrived as part of the early pioneering settlers at the beginning of the twentieth century; and other migrant groups such as the Portuguese, Italians, Greeks and Poles. The rest of the population comprises Asians and mixed-race Zimbabweans known locally as Coloureds, comprising 1 per cent of the country's population. Zimbabwe has three official languages – English, Shona and Ndebele – although English is the main language of business.

Religion and Culture

The Zimbabwean population subscribes to a wide range of religions, with approximately 70 per cent being members of mainstream Christian churches; the main denominations are the Roman Catholic, Anglican, Seventh Day Adventist, Dutch Reformed Church and Methodist. Over the years, however, indigenous churches, mostly breakaways from the orthodox churches, and several Pentecostal and Apostolic churches emerged and grew rapidly. The situation is complicated by the fact that many African Christians are also adherents of traditional religious practices and move between the two seamlessly, attending Christian church services regularly but also consulting traditional spiritual leaders when necessary. There are, however, many Africans who subscribe only to traditional religions. The largest Christian denomination in the country, the Roman Catholic, accounts for approximately 7 per cent of the population. Approximately 1 per cent of Zimbabwe's population is Muslim and consists mainly of people of Asian, North African and Middle Eastern origin and some indigenous Southern Africans, including Zimbabweans. Other religions represented in the country are Judaism, Hinduism, Buddhism, the Bahai Faith and Greek Orthodoxy.

Zimbabwe is a land of many cultures that reflect its multi-ethnic and multiracial character. The most dominant cultural traits are those associated with the Shona-speaking peoples who comprise the majority. Other cultures include those of the Ndebele, White, Indian, Coloured and other African minority groups. Like most African countries, Zimbabwe was an artificial creation of Western colonialism which drew its present boundaries without any real understanding of the demographic/cultural realities on the ground; as such, it lacked a homogenous precolonial ethnic or cultural united entity and instead brought together different cultures and ethnicities into an imagined country, to be called Rhodesia. It is, therefore, not possible to speak of a collective Zimbabwean culture but only of Zimbabwean cultures.

Brief Historical Outline

Until British colonisation in 1890, the country was the home of indigenous black people, beginning with Stone Age hunter-gatherers, the San, from as far back as 200 BC. The San were later displaced by Bantu-speaking peoples, the ancestors of present-day Shona-speaking inhabitants of Zimbabwe. In the early nineteenth century, a series of incursions from Bantu-speaking peoples of Nguni stock from present-day South Africa introduced the Ndebele people, the majority of whom now inhabit south-western Zimbabwe and whose major urban centre is Bulawayo.

Other Nguni groups, such as the Gaza-Nguni, settled in the south-eastern regions of the country and intermarried with the local Shona population to produce the present-day Ndau ethnic group. British occupation began with the arrival of Cecil John Rhodes-sponsored Pioneer Column in 1890, marking the beginning of an eighty-year-long colonial dispensation that saw the gradual expansion of a white settler population and the development of a modern economy based largely on mining, agriculture and, eventually, manufacturing heavily dependent on cheap African labour.

A racially based sociopolitical regime prevailed throughout the colonial period in which whiteness equalled power and privilege while blacks were marginalised economically, politically and socially. The tensions spawned by this discriminatory system resulted in many incidences of racial friction. In the meantime, Southern Rhodesia was granted self-government by the British in 1923, following a whites-only referendum in which the settlers had to decide whether to join South Africa as that country's fifth province or to govern themselves; they chose the latter. Under this arrangement, Southern Rhodesians could govern themselves in all but a few areas.

In 1953, for a variety of economic and political reasons, Southern Rhodesia joined its neighbours, Northern Rhodesia (Zambia), and Nyasaland (Malawi), in the Federation of the Rhodesias and Nyasaland, also known as the Central African Federation. The Federation collapsed in 1963 partly because of African opposition to it. In 1965, Southern Rhodesia unilaterally declared its independence from Britain, having failed to persuade the colonial power to grant such independence voluntarily. Thereafter, the country was caught in the throes of an armed conflict that only ended with Zimbabwe's independence in 1980 and the installation of a black majority rule government of the Zimbabwe African National Union-Patriotic Front (ZANU-PF) party under the leadership of Robert Gabriel Mugabe.

In 2000, Zimbabwe entered a major crisis period which was sparked by a controversial land reform programme referred to by government proponents as the fast-track land reform programme, which also involved violent farm invasions by government supporters, some of whom were veterans of the anti-colonial armed struggle. The international outcry that followed this campaign and the increasingly intolerant attitudes of the ruling party towards any political opposition led to a massive exodus of skilled professionals from the country, the ostracism of the country by some of its major trading partners and investors and an economic downward spiral that was the hallmark of what came to be known as the Zimbabwean Crisis of the first decade of the twenty-first century.

This book traces the history outlined earlier in the chapter in greater detail in order to identify the forces that have shaped Zimbabwe's recent lived experience and the trajectory of its development in the hope that this will best contextualise the country's present situation. Chapter 1 introduces the study, while Chapter 2 traces the history of the early pre-colonial states from the original societies of the San and the early state of Mapungubwe, through the Great Zimbabwe, Mutapa, Rozvi and Torwa states to the Nguni conquest state in the mid-nineteenth century. Chapter 3 focuses on the coming of British colonisation in 1890 and African responses, including the Anglo-Ndebele War of 1893 and the *Chimurenga/Umvukela* uprisings of 1896–7. Chapter 4 discusses colonial society and economy under the colonial state until 1953, highlighting the growth of the modern state and the colonial contradictions that were later to shape the racial confrontation of the 1960s and beyond. Chapter 5 briefly examines the Federation of Rhodesia and Nyasaland from 1953 to 1963 and its subsequent break-up. Chapter 6 traces the rise of Zimbabwean African nationalism from the interwar period, African nationalism's radicalisation during World War II and the rise of mass African confrontational nationalist politics in the immediate post-war period. Various post-war African nationalist parties are examined until the banning of the two largest parties by the government of Ian Smith in 1963.

Chapter 7 traces the coming of the unilateral declaration of independence from Britain by the government of Ian Smith and international reaction. The chapter also focuses on the reaction of black Zimbabweans to the Unilateral Declaration of Independence (UDI) in the form of the armed guerrilla struggle which was to last until 1979. The scope, nature and impact of the guerrilla campaign by African liberation movements and other forms of African protests are also analysed. The chapter ends with a discussion of the Lancaster House negotiations that ushered in Zimbabwe's independence in 1980. Zimbabwe's independence experience from 1980 to 2000 is discussed in Chapter 8, while Chapter 9 analyses the Zimbabwean crisis from 2000 to 2009. Chapter 10 concludes the study by focusing on the challenges that have faced the country in its quest to build a common sense of nationhood and the prospects for the future. The book fills a big gap in Zimbabwe's historical literature where much has been written on various aspects and themes of the country's experience but there is a glaring absence of a comprehensive, informative and accessible one-volume study that those who seek to understand the forces that shaped the country's experience can read. It will also be useful as a textbook in university courses on African history and politics.

2

Early States, c. 900–1900

Introduction

The colonisation of Africa at the end of the nineteenth century was often justified by claims that the colonised lands were 'uncivilised' and inhabited by a barbaric people without any history or, in the case of the South African interior and Zimbabwe, that the land was, in any case, empty and there for the taking. Both alleged attributes of pre-colonial Africa appear in a statement by the former Rhodesian Prime Minister Ian Smith in 1997, in which he justified the occupation of Zimbabwe by a group known as the Pioneer Column that were sponsored by the arch-imperialist Cecil John Rhodes by claiming that these invaders were

going into uncharted country, the domain of the lion, elephant, the buffalo, the rhinoceros – all deadly killers –the black mamba, the most deadly of all snakes, and the Matabele [sic], with Lobengula's impis, the most deadly of all black warriors.... But if the mission was to raise the flag for queen and country, no questions were asked. Moreover, their consciences were clear: to the west the Matabeles had recently moved in.... The eastern parts of the country were settled by a number of different tribes, nomadic people who had migrated from the north and east, constantly moving to and fro in order to accommodate their needs and wants. To the south were scattered settlements of Shangaans from Mozambique and Northern Transvaal. *Clearly it was no man's land, as Cecil Rhodes and the politicians back in London had confirmed, so no one could accuse them of trespassing or taking part in an invasion.*[1]

---

[1] I. D. Smith, *The Great Betrayal*, (London: Blake Publishing, 1997), 1–2 (italics added).

The dominant European view of non-European peoples then was based on racist assumptions of their inferiority as a justification for their conquest and colonisation. Thus, invariably, the lands occupied by indigenous peoples were regarded as either empty or uncivilised. The alleged 'emptiness' of colonised lands in Africa was based on a logic that maintained that areas that were not inhabited by Europeans were empty and there for the taking and that, where indigenous people were present, they were only nomadic wanderers without legal claim to the territory. It was also argued that such indigenous societies had no understanding of private property and, therefore, the land they occupied was not owned by anyone and thus available to the incoming Europeans. Lastly, proponents of this view insisted that indigenous people were not 'rational' beings and, therefore, had no institutions, culture or beliefs worthy of respect.[2]

This dismissive view of the African past was most clearly articulated by Professor Hugh Trevor-Roper of Oxford, first in a public lecture in 1960 and then, again, in 1969 when he categorically asserted that there was no African history before the arrival of the white man on the continent and insisted that the entire African continent, including Ethiopia and Egypt, was 'unhistoric'.[3] He stated:

Perhaps in the future ... there will be some African history to teach. But at present there is none: there is only the history of Europeans in Africa. The rest is largely ... darkness. And darkness is not a subject of history.

He added, in what can be regarded as a forerunner of the 'West and the Rest' worldview:

The history of the world for the past five centuries, in so far as it has significance, has been European history.... It follows that the study of history is and must be Eurocentric. For we can ill afford to amuse ourselves with the unrewarding gyrations of barbarous tribes in picturesque but irrelevant corners of the globe.[4]

The prevailing Western colonial view of precolonial Africa, therefore, was that there was no usable past and that there existed no coherent, organised and functioning political systems and structures until the white people arrived on the continent.

---

[2] J. M. Blaut, *The Colonizer's Model of the World: Geographical and Eurocentric History*, (New York: The Guilford Press, 1993), 15.

[3] The statement was originally made during a series of lectures in the University of Sussex transmitted by BBC Television. The lectures appeared in print in *The Listener* in 1963 and finally became a book: *The Rise of Christian Europe*, (London, 1965), 9–11.

[4] Hugh Trevor-Roper, 'The Past and Present: History and Sociology', *Past and Present*, 42 (1969): 3–17.

However, contrary to the claims of colonial historiography which portrayed the land between the Limpopo and Zambezi Rivers as a land that was either empty or inhabited by a savage people without a history or culture and who were only 'civilised' by the incoming white colonial settlers at the end of the nineteenth century, the country that became the British colony of Southern Rhodesia in 1890 and Zimbabwe at its independence in 1980 had, in fact, been home to centuries-old civilisations that dated back to the original San stone-age hunter-gatherers.

The arrival of Bantu-speaking migrants into the territory more than 2,000 years ago laid the foundation for a series of large and prosperous political entities or states that included, in chronological order, Mapungubwe, Great Zimbabwe, Mutapa and the Torwa/Rozvi states, all of which were established by ancestors of the present Shona-speaking people of Zimbabwe. The mid-nineteenth century saw the demise of the last of the Shona states, the Rozvi Empire, at the hands of Nguni invaders from the south, who established the Ndebele state under King Mzilikazi. This state was, in turn, destroyed by the incoming white colonial state in the 1890s. Caution must be taken, however, not to regard Zimbabwe's precolonial history as nothing more than a succession of large and powerful states, for while powerful states did exist prior to British colonisation, many groups lived outside the borders and control of such states, even though they interacted with them. Moreover, while precolonial Zimbabwean history has tended to be presented as a series of 'Shona 'empires' or states succeeding each other until the nineteenth century, the reality was that, until the usage of the term on the eve of British colonialism in the early twentieth century, no one in the territory that became Zimbabwe ever called themselves Shona, and neither was there a language with such a name.

The term 'Shona' is thus a creation of colonial rule, which is now used to describe people with a similar linguistic, cultural and political past, but who referred to themselves and were known by others by various names, such as the 'Karanga' of Great Zimbabwe (1270–1550); the 'Togwa' (Torwa) of the north-west (1450–1690), the Mutapa in the north (1450–1902) and the 'Rozvi' in the south-west (1690–1830), and other numerous small groups who never belonged to one monolithic group.[5] Nevertheless, these various groups did belong to what has been called

[5] G. Mazarire, 'Reflections on Pre-Colonial Zimbabwe, c.850–1880', in B. Raftopoulos & A. Mlambo (eds.), *Becoming Zimbabwe: A History from the Pre-Colonial Period to 2008*, (Harare: Weaver/South Africa: Jacana Media, 2009), 1–38.

the 'Zimbabwean Culture',[6] which evolved over time to produce the various phases of the political formations of the people of the Zimbabwean Plateau. In addition, apart from the aforementioned large political entities, there were also several autochthonous communities that lived in smaller units in the same area.

The Peopling of Zimbabwe

The San

Archaeological evidence of Stone Age cultures going back some 100,000 years, such as stone implements and arrowheads, as well as thousands of sites containing rock paintings throughout Zimbabwe, suggests that the San, hunter-gatherers whose descendants now live in the Kalahari Desert, were the first inhabitants of Zimbabwe, who were subsequently driven off their ancestral lands or incorporated by incoming Iron Age Bantu-speaking groups around the tenth and eleventh centuries AD. The San are reportedly the descendants of the original *Homo sapiens* (thinking man or modern-day man) and have the oldest gene pattern among all human beings. This means that most, if not all, other humans on the planet are descendants from that one gene type, and that these were the ancestors of most mankind. Early San society left a rich legacy of magnificent cave paintings that abound throughout southern Africa in general and in Zimbabwe, particularly notable in the Matopos Hills south of the modern city of Bulawayo, which depict animals, human beings and human activities such as hunting and dancing, while some seem to symbolise spiritual beliefs.[7] (See Figure 2.1.)

---

[6] I. Pikirayi, *The Zimbabwe Culture: Origins and Decline of Southern Zambezian States*, (Oxford: Rowman and Littlefied Publishers, Inc., 2001).

[7] Over 3 000 sites have been catalogued at Matopos Hills alone, with two major periods of painting activity established, from the 8th to the 6th millennium BC and then again from 200 BCE to 500 CE. See P. S. Garlake, *The Painted Caves: An Introduction to the Prehistoric Art of Zimbabwe* (Harare: Modus Publications, 1987), 6, 30, 32, cited in A. D. C. Hyland and S. I. K. Umenne, 'Place, Tradition and Memory: Tangible Aspects of the Intangible Heritage in the Cultural Landscapes of Zimbabwe: A Case Study of the Matobo Hills' (2006), Presented at the Forum UNESCO University and Heritage 10th International Seminar *Cultural Landscapes in the 21st Century, Newcastle-Upon-Tyne*, April 2005, available at www.ncl.ac.uk/unescolandscapes/files/UMENNESampson%20 HYLANDAnthony.pdf (accessed 10 June 2012). See also P. S. Garlake, 'Structure and Meaning in the Prehistoric Art of Zimbabwe', Seventeenth Annual Mans Wolff Memorial Lecture, 15 April, 1987, Indiana University, Bloomington, Indiana, available at https:// scholarworks.iu.edu/dspace/bitstream/.../StructureGarlake.pdf? (accessed 20 March 2012).

FIGURE 2.1. San rock art showing human figures, antelopes and a predator.

What little is known about the San indicates that theirs was a stateless society that subsisted on gathering plants and hunting wild game, and whose population lived in relatively small, independent, self-sufficient family groups with no sense of a pan-San identity. Decisions among groups were based on consensus, as San society was an essentially egalitarian one in which material possessions were distributed equitably. While men and women played different roles in society, with men responsible for hunting while women were the gatherers, there was no apparent gender discrimination among them.

Bantu-Speaking Peoples

The next inhabitants after the San were Iron Age Bantu-speaking peoples. Pottery discovered at various archaeological sites suggests that stone-using herders of cattle and sheep had entered the region, possibly from the north, around 150 BC. These were groups of migrants from the northern parts of the African continent, who spoke languages that belong to a cluster that linguists have identified as Bantu. By the fourth century AD, groups of Bantu-speaking people had established farming villages on the Zimbabwean Plateau south of the Zambezi River

These Iron Age agriculturalists grew a variety of cereals, including millet and sorghum, and beans using a slash-and-burn form of agriculture.

They also kept cattle, sheep and goats. They produced a distinctive comb-stamped pottery that has been identified at various archaeological sites throughout the country. In addition, they worked iron to produce a variety of implements such as hoes, axes, spears, arrows and knives and made bracelets, necklaces, bangles and other ornaments from copper. These items as well as ivory, skins and precious metals were traded by the emerging entrepreneurial and ruling elites with the Swahili Coast on the Indian Ocean from the seventh century onwards, in exchange for imported glass beads from India and Persia, ceramics from the Persian Gulf and the Far East and other luxuries. As more wealth was accumulated and society became progressively differentiated, the states that would dominate the Zimbabwean Plateau for so long emerged. By the end of the first millennium, the southern African coast and interior had become integrated into the Indian Ocean commercial network.[8]

With long-distance trade came social differentiation and the development of state systems. For this reason, the growth of external trade has often been identified with the growth of societies in precolonial Africa and their social stratification. As participation in external trade increased, society became more differentiated and stratified, as evidenced in the existence of different residential structures in some archaeological sites in the region where those belonging to the more powerful elites were built on hilltops, while those of the ordinary folk were located on lower ground.[9] Arguably, the increasing complexity of societies in the region owed its origin to the growth in wealth afforded, in part, by expanding external trade benefits which could be invested in cattle and thus enhancing an individual's standing and influence in society and enabling such an individual to gain even greater control of the trade.

Thus, rather than being the result of imported cultural systems and practices from the Middle East or anywhere else or of predominantly the impact of external trade as was previously propagated by colonial historiography, the development of more complex and hierarchically ordered and entrepreneurial indigenous societies seems to have been autochthonous and the product of internal social, religious and economic dynamics

---

[8] The section on the Bantu and the Zimbabwe culture is heavily dependent on studies by one of Zimbabwe's most accomplished archaeologists, I. Pikirayi, especially his *The Zimbabwe Culture*.

[9] Pikirayi, *Zimbabwe Culture*, 87; G. Pwiti, 'Iron Age (Later): Southern Africa: Characteristics and Origins, South of Zambezi', available at http://patachu.com/iron-age-later-southern-africa-characteristics-and-origins-south-of-zambezi/ (accessed 15 March 2012).

that promoted wealth accumulation and social and political differentiation associated with the early Zimbabwean states. The argument by
colonial scholars that 'the socio-cultural and economic changes around
the end of the first millennium AD could be best explained in terms of
another set of migrations into southern Africa' bringing in 'people with
a different and perhaps more advanced culture system' who ostensibly
possessed large numbers of cattle and 'the rudiments of social structures
which eventually developed into state systems' is thus untenable.[10]

The Iron Age prehistory of the region can be classified into four
epochs. The first stage was characterised by farming communities living
in scattered villages which did not seem to have any form of hierarchical
organisation. The second stage, dating from about the seventh century,
coincided with the introduction of external trade and witnessed a shift
towards goods with exchange value, such as gold and ivory. The third
stage from about the tenth century sees an increase in the volume of trade
and is characterised by villages that begin to show signs of social differentiation. The fourth stage witnessed the emergence of state structures such
as Mapungubwe and further social stratification. These developments
reached a climax with the establishment of the Great Zimbabwe state.

Early state formation on the Zimbabwean Plateau is associated with
the cattle-based chiefdoms of the Zhizo and Leopard's Kopje agriculturalist communities of Matopos and Tabazikamambo in south-western
Zimbabwe, Toutswemogala in eastern Botswana, and the Mapungubwe
State of the Shashe-Limpopo River basin. Based around Ntabazingwe
(Leopard's Kopje), north-west of the present city of Bulawayo, the Zhizo
or Leopard's Kopje community, arguably the ancestors of the present
Karanga/Shona people of Zimbabwe, flourished between the ninth and
thirteenth centuries based on cattle rearing and the cultivation of cereals,
especially millet and sorghum. The subsequent decline and demise of this
state was probably the result of environmental changes that could possibly have affected the community's herds.[11]

Meanwhile, further to the south-west, founded most likely by Zhizo
migrants, the Toutswemogala or Toutswe chiefdom emerged and flourished in the tenth and eleventh centuries. In addition to cattle, its economy

[10] G. Pwiti, *Continuity and Change: An Archaeological Study of Farming Communities
in Northern Zimbabwe, AD 500–1700* (Uppsala: Department of Archaeology, 1996),
17–18.
[11] Pikirayi, *Zimbabwe Culture*, 95–7.

was also based on iron, gold and copper mining, the manufacture of ceramics for local use and for trade, and trade in ivory, gold and skins with the Swahili coast. Increased wealth and food production led to a larger population and the rise of a wealthy elite who increasingly asserted their leadership positions in society.[12]

From the eleventh to the nineteenth century, the Zimbabwean Plateau civilisation or Zimbabwean culture falls into three distinct periods: the Mapungubwe phase located in the Shashe-Limpopo Basin of southern Zimbabwe from 1040 to 1270; the Great Zimbabwe phase from 1270 to 1550 and the last phase comprising the Mutapa state in north-eastern Zimbabwe from 1450 to 1900; and the Torwa state of Khami in south-western Zimbabwe from 1450 to 1650, which was succeeded by the Rozvi-Changamire state between 1680 and 1830.[13]

Mapungubwe (1040–1270)

Of the early Zhizo/Leopard's Kopje states, the most prominent was Mapungubwe (1040–1270), situated in the Shashe-Limpopo Basin in southern Zimbabwe where the modern states of Botswana, Zimbabwe and South Africa meet. As the state was located in a semi-arid environment, prone to droughts, inhabitants relied on cattle rearing, an economic activity made possible by the presence of several wetlands in Shashe-Limpopo river system. The cattle economy and some crop agriculture ensured the accumulation of wealth enough to support a growing population and to promote social differentiation, with those who owned the largest herds becoming the most influential members of the community. The capital city at Mapungubwe Hill at the confluence of the Limpopo and Shashe rivers is estimated to have had a population of about 5,000 at its height, while the state's influence extended far north into the Zimbabwe Plateau. In addition to cattle, Mapungubwe's economy included the production of domestic pottery and iron products, spinning and weaving of fabrics and ivory and bone carving. Mapungubwe also controlled the gold trade to the Indian Ocean towns of Kilwa (founded in 957), Sofala and other coastal settlements. Some gold was processed in the state, as evidenced

---

[12] Munyaradzi Manyanga, *Resilient Landscapes: Socio-Environmental Dynamics in the Shashi-Limpopo Basin, Southern Zimbabwe c. AD 800 to the Present* (Uppsala: Dept. of Archaeology and Ancient History, 2007), 143; Pikirayi, *Zimbabwe Culture*, 94–5.

[13] Pikirayi, *Zimbabwe Culture*, 1–3.

FIGURE 2.2. The famous golden rhino excavated at the Mapungubwe site and dated between AD 1040 and 1270.

by the small golden rhino (see Figure 2.2) and gold beads excavated at Mapungubwe. Also traded were ivory, skins and other locally produced goods in exchange for fish, metals, cowrie shells, copper, iron, silk, cotton cloth, and glass beads from India or Persia. Spinning spindles found at Mapungubwe suggest that the inhabitants of Mapungubwe also wove cloth from local cotton and other materials. Accumulation of wealth from such activities and control of the growing commerce and economy, among other factors, transformed traditional political structures and led to political hierarchy and centralisation.[14]

Mapungubwe went into decline in the late twelfth century. This may have been the result of changing environmental conditions, persistent droughts, possible overgrazing or the decline in the Indian Ocean trade as traders moved further north on the coast to take advantage of the richer goldfields of the Zimbabwean Plateau. After 1300, Mapungubwe was no longer inhabited, while political power had shifted 300 kilometres northward to Great Zimbabwe.

[14] Pikirayi, *Zimbabwe Culture*, 91–193; Manyanga, *Resilient Landscapes*, 43.

Great Zimbabwe (1270–1550)

As Mapungubwe went into decline, new centres of power emerged among Leopard Kopje farmers in the north, based on the Gumanye culture around Great Zimbabwe Hill, where the soils and environmental conditions were conducive to grain production and livestock rearing. Located just south-east of the present city of Masvingo, the area receives good rains that enable grain cultivation and cattle rearing. Its location at the head of the Save River which flows to the Indian Ocean stood it in good stead to make the most of the commercial networks of the Swahili Coast of the Indian Ocean. Great Zimbabwe controlled trade with Sofala and other Indian Ocean coastal towns, channelling ivory, gold, iron and other commodities to these places for onward transmission to Arabia, India and, possibly, China, in exchange for glass beads, cotton and silk cloths, exotic ceramics from China and Persia, and other products. Persian bowls, dishes from China, glass from the Near East and several other items have been excavated at Great Zimbabwe, suggesting trade links with these and other foreign places. It was also a hub for internal trade in which products such as salt, cattle, grain and copper were traded as far north as the present-day Democratic Republic of the Congo. A treasure trove of iron hoes, axes, copper and iron wire, and soapstone carvings on decorated monoliths have also been excavated next to the Great Enclosure, suggesting that Great Zimbabwe was not only a trading but also an important craft centre and a place of great religious significance. Thus, Great Zimbabwe's wealth was based on cattle rearing, crop cultivation and the domination of trade routes between the goldfields of the Zimbabwean Plateau and the Indian ocean to the east.[15]

Great Zimbabwe was the largest precolonial state in southern Africa and the capital of the kingdom of the ancestors of the present Shona-speaking people of Zimbabwe. Its capital, Great Zimbabwe, was a large town with an estimated 11,000 to 18,000 people at its peak in the fourteenth century. It comprised elite residences, ritual centres, houses of the ordinary people and, possibly, markets and occupied nearly 720 hectares. The oldest part and hub of the town was the hill to the north (the Acropolis), the Great Enclosure to the south and the valley to the east. The name Zimbabwe is derived from a Shona term *dzimbahwe* or

---

[15] Pikirayi, *Zimbabwe Culture*, 123–32; David Chanaiwa, *The Zimbabwe Controversy: A Case of Colonial Historiography* (New York: Syracuse University Maxwell School of Citizenship and Public Affairs, 1973), 17–18.

FIGURE 2.3. Part of the Great Enclosure at Great Zimbabwe.

dzimbabwe, meaning houses of stone, because the town was built of un-bonded granite quarried from the surrounding hills, with walls up to four metres thick in places. It was a prototype of more than 200 Iron Age settlements whose ruins are scattered in Zimbabwe, Botswana, Mozambique and South Africa at Khami, Domboshava, Manyikeni and Mapungubwe, respectively (see Figure 2.3). It was constructed over a long period stretching from the ninth to the fifteenth century.[16]

By the end of the fifteenth century, Great Zimbabwe was in decline and was largely abandoned by the following century. Reasons for the decline probably included environmental deterioration resulting from the concentration of population in one area and the resultant pressure on natural resources, as well as the shift of the gold trade route northwards to the Zambezi following the rise of the rival states of Mutapa and Torwa to the north-east and south-east, respectively.

Although abandoned by the majority of its inhabitants, Great Zimbabwe remained important to the Shona people as evident in the fact that, as late as the nineteenth century, the settlement was still being used as a religious shrine by people in the region. Indeed, its symbolic

---

[16] Pikirayi, *Zimbabwe Culture*, 129–32.

importance is clear in the fact that, at independence, the country adopted Zimbabwe as its name.

The Zimbabwe Controversy

Historically, there has been much controversy over the origins of Great Zimbabwe. Known as the Zimbabwe controversy, the debate pitted those who argued that Great Zimbabwe structures were built by foreign, namely non-African people, because Africans were judged inherently inferior and not capable of having built such architecturally impressive structures, on one side, and those who maintained that these were the products of the indigenous people of Zimbabwe, on the other. The Great Zimbabwe stone structures were clearly evidence that a great civilization had once flourished on the Zimbabwean Plateau. For members of the former school, which included European travellers, journalists, company promoters, professional and amateur archaeologists and anthropologists – and Rhodes himself – that civilisation would only have been external to Africa, as they considered Africans incapable of such an undertaking.[17] Members of this school of thought attributed the structures and the civilisation that built them to anything from Sabaeans, Greeks, Egyptians, Jews, Phoenicians, Arabs, Russians, the Semites, Persians and King Solomon to the Queen of Sheba, but not to the indigenous people.[18] Great Zimbabwe was sometimes associated with the legend of Ophir, reputed to be the source of King Solomon's gold, or with the imaginary world of *King Solomon's Mines* by Rider Haggard, which depicted a great white civilisation that once flourished in the African interior. The thinking behind such views was that the stone structures were clearly

evidence that a great civilization had once flourished on the plateau and that that civilization, like Europe's own greatness, had sprung from a Mediterranean root-stock. This belief constitutes the Great Zimbabwe myth and its mythologies can be found in the writings of travellers, journalists, company promoters, Rhodes' political allies in the Cape, professional and amateur archaeologists and anthropologists, and in numerous later accounts of Rhodesia written by the settlers themselves.[19]

---

[17] A. J. Chennels, 'Settler Myths and the Southern Rhodesian Novel', Ph.D. Thesis, University of Zimbabwe, (1982), 6.

[18] A. J. Bruwer, *Zimbabwe: Rhodesia's Ancient Greatness* (Johannesburg: Hugh Keartland Publishers, 1965), for instance, argues that Great Zimbabwe was built by the Phoenicians.

[19] Chennels, 'Settler Myths', 1.

Fuelling this view were the dominant racial ideas at the time that have
come to be known as Social Darwinism or Scientific Racism, advanced
by a number individuals in the United States and Western Europe, among
them Spencer and Alfred Mahan and others, which regarded the Anglo-
Saxon race as the most developed and the darker races as being at the
lower rungs of the evolutionary ladder.[20] Thus, Richard Hall argued that
the Zimbabwe civilisation came about due to the

importation of Asiatic culture in its most perfect form consequent upon the exploitation of Rhodesia for gold by Arabs, Persians, and Indians in prehistoric times.…
The Semites are supposed to have settled in Rhodesia and initiated both mining
and stone building between 2000 and 1000 BC to 900 AD. By 900 AD … the
Bantu arrived on the scene and brought about the tragic extinction of the Semitic
race and the inevitable 'kafirization' of the Zimbabwe Civilisation. The Semites
were either exterminated or absorbed by the Bantu through intermarriage or else
were wiped out by endemic tropical disease … the Zimbabwe Civilisation [then]
retrogressed into oblivion until it was discovered by European explorers.[21]

Clearly, early colonial settlers denied the existence of a vibrant and creative precolonial African civilisation in order to justify the conquest, occupation and domination of the country, for to admit otherwise would have
undermined the entire colonial project and its justification of the need
to 'civilise' the African people. Not surprisingly, colonial novelists also
perpetuated this myth in their writings, insinuating that an old European
civilisation had somehow 'completely succumbed to savagery and the vic-
tors now lived uncomprehendingly amidst its relics'. Thus,

almost invariably the mythopoeses of Great Zimbabwe serviced the settlers' own
racism. For the most important function of the myth was to deny that Africans
were capable of taking initiative, of ordering their lives or of being creative without the authority and example of some higher race.[22]

In contrast, a number of commentators at the time who can be called
the indigenists insisted that the Zimbabwe civilisation was indigenous
and that the Zimbabwe stone structures had, in fact, been built by the
ancestors of the present-day Shona people of Zimbabwe. Leading among
this group was Archaeologist Peter Garlake whose 1973 book entitled
Great Zimbabwe and other subsequent publications challenged the racist

[20] H. Cairns, *Prelude to Imperialism: British Reactions to Central African Society 1840–
1890* (London: Routledge and Kegan Paul, 1965), 74–6, cited in Chennels, 'Settler
Myths', 310.
[21] Chanaiwa, *The Zimbabwe Controversy*, 3–4; Pikirayi, *Zimbabwe Culture*, 6.
[22] Chennels, 'Settler Myths', 6.

view of Great Zimbabwe as a product of non-indigenous civilisations and pointed out that white Rhodesian settlers were deliberately manipulating research and interpretation of the site's history in order to deny any links with the African past for fear of encouraging the rising tide of African nationalism. Risking the ire of his fellow white Rhodesians, Garlake wrote in 1973:

Great Zimbabwe must be recognized for what it is – a building of peculiar size and imposing grandeur, the product of two or three centuries of development of an indigenous stone-building technique, itself rooted in long traditions of using stone for field walls, buildings platforms and terraces. The structure reflects the economic dominance and prestige of a small oligarchy that had arisen within an Iron Age subsistence economy.

For his views, which were not welcome to the then white minority government of Ian Smith, he was forced to go into exile to Nigeria where he taught at a local university. He only returned to Zimbabwe after independence.[23]

Another indigenist was David Chanaiwa who argued in 1973 that 'the founders of the Zimbabwe Civilization, which has so far been called the Rhodesian Iron Age, were Bantu-speaking ancestors of the present-day Shona-speaking peoples'. He charged that the colonial settlers had 'created and perpetuated the Semitic origin of the Zimbabwe Civilization as a pseudo-scientific justification for the occupation, conquest and domination of Southern Rhodesia' because any admission 'of a "native" Zimbabwe Civilization would have eradicated colonial legitimacy'.[24] The indigenist group of scholars gained greater prominence after Zimbabwe's independence with the new crop of Zimbabwean archaeologists, some of whom had been Garlake's students during his short stint as a lecturer at the University of Zimbabwe after independence.[25]

[23] See, for example, P. S. Garlake, *Great Zimbabwe Described and Explained*, (London: Thames and Hudson, 1973); P. S. Garlake, *Great Zimbabwe* (Harare: Zimbabwe Publishing House, 1982); P. S. Garlake, 'Great Zimbabwe: A Reappraisal', available at www.panafprehistory.org/images/papers/GREAT_ZIMBABWE_A_REAPPRAISAL_PS_Garlake.pdf

[24] Chanaiwa, *The Zimbabwe Controversy*, 7–8.

[25] This group includes, Pikirayi, *The Zimbabwe Culture*; G. Pwiti (ed.), *Caves, Monuments and Texts: Zimbabwean Archaeology Today* (Uppsala: Department of Archaeology and Ancient History, 1997); Godfrey Mahachi and Weber Ndoro, 'The Socio-Political Context of Southern African Iron Age Studies with Special Reference to Great Zimbabwe', in G. Pwiti, *Caves, Monuments and Texts*, 89 – 107; Chanaiwa, *The Zimbabwe Controversy*.

Mutapa Empire (1450–1629)

Beginning in the fifteenth century, a successor state to Great Zimbabwe emerged in north-eastern Zimbabwe under founder Nyatsimba Mutota, a migrant from Great Zimbabwe who conquered the local groups, earning himself the title of Mwene Mutapa (the owner of conquered lands or master pillager). His title has been variously presented in historical sources as Mutapa, Mhunumutapa, or Monomotapa. With its capital at Mount Fura near the Zambezi River, the Mutapa state expanded under Mutota's successor, Mutapa Matope, to cover most of the Zimbabwe Plateau, extending eastwards to cover the Manyika territory and the coastal kingdoms of Kiteve and Madanda all the way to the Indian Ocean and southwards to the Limpopo River. The Mutapa state was the largest political entity in the subregion at the time the Portuguese arrived in south-eastern Africa in the fifteenth century.[26]

Having established their presence on the coast with the conquest of the coastal towns of Sofala and Kilwa in 1515, the Portuguese established contact with the Mutapa state soon afterwards by sending one Antonio Fernandes to the Mutapa court to negotiate terms of trade. By the 1560s, Portuguese-Mutapa relations were fully established, although the Portuguese had to compete with the older established Swahili Muslim traders for influence and for control of the lucrative gold trade.

Portuguese influence was strengthened following the conversion of the Mutapa by Jesuit missionary Gonçalo da Silveira in 1560. However, soon afterwards, the king changed his mind and denounced Christianity, resulting in da Silveira being killed, possibly because of palace intrigues involving Muslim Swahili traders who were opposed to growing Portuguese influence. Using this as an excuse, the Portuguese invaded the Mutapa state with 1,000 soldiers under Francisco Barreto in 1568 in support of a rival claimant to the throne, Mamvura, who was then prevailed upon to sign treaties accepting vassalage to the Portuguese. Meanwhile, despite these upheavals, the Mutapa state continued to thrive and became the hub in the interior for trade with the Indian Ocean in silk, ceramics, silver, and glassware, among other imports, in exchange for gold, ivory, skins and local cloth known as Machira, woven from local cotton. The Portuguese maintained their presence in the state, benefitting from

---

[26] Chanaiwa, *Zimbabwe Controversy*, 37–45; Per Zachrisson, *An African Area in Change: Belingwe 1894–1946* (Gothenburg: University of Gothenburg, 1978), 13–14.

working with several puppet Mutapas and maintaining vibrant trading stations at Dambarare, Luanze, Massapa and other places.[27]

The state went into decline in the seventeenth century, for a variety of reasons, including the presence of the Portuguese *prazeiros* (landowners) in the coastal interior and in the state capital. By playing one claimant to the Mutapa throne against another, they progressively weakened the state. The succession to the throne of Mutapa Makombwe in 1663, however, marked the beginning of the decline of Portuguese power and influence, especially after Makombwe had succeeded in driving the Portuguese off their prazos by 1674. At this time, however, the Mutapa state came under increasing competition from a rival power emerging in the southwest of the Zimbabwean Plateau in the form of the Torwa/Rozvi state of Guruuswa or Butwa under Changamire Dombo. Meanwhile, in the succession crisis following the death of Mukombwe in 1693, the demise of the Mutapa state was hastened when Changamire Dombo backed one side while the Portuguese backed the other. In the ensuing armed conflict, Dombo overran the Portuguese fair of Dambarare, killing all Portuguese traders in it, capturing the gold-rich Manyika territory and becoming the undisputed power in the subregion. What remained of the Mutapa state collapsed in the 1820s and 1830s under attack by Nguni groups from the south, under the leadership of Zwangendaba and Nxaba and Maseko. By the 1880s, the Mutapa state was no more.

Togwa (Torwa)/Rozvi

With its capital at Khami in south-western Zimbabwe, near the modern-day city of Bulawayo, the Togwa (Torwa) state, also known as Butwa, flourished between 1450 and 1685 and was ruled by a king known as Mambo. Also built of stone as Great Zimbabwe, Khami is estimated to have been home to some 7,000 people at its height. Archaeologists have found copper, iron, bronze and gold ornaments at Khami. There is also evidence of cotton spinning, weaving, soapstone carving and the working of wood and ivory. Imported pottery from China, Egypt and Europe and glass beads suggest trading activities with the Indian Ocean coast down the Zambezi and Sabi Rivers in which such imports were exchanged for gold. Like its predecessors, Khami was also a cattle rearing society in addition to owning goats and sheep and growing crops.

---

[27] Zachrisson, *Belingwe*, 14–25.

The Togwa (Torwa) state split into two in 1644 as a result of a civil war. Khami was abandoned and a new capital at Danangombe (Dhlo Dhlo) east of Khami was established by the victorious Mambo, while the western part went its own way. Danangombe was attacked by the Portuguese between 1644 and 1685 when the Togwa under Mambo Tshibundule were defeated by the Rozvi. The new Rozvi rulers under Changamire Dombo had become so strong that they defeated the then-Mutapa Mukombwe in 1684 and, thereafter, consolidated their power in the western Butwa. Dombo was the first of seven successive rulers of the Rozvi dynasty who dominated south western Zimbabwe. Togwa (Torwa)-Rozvi rule went into decline in the eighteenth century and finally collapsed in the mid-nineteenth century under increasing attacks by Nguni groups from the south. Five different Nguni groups passed through or settled in the region between 1826 and 1838, each putting pressure on the Rozvi state. Nguni attacks eventually forced the Rozvi Changamire to evacuate his capital at Danangombe.[28]

The Conquest States: The Ndebele and the British

The 1820s witnessed a new intrusion from the south by various Nguni-speaking groups who were driven north by the upheavals associated with the Mfecane (Nguni for "the crushing") or Difaqane (Sotho-Tswana meaning "the scattering") – a period of continuous warfare and unrest in Southern Africa between 1816 and the 1840s that began at the time of the rise of the Zulu Kingdom under King Shaka. Starting in the eastern region of present-day South Africa, wars spread into the interior and resulted in large-scale migration out of the area by various groups, such as the AmaNdebele under Mzilikazi and the Makololo, that later established their own kingdoms throughout southern Africa.

Scholars are not agreed as to the causes of these wars, with some maintaining that they were the result of population pressure as population increased rapidly due to the introduction of maize (corn) by the Portuguese – a crop capable of supporting larger populations than traditional grain crops were. This, it is argued, resulted in competition for space among local ethnic groupings. Others point to the growing European influence in the region as Afrikaners moved ever northwards from the Cape Province where they had first settled and thus put pressure

---

[28] G. Liesegang, 'Nguni Migration between Delagoa Bay and the Zambezi, 1821–1839', *African Historical Studies*, 3, 2 (1970), 317–37.

on African groups in the interior, while Portuguese presence on the Indian Ocean also exerted its own pressures. Yet others highlight the impact of environmental factors, including a ten-year drought in the early 1800s, which increased competition for land and water. Finally, some scholars single out growing competition among the various African groups for trade with the Portuguese in guns, ivory and slaves.[29] Whatever the causes, the events that unfolded in the region at the time were closely linked with the rise of Shaka, king of the Zulus, whose military tactics and strategies made his people a formidable fighting power who were able to unleash more destructive power than in the past and fuelled outward migrations by groups fleeing this rising military machine.

Some groups fled northwards, attacking other groups in their path, using the very effective military tactics that had been pioneered by Shaka. The wars in Nguni territory thus had a ripple effect that spread violence and destabilisation, which affected numerous communities through-out southern Africa, destroying some old kingdoms and creating new ones. With respect to Zimbabwe, the migration of at least five Nguni groups between 1826 and 1835 changed the political landscape of the Zimbabwean Plateau. The Mfecane population dispersals are shown in Map 2.1.

The first groups of the Nguni to enter Zimbabwe were those of Soshangane and Zwangendaba. After a crushing defeat by Shaka's forces in 1818, Soshangane and his Ndwandwe followers fled to Mozambique where they dominated the local people to establish the Gaza Kingdom whose territory spread into present-day south-eastern and eastern Zimbabwe, and brought some Shona groups under its con-trol. Meanwhile, Zwangendaba of the Jere clan also fled to Mozambique with Soshangane, but the two fell out and Zwangendaba was forced to proceed westwards where he contributed to the collapse of the Rozwi Empire. Afterwards, he moved northwards across the Zambezi River with his followers in 1835 and established the Ngoni kingdom between present-day Lakes Malawi and Tanganyika. Another Nguni group led by a woman called Nyamazana killed the Rozvi king in 1836 and

---

[29] For debates on the causes of the Mfecane, see Julian Cobbing,' The Mfecane as Alibi: Thoughts on Dithakong and Mbolomo', *Journal of African History*, 29 (1988), 487–519. See also J. D. Omer-Cooper, *The Zulu Aftermath: A Nineteenth-Century Revolution in Bantu Africa* (Longmans, 1978); Norman Etherington, *The Great Treks: The Transformation of Southern Africa, 1815–1854* (Longman, 2001); Carolyn Hamilton, *The Mfecane Aftermath: Reconstructive Debates in Southern African History* (Indiana University Press, 1995).

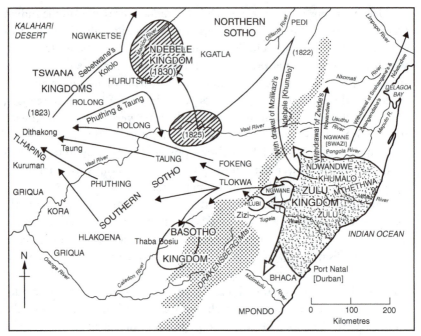

MAP 2.1. Map showing the rise of the Zulu Kingdom and the *Difaqane* on the Highveld, 1818–1835.

Source: Map 18.1 from 'The rise of the Zulu kingdom and the *Difaqane* on the Highveld 1818–35', in Kevin Shillington, *History of Africa*, revised 2nd edition, Oxford: Macmillan Education, 2005, 257, available at http://www.palgrave.com/history/shillington/resources/maps.html

subsequently merged with the Ndebele around 1840. Other smaller Nguni groups that entered Zimbabwe, led by Nxaba and Maseko, clashed with the waning Mutapa state in the 1830s before making their way northwards across the Zambezi.[30]

The second group was that of the AmaNdebele under Mzilikazi. A close ally of Shaka, Mzilikazi, chief of the Khumalo, fell out with the Zulu king and decided to flee northwards into the Transvaal (present-day Gauteng) Province of South Africa. There he incorporated other groups, including the Sotho-speaking communities through whose territory he travelled. From these disparate groups he was able to meld together a

[30] Gerald Mazarire, 'Who Are the Ndebele and the Kalanga in Zimbabwe?' Paper Prepared for Konrad Adenuer Foundation Project on 'Ethnicity in Zimbabwe' November 2003, available at http://ir.uz.ac.zw/jspui/bitstream/10646/314/1/Mazarire-Ndebele-and-Kalanga.pdf (accessed 4 December 2012).

nation that came to be known as the AmaNdebele. Mzilikazi and his followers settled north of present-day Pretoria for a while but were forced by pursuing Shaka military units to relocate further westwards. Mzilikazi was forced to move further northwards still in 1837 when he was attacked by incoming Boer settlers from the south and eventually settled in Matebeleland in southwest Zimbabwe. There he established a powerful kingdom with its capital at Bulawayo. The AmaNdebele found the local Rozvi kingdom seriously weakened by the attacks of the earlier Nguni groups of Nyamazana and Zwangendaba, and proceeded to set up their state on the territory previously ruled by the Rozvi. The Ndebele state's influence spread to other Shona groups to the north before it was finally broken up by the incoming British colonial settlers in the Anglo-AmaNdebele War of 1893.

In colonial historiography, the Ndebele were often portrayed as a war-like, predatory people who lived mainly on plunder of the neighbouring Shona people whom they terrorised, and whose defeat by the incoming British colonisers was welcomed with gratitude and relief by the Shona. This was a self-serving depiction of Ndebele society which justified the military destruction of Ndebele power in the name of 'pacification' and was part of European colonisers' divide-and-rule propaganda that was essential to safeguard colonial rule by preventing any concerted action by the colonised groups. Thus, the 'myth of the Ndebele always raiding the Shona' was 'generated by white settlers' who presented the Ndebele as 'bloodthirsty savages harassing the weaker Shona people'. Such views were also partly influenced by ignorance of Ndebele society and how it functioned and by the missionaries' need to justify their presence as 'saviours' of Ndebele souls.[31] Some Ndebele groups may also have per-petuated this myth for other reasons. Thus, the history of the Ndebele became the subject of 'exaggerations and distortions, repeated by both the Ndebele people themselves and outsiders', in which the 'Ndebele peo-ple have been invariably represented as "heroic warriors", "noble sav-ages" or "bloodthirsty savages" in the historical and popular accounts that abound'.[32]

[31] Zachrisson, *Belingwe*, 26; James Muzondidya, 'Historicizing the Ndebele Nation: Reflections on Hegemony, Memory and Historiography', available at http://www.aca-demia.edu/663157/Historicizing_the_Ndebele_James_Muzondidya_The_Ndebele_Nation_Reflections_on_Hegemony_Memory_and_Historiography (accessed 20 November 2012).

[32] Sabelo J. Ndlovu-Gatsheni, 'The Ndebele Nation: Reflections on Hegemony, Memory and Historiography', in James Muzondidya, *Historicising the Ndebele* (Amsterdam: Rosenberg/Pretoria: UNISA Press, 2009), 9–11.

The reality was that, while the AmaNdebele did periodically invade some Shona groups, relations between the two groups were not always antagonistic, and the AmaNdebele were not always victorious in such military clashes as was often asserted by early colonial accounts. Equally doubtful were claims that the Ndebele state was a highly centralised military state; evidence suggests that it was, in fact, 'a more loosely-knit affair consisting of decentralised settlements making the state flexible in its extensions and also making a more irregular impact on the Shona. The majority of the Ndebele settlements were small-scale.'[33] Also clear is that the Ndebele economy was based mainly on cultivation of mostly millets grain crops, with cattle rearing a close second, in addition to manufacturing and hunting. Tribute collection was more a means of imposing political control rather than a source of economic survival.[34]

Another colonial historical distortion was the presentation of the Ndebele state as comprising mainly descendants of the Nguni from Zululand. The reality is somewhat more complex. In fact, what became the political state of the Ndebele comprised an amalgam of ethnic groups that had been incorporated over the years it took Mzilikazi and his original core group to reach present-day Zimbabwe. On the way, the original core group from Zululand (*Abezansi*) had incorporated the Sotho-Tswana (*Abenhla*) from the northern part of South Africa (Gauteng, Limpopo and Northwest provinces), the Kalanga from south-eastern Zimbabwe and the indigenous Rozvi (*Amahole*) whose territory they now ruled over. Intermarriage over time tended to soften differences between the categories[35] and, indeed, to render them meaningless in the long run, as offspring of intermarriage took on the caste designation of their fathers.

Conclusion

As noted in this chapter, far from being uninhabited or from being inhabited by lawless and unorganised peoples, the territory of what became Zimbabwe was for long the home of several organised polities or civilisations that included the states of Mapungubwe, Great Zimbabwe, Munhumutapa and the Rozvi, dominated by ancestors of the present-day Shona-speaking people. In addition, in the middle of the nineteenth

---

[33] Zachrisson, *Belingwe*, 19.
[34] J. Cobbing, 'The Absent Priesthood: Another Look at the Rhodesian Risings of 1896–1897', *Journal of African History*, 18, 1 (1977), 61–84.
[35] J. Cobbing, 'The Absent Priesthood'.

century, new ethnic groupings, in the form of the Nguni, entered the area, bringing with them a new culture and different political organisational structures. Clearly, when the British colonisers arrived at the end of the nineteenth century, they were not marching into an empty land which was there just for the taking, as Rhodesian Prime Minister Ian Smith seemed to be implying in the passage quoted earlier.

At the same time, the country that was to become Rhodesia, and later Zimbabwe, was not yet a nation in the sense of a unified political, economic and cultural unit consisting of people who all shared a common history and values, as was the case in the emerging countries such as Italy and Germany in the nineteenth century, which were concrete manifestations of a nationalist spirit born of a common heritage. Because of its diverse history and ethnic groups, the territory that became Rhodesia was in the process of becoming a nation and may, indeed, have evolved to become such had Western colonialism not intervened to bring about an entirely new dynamic that was to influence the country's future development, as shown in the discussion that follows.

3

The British Conquest State

British colonialism destroyed the Ndebele state at the end of the nineteenth century. In 1890, a group of adventurers known as the Pioneer Column, sponsored by South African-based British arch-imperialist Cecil John Rhodes, occupied Zimbabwe and claimed the country for the British. British colonisation of Zimbabwe was part of nineteenth-century European expansionism in which European countries imposed political and economic control over territories in various parts of the globe. This was, in fact, the second wave of European imperialism and resulted in the African continent being carved up like the proverbial turkey and shared among the major European countries by the end of the century. The first wave occurred in the sixteenth century, following Christopher Columbus's crossing of the Atlantic Ocean, which linked the New World of the Americas to Europe and paved the way for Spanish, British, French, Portuguese and other European countries' acquisition of colonies in North and South America and the Caribbean. Sixteenth-century European imperialism ushered in the Transatlantic slave trade which was to see millions of Africans forcibly translocated to the Americas to work on sugar and cotton plantations and other sectors of the economy of the New World. Because of its distance from the sea, however, Zimbabwe was not directly affected by the Transatlantic slave trade.

In Africa, the speed with which European countries acquired territories was so rapid that it was a veritable scramble. In the 1870s, most of Africa was self-governing, with the exception of South Africa under the British and the Afrikaners, Algeria under the French, parts of North Africa under the Ottoman Empire, Mozambique and Angola under Portugal, and Lagos and Sierra Leone under the British. By 1910, the entire African continent

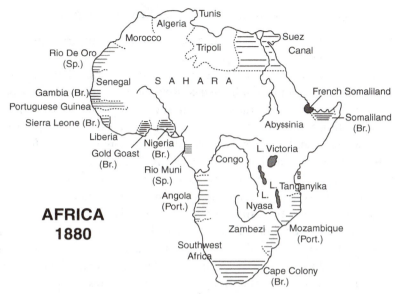

MAP 3.1. Africa in 1880.

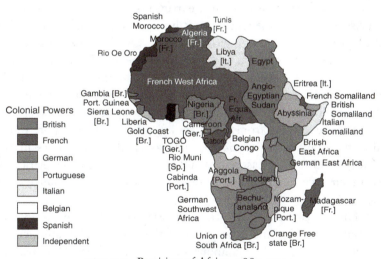

MAP 3.2. Partition of Africa, 1885–1914.

was under European rule, except for Ethiopia and Liberia. The European grab for colonies was accelerated following the Berlin Conference of 1884, which brought together representatives of the European countries that were interested in acquiring territory in Africa to establish rules of engagement in the colonisation process (Maps 3.1 and 3.2).

Accounting for Nineteenth-Century European Imperialism

There were many reasons for aggressive European imperialism in this period. Among these were the growing demands for markets, raw materials and investment opportunities by the rapidly expanding European economies in the era of the Industrial Revolution. Beginning in England in the eighteenth century, the Industrial Revolution transformed methods of production and national economies in ways that exerted new pressures on the societies and economies. Increasingly, it became necessary for these nations to find new markets for the mass-produced goods from the mushrooming factories, as well as raw materials to feed the production process. At the same time, as individual entrepreneurs amassed wealth, they needed to find new areas to invest in so as to maximise profits.

These economic imperatives coincided with mounting European nationalism that witnessed the unification of countries such as Italy and Germany and the cut-throat competition that accompanied the creation of such nation-states as they sought international prestige and material rewards in order to be stronger than their neighbours. Into this mix was added the ideology of European superiority that provided motivation for and justification of European expansionism. Known variably as the 'civilising mission', 'the white man's burden' and 'manifest destiny', this ideology argued that the Anglo-Saxon race was the most advanced of all races and, therefore, had a god-given mandate to rule the 'lesser hordes' and to spread the benefits of their superior civilisation to the 'darker corners' of the world.[1] Coupled with the civilising mission imperative was the determination of the various religious groups to 'save' the people of Africa and elsewhere from paganism by spreading Christianity to them. Also important were individuals such as Cecil John Rhodes in South Africa, Karl Peters in East Africa and George Goldie in West Africa, who used their own initiative and resources to expand their countries' influence in Africa.

Scholars have advanced various theories to explain European expansionism into Africa and other parts of the world in the late nineteenth century. One view, the economic or capitalist theory of imperialism, which emphasises the role of European economic interests in fuelling late-nineteenth-century imperialism, is associated with the writings of British commentator J. A. Hobson and the leader of the 1917 Bolshevik

[1] Richard Hofstadter, *Social Darwinism in American Thought* (Boston: Bacon Press, 1944).

Revolution and first Russian Soviet ruler Vladimir I. Lenin, respectively.[2] Broadly, the theory argues that Europe's expansionism was driven by its needs for markets and sources of raw materials in response to the demands of its rapidly industrialising economy in the context of the Industrial Revolution, while excess capital needed new investment areas.

Furthermore, industrialisation and mechanisation were fuelling unemployment and impoverishment in Europe and raising the danger of popular uprisings. Hence there was the need for an outlet for the 'surplus' European population. This, reportedly, prompted Cecil John Rhodes in 1885 to observe:

I was in the East End of London (a working-class quarter) yesterday and attended a meeting of the unemployed. I listened to the wild speeches, which were just a cry for 'bread! bread!' and on my way home I pondered over the scene and I became more than ever convinced of the importance of imperialism.... My cherished idea is a solution for the social problem, i.e., in order to save the 40,000,000 inhabitants of the United Kingdom from a bloody civil war, we colonial statesmen must acquire new lands to settle the surplus population, to provide new markets for the goods produced in the factories and mines. The Empire, as I have always said, is a bread and butter question. If you want to avoid civil war, you must become imperialists.[3]

An important difference between Hobson's and Lenin's views of imperialism, however, was that whereas the former believed that imperialism could have been avoided had the distribution of wealth under capitalism been more equitable in order to avoid the twin problem of underconsumption and over-saving that was the 'tap-root' of imperialism, the latter argued that imperialism was the inevitable outcome of capitalism at the highest stage of its development. For Lenin, unlike Hobson, capitalism could not be reformed and had, of necessity, to become imperialist at a certain stage of its development. This stage, he argued, had been reached in Western Europe, hence the nineteenth-century expansionism.

A second group of theories emphasises psychological factors, such as the idea of expansionism as the product of the Europeans' belief in the 'white man's burden', 'civilising mission' or 'manifest destiny'. Based on an adaptation of natural scientist Charles Darwin's *The Origin of Species*

---

[2] J. A. Hobson, *Imperialism: A Study* (London: George Allen & Unwin, 1902) and V. I. Lenin, *Imperialism: The Highest State of Capitalism* (Petrograd: Progressive Publishers, 1917).

[3] Quoted by V. I. Lenin, 'Imperialism, the Highest Stage of Capitalism', *Lenin: Collected Works*, 22 (Moscow: Progress Publishers, 1974), 256–7.

by Means of Natural Selection published in 1859, a theory collectively known as Social Darwinism emerged in the United States and Europe in the late nineteenth century. It maintained that, like the natural world, societies and races also were engaged in an ongoing struggle for the survival of the fittest and that the most evolved and, therefore, fittest race at that time was the Anglo-Saxon race. Consequently, Western Europe was placed at the summit of some imagined process of social evolution. Those societies that least resembled its habits of organisation were placed at the opposite end of the scale and the people of such societies were regarded as less developed than their European counterparts were.[4] The logical conclusion was, therefore, that the Anglo-Saxon race was the most suitable to rule the lesser or 'backward' races and had a god-given duty to spread its civilisation to all the 'darker' corners of the world. In fact, it was argued, the 'lower' races stood to benefit from being ruled by the superior race.[5] One of its most committed adherents was American politician Albert Beveridge who argued at the end of the nineteenth century that

God has not been preparing the English-speaking and Teutonic peoples for a thousand years for nothing but vain and idle self-contemplation and self-admiration. No! He has made us the master organisers of the world to establish system where chaos reigns. He has made us adept at government that we may administer government among savages.[6]

This view was celebrated in Rudyard Kipling's poem entitled 'The White Man's Burden', written to commemorate the United States' defeat of Spain in the Spanish-Cuban-American War of 1898. It enjoined members of the Anglo-Saxon race to

Take up the white man's burden
Send forth the best ye breed
Go bind your sons to exile
To serve your captives' need;
To wait in heavy harness,

[4] H. Cairns, *Prelude to Imperialism: British Reactions to Central African Society 1840–1890* (London: Routledge and Kegan Paul, 1965), 74–6, cited in Chennels, 'Settler Myths', 310.

[5] P. Curtin, *The Image of Africa: British ideas and Action 1780 – 1850* (Madison: University of Wisconsin Press, 1973), 272–3 and Cairns, *Prelude to Imperialism*, 234–5, cited in Chennels, 'Settler Myths', 310.

[6] Albert J. Beveridge in Congress, cited in Hofstadter, *Manifest Destiny*, (1992). For a detailed examination of Social Darwinism, see Hofstadter, *Social Darwinism*.

On fluttered folk and wild –
Your new-caught, sullen peoples,
Half devil and half child.[7]

Other explanations highlight the role of evangelical Christianity and the compulsion to save the souls of heathens around the world and European countries' concerns with the balance of power, national prestige and national security during a period of intense nationalism on the continent in the nineteenth century. Also contributing to the scramble for Africa were the various associations of geographers, explorers and adventurers, various individuals on the spot, such as Cecil John Rhodes in southern Africa and George Goldie in West Africa, and Europe's technological capacity to conquer and rule over other societies, particularly following the invention of the Maxim and the Gatling machine guns, which they used to devastating effect against the Africans' spears and bows and arrows.[8] Faced with the determined European onslaught, Africans could not adequately resist also partly because they were not united and mistakenly believed in the principle of 'my enemy's enemy is my friend'. Indeed, there were many Africans who fought as soldiers in the conquering European colonial armies against fellow Africans. In addition, Africans lagged behind Europe technologically and had no professional standing armies as the invading European powers had had for a long time. Moreover, they did not co-ordinate their responses, making it easier for incoming European colonising forces to defeat them one by one.

From the Berlin Conference to Occupation

To prevent possible conflicts among the countries competing for colonies in Africa, all the European countries interested in acquiring territory on the African Continent met in Berlin at the end of 1884 to discuss ground rules that would govern territorial acquisition and the colonisation process.

---

[7] Modern History Sourcebook: Rudyard Kipling, The White Man's Burden, 1899, http://www.fordham.edu/halsall/mod/kipling.asp (accessed 24 June 2012).

[8] For more on theories of imperialism and surrounding debates, see I. Phimister, 'Africa Partitioned', *Review* (Fernand Braudel Center), 18, 2 (Spring, 1995), 355–81; N. A. Etherington, *Theories of Imperialism: War, Conquest and Capital* (London: Croom Helm, 1984); D. K. Fieldhouse, *Theory of Capitalist Imperialism* (New York: Barnes and Noble, 1967); C. N. Uzoigwe, 'European Partition and Conquest of Africa', in A. Adu Boahen (ed.), *Africa Under Colonial Domination 1880–1935* (London: Heinemann, 1985), 19–44.

Gathered at Berlin were representatives of Britain, France, Portugal, Spain, Germany, Holland, Belgium, and Italy. The United States and the Ottoman Empire also sent their observers to the meeting. Under the chairmanship of German Chancellor Otto von Bismarck, the conference agreed that:

1. Countries should declare their intention to claim lands to others to enable them to make good on their own claims should they wish to do so.
2. Only those countries 'effectively occupied' would be respected as the spheres of influence of the claiming European country; effective occupation meant military conquest and the establishment of a colonial administration.
3. Major waterways such as the Congo, the Niger and the Zambezi rivers were to be open to all traders.
4. All countries should undertake to end slavery.

Significantly, there was not a single African represented at this conference which was deciding the future of the continent.

Colonisation of Zimbabwe

British expansionist Cecil John Rhodes (see Figure 3.1) spearheaded the colonisation of Zimbabwe using his considerable wealth that he had obtained from gold and diamond mining in South Africa in the late nineteenth century, as well as his political clout as the then-prime minister of the Cape Province of South Africa. Rhodes was a staunch believer in the superiority of British civilisation and was determined to bring under British rule as much of the world as possible because he firmly believed that this was beneficial to humankind. In his words,

I contend that we are the finest race in the world and that the more of the world we inhabit the better it is for the human race. Just fancy those parts that are at present inhabited by the most despicable specimens of human beings what an alteration there would be if they were brought under Anglo-Saxon influence, look again at the extra employment a new country added to our dominions gives ... Africa is still lying ready for us, it is our duty to take it. It is our duty to seize every opportunity of acquiring more territory and we should keep this one idea steadily before our eyes that more territory simply means more of the Anglo-Saxon race more of the best, the most human, most honourable race the world possesses.[9]

---

[9] Cecil Rhodes's Confession of Faith, 1877, http://pages.uoregon.edu/kimball/Rhodes-Confession.htm (accessed 15 June 2012).

FIGURE 3.1. Cecil John Rhodes (www.wikipedia.com).

Rhodes's ambition was to extend British rule over as many territories as possible. His vision was all-encompassing and involved

the establishment, promotion and development of a Secret Society, the true aim and object whereof shall be for the extension of British rule throughout the world, the perfecting of a system of emigration from the United Kingdom, and of colonisation by British subjects of all lands where the means of livelihood are attainable by energy, labour and enterprise, and especially the occupation by British settlers of the entire Continent of Africa, the Holy Land, the Valley of the Euphrates, the Islands of Cyprus and Candia, the whole of South America, the Islands of the Pacific not heretofore possessed by Great Britain, the whole of the Malay Archipelago, the seaboard of China and Japan, the ultimate recovery of the United States of America as an integral part of the British Empire.[10]

In Africa, specifically, his intention was to establish British rule from the Cape in the south to Cairo in the north. (Rhodes's African ambitions are depicted in a cartoon as shown in Figure 3.2.) Rhodes subsequently

[10] Cecil Rhodes's Confession of Faith, 1877.

FIGURE 3.2. The Rhodes Colossus (http://en.wikipedia.org)

succeeded in establishing a British Empire north of the Limpopo River that encompassed Zimbabwe (Southern Rhodesia), Zambia (Northern Rhodesia) and Malawi (Nyasaland). Before he could do this, however, he needed legal authorisation from the British government. Such authorisation would be obtained if Rhodes could demonstrate that he had secured a treaty of friendship with local rulers in what was to become Southern Rhodesia. To secure such an agreement, Rhodes resorted to deception.

He sent his business partner Charles Rudd, accompanied by Rochfort Maguire and Francis Thompson, to persuade Ndebele King Lobengula (see Figure 3.3), successor to the founding leader of the Ndebele nation, Mzilikazi, to enter into a treaty of friendship with him. Lobengula was reluctant to sign such an agreement until he was persuaded by Reverend Helm, the London Missionary Society (LMS) representative then resident in Lobengula's capital of Bulawayo, that the document he was being asked to sign was harmless. Being unfamiliar with the English language, he could not verify this claim. In any case, even if he had been familiar with the language, Lobengula could not have fully understood the

FIGURE 3.3. Lobengula Khumalo, King of the Ndebele between 1868 and 1894 (http://en.wikipedia.org).

document which was 'couched (by Maguire a barrister and Fellow of All Souls) in the turgid language of the Inns of Court' and which was, in any case, misrepresented, with the king being disingenuously informed that under the terms of the document he was being asked to sign, the concession seekers would 'not bring more than ten men to work in the country'[11]

In return for this friendly gesture, Lobengula was promised guns, a gun-boat on the Zambezi River and some cash. Because the assurance came from an individual that he had no reason not to trust, given his missionary status, Lobengula signed the document that became known as the Rudd Concession. Shortly afterwards, however, Lobengula discovered that he had been conned and that the document he had signed contained more than what he had been told it said. He discovered that he had, in

[11] Arthur Keppel-Jones, 'The Occupation of Mashonaland', http://www.memoriesofrhodesia.com/media/documents/occupationofmashonaland.pdf (accessed 10 June 2012).

fact, signed away his territory and sovereignty and placed his territory and its people, as well as the people of Mashonaland over whom he had no jurisdiction, under British rule. The Rudd Concession is reproduced in full in the following insert.

The Rudd Concession, 1888

Know all men by these presents, that whereas Charles Dunell Rudd, of Kimberley; Rochfort Maguire, Of London; and Francis Robert Thompson, of Kimberley, hereinafter called the grantees, have covenanted and agreed, and do hereby covenant and agree, to pay to me, my heirs and successors, the sum of one hundred pounds sterling, British currency, on the first day of every lunar month; and, further, to deliver at my royal kraal one thousand Martini-Henry breech-loading rifles, together with one hundred thousand rounds of suitable ball cartridge, five hundred of the said rifles and fifty thousand of the said cartridges to be ordered from England forthwith and delivered with reasonable dispatch, and the remainder of the said rifles and cartridges to be delivered as soon as the said grantees shall have commenced to work mining machinery within my territory; and further, to deliver on the Zambesi River a steamboat with guns suitable for defensive purposes upon the said river, or in lieu of the said steamboat, should I so elect to pay to me the sum of five hundred pounds sterling, British currency. On the execution of these presents, I, Lo Bengula,[sic] King of Matabeleland, Mashonaland, and other adjoining territories, ..., do hereby grant and assign unto the said grantees, their heirs, representatives, and assigns, jointly and severally, the complete and exclusive charge over all metals and minerals situated and contained in my kingdoms, principalities, and dominions, together with full power to do all things that they may deem necessary to win and procure the same, and to hold, collect, and enjoy the profits and revenues, if any, derivable from the said metals and minerals, subject to the aforesaid payment; and whereas I have been much molested of late by diverse persons seeking and desiring to obtain grants and concessions of land and mining rights in my territories, I do hereby authorise the said grantees, their heirs, representatives, and assigns, to take all necessary and lawful steps to exclude from my kingdom, principalities, and dominions all persons seeking land, metals, minerals, or mining rights therein, and

I do hereby undertake to render them all such needful assistance as they may from time to time require for the exclusion of such persons, and to grant no concessions of land or mining rights from and after this date without their consent and concurrence; provided that, if at any time the said monthly payment of one hundred pounds shall cease and determine from the date of the last-made payment; and, further, provided, that nothing contained in these presents shall extend to or affect a grant made by me of certain mining rights in a portion of my territory south of the Ramaquaban River, which grant is common known as the Tati Concession.

This, given under my hand this thirtieth day of October, in the year of our Lord 1888, at my royal kraal.

LO BENGULA X his mark.

C. D. RUDD.

Witnesses: CHAS. D. HELM. ROCHFORT MAGUIRE. F. R. THOMPSON[12]

The insertion of 'Mashonaland and other adjoining territories' into the agreement, even though Rhodes and his team knew very well that Lobengula did not have jurisdiction over these lands, was, of course, disingenuous but shrewdly calculated to enhance future British territorial claims.

After discovering the duplicitous nature of the document, Lobengula sent two envoys to the queen in England to inform her that he had been duped and that the document had been obtained fraudulently. Part of Lobengula's message to the British queen read:

Some time ago a party of men came into my country, the principal being a man named Rudd. They asked me for a place to dig gold and said that they would give me certain things for the right to do so. I told them to bring what they would give me and I would show them what I would give.

A document was written and presented to me for signature. I asked what it contained and was told that in it were my words and the words of those men. I put my hand to it.

---

[12] Sir Lewis Mitchell, *The Life of the Right Honourable Cecil Rhodes*, 2 vols. (London, 1910), 1:244–45 at weblearn.ox.ac.uk/.../1888%20A%20Rudd%20Concession%20 1888.pdf (accessed 20 May 2012).

About three months afterwards I heard from other sources that I had given, by that document, the right to all the minerals in my country, I called a meeting of the Indunas [chiefs] and also of the white men and demanded a copy of that document. It was proved to me that I had signed away the mineral rights of my whole country to Rudd and his friends.

I have since had a meeting with my indunas and they will not recognise the paper as it contains neither my words nor the words of those who got it ... I write to you that you may know the truth about this thing, and not be deceived.[13]

Apparently, Lobengula later sent a second message repudiating the Concession, but the letter was delayed in the post. According to one source:

On August 10, Lobengula wrote to the Queen again, repudiating the concession and this time took care to have Moffat (the LMS Missionary stationed in Matebeleland at the time) sign as a witness. If the Post Office had functioned at its usual speed, this letter would have been delivered in London about September 26. But it did not in fact reach its destination until November 18; three weeks after the Great Seal had been affixed to the charter. The only reasonable inference is that Rhodes had friends in the Post Office, as well as in the customs, railways and harbours.[14]

Despite Lobengula's serious charges about the fraudulent nature of the Rudd Concession, the British government still went ahead to recognise the concession as binding and to grant Cecil Rhodes a charter authorising his recently established British South Africa Company (BSAC) to colonise Zimbabwe on Britain's behalf. The Charter authorised Rhodes' BSAC to

[m]ake treaties, promulgate laws, preserve the peace, maintain a police force and acquire new concessions ... [and to] make roads, railways, harbours or undertake other public works, engage in mining or any other industry, establish banks, make land grants and carry on any lawful commerce, trade, pursuit or business.[15]

The dishonest manner in which the Rudd concession had been secured was not atypical of the tactics of early European expansionists in Africa, who were determined to acquire territories for their countries in whatever way possible. Thus, for instance, in Namibia, Adolf Luderitz, a German businessman who travelled to the territory in search of precious minerals, signed a treaty in 1883 with Joseph Fredericks, a local chief of the Nama

[13] Louis L. Snyder, *The Imperialism Reader* (New York: D. Van Nostrand Co, Inc., 1962), 218–20; H. Marshall Hole, *The Making of Rhodesia* (London: Cass, 1967), 108.
[14] Arthur Keppel-Jones, The Occupation of Mashonaland, http://www.memoriesofrhodesia.com/media/documents/occupationofmashonaland.pdf (accessed 23 May 2012).
[15] C. Chavunduka and D. W. Bromley, 'Beyond the Crisis in Zimbabwe: Sorting out the Land Question', *Development Southern Africa*, 27, 3 (September 2010), 9.

people. The treaty provided for the sale to Luderitz of a stretch of land along the coast 20 miles wide and 250 miles in length for the sum of £500 and sixty British rifles. However, while the Nama chief was made to believe that he had sold land in English miles, equivalent to 1.4 kilometres each, the agreement, written in German, actually recorded the sale in German miles, which were the equivalent of 7.4 kilometres each. This meant that, in effect, the Nama chief had signed away all his territory. Later protests to the German government yielded no response. The result was that the agreement formed the basis of German colonisation a few years later.[16] Other examples of such fraudulent strategies exist. Later African anti-colonial responses in such countries as Zimbabwe and Namibia were to be coloured by memories of such earlier sharp colonial practices.

Meanwhile, Rhodes faced the problem that the Rudd Concession merely granted his company mining rights, but not land rights. To obtain these rights, he connived with one Eduard Lippert, a German adventurer who also fraudulently secured a concession from Lobengula in 1889 granting him land rights. Acting on a prior agreement, Rhodes bought the Lippert Concession in 1894, thus enabling Rhodes to claim land rights in the territory. In any case, by this time, the BSAC had already made extensive land awards to the settlers in Mashonaland.

With the Charter in hand, Rhodes assembled the Pioneer Column, a group of hired hands and adventurers and their African and Coloured servants, to march into the territory north of the Limpopo River and claim it for Britain. He promised each member of the Column more than 3,000 acres of land and several mining concessions upon successful occupation of the territory. Because he was aware of the fraudulent nature of the Rudd Concession, Rhodes instructed the Column to skirt Lobengula's land and to enter Mashonaland to the east instead. If Lobengula took no action against the advancing Column, the BSAC would occupy Mashonaland, but,

[i]f on the other hand, Lobengula attacks us, then the original plan (the armed invasions of Matebeleland) ... will be carried out to the very letter ... he must expect no mercy and none will be given him ... if he attacks us, he is doomed ... the desired result, the disappearance forever of the Matebele as a power ... is yet the more certain.[17]

---

[16] Horst Drechsler, *Let Us Die Fighting: The Struggle of the Herero and Nama against German Imperialism, 1884–1915* (London: Zed Press, 1980).

[17] Richard Brown, 'Aspects of the Scramble for Matabeleland', in E. Stokes and R. Brown (eds.), *The Zambezi Past: Studies in Central African History* (Manchester: Manchester University Press, 1966), 90.

Apparently, 'the original plan' referred to a secret agreement that Rhodes had earlier entered into with two 'soldiers of fortune, Frank Johnson and Maurice Heany' that, should Lobengula prove difficult, they were to invade and destroy Bulawayo with a force of 500 men.[18]

Subsequently, the Ndebele state did collapse in 1893 after the British occupation of Mashonaland in 1890, when the Pioneer Column hoisted the British flag at Fort Salisbury (now Harare) and claimed for Britain the territory soon to be named Southern Rhodesia. Coveting the land of the Ndebele, which was reputed to contain large amounts of gold, the BSAC Company's administrator, Leander Starr Jameson, used the pretext of a Ndebele army attack on a Shona-speaking community living in the vicinity of the new colonial settlement of Fort Victoria (now Masvingo) to attack the Ndebele people in reprisal. Jameson raised a volunteer settler army with promises of 6,000 acres, 20 mining concessions and a share of the loot from Lobengula's territory to each volunteer.[19] Thus, in 1893, settler forces attacked and destroyed Lobengula's capital at Bulawayo, forcing the Ndebele king, after an unsuccessful attempt to sue for peace, to flee northwards where he later perished in unclear circumstances. An armed party under settler leader Alan Wilson, which went in pursuit of the fleeing king, was ambushed and massacred by Ndebele forces just north of Bulawayo. It was later eulogised in colonial accounts of the conflict as the epitome of Rhodesian heroism. Not surprisingly, the Ndebele people had a very different view of this incident.

The crushing of Ndebele power paved the way for the full establishment of British colonial rule. The colonial administration immediately annexed Matebeleland and parcelled land out to colonial settlers for mining and agricultural purposes. In 1898, a British Government Order in Council recognised the new colony of Rhodesia. The Order in Council remained the country's governing document until 1923 when BSA Company rule ended and Southern Rhodesia obtained Responsible Government status.

The First Chimurenga/Umvukela War (1896)

In 1896, the British colonial administration and the white settler community faced a serious armed insurgency as groups of Africans made a

[18] Assa Okoth, *A History of Africa: African Societies and the Establishment of Colonial Rule 1800–1915*, Vol. 1 (Nairobi: East African Educational Publishers, 2006), 148.

[19] A. J. Hanna, *The Story of the Rhodesia and Nyasaland* (London: Oxford University Press, 1960), 136.

last-ditch effort to dislodge colonialism. Referred to in Zimbabwe's two main indigenous languages of Shona and Ndebele as Chimurenga and Umvukela, respectively, the uprising failed to end white rule but later inspired anti-colonial African nationalism, with African nationalist leaders using what was now called the First Chimurenga/Umvukela War to mobilise support against colonial rule. Another armed uprising in the 1960s and beyond was, significantly, to be called the Second Chimurenga/Umvukela war.[20]

Much to the surprise of the settler community, in 1896, African groups across the country launched armed attacks against the white community, killing some and forcing others to flee into the towns for safety. As the Ndebele had only recently been defeated in the Anglo-Ndebele War of 1893 and the Shona had never resisted the imposition of settler rule, colonial white society had no reason to expect any trouble from the African population. With regard to the Shona-speaking people, especially, the settlers regarded them as cowards who should, in any case, be grateful to the whites for having rescued them from Ndebele overlordship and who would, thus, never rise up. Consequently, the Shona uprising was described by the BSAC as causing 'the greatest surprise to those who, from long residence in the country, thought they understood the character of these (people)'. Explaining why this was so, the 1898 BSAC report continued:

The Mashona race had always been regarded as composed of disintegrated groups of natives ... cowed by a long series of raids from Matabeleland ... and incapable of planning any combined premeditated action. The result has proved that their intelligence has been underrated and their cunning, it cannot be courage ... had not been sufficiently appreciated.... With true Kaffir deceit they have beguiled the Administration into the idea that they were content with the government of the country and wanted nothing more than to work and trade and become civilised; but at a given signal they cast all pretence aside and simultaneously set in motion the whole of the machinery which they had been preparing.[21]

Why did the Ndebele and Shona groups, who, according to settler accounts, were sworn enemies until British colonisation, unite in a common bid to

---

[20] Apparently, 'the term *Chimurenga* comes from the name of a legendary *Shona* ancestor, *Murenga Sororenzou* ... (who) was well known for his fighting spirit and prowess'. For more on this, see M. T. Vambe, 'Versions and Sub-versions: Trends in Chimurenga Musical Discourses of Post Independence Zimbabwe', *African Study Monographs*, 25, 4 (2004), 167–93.

[21] British South Africa Company, *Reports on the Native Disturbances in Rhodesia, 1896–1897* (London: BSAC, 1898).

dislodge British rule? Were the uprisings part of one united movement, or were there many small uprisings occurring separately? Zimbabwean historiography is divided on this issue, with one school of thought arguing that the uprisings were well coordinated by African spirit mediums (religious leaders known among the Shona as ma*Svikiro*) who harmonised the activities of both Shona and Ndebele groups. This school, therefore, sees the first Chimurenga/Umvukela as evidence of pan-Zimbabwean national consciousness.[22] This view has been challenged by a revisionist interpretation that argues that there were, in fact, many separate uprisings, zvimurenga (plural of chimurenga) rather than one pan-national one, and that various groups across the country responded according to their perceived interests rather than as part of any kind of pan-nationalist sensibility. Indeed, some groups decided to remain neutral or to side with the whites, while others took up arms against the settlers according to their analyses of what would best serve their interests at the time.[23] The idea that there was a priesthood or religious leadership coordinating the uprisings has, thus, been strongly challenged.[24]

Causes

Several factors account for the Chimurenga/Umvukela uprisings. Among the Shona-speaking groups, the colonial disruption of traditional life and economy caused much resentment. British colonial rule robbed the Shona of their independence and the right to be ruled by their own leaders according to their customs. Moreover, the new rulers did not respect indigenous institutions and practices and often punished chiefs and their subjects using an alien legal system that the Shona found incomprehensible. In addition, settler colonialism disrupted the indigenous people's long-established trade network with the Portuguese on the Indian Ocean coast, which had supplied them with guns and other valued imports in return for ivory, gold and other commodities. No longer could they access these affordable and much-valued trade goods; they now had to purchase

[22] T. O. Ranger, *Revolt in Southern Rhodesia, 1896–7: A Study in African Resistance*, (Evanston: Northwestern University Press, 1967); T. O. Ranger, 'The Role of Shona and Ndebele Religious Authorities in the Rebellions of 1896 and 1897', in E. Stokes and R. Brown (eds.), *The Zambezi Past: Studies in Central African History*, (Manchester: Manchester University Press, 1966), 94–136.

[23] Ian Phimister, *An Economic and Social History of Zimbabwe, 1890–1948: Capital Accumulation and Class Struggle* (London and New York: Longman, 1988), 20.

[24] Julian Cobbing, 'The Absent Priesthood: Another Look at the Rhodesian Risings of 1896–1897' *Journal of African History*, 18, 1 (1977), 61–84; D. N. Beach, '"Chimurenga": The Shona Rising of 1896–97', *Journal of African History*, 20, 3 (1979), 395–420.

unfamiliar and more expensive South African and British imported goods from settler-run stores.

Even more galling was the settlers' land grabbing which dispossessed the indigenous people of their land and transformed them into squatters and farm labourers overnight. On the basis of British jurisprudence regarding property ownership and rights, the incoming colonial rulers determined that Africans did not have legal ownership of the land on which they lived. They also maintained that most of the land was empty, as there were no people actually occupying the particular stretches of land at the time of colonisation. For these reasons, it was decided that such land was there for the taking. This, of course, violated the indigenous people's sense of land ownership and traditional jurisprudence which did not recognise individual ownership of land but regarded land as communally owned under the spiritual and customary guardianship of the chief.[25]

Acknowledging the role of grievances over land in fuelling the uprising, a Catholic missionary, Fr. Richartz, recalled how, at the time, in Chishawasha, just outside Salisbury, whites 'came and acted as sole proprietors' of the land.

Often the Natives were simply driven away or told that they had to do certain services if they would like to continue to make gardens on their old place. Though we had no native Kraal or Garden on our farm when we arrived, nevertheless old [Chief] Chinamora very often showed his surprise when we spoke of 'our ground, boundaries, beacons etc' – Who gave you this land' he would often ask.[26]

Worse still, the new rulers made numerous tax demands that the indigenous people found intolerable. In order to raise revenue to fund the nascent colonial administration, as well as to force African males into the European labour market of the mines and farms, the colonial administration imposed a variety of taxes, payable in cash, livestock or labour. Among the main sources of resentment were the hut tax imposed in 1893, a dog tax, head tax and a tax on wives in excess of one. To collect these various taxes, the colonial administration created the Native Department in 1895.

Meanwhile, where tax demands did not yield the required number of workers for the local white economy, the settlers resorted to coercion,

[25] A. S. Mlambo, 'This Is Our Land': The Racialization of Land in the Context of the Current Zimbabwe Crisis', *Journal of Developing Societies*, 26 (2010), 39–69.

[26] Jesuit missionary, Father Richartz of Chishawasha, cited in Elizabeth Schmidt, *Peasants, Traders and Wives: Shona Women in the History of Zimbabwe, 1870–1939* (Harare: Baobab, 1992), 37.

rounding up African males and forcing them to work on the mines and farms. In some cases, the workers' wives were taken as hostages to ensure that their husbands did not abscond. Meanwhile, the liberal use of corporal punishment by white employers did not exactly endear them to the African population.[27] Commenting on the abuse of the Africans by the colonial regime, missionary John White reportedly informed his superior overseas in 1894 that some white settlers 'think less of shooting a Mashona than they do of shooting their dog. The burning of huts, stealing of meal and raping of their women are common occurrences'.[28]

Even more loathed were the African policemen, the so-called Native Police, who exceeded their mandate and abused their powers in the enforcement of colonial laws. On missions to round up labourers, to collect taxes or to punish tax dodgers, they often acted like warlords, taking whatever they wanted in the form of goats, cattle and even women. For example, the people of the Mtoko District in the north-eastern part of the country refused to pay taxes and for that they were attacked by groups of government tax collectors and had their cattle and goats confiscated and their homes torched. As further punishment, several hundred males were conscripted for work in the mines.[29] Such actions alienated many Shona-speaking groups and contributed to the uprising. Summing up the Shona people's grievances, one elderly man was quoted saying:

We saw you come with your wagons and horses and rifles ... we said to each other 'they have come to buy gold, or it may be to hunt elephant; they will go again'. When we saw you continue to remain in the country and were troubling us with your laws, we began to talk and to plot.[30]

Equally unhappy were the Ndebele people who, in any case, were still smarting from their defeat and the destruction of their kingdom in 1893 and who were subjected by the settlers to abuses similar to those suffered by the Shona-speaking groups. They particularly resented the manner in which the new rulers were subverting their traditional systems and customs, especially the abolition of the Ndebele monarchy and the exile of Lobengula's two sons to South Africa. Further alienating the Ndebele people and assuring their resentment given their cattle-based economy, the settlers confiscated Ndebele cattle as loot in the wake of the Ndebele

[27] Phimister, *Economic and Social History*, 16.
[28] Cited in Richard Hodder-Williams, *White Farmers in Rhodesia, 1890–1965* (London: Macmillan Press, 1983), 23.
[29] Phimister, *Economic and Social History*, 16.
[30] Hodder-Williams, *White Farmers in Rhodesia, 1890–1965*, 31.

defeat in the war. From October 1893 to March 1896 'anything from 100 000 to 200 000 cattle were seized from the Ndebele. Armed gangs of settlers and contingents of BSA police equipped with Maxim guns roamed across the countryside, taking what they could.... By October–November 1895, Ndebele cattle holdings had been reduced to an estimated 74 000 head ... as the BSA company quickened the pace of cattle confiscation'.[31]

Added to cattle loss was the settlers' indiscriminate expropriation of Ndebele land after the 1893 war, which resulted in the indigenous people being herded into the malarial, tsetse fly–infested and arid Gwaai and Shangani African Reserves created in 1894 in order to free most of the land for white settlement. This policy prompted Ndebele *Induna* (Chief) Gambo to complain in 1897: 'One cause of dissatisfaction and unrest is that after we have lived many years in a spot, we are told that a white man had purchased it and we have to go'.[32] The situation was worsened by hardships which followed a series of unfortunate natural 'disasters' on the eve of the uprising. Reporting on causes of the 1896 uprisings, the Chartered Company highlighted the role of three 'physical plagues' which afflicted the territory in the run-up to the troubles, namely drought, a locust invasion and the outbreak of a cattle disease called rinderpest. In the words of the Company's official report in 1898, the uprising might not have occurred had it not been for 'the phenomenal combination of physical plagues' which Africans attributed to 'the advent and continued presence of the white man'. These were

A drought, abnormal alike in its duration and intensity, had set in ... and continued ... locusts which ... had never made their presence felt, now appeared in swarms that literally darkened the sky, devastating both the veld and the gardens of the country, eating up the crops on which the natives depended for their food.... The simultaneous advent in Rhodesia of the white man and of swarms of locusts, of a kind unknown in the country for forty years, and much more destructive than the ordinary species, caused the locusts to be called by the Matabele *Zintethe za Makiwa* (Locusts of the white man).... And if these plagues were not sufficient, the rinderpest, an absolutely new and unknown disease, suddenly seized the cattle of the Matabele and mowed them down in herds. The action of the government in shooting live and healthy cattle with the view to checking the spread of the disease ... appeared to them more terrible and unaccountable than the rinderpest itself.[33]

[31] Phimister, *Economic and Social History*, 16.
[32] Okoth, *A History of Africa*, 225.
[33] The British South Africa Company, *Reports on the Native Disturbances in Rhodesia, 1896–97* (London: BSAC, 1898).

Meanwhile, both the Shona and Ndebele were subject to forced labour. By 1895, labour requirements on the mines were higher than available African cheap labour, necessitating resort to compulsory labour recruitment in which the settlers, with the help of the Native Department, forced African males to work on the mines. These and other abuses fuelled the 1896 armed uprisings.

Taking advantage of the absence from the country of a large contingent of policemen and soldiers who had left on the ill-fated Jameson Raid on the South African Boer Republic of the Transvaal, the Ndebele rose on 20 March 1896, soon to be followed by the Shona. Armed conflicts between colonial soldiers and African insurgents continued into 1897 when reinforcements brought in from South Africa and England and a determined scorched-earth policy enabled the colonial administration to quell the uprisings. In Matebeleland, the conflict ended with Rhodes' open-air meeting with Ndebele chiefs at Matopos in late 1896 at which the Ndebele were promised amnesty and the withdrawal of imperial troops from their part of the country. In Mashonaland, on the other hand, fighting ended only with the capture of two prominent leaders of the uprising, Nehanda and Kaguvi. By the end of the armed conflict, 450 whites had died and 189 had been wounded. There are no statistics of African casualties, but they probably amounted to many hundreds of people.

Conclusion

The defeat of African resistance had far-reaching political, economic and cultural consequences which were to transform African society and way of life considerably and to contribute to African anti-colonial sentiment that was ultimately to end in another armed conflict between the two races half a century later. The first casualty of the defeat was African self-determination and independence, as Africans became British colonial subjects, governed according to foreign laws. Secondly, the African people lost their land through a series of laws that allowed for its expropriation by the colonial administration for white occupation and use, while Africans were confined to specially designated areas known as African Reserves. They were also increasingly drawn into the capitalist economy, mainly as suppliers of cheap labour, while their culture and religion came under intense and sustained pressure from Western culture, ideologies and organisational principles. As a vanquished people, the Africans became, in effect, second-class citizens, with minimal political rights and economically marginalised and looked down upon. On the part of the white people, victory over African insurgency gave them increased confidence in their right to rule, if only by right of conquest, and strengthened their determination to prevent any future African armed uprising. At the same time, it made the fear of such a potential uprising an ever-present reality that was to influence future African policy which was informed by the fear of being swamped by the black majority as well as fear of the so-called black peril.

The results were, of course, not all despondent for the African people; failure to dislodge colonial rule notwithstanding, the uprisings had set a precedent of armed resistance to, and relatively coordinated action against, foreign rule – a lesson that would prove useful later. The uprising also provided 'martyrs' to the anti-colonial cause in the form of leaders of the insurgency, such as Nehanda, Kaguvi and others whose names could be invoked effectively later to inspire the anti-colonial struggle and to mobilise the future cohort of anti-colonial fighters. In this sense, therefore, one of the long-term results of the First Chimurenga/ Umvukela uprisings was the Second Chimurenga/Umvukela armed anti-colonial uprising of the 1960s to 1979. Meanwhile, between the two armed uprisings, colonial rule exposed Africans to new ideas, Western education and Western medicine as schools, clinics and hospitals were established, mostly by the missionaries.

4

Colonial Economy and Society to 1953

Introduction

From the collapse of the first concerted African armed resistance to British colonialism in 1896–7 until the creation of the political and economic bloc known as the Central African Federation or the Federation of the Rhodesias and Nyasaland in 1953, Southern Rhodesia went through tremendous economic and political changes that established a modern state and changed the way in which the African majority lived. Significant economic advances were registered in mining, agriculture, transportation and manufacturing, while Africans were increasingly incorporated into the evolving capitalist economy, mostly as suppliers of cheap labour. The period also witnessed the advance of Christianity and Western education, which impacted extensively on the African population's culture, belief systems, tastes and self-perception and which, arguably, facilitated the entrenchment of white colonialism in the country while at the same time contributing to the growing African political awareness that was to culminate in the anti-colonial struggle beginning in the 1950s. As the numerically inferior but politically and economically dominant white society worked hard to develop the economy for its own benefit and to keep a tight reign on the country's political structures and systems, with an eye on controlling African aspirations, Africans explored various ways of challenging the status quo, ranging from peaceful mutual-help or solidarity associations and organisations, to workers movements, African independent churches and ultimately to political parties. This chapter traces these various developments that characterised colonial society and economy in the first half-century of European colonialism in Zimbabwe.

The Economy

Cecil John Rhodes's 'Cape-to-Cairo' dream of colonising the entire African continent was inspired partly by his strong belief in the beneficial nature of British rule on the 'lower' races in accordance with the dominant race theories of the time and partly by the belief that great fortunes could be made there. With respect to Zimbabwe, in particular, it was believed at the time that there were abundant gold resources there that would dwarf those found on the Rand in South Africa. This idea of the Second Rand was fed by myths about an Eldorado or the land of Ophir in the African interior that were constantly fed by novelists such as Rider Haggard and his *King Solomon's Mines*, a book that was popular at the turn of the nineteenth century. The myth was also fed by the exaggerated accounts of early white travellers into the interior such as Thomas Baines who travelled in Matebeleland in 1868 and German explorer, Carl Mauch, who visited Great Zimbabwe in 1871, which spoke of rich goldfields in the lands north of the Limpopo. Indeed, in 1889, great publicity was given in South African and British newspapers to Mashonaland as the legendary land of Ophir, while the

BSA Company published a propaganda pamphlet comprising articles from various journals and newspapers ... (with) several references to Mashonaland's ancient past ... (including) an anonymous writer's remarks that 'close to Lobengula lies the land of Ophir, rich beyond imagination with alluvial gold awaiting the expected rush of myriads of diggers.[1]

Not surprisingly, therefore, early settlers such as members of the Pioneer Column firmly believed that they would make their fortunes in the new land very quickly, especially in the light of the numerous mining claims they were promised as reward for their participation in the colonisation process. By the end of 1891, however, it had become clear that the territory was not as well endowed with gold resources as had been claimed, resulting in both the BSAC and the settlers having to review their expectations and to seek other avenues for developing the colony and making a living, including taking up and promoting agriculture.

---

[1] BSA Company, *General Information of the Country and Press Notices* (1889) and 'Painting the African Map Red', *Pall Mall Gazette*, 29 May 1889; cited in A. Chennels, 'Settler Myths', 11.

Agriculture and the Land Question

While mining continued to be very important to Southern Rhodesia's economy, agriculture increasingly became a focus of government economic policy, beginning with the adoption of an official 'white agricultural policy' by the colonial administration in 1908. Before then, all attention had been on mining. Thus, although both individuals and companies owned large tracts of land in the early years, much of it was unutilised. As the Second Rand dream became jaded, some settlers sold off their land claims to companies and either left the country or turned to other economic activities. As a result, large companies, such as John Willoughby's and Rhodesia Land Ltd, bought up large tracts of land, mainly for speculative purposes. Until state support emerged seriously after 1908, therefore, land also remained underutilised for agricultural purposes because there was no domestic market for farm products, as the mines and emerging towns obtained all their agricultural products from African farmers who had sufficiently increased their productivity to take advantage of the new market opportunities. Settlers who called themselves farmers then were, in fact, nothing of the kind, being merely 'storekeepers or small-time prospectors' who hardly cultivated anything and who, reportedly,

used to go out on bartering expeditions to purchase grain, hay, beans, pumpkins or chicken for retailing in ... [urban centres, such as Salisbury, the administrative capital] in exchange for the usual calico and beads ... It was the exceptional one who grew a little tobacco, maize and vegetables, but farming even in these cases was never much more than market gardening.[2]

Eight years after colonisation, there were only an estimated 250 white 'farmers' in the country, whose activities were characterised as mostly 'trading, wood cutting and transport riding' and, possibly, 'cultivating a small patch of mealies'.[3] White agriculture was slow in developing also because of the shortage of cheap labour, lack of capital, the absence of a good transportation system and the smallness of the internal market. Although the domestic market for agricultural products improved slightly during the Anglo-Boer War period (1899–1902) as a result of a decline of imports from South Africa, which resulted in better local prices for grains and other products, as well as because of the development of

[2] Richard Hodder-Williams, *White Farmers in Rhodesia, 1890–1965* (London: Macmillan Press, 1983), 25.

[3] Hodder-Williams, *White Farmers*, 58.

railway transportation that facilitated the movement of products, white agriculture remained largely undeveloped and the white farming community small. In 1901 came East Coast Fever which impacted badly on the country's nascent livestock-rearing sector. Gradually, however, the sector began to grow so that, by 1914, there were an estimated 2,040 white-occupied farms cultivating about 183,400 acres where they grew maize and tobacco, although competition from African farmers made white farming a precarious venture. Indeed, because of growing African peasant production, maize prices on the local market declined considerably between 1903 and 1912, while the tobacco market was equally affected between 1911 and 1914.[4]

In contrast, African peasant production prospered in the first few years of the twentieth century, as African producers serviced the settler population, which numbered some 11,100 in 1901. The prosperity of peasant agriculture in this period can be explained by a number of factors. The Africans were then still living in the fertile areas of the Highveld, within easy reach of markets. The population was still small and, therefore, there was little pressure on land, while the growing number of mines provided markets for the peasant producers. In addition, because white settlers were more concerned with prospecting for gold, they depended on the African producers for their food needs, in some areas creating opportunities for African women to market their agricultural products such as sorghum, beans, pumpkins and potatoes. In areas close to mines and urban centres, 'African agriculturalists were among the first to respond to the ... market' provided by the new dispensation, as 'peasant producers expanded their acreage under cultivation and sold grain, green vegetables, beef, and beer to traders, urban dwellers, and migrant workers on the mines'.[5]

Until white agriculture became established, however, the expansion of peasant production was allowed, as the settler community depended on it. This was soon to change as white commercial agriculture developed as a result of a vigorous state policy and a concerted campaign to promote white agriculture which was based on a multi-pronged white agriculture policy. This began with the creation of an Estates Department in 1908 to promote European settlement and to handle all applications for land.

[4] Ian Phimister, *Economic and Social History*, 60–1.
[5] Elizabeth Schmidt, 'Farmers, Hunters and Gold-Washers: A Re-Evaluation of Women's Roles in Pre-Colonial and Colonial Zimbabwe', *African Economic History*, 17 (1988), 45–80.

In addition, government made available free agricultural training and extension services and set up a Land Bank in 1912 in order

to provide white farmers with loans for the purchase of farms, livestock and agricultural equipment as well as for farm improvements such as irrigation and fencing. Fertilizers, seeds, and stock were made available at subsidised prices. Roads and irrigation works were constructed in close proximity to European settlements. As a result of these incentives, the number of European farmers increased by 82% between 1907 and 1911.[6]

As these services and support structures were restricted to whites only, 'white settlers, from the outset, were placed in an advantageous position compared to their African competitors'.[7] As African agriculture increasingly came under pressure, African farmers were forced to innovate by adopting new technology in the form of the ox-drawn plow, which led to greater rural stratification as output increased for those using the new technology in comparison with those who could not afford it. Another effect of this was to increase the labour burden of women in terms of planting, weeding and threshing, apart from the fact that they also now had to take over other roles and chores that were traditionally the preserve of men when African males migrated to cities and mines as labourers.[8]

Meanwhile, the colonial state intensified its efforts to recruit more settlers by deploying several information officers in Britain. It also engaged the services of a scientist from the Cape, Dr. E. A. Nobbs, to reorganise the Department of Agriculture which had originally been created in 1903. He was tasked with promoting agricultural research and providing advice to farmers through the Department's publication, the *Rhodesian Agricultural Journal*. The government also opened an experimental station near Salisbury, while the BSAC became directly involved in tobacco and citrus fruit agriculture at its various farms in the colony. As a result of these measures, production on white farms increased so that by 1914, 2,040 white farmers were cultivating an estimated 183,400 acres, while tobacco production amounted to 3 million pounds in 1914, compared to merely 147,000 pounds in 1904.[9] By the early 1920s, white agriculture had consolidated itself, with large areas under big companies dominating production and several small farmers estimated at 2,500 in 1925. Farming

---

[6] Elizabeth Schmidt, *Peasants, Traders and Wives*, 66.

[7] Schmidt, 'Farmers, Hunters and Gold-Washers'.

[8] Schmidt, *Peasants, Traders and Wives*, 68; Schmidt, 'Farmers, Hunters and Gold-Washers'.

[9] Hodder-Williams, *White Farmers*, 60.

methods were, however, still poor, with farmers reportedly 'mining' the soil for quick profits rather than using proper scientific methods of agriculture.[10] Overproduction of tobacco in the late 1920s by white farmers resulted in tumbling prices in 1928 when Britain, Rhodesian tobacco's main market, reduced purchases because of overstocking, leaving Rhodesian farmers facing possible bankruptcy. Given this situation, the colonial state had to quickly develop strategies to protect the white farmers in the 1930s, as will be shown in the later discussion.

Not surprisingly, as white agriculture grew, African peasant agriculture gradually declined, partly as a result of stiff competition from white farmers who were heavily supported by the state and also partly because Africans were systematically pushed out of the productive lands to African Reserves which received low rainfall and were less productive and were also becoming increasingly overcrowded. Moreover, as more whites took to farming, demands increased for African production to be curbed in order to reduce harmful competition in the market and to force Africans to provide labour on the farms. As long as African peasants were self-sufficient, it was argued, white farmers and miners would always face the problem of labour shortage. Reflecting this awareness, one government official commented on how ' the local native is getting rich and he sees the day not far distant when he need not work at all' as evidenced by the fact that

[o]ne can hardly see the smallest kraal without its accompaniment of a herd of 20 to 50 head of cattle, plus sheep and goats; and I am told that some kraals possess hundred – up to 600 head of cattle – a good sign so far as the welfare of the native is concerned, but not encouraging from a labour point of view.[11]

Thus it was argued that it was necessary to develop measures to curb African economic self-sufficiency in order to force the Africans into the labour market and to minimise competition from African produce in the marketplace. Among the many steps taken to squeeze the Africans off the land and into the workplace were the increase in hut tax in 1904, the passage of the Private Locations Ordinance in 1908, the Kaffir Beer Ordinance of 1912, prohibiting Africans from brewing and selling African beer, the introduction of a dog tax in 1912 and cattle dipping fees in 1914, as well as the requirement for all Africans living on so-called unalienated land

[10] Phimister, *Economic and Social History*, 125.
[11] Bulawayo Mining Commissioner, cited in Phimister, *Economic and Social History*, 65.

to pay rent and grazing fees to the Chartered company.[12] These measures were reinforced by African land alienation which dispossessed the indigenous people of most of the land and confined Africans to marginally productive land.

Land Alienation

One of the most contentious issues in Zimbabwe's history was the colonial alienation of land, starting with the arrival of the Pioneer Column in 1890, as each member pegged 3,000-acre land claims, in addition to receiving several mining concessions.[13] Thereafter, Africans lost even more land, as the government passed a series of enabling legislation, beginning with the creation of the first African or 'Native' reserves in Matebeleland in 1894, following the recommendations of the 1893 Commission of Enquiry on future land policy to create reserved areas for African occupation in the districts of Gwaai, Tsholotsho and Nkai – malarial regions with poor sandy soils and very little rainfall.[14] By 1905, sixty reserves were already in existence. Land ownership and use were to remain thorny issues throughout the colonial period and eventually helped to fuel the armed liberation struggle of the Second Chimurenga in the 1960s.

At the heart of the dispute was the question of who were the rightful owners of the land – the colonising settlers, or the indigenous people. The colonial settlers claimed ownership by conquest and proceeded to parcel land out on the basis of English law, which was based on individual private ownership of land. African jurisprudence, on the other hand, did not operate on the basis of individual ownership, but regarded land as a communal asset which individuals could use for private sustenance. The colonising authorities took it for granted that the land belonged to the BSAC by virtue of the Charter granted by the British Government declaring it the governing authority of the new territory. The British South Africa Company (BSAC) was thus empowered to dispose of the Territory's land on behalf of the British Crown, as it saw fit. Consequently, the Company sold what it regarded as 'unalienated' land to incoming white settlers for very low sums, at the expense of the African majority.

---

[12] Phimister, *Economic and Social History*, 66.

[13] Parts of this section were originally published in two earlier publications: A. S. Mlambo, 'This Is Our Land: The Racialisation of Land in the Context of the Current Crisis in Zimbabwe', *Journal of Developing Societies* (2010), 26–39 and A. S. Mlambo, 'Land Grab or Taking Back Stolen Land: The Fast Track Land Reform Process in Zimbabwe in Historical Perspective', *Compass*, July 2005.

[14] E. Mlambo, *Rhodesia: The Struggle for a Birthright* (London: Hurst, 1972), 16.

The belief that the land was there for the taking was also based partly on the colonisers' misconception of the nature of African land tenure systems and practices, which led them to assume that the land that was not physically occupied and utilized at the time of their arrival was unspoken for and, therefore, available for their occupation. According to R. Palmer, this misconception was partly born of the fact that the indigenous population was very small at the time, so that it appeared to the incoming white settlers like much of the land was unclaimed. Yet,

if there was much unoccupied land, there was very little which was unclaimed. Shona chiefdoms covered the greater part of the country and their boundaries are always contiguous and precisely defined ... [so that] almost any European occupation of land would have resulted in the alienation of tribal lands.[15]

This initial misunderstanding became, over the years, a very convenient and self-serving justification for the perpetuation of injustices with regard to the marginalisation of Africans in the country's land tenure arrangements. Apparently, the notion of empty or unoccupied lands in occupied colonial territories emerges from

the doctrine of *territorium nullius*, empty land, which asserts that lands occupied by foraging peoples at the time of settlement by Europeans became the sole property of the 'original [European] discoverers' because such native peoples were deemed to be even more primitive than others encountered in European expansion.... (Since) indigenous peoples did not have the usual artefacts that colonisers took to imply 'ownership' (fences, stone houses, adjacent cultivated fields) it was too easy to assume that the locals did not need or want the land and it was therefore vacant or 'empty'. Regarding land as empty was a convenient excuse to lay claim to as much of it as possible.[16]

Thus, in order to make room for incoming settlers, the colonial state introduced a policy of settling Africans in specially designated areas known as Native Reserves. This segregationist position on land tenure was sanctioned by the British government's Southern Rhodesia Order in Council of 1898, which authorised the BSAC to provide land to the Africans 'sufficient for their occupation and suitable for their agricultural or pastoral requirements'. The colonial state created more Reserves following the 1913 Reserves Commission's recommendations, most of them located in the marginal areas of the country, with little rainfall and far away from major transportation lines and market towns located on the

[15] R. Palmer, 'Red Soils in Rhodesia', *African Social Research*, 10 (December 1970), 747–58.
[16] C. Chavunduka and D. W. Bromley, 'Beyond the Crisis in Zimbabwe: Sorting out the Land Question', *Development Southern Africa*, 27, 3 (September 2010), 11.

TABLE 4.1. *Land Distribution Structure in 1914*

Category	Area (million ha)
White land	5.28
BSAC	19.51
Other private companies	3.66
Native areas	9.76

Source: Ministry of Information (2001).[17]

Zimbabwean Highveld running from Salisbury in the north to Bulawayo in the south-west. This was done partly to eliminate African competition, as the quickest way to do this was to 'put ... the native cultivator ... in reserves ... so far away from railways and markets that the white trader will not be able to buy from him and compete with the white farmers'.[18] Table 4.1 presents the country's land allocation by 1914.

As the total white population in the country in 1914 was a mere 28,000, compared to 836,000 Africans, this meant that 3 per cent of the population controlled 75 per cent of the productive land, while 97 per cent were limited to only 23 per cent of the land in the marginal areas of the country.[19]

To justify the location of Reserves in the marginal areas of the country, a new fiction was created, which claimed that Africans preferred to be in those areas because they had a natural aversion to red loamy soils that were harder to work without modern technology. It was argued that Africans naturally preferred the sandy soils in the marginal areas of the country.[20] This was clearly not true given that the colonial authorities had to forcibly remove Africans from the areas taken over by the white settlers and dump them in the reserves. Indeed, as late as the 1940s, government undertook massive removals of Africans from what were redesignated as white areas into malaria-infested parts of the country, hitherto uninhabited, in order to make way for incoming British immigrants after the Second World War, thus giving the lie to the claim that Africans naturally preferred to live in marginal areas.[21] Indeed, the following statement

---

[17] Cited in Abyssinia Mushunje, 'Farm Efficiency and Land Reform in Zimbabwe', Ph.D. dissertation, University of Fort Hare, Alice, South Africa (April 2005), 13.

[18] Phimister, *Economic and Social History of Zimbabwe*, 65.

[19] Mushunje, 'Farm Efficiency and Land Reform', 13.

[20] R. C. Haw, *No Other Home*, (Bulawayo: Stuart Manning, 1960), 74, cited in W. Roder, 'The Division of Land Resources in Southern Rhodesia', *Annals of the Association of American Geographers*, 54, 1 (March 1964), 53–58.

[21] P. S. Nyambara, 'Madheruka and Shangwe: Ethnic Identities and the Culture of Modernity in Gokwe, Northwestern Zimbabwe, 1963', *Journal of African History*, 42

from the then-director of land settlement, F. W. Inskipp in February 1915 suggests the dominant colonial administrator's attitude regarding what lands were suitable for Africans who had been kicked out of their traditional lands:

I see no objection [to making it a Native Reserve] as the area in question, which is practically a conglomeration of kopjes [hills] with very small cultivable valleys in between, is infested with baboons and is only traversable by pack animals.[22]

The 1930 Land Apportionment Act

In 1930 came what became the Magna Carta of racial segregation on land in Zimbabwe in the form of a highly controversial law called the Land Apportionment Act (LAA). This Act divided the land along racial lines, spelling out white areas where Africans could never acquire land, African purchase areas reserved for those Africans who wanted to and could afford to purchase land, and Tribal Trust Lands (TTLs) which were the African Reserves of old where land was owned in Trust on behalf of the Africans. Another category was that of Crown lands that were owned by the state in reserve for future allocation as need arose, as well as for public parks and state forests. It allocated 51 per cent of the total land area of the country to approximately 50,000 whites and only 29.8 per cent to more than 1 million Africans. The land division is documented in Table 4.2.

While racial segregation had always been present since the establishment of the colony in 1890, it had not been formalised in law. The LAA made segregation formal by making land tenure permanently dependent on race, thus aping the South African Land Act of 1913. Describing the racialisation of land in Zimbabwe, the veteran African nationalist Joshua Nkomo said:

The introduction of the Land Apportionment Act was, therefore, the beginning of the permanent divisions of our people into separate sections based on the concept of master and servant, and ruler and ruled (i.e. white versus black).... The whole pattern of life was guided by and resolved round this separation law – the

(2002), 287–306; P. S. Nyambara, 'The Politics of Land Acquisition and Struggles Over Land in the "Communal" Areas of Zimbabwe: The Gokwe Region in the 1980s and 1990s', *Africa*, 71, 2 (2001), 54–108; R. Palmer and I. Birch, *Zimbabwe: A Land Divided* (Oxford: Oxfam, 1992), 8.
[22] F. W. Inskipp, Acting Director of Land Settlement, to P. S. Inskipp, 23 February 1915, cited in Phimister, *Economic and Social History*, 45.

TABLE 4.2. *Land Allocation under the 1930 Land Apportionment Act*

Category	Acres	% of Country
European area	49,149,174	51.0
Native reserves	21,127,040	22.0
Unassigned area	17,793,300	18.5
Native area	7,464,566	7.8
Forest area	590,500	0.6
Undetermined area	88,540	0.1
Total	96,213,120	100.0
Total for African use	28,591,606	29.8

Source: H. V. Moyana, *The Political Economy of Land in Zimbabwe* (Gweru: Mambo Press, 1984), 70.

Land Apportionment Act. Our political, social, economic, educational, and even religious life was coloured, controlled, and directed by this act.[23]

As the African population grew over the years and more and more Africans were evicted from the areas now designated as European areas, there was increasing overcrowding in the Reserves. With overcrowding came the problems of environmental degradation in the form of soil erosion due, in part, to overgrazing and overcultivation. Not surprisingly, agricultural yields declined correspondingly. The colonial state worsened the plight of the African farmers by passing a range of discriminatory laws in the 1930s, such as the Maize Control Act of 1931 and the various slaughter fees charged for all cattle slaughtered for domestic consumption – measures that were designed to promote the white-controlled agricultural export industry at the expense of the African population. Indeed, so effective were the colonial attacks on African agricultural self-sufficiency that by the end of the 1930s, the agricultural economy of the Shona and Ndebele had been destroyed, and Africans were reduced to providing labour 'in the modern sectors of the economy which are controlled and owned by Europeans and local and foreign-based companies'.[24]

African agriculture had started to decline seriously in the 1920s because of a combination of a sharp fall in grain and livestock prices and

[23] J. Nkomo, cited in W. Cartey and Martin Kilson, *The Africa Reader: Independent Africa* (New York: Vintage, 1970), 264.
[24] R. Riddell, 'Zimbabwe's Land Problem: The Central Issue', in W. H. Morris-Jones (ed.), *From Rhodesia to Zimbabwe: Behind and Beyond Lancaster House* (London: Frank Cass, 1980), 1–13.

a drought in 1922, making it difficult for many Africans to meet their fiscal obligations to the state. Alarmed by this trend, the colonial state had introduced corrective measures. The first was to train agricultural demonstrators at the newly opened industrial training schools at Domboshawa outside Salisbury and Tjolotjo in Matebeleland, established in 1920 and 1922, respectively. In addition, the government set up a Native Trust Fund to allocate money from livestock dipping fees for the improvement of cattle and agriculture, and also appointed former American missionary, E. D. Alvord, in 1926, as Agriculturalist for the Instruction of Natives, tasked with training Africans in better farming methods. During his tenure, Alvord insisted on African farmers building contour ridges to lessen soil erosion and encouraged agricultural demonstrators to establish demonstration plots designed to teach the rest of the African population good farming methods by example. He also promoted the establishment of irrigation schemes, apart from insisting on separating grazing and arable areas through centralisation, which involved building homes in a straight line between the two types of land to prevent livestock from straying into the fields. African farmers were suspicious of these measures, which they saw as government's ploy to increase the carrying capacity of the already overcrowded Reserves so that the government would avoid having to allocate more land to the growing African population.[25]

When the 1938 Natural Resources Commission reported on the alarming deterioration of land in the reserves because of overstocking, government passed the Natural Resources Act of 1941 'permitting the authorities to carry out soil erosion protection control and compulsory de-stocking to protect the environment'.[26] Section 36 of the Act provided for the limitation of the numbers of livestock in African areas which were experiencing environmental degradation because of overstocking.[27] Thereafter, pressure on Africans to sell their 'surplus' stock was intensified so that the recently established Cold Storage Commission acquired large numbers of African cattle at its compulsory cattle sales countrywide. As

[25] E. Punt, 'The Development of African Agriculture in Southern Rhodesia with Particular Reference to the Inter-War Years', M.A. Thesis, University of Natal (1979); T. Hove, 'Peasant Agriculture in Mberengwa, 1890–1945: Some Aspects of Economic Disarticulation', B.A. Special Honours dissertation, University of Zimbabwe (1990), 21.

[26] Dale Dore, 'Transforming Traditional Institutions for Sustainable Natural Resource Management: History, Narratives and Evidence from Zimbabwe's Communal Areas', *African Studies Quarterly*, 5, 3 [online], http://web.africa.ufl.edu/asq/v5/v5i3a1.htm (accessed 3 December 2012).

[27] A. S. Mlambo, 'The Cold Storage Commission: A Colonial Parastatal, 1938–1963', *Zambezia*, 23, 1 (1996), 53–72.

a result, more than 1 million head of cattle were forcibly acquired from the Reserves through supervised sales programmes.[28] De-stocking and other state measures did not resolve the problem of environmental degradation which was due mostly to overpopulation, for as the Godlonton Commission discovered in 1944, an estimated '24 reserves were more than 5% overpopulated; 19 were 50 to 100% overpopulated; and 19 were overpopulated by 100% or more'.[29] This made the state even more determined to enforce stricter measures to 'discipline' African peasants. The result was the Native Land Husbandry Act of 1951.

De-stocking was highly unpopular among the African farmers, especially since, in some areas, they 'were being forced to sell cattle against their own wishes ... (and) prices paid for the cattle were very low'. Moreover, 'cattle belonging to Africans who were absent at the time of sale were sold without their knowledge or consent', while Africans who refused to sell their cattle 'were punished or threatened with punishment'. Meanwhile, immature African cattle and cattle otherwise unfit for immediate slaughter were often entrusted by the Cold Storage Commission to white farmers under the Commission's grazier system, in which the farmers were paid handsomely to look after them until such time as they were required by the Commission. Approximately 45,000 cattle per annum, mostly 'graziers and females suitable for breeding', were transferred from African to white areas under this scheme.[30]

African agriculture came under more pressure at the end of the Second World War with a major influx of European immigrants into the country, which increased the white population from 68,954 in 1941 to 218,000 in 1960.[31] To accommodate these incoming settlers and as a reward to white ex-servicemen returning from the front, the Southern Rhodesian Government forcibly removed thousands of Africans from their traditional home areas under the 1944 Land Settlement Act and relocated them in remote, arid and tsetse-infested reserves on the Zambezi escarpment, such as Gokwe and Muzarabani on the northern edges of the country. Ex-servicemen were either given or assisted to acquire farms and were provided with affordable loans for the purchase of equipment and livestock. Further concerned about the continued deterioration of the African

[28] Todd Leedy, 'The Soil of Salvation: African Agriculture and American Methodism in Colonial Zimbabwe, 1939–1962', Ph.D. Dissertation, University of Florida (2000).
[29] Dore, 'Transforming Traditional Institutions'.
[30] Mlambo, 'The Cold Storage Commission'.
[31] A. S. Mlambo, White Immigration into Rhodesia: From Occupation to Federation (Harare: University of Zimbabwe Publications, 2002), 4.

reserves because of overcrowding and what the state regarded as poor farming methods, and also desirous of stabilising labour in the light of the country's emerging manufacturing industry which was in need of permanent urban-based African labour rather than the seasonal migratory labour of the past, the government passed the 1951 Land Husbandry Act (LHA). The thinking behind the Act was evident in the Good Husbandry Bill of 1948 which maintained that the time had come to end the system under which Africans worked in the European economic sector for a wage for part of the time before returning to the Reserves to till their lands for the rest of the year because this

did not conduce to efficiency in either area, nor can the economy of the colony afford to offer satisfactory conditions in both areas for the dual mode of life.... If the principle of the limitation of numbers [allowed to farm in the Reserves] is accepted, then we have to accept that an increasing number will become permanently divorced from the land. Most of these will find a livelihood in the European area.[32]

Specifically, the Act sought to

- provide for a reasonable standard of good husbandry and for the protection of natural resources by all Africans using the land;
- limit the number of stock in any area to its carrying capacity, and, as far as practicable, to relate stock holding to arable land holding as a means of improving farming practice;
- allocate individual rights in arable areas and in communal grazing areas as far as was possible in terms of economic units and, where this was not possible due to overpopulation, to prevent further fragmentation and to provide for the aggregation of fragmentary holdings in economic units;
- provide individual security of tenure of arable land and individual security of grazing rights in communal grazing areas; and
- to provide for the setting aside of land for towns and business centres in the African areas.[33]

The NLHA was similar to the Swynnerton Plan introduced in Kenya in 1954, which also sought to reform the African land tenure system away

[32] Cited in Ian Phimister, 'Rethinking the Reserves: Southern Rhodesia's Land Husbandry Act', *Journal of Southern African Studies*, 19, 2 (June 1993), 225–39.
[33] Victor E. M. Machingaidze, 'Agrarian Change from Above: The Southern Rhodesia Native Land Husbandry Act and African Response', *The International Journal of African Historical Studies*, 24, 3 (1991), 557–88.

from communal to individual ownership in order to improve African agricultural output.[34] Similar policy initiatives called betterment schemes were introduced in South Africa from the 1930s and intensified under the apartheid system in order to make African Bantustans more productive as a way of legitimising the separate development policy of the South African government.[35]

The envisaged revolution in African land ownership under the Act did not materialise, and the exercise was abandoned a few years later mainly because of African hostility to the measure, which sometimes took the form of violence against the African and white implementers of the Act and those seen to be collaborating with them. This was because Africans were not persuaded that the environmental problems in the Reserves were the result only of their alleged poor agricultural practices and maintained that overcrowding due to land alienation by the settlers was the real cause. In the words of one nationalist, 'The problem of the African, the cause being this story of the people's agony, is landlessness'.[36] Consequently, in defiance of state efforts to demarcate arable areas, Africans resorted to 'freedom ploughing', namely defiantly ploughing wherever they wanted regardless of the prescriptions of the Act. Refusal to cooperate with the state's administrative structures in the Reserves made the implementation of the Act difficult, ultimately leading to its suspension in 1962.

Spearheading African resistance to the LHA and equally fuelled by African grievances against the legislation were the emerging militant mass African nationalist organisations of the 1950s, such as the Rhodesia Bantu Voice Association (RBVA) and the Southern Rhodesian African National Congress (SRANC) and its successor the National Democratic Party (NDP). Thus the LHA became, according to George Nyandoro, one of the leaders of the ANC, 'the best recruiter Congress ever had'.[37] By 1961, resistance was assuming alarming proportions, with reports from across the country of

school buildings, teachers' houses, cattle-dipping tanks, beer-garden shelters being burnt down or destroyed ... (while) land allocation maps were torn up by angry

---

[34] N. E. Makana, 'Peasant Response to Agricultural Innovations: Land Consolidation, Agrarian Diversification and Technical Change: The Case of Bungoma District in Western Kenya, 1954–1960', *Ufahamu: A Journal of African Studies*, 35 (1), 2009, 1–17.

[35] G. C. Seneque, *'Betterment Planning in South Africa'*, Master Thesis, University of Natal, Durban (1982).

[36] M. Yudelman, *Africans on the Land* (London: Oxford University Press, 1964), 83. Cited in Dore, 'Transforming Traditional Institutions'.

[37] Phimister, 'Rethinking the Reserves'.

villagers, and Land Development Officers and their assistants assaulted … DCs [District Commissioners] could no longer hold meetings and the administration was grinding to a halt.[38]

The Land Tenure Act (1969)

The last major piece of land legislation in the colonial period was the Land Tenure Act of 1969 which replaced the Land Apportionment Act. The Act allocated an equal amount of land to Africans and whites, despite the fact that whites accounted for only 5 per cent of the population. Under the Act, Africans were not 'permitted even to lease land for entrepreneurial purposes' outside the designated African areas and, therefore, were 'effectively excluded from any meaningful participation in the free enterprise system in all the developed areas of the economy'. In the words of Advocate Bernard Whaley in 1976, 'the Land Tenure Act is, metaphorically speaking, the "constitution" of racial discrimination in this country'.[39] Land was allocated as shown in Table 4.3.

What made colonial land distribution irksome to the African majority was that most land allocated to them was in marginal rainfall and unproductive areas. Zimbabwe's total land area of 39.6 million hectares can be classified into five natural regions on the basis of land use potential and average rainfall patterns. Region I, covering 2 per cent of the land area, receives the highest rainfall and is characterised by specialised and diversified farming. Region II accounts for 15 per cent of the land area and receives lower rainfall than Region I but also sustains intensive crop and livestock farming. Nineteen per cent of the country's land area falls into Region III which is characterised by semi-intensive farming, with emphasis on livestock farming because it is marginal land for crop agriculture, while Region IV (38 per cent of the land area) is good only for semi-extensive agriculture, as rainfall is low and the region is prone to recurrent droughts. Natural Region V covers 27 per cent of the land area and is suitable only for extensive livestock farming. Rainfall in this region is too low and erratic for any crop production. Zimbabwe's agro-ecological zones are as documented in Table 4.4 and Map 4.1.

[38] Phimister, 'Rethinking the Reserves'.
[39] N. Jardine, 'Rhodesia to Zimbabwe: Why Did Things Go So Badly Wrong? A Personal View'. Paper Delivered to the University of the Third Age, Johannesburg, 21 October, cited in Mlambo, 'This Is Our Land'.

TABLE 4.3. *Principal Land Categories under the Land Tenure Act (1969)*

Land Category	Area (ha)	% of Total
European land	18,145,116	46.5
African land	18,202,084	46.6
National land	2,727,617	6.9
Total Zimbabwe	39,074,817	100.0

Source: Mushunje Thesis, 16. Adapted from Moyo (1994).

TABLE 4.4. *Agro-Ecological Zones of Zimbabwe and Recommended Farming Systems in Each Zone*

Natural Region	Area (km2) and % of Land Area	Rainfall (mm per yr)	Farming System
I	7,000 (2%)	>1,000	Specialised and diversified farming
II	58,600 (15%)	750–1,000	Intensive farming
III	72,900 (19%)	650–800	Semi-intensive farming
IV	147,800 (38%)	450–650	Semi-extensive farming
V	104,400 (27%)	<450	Extensive farming

Source: V. Vincent and R. G. Thomas, *An Agricultural Survey of Southern Rhodesia: Part I: Agro-Ecological Survey* (Salisbury: Government Printer, 1960).

The majority of African Reserves, hosting nearly 80 per cent of the population, were in Regions IV and V where crop production was difficult because of their marginal soils and erratic rainfall patterns.

Furthermore, while the African population in the reserves shared increasingly scarce land resources, most white-owned land remained idle and was held mostly for speculative purposes. In 1957, for instance, it was reported that only a million acres were under cultivation out of a total 31.7 million owned by white farmers. Catholic Bishop Donal Lamont denounced this grossly inequitable distribution of land in 1959, which fuelled African resentment, especially when, in contrast to his own dire situation, he saw nearby

hundreds of thousands of hectares of fertile soil which he may not cultivate, not occupy, not grace, because although it lies unused and unattended, it belongs to some individuals or group of individuals who perhaps do not use the land in the hope of profit from speculation.[40]

[40] 'Background to Land Reform in Zimbabwe', http://www.zimembassy.se/land_reform_document.htm (accessed 3 December 2012).

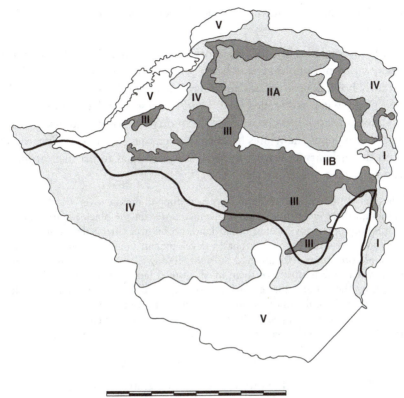

MAP 4.1. Zimbabwe's five natural regions.
Source: FAO – 'Fertiliser Use by Crop in Zimbabwe', http://www.fao.org/
docrep/009/a0395e/a0395e00.htm

Given this situation, it is not surprising that the land issue remained a bone of contention throughout the colonial period and was one of the factors that fuelled the anti-colonial armed struggle of the 1960s known as the Second Chimurenga/Umvukela War, when nationalist forces of both ZANU and ZAPU took up arms to overthrow colonial rule. It is significant, for instance, that nationalists referred to each other as *mwana wevhu* (child of the soil). To underscore the central importance of the land issue in the anti-colonial struggle of the Second Chimurenga/Umvukela, the chairman of ZANU, Herbert Chitepo, said:

I could go into the whole theories of discrimination in legislation, in residency, in economic opportunities, in education. I could go into that, but I will restrict myself to the question of land because I think this is very basic. To us the essence of exploitation, the essence of white domination, is domination over land. That is the real issue.[41]

Until independence in 1980, therefore, land remained divided along racial lines, with whites holding, and being perceived by the African majority to unfairly hold, the biggest and most fertile share of the available land. This was partly what had fuelled the liberation struggle and accounted for the widespread support it received in the countryside where promises of land restoration, once the whites had been driven out, resonated very strongly with the ordinary peasants' present grievances and future aspirations. It can be argued, therefore, that

The war of liberation in Zimbabwe was fought mainly over the land issue. Although there were other repressions meted out on the black population such as prohibitions from owning urban land, prohibitions from developing in certain areas as well as subtle separate development, land constituted the major bone of contention. Africans had no rights to any land, even land in communal areas where the majority of them lived. Instead land rights were held on their behalf by the administrative machinery set up by colonial governments such as the District Commissioners. Traditional chiefs who were the true representatives of the people were stripped of their powers most of which were now exercised by the District Commissioners.[42]

Labour and African Migration

From the onset, the colonial settlers and the economy depended almost entirely on African labour. A perennial problem in the early years was the shortage of labour resulting partly from the reluctance of the indigenous population to work for a wage when they could meet most of their needs through independent agriculture and the sale of their produce to the growing settler market. This is what prompted white farmers and miners to continually demand that the state pass measures to force Africans into the labour market and partially explains the many taxes the colonial state levied on African males. Continued shortage of labour led to the Chibharo, or coerced labour system where African males were press-ganged to work on both private and public projects for no pay.[43] It

---

[41] Cited in Tom Lebert, 'Backgrounder – Land and Agrarian Reform in Zimbabwe'. Land Research Action Network, 21 January 2003.

[42] S. Pazvakavambwa, at www.sarpn.org.za/d000269/Zimbabwe_redistribution.pdf

[43] Most of this section first appeared in J. Crush and D. Tevera (eds.), *Zimbabwe Exodus: Crisis, Migration, Survival* (Cape Town and Ottawa: SAMP and IDRC, 2010) as a chapter 'A History of Zimbabwean Migration to 1990' by the present author and is reproduced

was sometimes disingenuously argued that 'this had a beneficial effect on the Africans because it brought them into contact with civilization and accustomed them to the presence of Europeans in the country'.[44] Instead, this practice roused African resentment and contributed to the 1896 uprisings. In addition, as noted, in order to force African males to join the labour market, colonial authorities imposed a wide range of taxes, including a ten-shilling tax 'for every wife after the first'[45] Arrighi pointed out that white settlers forced Africans into the white labour market through a variety of measures, including expropriation of land and requiring those that remained on such expropriated land to pay rent in the form of labour, and imposing a variety of taxes and a pass system 'intended to direct labour where it was wanted'. Meanwhile, care was taken not to destroy the peasant agricultural sector entirely because by leaving some land in the hands of the Africans, the settlers would keep labour costs low, 'since part of the real cost of the means for the subsistence of the migrant workers' families would be borne by the peasantry'.[46]

Because African workers were still only partially involved in wage labour and tended to maintain one foot in peasant agriculture – a situation that was not satisfactory to the white farmers and mine owners – there were increasing calls for measures to stabilize the labour force. The result was the 1901 Masters and Servants Ordinance and the 1902 Natives Pass Ordinance which were meant to regulate black labour mobility and enforce labour contracts. The first regulated the relations between white masters and their African servants in ways that gave the former unchallenged control over the latter, while the Native Pass Ordinance, passed as a result of pressure from the Chamber of Mines and requiring all male Africans over the age of fourteen to have a registration certificate and a pass in order to seek work, was designed to reduce labour 'desertions and to control the flow of migrant labour'.[47]

In a bid to better control and discipline labour, mine owners adopted the compound system that enabled them to keep their workers in prison-like institutions where they were closely monitored and disciplined by compound management with the help of the assistance of the so-called African 'Police boys'. In order to mitigate the constant

---

with the kind permission of Prof. Jonathan Crush of the Southern African Migration Programme (SAMP).

[44] Per Zachrisson, *Belingwe*, 50.
[45] Schmidt, *Peasants, Traders, and Wives*, 58.
[46] G. Arrighi, 'The Political Economy of Rhodesia', *New Left Review*, 13 (1966), 39.
[47] Zachrisson, *Belingwe*, 150.

shortage of labour, employers set up several recruiting organisations, including the Labour Board of Southern Rhodesia (1899–1901), established by the Rhodesia Chamber of Mines, with the support of the BSA Company; the Rhodesia Native Labour Bureau (RNLB) (1903–1906); a reconstituted Labour Bureau (1906–1912; and a second Rhodesia Native Labour Bureau (1912–1933). Under this system, labour agents recruited contract workers and sent them to the various mines, as needed. Most of the organisations collapsed mainly because of lack of adequate funding.[48] After it was established, the Native Department also recruited labour for the mines.

Persistent shortages of labour were also fuelled by ill treatment of workers by some employers, as, sometimes,

> underground workers who failed to complete their tasks forfeited a day's pay and were sometimes assaulted by white miners ... recalcitrant workers were fined and sometimes imprisoned ...most often, they were whipped. flogging was between six and twelve lashes of the *sjambok* ... sometimes resulting in death.[49]

Workers hit back in a variety of ways, such as sabotaging equipment or farm animals, loafing and desertions, among other actions. Others stopped just long enough to earn some money before moving on to the better-paying South African mines, so that labour shortage remained a major challenge for Southern Rhodesian employers.[50] In frustration, employers turned to migrant labour. After unsuccessful efforts to recruit workers from as far afield as the Red Sea area, China and India, employers concentrated on securing labour from the neighbouring countries, mostly of Mozambique, Nyasaland (Malawi) and Northern Rhodesia (Zambia). Thus, Southern Rhodesia became part of an expanding southern African labour migration network that fed the growing capitalist economies of the region.

Labour migrancy in southern Africa dates back to the 1850s with the development of the sugar plantations of Natal in South Africa. Thereafter, it intensified with the discovery of diamonds at Kimberley in 1870 and gold on the Witwatersrand in 1886. The uneven development of capitalism in southern Africa, with its emerging mining and agricultural economic centres in South Africa in the nineteenth

---

[48] Zachrisson, *Belingwe*, 150; Phimister, *Economic and Social History*, 23.
[49] Phimister, *Economic and Social History*, 88.
[50] Phimister, *Economic and Social History*, 88, Zachrisson, *Belingwe*, 150.

TABLE 4.5. *Africans Employed in Mining, 1906–1910*

Year	Mining			Other		
	Local	Foreign	Total	Local	Foreign	Total
1906	6,345	11,359	17,704			
1907	7,673	17,937	25,610			
1908	10,368	20,563	30,931			
1909	10,689	21,948	32,637	14,518	11,425	25,943
1910	12,739	25,086	37,825	15,962	13,548	29,510

Source: *Report of the Native Affairs Committee of Enquiry*, 1910–11 (Southern Rhodesia Government, 1911), para. 214.

and Southern Rhodesia in the twentieth century, led to new forms of migration, as workers from neighbouring countries migrated in search of work. These 'southernmost centres, where capital was best developed and entrenched, each in turn fed off the less developed northern periphery for part of its labour supplies'.[51] In this regional migration network, Southern Rhodesia played a dual role as both a receiver of migrant labourers from its neighbours and as a supplier of migrant labour to South Africa. Sometimes it was used merely as a conduit by migrant labourers from Malawi and Zambia en route to South Africa, who would work in Zimbabwe for a while to earn enough to finance their journey southward and then move on.

As noted, the general reluctance of local Africans to enter the colonial labour market led to growing reliance on foreign migrant workers who grew to dominate the wage labour market in the early colonial years, not just on the mines and farms, but also in the urban centres. As documented in Table 4.5, foreign migrant labour became increasingly important in the Southern Rhodesian economy before 1910.

Between 1903 and 1933, a government agency, the Rhodesia Native Labour Bureau (RNLB), recruited foreign labour and supplied an average of 13,000 workers to employers each year.[52] Many other workers migrated on their own. By 1912, there were 10,000 Malawian workers in Southern Rhodesia, accounting for 35 per cent of the country's entire

[51] C. van Onselen, *Chibaro: African Mine Labour in Southern Rhodesia, 1900–1933* (Johannesburg: Ravan Press, 1976), 120.
[52] van Onselen, *Chibaro*, 25.

African mine labour force of 48,000.[53] From 1920 onwards, Malawian migrant workers 'exceeded even Southern Rhodesian Africans'.[54]

The colonial state assisted employers to secure labour by concluding labour agreements with Mozambique, Zambia and Malawi. These included the Tete Agreement of 1913 with Mozambique and the Tripartite Labour Agreement of 1937 with Malawi and Zambia. Malawian labour migration was boosted by the introduction of a free transport service for migrant workers in 1927.[55] The Free Migrant Labour Transport Service enabled workers to travel to and from Zimbabwe free of charge and provided them with free rations and accommodation.[56] Until the end of the Second World War, Malawian immigrants were in the majority in Salisbury (Table 4.6) and the rest of the country (where they accounted for between 35 per cent and 50 per cent of all migrant workers).[57] Meanwhile, the capital city of Salisbury remained dominated by migrant workers for a long time, as local Africans were still self-sufficient from their agricultural and market-gardening activities outside the city.

In 1946, the government established the Rhodesia Native Labour Supply Commission (RNLSC) to recruit foreign workers for the country's farming sector. The RNLSC imported an average of 14,000 workers per year from 1946 to 1971.[58] Migrant labour inflows were further encouraged during the Central African Federation from 1953 to 1963 when Malawian migrants coming into Zimbabwe were allowed to bring their families with them. Others were allowed to settle in Southern Rhodesia after a stipulated period of service. An estimated 150,000 Malawians and Zambians took this opportunity to settle in the country.[59] In 1958, an estimated 123,000 Malawian men, out of a total of 169,000 then outside the country, were in Zimbabwe.[60]

---

[53] van Onselen, *Chibaro*, 81–83.

[54] F. Sanderson, 'The Development of Labour Migration from Nyasaland, 1891–1914', *Journal of African History*, 2 (1961), 259–71.

[55] D. G. Clarke, *Agricultural and Plantation Workers in Rhodesia* (Gwelo: Mambo Press, 1977).

[56] P. Scott, 'Migrant Labor in Southern Rhodesia', *Geographical Review*, 44, 1 (1954), 36.

[57] Scott, 'Migrant Labor in Southern Rhodesia', 32.

[58] J. Chadya and P. Mayavo, '"The Curse of Old Age": Elderly Workers on Zimbabwe's Large-Scale Commercial Farms, with Particular Reference to Foreign Farm Labourers up to 2000', *Zambezi*, 19, 1 (2002), 12–26.

[59] F. Wilson, 'International Migration in Southern Africa', *International Migration Review*, 10, 4 (1976), 451–88.

[60] A. Hanna, *The Story of the Rhodesias and Nyasaland* (London: Faber & Faber, 1960), 230.

TABLE 4.6. *African Population by Nationality, Salisbury, 1911–1969*

Origin	1911	1921	1931	1936	1941	1946	1951	1962	1969
Local	2,052 (49%)	3,346 (41%)	6,406 (49%)	9,550 (55%)	12,935 (49%)	15,810 (44%)	30,958 (41%)	154,80 (72%)	231,980 (83%)
Malawi	–	3,219 (40%)	4,637 (36%)	5,406 (31%)	7,665 (29%)	9,509 (26%)	16,399 (22%)	41,530 (19%)	28,830 (10%)
Zambia	1,155 (28%)	366 (4%)	791 (6%)	774 (4%)	935 (4%)	1,355 (4%)	2,339 (3%)	4,800 (2%)	2,770 (1%)
Mozambique	879 (21%)	1,149 (14%)	1,008 (8%)	1,612 (9%)	4,665 (18%)	9,486 (26%)	25,367 (34%)	13,350 (6%)	13,460 (5%)
South Africa & Others	70 (2%)	59 (1%)	161 (1%)	119 (1%)	161	198	425	1,260 (1%)	1,870 (1%)
Unspecified	66	–	–	–	–	–	–	–	1,180
Total	4,222	8,139	13,003	17,461	26,361	36,358	75,488	215,810	280,090

Source: T. Yoshikuni, *African Urban Experiences in Colonial Zimbabwe: A Social History of Harare before 1925* (Harare: Weaver Press, 2007), 160.

TABLE 4.7. *Origin of African Male Employees in Zimbabwe, 1911–1951*

Year	Zimbabwe	Zambia	Malawi	Mozambique	Other Territories	Total
1911	35,933	17,012	12,281	13,588	5,341	84,155
1921	52,691	31,201	44,702	17,198	1,524	147,316
1926	73,233	35,431	43,020	13,068	2,218	171,970
1931	76,184	35,542	49,487	14,896	2,983	179,092
1936	107,581	46,884	70,362	25,215	2,440	252,482
1941	131,404	48,163	71,505	45,970	2,468	299,510
1946	160,932	45,413	80,480	72,120	4,399	363,344
1951	241,683	48,514	86,287	101,618	10,353	488,455

Source: P. Scott, 'Migrant Labor in Southern Rhodesia', *Geographical Review*, 44, 1, (1954), 31.

TABLE 4.8. *Foreign Workers in Zimbabwe, 1956*

Sector	Zambia		Malawi		Mozambique	
	M	F	M	F	M	F
Mining	9,718	63	15,976	91	11,579	44
Commercial Farming	12,218	1,027	57,226	4,315	54,896	8,441
Manufacturing	5,762	154	14,694	326	13,050	201
Construction	4,478	2	10,435	12	14,870	7
Services	704	0	1,694	0	1,411	2
Commerce	1,380	17	4,567	17	3,599	7
Transport	1,801	0	3,316	13	2,517	2
Domestic Work	4,847	127	19,534	284	16,281	28
Total	40,908	1,390	127,442	5,058	118,203	8,732

Source: J. Crush, V. Williams and S. Peberdy, 'Migration in Southern Africa', *Report for SAMP* (Cape Town, 2005), 4.

The number of male labour migrants from Zambia, Malawi and Mozambique continued to increase (Table 4.7). By the 1950s, they were well represented in all sectors of the economy (Table 4.8). With the exception of commercial agriculture, there were few female migrants from these countries. Foreign workers continued to be very significant in that sector until the 1970s (Table 4.9).

TABLE 4.9. *Foreign Workers in Commercial Agriculture, 1941–1974*

Year	No.	% of Total Employment
1941	56,083	–
1946	84,089	56
1951	114,878	62
1956	137,030	60
1961	135,330	50
1969	130,235	43
1970	114,693	39
1971	119,275	39
1972	120,964	36
1973	118,000	34
1974	119,000	33

Source: D. Clarke, *Agricultural and Plantation Workers in Rhodesia* (Gweru: Mambo Press, 1977), 31.

White Migration 1890–1990

From a handful of white settlers that came with the Pioneer Column, numbering some 700 or so people, the white population of Southern Rhodesia slowly increased in the coming years,[61] not at as fast a pace as Cecil John Rhodes would have wanted, given his determination to develop Rhodesia as a 'white man's country'.[62] Before colonisation, white hunters, adventurers, explorers and missionaries had long traversed the land between the Limpopo and the Zambezi, but none had settled permanently in the region. This was all to change following the hoisting of the British Union Jack at Fort Salisbury (now Harare) in 1890 when the BSAC and subsequent administrations made determined efforts to encourage white immigration into the country. Figure 4.1 shows a British South Africa Company Prospectus promoting British emigration to Rhodesia.

Pre–First World War immigration was fuelled in the run-up to the establishment of the Union of South Africa in 1910 when a large inflow of mostly English-speaking immigrants, rising from 11,000 in 1901 to 23,000 in 1911, entered the country from South Africa, making this the

---

[61] Originally published as Mlambo, *White Immigration into Rhodesia*.
[62] A. Keppel-Jones, *Rhodes and Rhodesia: The White Conquest of Zimbabwe, 1884–1902* (Montreal and Kingston: McGill-Queen's University Press, 1983).

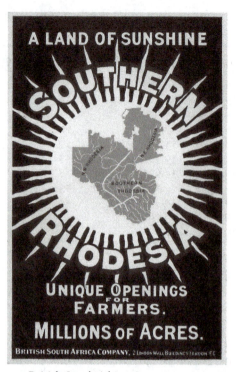

FIGURE 4.1. British South Africa Company prospectus, 1909.
Source: http://www.latrobe.edu.au

fastest white population growth decade in the entire period of colonial rule (Table 4.10). Many of the English-speaking South Africans were escaping what they regarded as an unfairly pro-Afrikaner Union.

After a hiatus during the First World War, white immigration picked up again.[63] The end of Company government in 1923 and Southern Rhodesia's attainment of responsible government and the subsequent provision of development assistance by the British government together with the British inauguration of a sponsored three-year settlement scheme led to substantial immigration from 1924 to 1928. The numbers declined from 1931 to 1936 because of the Great Depression and the deliberate Southern Rhodesian government policy of discouraging immigration in order to minimize unemployment. Immigration also declined considerably during the Second World War because of the difficulties of overseas travel.

[63] *Rhodesia: Official Yearbook* (Salisbury: CSO, 1924), 37.

TABLE 4.10. *White Population Increase,*
1891–1969

Year	Total	% Increase
1891 (Est.)	1,500	–
1904	12,596	14.0
1911	23,606	87.0
1921	33,620	42.0
1931	49,910	48.0
1941	68,954	38.0
1951	136,017	97.0
1960	218,000	60.0
1969	262,000	14.0

Source: *Rhodesia, Census of Population 1904–*
1969 (Salisbury: CSO, 1969), 62.

After the war, immigration increased dramatically as hundreds of demobilised British soldiers entered the country as part of the Southern Rhodesian government's post-war settlement scheme. In 1948, a record 17,000 immigrants arrived.[64] More than 100,000 Africans were moved from their lands to accommodate the new arrivals.[65] Additional immigrants were attracted by jobs and other economic prospects in the rapidly industrialising Southern Rhodesian economy. Job reservation provided unlimited opportunities for white immigrants who could live 'a privileged, comfortable life.'[66]

Economic depression in the Central African Federation from 1956 to 1958, and the rise of militant African nationalism, led to a decline in white immigration. This decline continued in the 1960s when economic sanctions were imposed on Rhodesia after its unilateral declaration of independence (UDI) in November 1965. Subsequently, escalating military clashes between the regime and nationalist liberation forces made the country unattractive as a destination for European migrants. However, some immigrants entered the country fleeing black rule in African countries such as Kenya, Zambia and the Congo. The country also received large numbers of immigrants from Mozambique and Angola in 1975 following the end of Portuguese colonial rule in those countries.

[64] B. Schutz, 'European Population Patterns, Cultural Resistance and Political Change in Rhodesia', *Canadian Journal of African Studies*, 7, 1 (1973), 16.
[65] Palmer and Birch, *Zimbabwe: A Land Divided*, 8.
[66] Schutz, 'European Population Patterns', 16.

TABLE 4.11. *White Population by Country of Birth, 1901–1956*

Year	% Zimbabwe	% South Africa	% UK/Eire	% Other
1901	n/a	n/a	n/a	n/a
1904	10.1	27.3	44.4	18.2
1911	13.6	30.7	40.9	14.8
1921	24.7	34.6	31.4	9.3
1926	29.1	32.6	29.2	9.1
1931	29.2	34.5	27.1	9.2
1936	34.1	32.8	23.8	9.3
1941	34.1	27.9	26.4	11.6
1946	37.7	26.4	18.3	17.6
1951	31.4	30.4	28.8	9.4
1956	32.5	28.9	28.1	10.5

Source: A. Rogers and C. Frantz, *Racial Themes in Zimbabwe: The Attitudes and Behaviour of the White Population* (New Haven, CT: Yale University, 1962), 14.

TABLE 4.12. *White Population by Country of Birth, 1969*

Place of Birth	No.	%
Rhodesia	92,934	40.7
Britain	52,468	23.0
South Africa	49,585	21.7
Portugal	3,206	1.4
Elsewhere	30,103	13.2
Total	228,296	100

Source: *Southern Africa: Immigration from Britain, A Fact Paper by the International Defence and Aid Fund* (London: IDAF, 1975), 17.

Throughout the twentieth century, foreign-born whites outnumbered those born in the country (Table 4.11). The dominance of immigration over natural increase was still evident as late as 1969 when approximately 59 per cent of the white population were foreign-born. Of these, more than 55 per cent arrived after the Second World War.[67] Table 4.12 documents the white population by country of birth by 1969.

[67] Mlambo, *White Immigration into Rhodesia*.

TABLE 4.13. *White Net Migration and Natural Increase,*
1901–1969

Period	Net Migration	Natural Increase	Total Increase
1901–11	11,083	1,491	12,574
1911–21	5,835	4,179	10,014
1921–31	10,145	6,145	16,290
1931–41	11,025	9,019	19,044
1941–51	50,066	16,576	66,642
1951–61	47,097	38,811	85,908
1961–69	(-)13,914	20,706	6,792

Source: *Census of Population*, 1969, 3.

TABLE 4.14. *Racial Composition of Population,*
1911–1951

Year	White	Asian	Coloured	Black*
1911	23,730	880	2,040	752,000
1920	32,620	1,210	2,000	850,000
1930	47,910	1,660	2,360	1,048,000
1940	65,000	2,480	3,800	1,390,000
1947	88,000	3,090	4,750	1,781,000
1948	101,000	3,280	4,880	1,833,000
1949	114,000	3,400	5,000	1,895,000
1950	125,000	3,600	5,200	1,957,000
1951	136,017	4,343	5,964	2,000,000

*These were estimates based on periodic population counts. The first comprehensive census of the African population was not until 1962, although limited sample surveys were taken in 1948, 1953 and 1955.

Source: Southern Rhodesia, Central Statistical Office, *Official Yearbook of Southern Rhodesia* (Salisbury: Rhodesia Printing and Publishing Company, 1952), 130.

Until 1961, net migration consistently outnumbered natural increase (Table 4.13), while the white population was always a minority, as shown in Table 4.14. One reason for the slow increase of the locally born white population, at least in the early period, was the paucity of white women in the country. Until 1911, the gap between the sexes was very wide. Thereafter it narrowed as more vigorous efforts were made to attract female immigrants. The percentage of white women in the country rose from 34 per cent of total white population in 1911 to 44 per cent in

TABLE 4.15. *White Population Sex Ratio,*
1901–1956

Year	Sex Ratio (Male: Female x 100)
1901	278
1904	246
1911	194
1921	130
1926	126
1931	120
1936	116
1941	113
1946	116
1951	111
1956	107

Source: Rogers and Frantz, *Racial Themes in Southern Rhodesia*, 15.

1921. Increasingly, the white population began to resemble that of older settler societies (Table 4.15).[68]

A prominent feature of the history of white migration was its high turnover rate. For every ten immigrants who entered the country between 1921 and 1926, seven left.[69] Between 1926 and 1931, the ratio was 5:3 and between 1931 and 1936, it was 9:7. An analysis of net migration between 1921 and 1964 shows that, in this period, Rhodesia received a total of 236,330 white immigrants but lost 159,215, or 67 per cent, through emigration (Table 4.16).

The inflow of white immigrants into the country might have been larger had successive Rhodesian governments not been very selective about the type of immigrants they would accept. Determined to allow in only the 'right type' of immigrant, by which they meant British immigrants, the government discouraged other nationalities and ethnic groups from migrating to the country. Of the 33,620 whites in Rhodesia in 1921, 32,203 were British by birth or naturalization. By 1931, British settlers accounted for 92 per cent of the white population. Similarly, the majority of immigrants during the immediate post-war period were British-born and nearly half migrated directly from Britain to Rhodesia.[70]

[68] Schutz, B. 'European Population Patterns', 8. See also, Mlambo, *White Immigration into Rhodesia*, 8–9.
[69] *Census of Population of Zimbabwe, Pt. 1* (Salisbury: CSO, 1941), 5.
[70] Schutz, 'European Population Patterns', 17.

TABLE 4.16. *Net White Migration, 1921–1964*

Period	Immigrants	Emigrants	Net Migration
1921–26	9,400	6,676	+ 2,724
1926–31	20,000	12,685	+ 7,421
1931–36	9,000	7,058	+ 2,032
1941–46	8,250	6,192	+ 2,058
1946–51	64,634	17,447	+ 47,187
1955–59	74,000	39,000	+ 35,000
1960–64	38,000	63,000	− 25,000

Source: *Census of Population*, 1969, 168.

Urbanisation

Apart from the very early urbanisation thrust associated with the pre-colonial societies of Great Zimbabwe, Khami, Dhlodhlo and related archaeological sites which were relatively large population centres for the time, the country does not have a prominent history of urbanisation before European colonisation, so that the phenomenon can be regarded as one brought about by Western colonisation. Before then, the African population tended to live in dispersed settlements that were consistent with a pastoral life based on crop agriculture and livestock rearing. The country's first colonial urban centres were established in the last decade of the nineteenth century. Colonialism's infrastructural, economic and administrative needs necessitated the establishment of towns and later cities.

The first modern towns developed initially as military posts established as resting places by the Pioneer Column on its march from South Africa to Salisbury, the subsequent capital city of Southern Rhodesia. Not surprisingly, Fort Tuli, Fort Victoria (Masvingo), Fort Charter and, finally, Fort Salisbury were the first white settlements which later developed into towns. Thereafter, population clusters developed around mines and farming centres, giving rise to a chain of small settlements. The establishment of a railway network that linked South Africa to the port of Beira in Mozambique through Bulawayo and Salisbury in 1902 produced new major settlements.[71] The completion of a railway line linking Bulawayo and Victoria Falls on the Zambezi River in the north promoted the development of the mine and town of Wankie (Hwange) and the tourist town

[71] M. A. H. Smout, 'Urbanisation of the Rhodesian Population', *Zambezia*, 4, 2 (1975–6), 79–91.

of Victoria Falls. By 1923, Bulawayo was the largest town with a white population of 16,363, followed by Salisbury, with 6,462 whites, and Umtali (Mutare) and Gwelo (Gweru). Among the smaller towns were Fort Victoria (Masvingo), Que Que (Kwe Kwe) and Umvuma (Mvuma).[72] This early phase lasted from 1890 to the eve of the Second World War.[73]

The second phase, from the Second World War to the birth of the Federation of Central Africa in 1953, saw the expansion and consolidation of the country's urbanisation as a result of the development of the country's manufacturing sector which saw not only a rapid increase in the number of establishments and the volume of investment in the sector, but also an increase in government's active support for select industrial sectors such as iron and steel, meat-processing, textile and sugar industries, among others. The period also witnessed an influx of white immigrants from post-war Europe, most of who settled in the towns. Among the towns that benefitted from these developments were Kwekwe, which developed a thriving iron and steel industry at the Rhodesia Iron and Steel Company (RISCOM) site, and Gatooma (Kadoma) with its cotton and textile industrial complex and cotton research centre.[74]

The establishment of the Federation of Rhodesia and Nyasaland in 1953 gave a further boost to urbanisation, especially because Salisbury became the Federation's capital and thus attracted infrastructural and other investment. Among the institutions that were established in Salisbury at the time were the University of Rhodesia and Nyasaland (University of Zimbabwe) and one of the country's two largest public hospitals. The construction of the Kariba Dam provided the necessary electrical power. The period of the declaration of unilateral independence (UDI) from 1965 onwards, when international economic sanctions against the regime of Prime Minister Ian Smith were imposed in reprisal, forced the economy to resort to import substitution industrialisation. As a result, the country experienced rapid economic growth in the period, resulting in urban expansion. Also in this period, government embarked

[72] W. D. Gale, *The Years in between, 1923–1973: Half a Century of Responsible Government in Rhodesia* (Salisbury: Mardon Printers, n.d.), 11.

[73] Killian Munzwa and Jonga Wellington, 'Urban Development in Zimbabwe: A Human Settlement Perspective', *Theoretical and Empirical Researches in Urban Management*, 5, 14 (February 2010), 121–6.

[74] Munzwa and Wellington, 'Urban Development in Zimbabwe'; K. H. Wekwete, 'Urbanisation, Urban Development and Management in Zimbabwe', in K. H. Wekwete and C. O. Rambanepasi (eds.), *Planning Urban Economies in Southern and Eastern Africa* (Avebury: Belmont, 1994).

TABLE 4.17. *Population Trends in Selected Towns, 1936–1974*

Urban Area	1936	1941	1946	1951	1969	1974
Salisbury (Harare)	20,177	32,008	45,993	75,000	280,000	420,000
Bulawayo	15,322	21,340	33,322	56,000	187,270	270,000
Gwelo (Gweru)	2,165	5,100	7,237	9,800	36,840	51,000
Que Que (Kwekwe)	2,608	3,686	3,860	4,600	18,740	30,000
Gatooma (Kadoma)	1,718	1,564	2,380	4,600	18,740	30,000
Umtali (Mutare)	3,566	4,812	6,549	10,900	36,300	48,000
Totals	45,550	68,510	99,341	161,200	589,480	859,000

Source: D. Auret, *A Decade of Development, Zimbabwe* (Gweru: Mambo Press, 1990). Taking a wider range of towns in the period 1961 to 2002, the picture that emerges reveals a very rapid urban population growth, as Table 4.18 shows.

on the construction of African housing, with the result that many African townships were built in the major cities.[75]

Non-Africans, mainly whites, Indians and Coloureds, were the most urbanised population groups before the country's independence in 1980. According to the first census of 1904, 58 per cent of the country's non-African population was reported as resident in urban areas. By 1974, the figure had risen to 88 per cent.[76] Initially, there was a very small indigenous African population permanently resident in urban areas, as most people were migrant workers oscillating between the towns/mines and rural areas. As documented in Table 4.16, most of the Africans in the major towns in the early decades of colonisation were immigrant workers from neighbouring territories.[77] Increasingly, an urban-based African population developed, although links to the rural areas remained strong. However, the level of urbanisation of the African population was low, remaining at less than 20 per cent of the total African population by the mid-1970s.[78]

[75] Among the African townships built in this period in Harare were Kambuzuma (1964) and Glen Norah (1971).
[76] Smout, 'Urbanisation of the Rhodesian Population', 82.
[77] T. Yoshikuni, *African Urban Experiences in Colonial Zimbabwe: A Social History of Harare Before 1925* (Harare: Weaver Press, 2007), 160.
[78] Smout, 'Urbanisation of the Rhodesian Population', 89.

TABLE 4.18. *Zimbabwe's Urbanisation Trends, 1961–2002*

Name of Urban Centre	1961/62*	1969*	1982*	1992	2002
Harare	310,000	386,000	656,00	1,184,169	1,903,510
Bulawayo	211,000	245,000	414,000	621,742	676,787
Chitungwiza	-	15,000	172,000	274,035	323,260
Gweru	39,000	46,000	79,000	124,735	141,260
Mutare	43,000	46,000	70,000	131,367	170,106
Kwekwe	21,000	31,000	48,000	74,982	93,608
Kadoma	19,000	25,000	45,000	67,267	76,173
Masvingo	10,000	11,000	31,000	51,746	69,993
Chinhoyi	8,000	13,000	24,000	42,946	49,603
Redcliff	5,000	10,000	22,000	27,994	32,346
Marondera	7,000	11,000	20,000	39,384	52,283
Chegutu	7,000	9,000	20,000	30,122	42,959
Shurugwi	7,000	8,000	13,000	6,029	16,866
Kariba	6,000	4,000	12,000	21,039	24,210
Victoria Falls	2,000	4,000	8,000	15,010	31,519

* Estimates

Sources: K. H. Wekwete, 'New Directions for Urban Development and Management in Zimbabwe and Rapidly Urbanising Countries: The Case of Zimbabwe', *Habitat International* 16, 2 (1992), 53–63; Government of Zimbabwe, *Census Report* (Harare: Central Statistical Office, 2002).

After independence, the government built yet more housing and also embarked on what was known as the growth-point strategy which sought to develop industrial centres in the countryside in order to stem rural-to-urban drift and to provide jobs to people in their own localities. This also stimulated urban development in hitherto outlying centres such as Gokwe, Murambinda and other places. The growth of the country's urban centres between 1936 and 1974 is documented in Table 4.17, while Zimbabwe's urbanisation trends are documented in Table 4.18.

Transportation

Roads

In the first decade of colonisation, Zimbabwe had a very rudimentary transportation structure, comprised mostly of dirt tracks inherited from the trails made by the wagons of white hunters and adventurers who had traversed the country before 1890.[79] In this period, however, roads were mere adjuncts of the railway system which transported goods and people from the surrounding farms and population centres to the nearest railway stations. Gradually, however, they assumed a relatively separate identity and combined in their operations the dual functions of serving as feeder lines to the railways as well as being the railways' competitors. In 1891, the British South Africa Company contracted Frank Johnston and his associates to construct a good wagon road, to erect forts and to keep the country's communication lines open. Johnson's company constructed several roads connecting the country to South Africa and Mozambique and connecting various points within the country. However, travelling on these 'roads' was an adventure, with ox-drawn wagons having to plough through deep sand and black clay and often raising dense clouds of dust that reportedly 'chocked everything and reduced Europeans and Africans alike to a uniform grey'.[80]

So rudimentary and primitive were these roads that sometimes it was difficult for road users to tell them apart from the animal spoors around them, for as one Sir Crawford Douglas-Jones noted:

One of the chief difficulties [for road users] was that of keeping to the road they wished to follow. On leaving a town, the track would be distinct and easy to follow but a few miles out, unless one was familiar with the road, it became difficult to decide which was the correct way, either the well-defined spoor, or the indistinct one often hidden in the tall Tambookie grass.

Worse still, during the rainy season, interminable delays, sometimes of up to six weeks, were not uncommon as a result of flooded rivers which forced travellers to bide their time until the rivers were passable once more. Not surprisingly, the journey from South Africa to Salisbury could take as long as four months or more. As if the primitive condition of the roads was not enough trouble, travellers faced added hardships with the rinderpest outbreak at the turn of the century which decimated the country's draught power.[81]

[79] The sections on road and air transport were originally published as A. S. Mlambo, 'From Dirt Tracks to Modern Highways: Towards a History of Roads and Road Transportation in Colonial Zimbabwe 1890 to World War', *Zambezia*, 21, 2 (1994), 147–66; *Zambezia*, 22, 1 (1995), 99–116; A. S. Mlambo, 'A History of Civil Aviation in Zimbabwe, 1912–1980', *Zambezia*, 19, 2 (1992), 99–116; and A. S. Mlambo, 'A Decade of Civil Aviation in Zimbabwe: Towards a History of Air Zimbabwe Corporation 1980 to 1990', *Zambezia*, 22, 1 (1995), 79–100.

[80] B. Whyte, 'From Wagons to Wings', *Illustrated Life Rhodesia*, 4, 19 (1972), 16–31.

[81] Whyte, 'From Wagons to Wings'.

In an effort to resolve the problem, one enterprising settler, Lt-Colonel J. Flint, imported twenty baggage and fourteen riding camels and the requisite number of Sikh attendants in 1903. The camels' usefulness proved very short-lived, however, for in the words of one commentator,

Alas, Rhodesia's ships of the veld never really set sail; within a few months, one camel had died of what was a fairly common complaint in Rhodesia in those days – cirrhosis of the liver – and later foot and mouth disease broke out among the others.[82]

It was not only the main roads linking the country's towns which were in poor condition, for it was also reported that, even in the towns, the roads were in such an appalling state that many settlers resorted to the use of bicycles. An amusing account is given of the famous author and poet Rudyard Kipling's experience when riding a bicycle on Bulawayo's streets one day when it was reported that

[Kipling] hired a bicycle from Dulys for 7s 6d and set off for the Umgusa Hotel, where he arrived with a flourish. In a spirited moment he took a running leap over the low railing of the verandah. His style was admirable, but sad to relate, he lacked altitude and caught the top in his flight, landing heavily on a flower bed.[83]

The country's road system remained poor even after the Chartered Company Government created the Roads Department in 1895. Operating as a subsection of the Public Works Department and administered by the Secretary for Mines and Roads, the Roads Department was given the onerous task of constructing and maintaining roads throughout the country. The task was to prove very difficult to fulfil mainly because, for many years, the department remained underfunded and possessed neither the necessary manpower nor the required road construction equipment. It is not surprising, therefore, that the department accomplished little before the First World War. Meanwhile, throughout the years of the BSAC administration, farmers continued to demand better roads, particularly as they felt that the railways were taking advantage of their monopoly position as the sole carriers of goods within the country to charge unacceptably high transportation rates. Complaints became more vociferous following the increase in railway freight rates in 1916 when the rate on grain was hiked by 100 per cent from 1 d to 2 d in British

[82] Whyte, 'From Wagons to Wings'.
[83] Whyte, 'From Wagons to Wings'.

TABLE 4.19. *Number of Vehicles in Southern Rhodesia, 1928–1929*

	Municipalities		Elsewhere		Total	
Year	1928	1929	1928	1929	1928	1929
Motor cars	4,625	5,275	6,175	7,730	10,800	13,150
Other vehicles (iron-tired)	850	725	7,450	7,200	8,300	7,925

Source: NAZ, S482/477/39, Roads: General, Number of Vehicles in the Colony, Minister of Mines and Public Works to PM, 23 July 1930.

currency. In 1918, farmers complained bitterly about the railways' failure to give sympathetic treatment to Rhodesian farmers to enable them to exploit the lucrative Johannesburg market.

By the end of Company rule in 1923, the country's road system was still relatively primitive, although a number of gravel roads had been constructed throughout the country and travel was no longer as hazardous as it had been earlier in the century. With all its shortcomings over the years, the Roads Department had managed to construct more than 8,000 miles of public roads by the time it was transferred from the Public Works Department to the newly created Secretariat for Mines and Works in 1922.[84] However, much still remained to be done before the country could claim to have an efficient and viable road system. Road construction registered major advances in the post-Company period as successive governments made serious efforts to expand and improve the country's road network in order to promote white settlement and economic development. From 1923, government funding for road construction and maintenance increased steadily from the sum of £15,000 allocated to the Roads Department in that year to £58,000 in 1924, £112,000 in 1926 and £202,000 in 1927.[85]

Government's determination to develop the country's road system was partly in response to the growing number of vehicles in the country, as cars became more popular and car imports increased. Table 4.19 documents the increase in the number of cars between 1928 and 1929.

[84] Southern Rhodesia, *Report on Roads by the Acting Secretary for Mines and Works for the Year 1922* [Presented to the Legislative Council, 1923]; 'Transport in Rhodesia'; T. C. Salmon, 'A Short History of Rhodesian Roads', 850.

[85] National Archives of Zimbabwe, LE 3/1/1, Folios 728–733, Moffat to Coghlan, March 1926; *Report of the Chief Road Engineer for the Year Ended 31st December 1937*.

FIGURE 4.2. Strip road, Rhodesia, 1960s.
Source: http://www.flickr.com

In 1930, government introduced permanent asphalt-paved strip roads, as shown in Figure 4.2. By 1938, motorists could travel continuously on asphalt paving for 1,182 miles. By the outbreak of the Second World War, the country boasted a fairly modern highway system of asphalt strip roads and reasonably usable gravel roads linking major population centres to each other and with the surrounding countryside. Following a period of relative neglect during the war, as efforts were focused on the war effort, the road system was further improved by replacing the strips with the conventional bituminous mat, starting in 1946.

Railways
From the start, the BSAC administration showed great determination to develop the country's railways transport system to link Central Africa to the ports of South Africa and Mozambique by sponsoring several railway companies and raising the necessary funding to ensure the rapid

expansion of the railway network.[86] Consequently, already in November 1897, the railway line from South Africa reached Bulawayo in the south-western part of the country, while Umtali (Mutare) in the east was linked to the Indian Ocean in February 1898. In 1902, the link between Salisbury and Bulawayo and Umtali was completed, providing a continuous line from Beira on the Indian Ocean coast in Portuguese-ruled Mozambique and South Africa. Then the line reached the northern holiday resort town of Victoria Falls from Bulawayo in 1905 and the border of the Congo (Democratic Republic of the Congo) in 1909. By the end of Company rule in 1923, the country's main railway network, linking the country with South Africa through Botswana, with the Indian Ocean through the Mozambican ports of Beira and Lourenco Marques (Maputo), and with Zambia through Victoria Falls was all in place. Until 1927, the railways were run by a private consortium, the Mashonaland Railway Company, after which it came under the Rhodesia Railways Company. Rhodesia Railways Limited acquired the railway system in October 1936, while, in April 1947, the Rhodesian government took over and created the Rhodesia Railways Company in 1949 to administer the railway system, including the lines in Zambia. Following the break-up of the Federation, Rhodesia Railways controlled only the Rhodesian-based lines from 1967 onwards until 1979 when the company's name changed to the Zimbabwe Rhodesia Railways and then to National Railways of Zimbabwe at independence in 1980. Map 4.2 documents the development of Rhodesia's railway system over time.

Air Transport

Civil aviation in Rhodesia was initially promoted by the Aeronautical Society of Rhodesia founded in Salisbury in 1912 under the patronage of Sir William Milton, the country's administrator. A decision by the British Air Ministry in 1918 to open an air route to Cape Town, South Africa, was followed two years later by the arrival in Bulawayo of the

---

[86] For insightful studies of the history of the railways of Zimbabwe, see Ian Phimister, 'Towards a History of Rhodesia Railways', *Zimbabwe History*, 12 (1981), 71–100; J. R. Lunn, '*Capitalism and Labour on the Rhodesian Railway System 1890–1939*', D.Phil. Thesis, Oxford University (1986); A. H. Croxton, *Railways of Zimbabwe: The Story of the Beira, Mashonaland and Rhodesia Railways* (London: David and Charles, 1982); P. Maylam, 'The Making of the Kimberley-Bulawayo Railway: A Study in the Operations of the British South Africa Company', *Rhodesian History*, 7 (1977); A. M. Kanduza, 'Railway Rates and Capitalist Agriculture in Southern Rhodesia 1918–1930', *Economic Symposium* (8–10 September 1980).

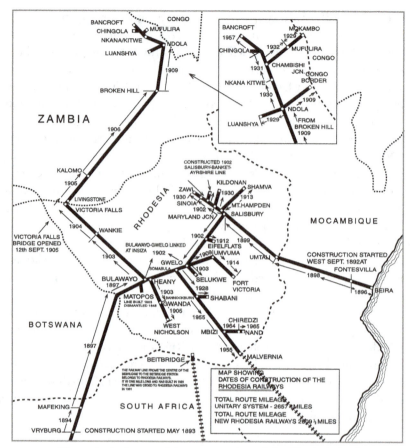

MAP 4.2. Chronological map of the construction of the Rhodesia Railways.
Source: D. Gale, *Rhodesia: The Years between 1923–1973: Half a Century of Responsible Government in Rhodesia* (Salisbury: H. C. P. Andersen, 1973). (Numerous attempts have been made by the author to identify and reach copyright owners for permission.)

first aircraft ever to land in the country. The excitement of the local population at the arrival of the first aeroplane ever to land in the country was described by the local newspaper, *The Chronicle*, as follows:

Arrangements had previously been made for the town to receive a warning of the aircraft's approach by means of gun signals, and at 10.20 am these signals sounded at the Police Camp. Cars and bicycles immediately hurried to the aerodrome. Excitement mounted. Work practically ceased throughout the town, as almost the whole population, black and white, assembled at the landing ground. At 12.30, a speck in the sky to the north-west heralded the approach of the Silver

Queen II and, within minutes, she touched down smoothly on the grass – the first aeroplane to land on the soil of Southern Rhodesia.[87]

Although, sadly, the aircraft crashed soon after take-off, its arrival had greatly stimulated local interest in aviation, although government did not show any enthusiasm for developing this sector until 1929 when it passed the Aviation Act (No. 555 of 1929) and created a Department of Civil Aviation.[88] In the 1930 financial year, the government voted £5,660 for the Department with the proviso that £3,760 of this sum was to be used for the preparation of emergency landing grounds on the Cape-to-Cairo air route, and for the salary of the supervisor of aerodrome construction in the country. The government also voted the standing sum of £750 per year as a subsidy for the instruction of seven pilots a year.[89] Civil Aviation received a further boost from a £50,000 grant provided by the Imperial Airways (Africa) Limited which inaugurated a mail service to England in January 1932 and, two months later, started a passenger service as well. In 1931, a road transport contractor in Nyasaland, C. J. Christowitz, set up Christowitz Air Services Limited and had started regular flights between Blantyre and Beira and Blantyre and Salisbury.

In October 1933, Christowitz's company was merged with the Rhodesia Aviation Company to produce Rhodesia and Nyasaland Airways (RANA), the largest air service venture in Central Africa up to that time. The Beit Trust, Rhodesia Railways and Imperial Airways were all financially involved in the new company, with the Beit Trust having the controlling interest, while Imperial Airways (Africa) Limited and Rhodesia Railways were both subscribers and technical advisers. Salisbury was the airline's headquarters.[90] By 1935, RANA was providing a regular mail and passenger service to Nyasaland, Northern Rhodesia and Mozambique.[91] By 1946, thirty-one other private airlines were servicing the country. Meanwhile in 1937, the British Airline (BOAC)'s introduced a Flying Boat service from England to South Africa in June 1937 and added the north-western tourist town of Victoria Falls to its flight route in December 1947.

[87] http://www.tothevictoriafalls.com
[88] Director of Civil Aviation, *Report on Civil and Military Aviation for the Year 1930* (Salisbury: Government Printer, 1931); P. McNamara, 'The Administration of Civil Aviation in Southern Rhodesia, 1920–1961' (Salisbury: unpubl., 1970), 3.
[89] Dir. Civil Aviation, *Report, 1930* (Salisbury: Government Printer, 1931).
[90] Dir. Civil Aviation, *Report, 1933* (Salisbury: Government Printer, 1934).
[91] Dir. Civil Aviation, *Report, 1933*, (Salisbury: Government Printer, 1934).

During the Second World War, the government of Southern Rhodesia took over RANA, now renamed Southern Rhodesia Air Services (SRAS), in order to meet national wartime transport requirements. After the war, the government relinquished control of SRAS and handed the airline over to a new civil aviation venture known as the Central African Airways Corporation (CAAC).[92] The creation of CAAC was the result of a growing interest among the three Central African countries – Southern Rhodesia, Northern Rhodesia and Nyasaland – to establish a regional airline which would be administered by one central authority and which would provide services to the three member states. In early 1949, therefore, each of the three territories passed legislation establishing the Central African Airways Corporation (CAAC) to be administered by a Central African Airways Authority (CAAA). CAAC was subsequently incorporated on 1 June 1946 with a capital of £500,000.[93] By 1947, the CAAC was not only servicing the regional market but had also successfully negotiated with the British government to permit it to run a twice-monthly end-to-end passenger service between Salisbury and London.

CAAC operated as a regional airline until the breakup of the Central African Federation in December 1963, when the three governments signed the Dissolution Order-in-Council reconstituting the airline as a corporate body jointly owned by Southern Rhodesia and the now-independent countries of Zambia and Malawi. In 1964, the three governments agreed to separate their air operations and set up three territorially based subsidiaries: Air Rhodesia, Air Malawi and Zambia Airways. The CAAC was dissolved and ceased operations on 31 December 1967.

Industry and Mining

Until the Second World War, the Rhodesian economy was primarily based on mining and agriculture. Manufacturing remained largely undeveloped. Initially secondary industries comprised primarily plants processing agricultural products, construction industries and the railways. For instance, among the earliest industries were tobacco-processing establishments, a brewery and creameries which were established before the First World War. However, because of the shortages created by the war and the

---

[92] McNamara, 'The Administration of Civil Aviation in Southern Rhodesia', 11.

[93] Zimbabwe National Archives, ME5/1/2/1 (Meredith [Chairman of CAA]: CAA Correspondence and Other Papers: General: 1947–1949), Internal Memorandum, 31 May 1949.

economic depression that followed it, the country was compelled to adopt import substitution industrialisation strategies which resulted in the establishment of a number of new industries, such as sawmills and factories producing fertiliser, vegetable oil, leather, bacon, biscuits, cereals, soaps and furniture.[94] The country's industrialisation drive slowed down in the 1920s after the world economy recovered from the war and traditional suppliers of goods reclaimed their world markets. While manufacturing surged noticeably in the early 1930s owing to a variety of factors, including the rapid pace of African proletarianisation, the growth of the local gold-mining industry and the devaluation of the pound sterling against an appreciating Southern Rhodesian currency, the country's manufacturing sector always faced the spectre of competition from its large neighbour, South Africa, and unfavourable trade arrangements which privileged the bigger economy against its neighbour. During these years, Rhodesian producers were clamouring for protection or, at least, more favourable trade terms with South Africa than already existed. Largely, however, successive governments left manufacturing to its own devices as they did not believe that the sector required any special attention.

Not surprisingly, in July 1939, a government-appointed committee of enquiry advised against an active policy of encouraging secondary industrialisation. Private enterprise, concluded the committee, 'could safely be left, without direct Government assistance, to develop worthwhile industries as opportunity occurred.... It was quite unnecessary for the Government to devote funds to hastening such developments'.[95] However, within months of accepting the committee's report, the government's laissez-faire attitude towards secondary industry was transformed by the outbreak of the Second World War. The war speeded up the country's import substitution drive as traditional sources of manufactured products dried up and government realised that drastic action was needed to overcome supply bottlenecks threatening to stifle the colony's war effort and its wider economic expansion.

Consequently, in 1940, the government established an Industrial Development Advisory Committee, which later became the Industrial Development Commission – a body which had access to public funding

[94] Ian Phimister, 'The Origins and Development of Manufacturing in Southern Rhodesia, 1894–1939', in A. S. Mlambo, E. Pangeti and Ian Phimister (eds.), *Zimbabwe: A History of Manufacturing 1890–1995* (Harare: University of Zimbabwe Publications, 2000), 9–30.

[95] *Report of the Economic Development Committee*, Salisbury, 1939, 38–40. This section draws heavily on A. S. Mlambo, E. Pangeti and Ian Phimister, *Zimbabwe: A History of Manufacturing 1890–1995*, 26.

TABLE 4.20. *Manufacturing Industries: Exports and Imports, 1951–1952*

Commodity	Domestic 1951 (£)	Exports 1952 (£)	Imports 1951 (£)	Exports 1952 (£)
1. Clothing	2,827,000	2,365,000	5,380,000	4,074,000
2. Cigarettes	653,000	723,000	25,000	26,000
3. Meats preserved	413,000	461,000	41,000	47,000
4. Sugar refined	403,000	592,000	1,000	1,600
5. Jute/Hessian (Excl. bags)	365,000	172,000	269,000	164,000
6. Footwear	340,000	344,000	1,067,000	935,000
7. Cotton piece goods	301,000	239,000	5,362,000	3,040,000
8. Cotton yarns	226,000	170,000	207,000	160,000
9. Asbestos cement manufactures	189,000	264,000	192,000	314,000
10. Groundnut oil	180,000	153,000	–	–
11. Furniture, Wooden	153,000	196,000	710,000	657,000
12. Blankets and Rugs	142,000	161,000	623,000	672,000

Source: W. A. E. Winterton, 'Secondary Industry in Southern Rhodesia', Department of Trade and Industrial Development, May 1953, 10.

for approved projects. The general idea was that where assistance was required 'to enable new industries, particularly those based on the processing of raw materials produced in the country, to become established', the government would either participate directly or it would create conditions conducive to the establishment of industries 'in the national interest'.[96] Thus, state interventions were designed to complement rather than compete with private enterprise. This was why the government invested directly in a number of parastatals (public enterprises), including the Cold Storage Commission, the Rhodesian Iron and Steel Commission, the Roasting Plant and the Sugar Industry Board.[97] Table 4.20 documents manufacturing industries' exports and imports from 1951 to 1952.

[96] N[ational] A[rchives] of Z[imbabwe] F295/51/26/51 Import Controls: Piece Goods – Department of Trade and Industrial Development, 'Secondary Industry in Southern Rhodesia', May 1953, [W. A. E. Winterton – Minister of Trade and Industrial Development].

[97] See variously, Mlambo, 'The Cold Storage Commission', and Mlambo and Pangeti, *The Political Economy of the Zimbabwean Sugar Industry, 1920–1990* (Harare: University of Zimbabwe Publications, 1996).

Missionaries, Education and Health

As in many other parts of the African continent, colonisation came in the wake of missionary activities in their quest to spread Christianity. Indeed, missionaries were later blamed by African nationalists in the immediate post–Second World War period for having facilitated the colonisation of Africa by softening the African people for colonial domination. Hence the popular expression among African nationalists is that 'white people came with the bible in one hand and a gun in the other', or its variant, 'When the white people first came, they told us to close our eyes to pray, but by the time we opened our eyes, our land was gone'.

It is now widely accepted that missionaries played a double role in the colonial history of Africa, facilitating its conquest but later also fuelling African nationalism through their Christian doctrines of justice and fairness and equality before God, in addition to the Western education they made available to the Africans in their various mission stations. There is evidence of collusion between imperialism and the missionary endeavour in Zimbabwe. A prominent example is the role that Reverend Helm of the London Missionary Society played in duping King Lobengula of the Ndebele into signing the Rudd Concession, as shown earlier in the book. Similarly, missionaries accompanied the Pioneer Column which occupied Zimbabwe in 1890. They consisted of a Jesuit priest who was the Column's chaplain and some Dominican Sisters who provided health services to members of the Column. It is also evident that some missionaries, such as a Jesuit priest, Fr. Prestage, were keen to destroy Ndebele power which they regarded as a stumbling block to proselytisation of the gospel, especially given that the Jesuits had not been able to make any converts among the Ndebele because, they believed, of the Ndebele system of government. On the eve of the Anglo-Ndebele War of 1893, Fr. Prestage expressed the hope that the 'Matabele kingdom will be smashed up' because 'it was founded upon a basis of injustice', as it was a military state designed for the 'self-aggrandisement of the king and his advisers at the expense of the denial and violation of the natural law to his subjects and his tributaries'. According to his Christian precepts, he had no doubt that the 'Matabele system of government was a system of iniquity and devilry'.[98]

Missionaries began work in Zimbabwe long before British colonisation. Already in the sixteenth century, Portuguese missionaries were active in Zimbabwe. However, it was only in the nineteenth century that

---

[98] C. J. M. Zvobgo, *A History of Christian Missions in Zimbabwe, 1890–1939*, (Gweru: Mambo Press, 1996), 6–7.

missionaries began to have some impact on the African populations. The leading missionary group operating in Zimbabwe on the eve of European colonisation was the London Missionary Society (LMS) whose most prominent representative was Robert Moffat, based at Kuruman in South Africa, who established contact with King Mzilikazi in 1829 during the Ndebele leader's northward migration at the time of the *Mfecane*. Mzilikazi later permitted Moffat's son, John Smith Moffat, to settle in Matebeleland. The LMS established two mission stations at Inyati and Hope Fountain in 1859 and 1870, respectively. Conversion was slow in coming at first because Africans were suspicious of the intentions of these newcomers, while African rulers were not keen to give missionaries a free hand in their territories for fear of subversion. Thus while 'for years on end the white preachers, with incredible perseverance, continued to argue, teach and exhort, to tend the sick, school the children, and hold short services for visitors who might chance to come to the station', all this 'proved ineffective' so that until 1887 the LMS 'could not boast of a single convert in Matebeleland'.[99] Before colonisation, therefore, missionaries in Matebeleland and other areas remained isolated, barely tolerated and with few converts.

With the establishment of colonial rule, missionary organisations flocked into the country. Among them were the Roman Catholics, Dutch Reformed Church, Anglicans, Methodists, Berlin Missionary Society, Lutheran Church, Paris Evangelical Mission and American Board of Foreign Missions. They vied with each other for territorial influence, while intensifying efforts to convert Africans to Christianity and to change their value system, habits and cultural practices. In seeking to modernise (read 'Westernise') the indigenous people, missionaries, whether wittingly or unwittingly, became part of the colonial project to undermine African culture and identity and to justify colonialism, especially as they tended to condemn everything African as un-Christian and barbaric and dismissed all indigenous knowledge systems out of hand, sparing no efforts to promote and privilege Western ideas and knowledge. As one scholar commented, European colonialists condemned African religion as 'idolatry' and African Gods as 'demons or fetishes'. Furthermore, it was claimed that the African people's

[a]ncestors were lost souls, having lived and died outside the Church; their feasts and ceremonies were all idolatrous and pagan; their dances were immoral; their

[99] L. Gann, *A History of Southern Rhodesia* (London: Chatto & Windus, 1965), 57.

diviners were sorcerers; their medicine was magic and quackery; their languages were hopelessly tone-infested cacophonies, while their names were unpronounce-able gibberish for which the ... names of European canonised saints had to be substituted. All was one irredeemable *massa damnata*.[100]

An example is a Jesuit priest Fr. Richartz who headed Chishawasha Mission just outside Salisbury soon after colonisation and who described the Shona-speaking indigenous people of the area as 'an altogether degraded race' whose principal vices were 'immorality and avarice' and who were 'extremely cowardish [sic], lazy, cruel, constantly quarrelling between themselves', and whose religion was merely 'a system of super-stitious rites' pursued mostly to 'pursue immoral objects'.[101]

Christian churches were generally unable to de-link themselves from the racial and cultural chauvinism that characterised colonial rule and saw themselves as duty bound to promote Christian civilisation, a euphe-mism for Westernisation. The missionary gospel at the time included

such tangibles as Lancashire cotton, cash crops, redbrick houses, Western med-icine, tombstones, books and money. The intangibles pertained not only to Christianity's transcendent God, but also to individualism, formal schooling, the nuclear family, middle-class values and virtues, skilled trades and ambition. All had religious meaning. Christian conversion aimed at a cultural, as well as a reli-gious conversion. As missionaries were fond of saying, the converted 'set them-selves apart'; they 'declared for a completely changed life'.[102]

While some of their attitudes and activities clearly buttressed colonialism, missionaries contributed immensely to the improvement of the quality of life of the African majority through, among other things, providing education and health care in mission schools and hospitals and impart-ing various skills and values that enabled the Africans to adapt to the changing world around them. For a long time after colonisation, mis-sion schools were the only places where Africans could obtain an edu-cation, as the colonial administration was slow in supporting African education. The impact of mission schools in the country is evident in the fact that many of the early nationalist leaders who were to lead Zimbabwe to independence received their education at mission schools. Missionaries also inspired and nurtured the desire for freedom that even-tually became full-blown anti-colonial nationalism in the post–Second

[100] Theophilus Okere, 'African Culture: The Past and the Present as an Indivisible Whole', at http://www.crvp.org/book/Series02/II-3/chapter1.htm (accessed June 20, 2012).

[101] Schmidt, *Peasant, Wives and Traders*, 100–1.

[102] K. Fields, 'Christian Missionaries as Anti-Colonial Militants', *Theory and Society*, 2 (1982), 96, cited in Phimister, *Economic and Social History*, 146.

World War period and which was to hasten the end of colonial rule in Africa. This was through providing opportunities for education and promoting the Christian principles of fair play, brotherhood of man and justice, enabling the African people to begin to question the colonial status quo. Some missionaries went on to play prominent roles in the fight for justice and fair play in the colonies, resulting in some of the missionaries being incarcerated or deported. Missionaries also developed indigenous language orthographies that helped to promote literacy and publishing in vernacular languages.

The first mission schools for Africans were established by the London Missionary Society at Inyati in 1859 and Hope Fountain mission in 1870. Thereafter, mission schools spread throughout the country. Government was not entirely happy with missionaries educating Africans, especially since it was suspected that Africans were being fed notions that would make them aspire to social ranks that were not available to them in the colonial setting. Chennels points out that the resentment against missionaries and their schools is reflected in the white novels of the time. The hostility stemmed from the suspicion that

the end of their work can only be to bridge the gap between Black and White. They encourage dangerous fantasies of equality by teaching Blacks that they have an immortal soul and by suggesting that they are heading for the same spiritual destinations as the settlers themselves.... The more sustained objection is to mission schools and in the novels educated Africans are invariably regarded as seditious to the settler order, sexually corrupt and dishonest.[103]

For example, a Native Commissioner character in a colonial novelist Gouldsbury's novel *God's Outpost* says, if he had his way, 'there wouldn't be a single missionary at large between the Zambezi and the Limpopo. They're the curse of the country, worse than Rinderpest and the labour problem together' especially because they delude the 'native into the idea that he has an immortal soul ... upon the same footing as the soul of a white man'.[104]

Concerned that a liberal education might encourage Africans to aspire beyond the role that colonialism had assigned them as suppliers of cheap labour, the colonial administration moved to influence the African school curriculum towards industrial education by passing the Education Ordinance of 1899 which provided a government grant of

[103] Chennels, Settler Myths, 338.
[104] H. C. Gouldsbury, *God's Outpost* (London: Everleigh Nash, 1907), 40–1, cited in Chennels, 'Settler Myths', 340.

10 shillings per pupil, up to a maximum of £50 per year per school, for schools which allocated at least two hours a day to industrial training, provided daily pupil attendance was fifty or more.[105] Thereafter, government provided annual grants to mission schools and consistently insisted on the inclusion of industrial education in the curriculum. For instance, H. S. Keigwin, the Director of Native Development in 1920, insisted that African schools should be concentrating more on 'developing skills in the fields of hides and skins, food production or agriculture, rope and mat making, basket and chair making, pottery and tiles, carpentry and smithing ... (as well as) ... food production or agriculture'[106] instead of providing a literary education. At his instigation, two industrial schools were established at Domboshawa in the Chinamhora Reserve in 1920 and Tjolotjo in the Gwaai Reserve in 1929, respectively, to provide industrial education.

Generally, early colonial African education was designed to produce students who would meet white labour requirements rather than to produce a well-rounded educated African. The education fare fed to African students was designed to underscore their inferiority and to validate white dominance. As social scientist Walter Rodney observed,

[Colonial education] was not an education system designed to give young people confidence and pride as members of African societies, but one which sought to instil a sense of deference towards all that was European and capitalist.[107]

Being repeatedly told that Africa was a 'dark continent' before the arrival of the whites and constantly being fed a diet of European history and European achievements and the 'heroic' exploits of European statesmen implanted a sense of awe and admiration for things European, as it was supposed to do. In the words of one ZANLA ex-combatant,

I remember my history teacher describing Dingaan [a precolonial Zulu king] as a brute, a savage and a primitive creature resisting European civilisation. The same teacher would talk of Rhodes [Cecil John Rhodes] as a man of varied talents, a genius, and a man whose whole life was developed and destined to deliver natives from savagery into civilisation.

As Franz Fanon noted, colonialism, by definition, seeks to hold its subjects in its grip partly by turning to the past of the colonised people and distorting or disfiguring it. Hence African students were taught that there

---

[105] Zvobgo, *Christian Missions*, 178.
[106] Zvobgo, *Christian Missions*, 183.
[107] A. S. Mlambo, *Economic Structural Adjustment Programme*, 56.

was nothing in the African past worth studying and were persuaded that colonialism had come to 'lighten their darkness'.[108] Indeed, one song that young black members of the International Scout Movement were required to sing had a stanza which contained the words: 'Let us thank Lord Baden Powell who came to Africa to help the African people', despite the fact that Baden Powell had been central in the suppression of the 1896 uprising in Matebeleland and had used harsh and ruthless methods that had led to an official enquiry to investigate charges of war crimes against him.[109]

Meanwhile, colonial intentions regarding African education were expressed in the following words of a Member of Parliament in the Legislative Assembly in 1927:

> We do not intend to hand over this country to the native population or to admit them to the same society or political position as we occupy ourselves.... We should make no pretence of educating them in exactly the same way as we do the Europeans.

Similarly, in the words of one Seventh Day Adventist minister at Solusi, it was not proper 'that we should teach or allow a Native to think that he is as good as a white man'.[110]

To drive this point home, government kept expenditure on African education much lower than that on European education, while African schools suffered from a chronic shortage of well-trained teachers and teaching materials and from an inferior curriculum throughout the period of colonial rule. African and European education systems and structures were maintained separately and were run by two separate administrative boards. African education was under the Native Affairs Department for African Education, whereas European education was under the Department of Education. As late as the 1960s and 1970s, the difference in the level of funding between the two education systems was very evident. For instance, in the 1967–8 financial year, the government spent approximately twenty times more per capita on white as compared to African students. In 1974, the total expenditure on African education was R$30.1 million, while that on white education in the same year was R$31.8 million. African enrolment in that year

---

[108] Franz Fanon, *The Wretched of the Earth* (New York: Penguin Books, 1978), 169.

[109] Tim Jeal, *Baden-Powell: Founder of the Boy Scouts* (London: Pimlico, 1991); 'Scouts founder Baden-Powell was a war criminal who had tribal chief executed illegally', *Daily Mail* (UK), 6 December 2009.

[110] Richard Gray, *The Two Nations* (London: Oxford University Press , 1960), 136.

was 863,596, giving a unit cost of R$34.90. On the other hand, white enrolment was a mere 69,061, giving a unit cost of R$461. The unit cost ratio between African and white education was thus 1:13. Similarly in 1977, R$31.7 million went to white education whereas R$42.8 million went to black education. This averaged to R$522 per white and R$52 per African pupil – reducing the ratio to approximately 1:10 but still representing a sizable gap.[111]

While education became compulsory for all white children since 1930, approximately 50 per cent of African children of primary school age were not attending school in 1979, while those who did attend school had to negotiate through a minefield of tests and examinations, applicable only to African students, which effectively eliminated the majority before they reached post-primary education. Thereafter, they sat three more examinations at two-year intervals before they could enter university. The system was structured in such a way that out of every 100 African pupils entering Grade 1, only 5 reached Form IV (Grade 12) and even fewer made it to university. As one source put it,

80% of African children in Southern Rhodesia got schooling up to Standard 2; 36% of the 80% went up to standard 4 and 18% of the 36% were able to get full primary education. Of these, only 4% got to Form 4, while only 1% of 3% got to Form 6 (full six years of secondary education).[112]

Of the 135,951 African pupils who started primary school in 1970, only 78,000 completed primary school in 1976, while only 14,000 proceeded to secondary school.[113]

Secondary school education for Africans became available only in 1939, with the establishment of St. Augustine's Secondary School at Penhalonga in the eastern part of the country by the Anglican Church. In 1946, the first government African secondary school opened its doors. Missionaries opened other secondary schools thereafter, the best known of which included Dadaya, Kutama, Tegwani and Gokomere.

---

[111] S. Mumbengegwi, 'Zimbabwe: A Diagnosis of an Educational System in a Rapid Change'. Paper presented to the Seminar on Education in Zimbabwe: Past, Present and Future, University of Zimbabwe, 27 August–7 September 1981, 41; Ministry of Finance, Economic Planning and Development, *Socio-Economic Review, 1980–1985 – Zimbabwe* (Harare: Government Printers, 1986), 169; Colin Stoneman, *Zimbabwe's Inheritance* (London: Macmillan Press; Harare: College Press, 1981), 65; Ruth Weiss, *Zimbabwe and the New Elite* (London: British Academic Press, 1984), 109.

[112] Mlambo *Economic Structural Adjustment Programme*, 56.

[113] D. Auret, *A Decade of Development, Zimbabwe 1980–1990* (Gweru: Mambo Press, 1990), 18.

Before 1939, Africans who wanted a secondary education had to go to South Africa where a number of schools, such as Marianhill, St. Peters and Adams College, provided study opportunities. Indeed, many future African nationalist leaders obtained their secondary education in South Africa.

Missionaries also made huge contributions in the provision of health services to the Africans by establishing clinics and hospitals at mission stations across the land. Among the major mission hospitals established in the first few decades of colonisation were Mount Selinda Hospital in Chipinge by the American Congregational Church in 1893, Morgenster Mission Hospital by the Dutch Reformed Church in 1894, Kwenda Mission Hospital in 1913, Nyadiri Mission Hospital in 1923 and Waddilove Mission Hospital in 1927.[114] Government funding for mission hospitals only came in 1928 when Government Notice No. 543 authorised grants to missionary societies that employed qualified medical missionaries and nurses working among Africans to cover the purchase of drugs, training for nurses and salaries. Government itself eventually established some state-run African hospitals, the largest of which were Mpilo Hospital in Bulawayo and Harare Hospital in Salisbury, as well as smaller hospitals and clinics throughout the country.

State health facilities were also racially structured, with whites receiving service from whites-only hospitals, such as Andrew Fleming in Salisbury. White hospitals were better staffed and better equipped than were African ones; African hospitals also suffered chronic overcrowding. For example, while there were approximately 280 doctors for the country's 232,422 whites, there were only 850 doctors for 7 million Africans in 1978. Similarly, while there was, on average, 1 hospital bed for every 219 whites, the African hospital average was 1 bed for every 525 people. For maternity cases, there was 1 bed for every 964 whites, as compared to 1 bed for every 6,339 Africans.[115] The African infant mortality rate was much higher at 122 per 1,000 and as high as 300 per 1,000 in more remote areas than that of whites at 17 per 1,000, which compared favourably with mortality rates in the industrialised North, which stood at 16 per 1,000 in England and Wales. Similarly, life expectancy for Africans was 49.8 years, whereas for whites it was 66.9 years. The distribution of medical personnel also reflected the racial structure of society.

---

[114] C. J. M. Zvobgo, 'Medical Missions: A Neglected Theme in Zimbabwe's History, 1893–1957', *Zambezia* 13, 2 (1986), 109–19.

[115] John Gilmurray et al., *From Rhodesia to Zimbabwe: The Struggle for Health* (London: Catholic Institute for International Relations, 1979), 36–7.

There were more doctors in the towns and cities than in the rural areas where the majority of the population lived.

Government funding was equally skewed in favour of white hospitals. For instance, 29.7 per cent of the health budget went to the Salisbury Group of Hospitals which served only 8.7 per cent of the population. In addition, African medical workers were paid less than their white counterparts. In 1979, of the 45,000 health workers in the country, 10,200 or 70 per cent were African and only 4,500 or 30 per cent were white, yet total African earnings amounted to 40 per cent of the total wage bill.[116] State rural clinics and hospitals were understaffed and overcrowded so that, without mission medical facilities, many Africans would have gone without medical care.

Moreover, colonial medicine focused on curative rather than preventive medicine, even though the majority African population's ailments pointed to the need to concentrate on the latter. Generally, Africans were prone to communicable diseases, as well as diseases caused by nutritional deficiencies, poor sanitation and unclean drinking water. Despite this, 86.7 per cent of the colonial health budget went to medical care, while only 9 per cent was allocated to prevention. This disparity led one doctor to claim that colonial medicine operated on the 'three quarters rule':

> Three quarters of our population are rural, yet three quarters of our medical resources are spent in the towns where three quarters of our doctors live. Three quarters of our people dies from diseases which could be prevented at low cost, yet three quarters of our medical budgets are spent on curative services.[117]

From Separate Development to Partnership

As noted, the British South Africa Company (BSAC) government ruled Southern Rhodesia from occupation in 1890 to 1923 when the country obtained self-government status from Britain. For many years, the country's settlers had been unhappy at the fact that the Company was putting its own commercial interests ahead of theirs and wanted to run their own affairs independent of the Company. Consequently, in October 1922, Britain held a referendum for the settlers to determine their future either as a self-governing entity or as part of the Union of South Africa. The majority voted for the former and in 1923, the country became a

---

[116] R. Carver and D. Saunders, 'Zimbabwe's Biased Health Service', *New African* (August 1980), 42.

[117] Carver and Saunders, 'Zimbabwe's Biased Health Service', 42.

self-governing territory with a high degree of autonomy, although Britain
retained control over foreign policy and the right to veto legislation that
impacted negatively on Africans. Charles Coghlan became the first prime
minster of self-governing Southern Rhodesia in 1924. In 1953, Southern
Rhodesia joined with the colonies of Northern Rhodesia (Zambia) and
Nyasaland (Malawi) in the Central African Federation.

Under successive self-government regimes, segregation became
entrenched in the country, as various measures were put into place to
ensure African subservience, especially during prime ministership of
Godfrey Huggins, leader of the Reform Party, who came to power in
1934. Until then, Sir Charles Coghlan and H. U. Moffat had led the
country in succession since the attainment of responsible government.
Underpinning the governments' adoption of racial segregation as national
policy was the perceived rising threat of African economic competition,
especially in the face of the economic hardships ushered in by the Great
Depression. Indeed, in 1931, Southern Rhodesia faced a great crisis as the
economy plummeted and white unemployment rose. The farming community bore the heaviest brunt of the Depression, as the country's unusu-
ally large tobacco and cotton crops could no longer be absorbed by the
shrinking British market, and many of the farmers drifted into the towns
in search of non-existent jobs. Given such circumstances, then–Prime
Minister Moffat was exploring appropriate measures to protect whites
from further hardship through African competition for such employment
and economic opportunities as did exist at the time.

The leading exponent of racial segregation, however, was Moffat's successor Godfrey Huggins, prime minister from 1934 to 1953, who advocated separate development of the races and promoted what he called a
Two Pyramid Policy from 1938 onwards. According to this approach, a
native policy that would ensure gradual differential development would
be pursued so as to preserve European supremacy and lessen economic
competition from the Africans, while also protecting African institutions
as the whites mentored them in the ways of civilisation.[118] Within their
own social pyramid, Africans could become lawyers, journalists or whatever they aspired to become, without fear of competition from whites.
Similarly, Europeans should not be subjected to competition from Africans
within their own social pyramid, with Africans serving only in the capacity of assistants and not competitors. Thus, 'the two races will develop
side by side under white supervision, and help, not hinder, each other's

---

[118] Gray, *The Two Nations*, 152.

progress'.[119] In both pyramids, however, white people would remain in charge in the interests of preserving civilisation. In Huggins's words,

The European in this country can be likened to an island of white in a sea of black, with the artisan and the tradesman forming the shores and the professional classes the highlands in the centre. Is the native to be allowed to erode away the shores and gradually attack the highlands? To permit this would mean that the leaven of civilisation would be removed from the country, and the black man would inevitably revert to a barbarism worse than ever before.... Rightly or wrongly, the white man is in Africa and now, if only for the sake of the black man, he must remain there. The higher standard of civilisation cannot be allowed to succumb.[120]

In order to protect white economic supremacy from African competition, especially in the economic depression of the 1930s when white artisans were in danger of being undercut by lower-paid Africans, the colonial administration enacted the Industrial Conciliation Act of 1934 which effectively made an employment colour bar part of the country's labour relations landscape. The Act provided for the establishment of trade unions and industrial councils for employers as part of an employer-employee conciliation system that would minimise confrontation in the workplace. It pointedly excluded Africans from the definition of employees, thus making it unlawful for them to form trade unions and, therefore, to bargain for better working conditions like their white counterparts could. Apprenticeships were also restricted to whites under the Act, while the 1931 Public Services Act excluded Africans from employment in the civil service, thus closing a possible avenue for personal career advancement for them. Effectively this meant that Africans could not be 'foremen, telegraphists, postal sorters, salesmen, typists, printers, dispensers or even mechanics employed by Government of industry'.[121]

At the same time, the economic problems facing the country's white agricultural sector were addressed at the African farmers' expense through various levies and control acts which essentially forced Africans to subsidise white farmers. The first such legislation was the Maize Control Act of 1931, amended in 1934, which established a state board to regulate white and African farmers' access to both domestic and international markets in a way that prejudiced African farmers to the white farmers' advantage. With the fall of prices on the international market where white farmers

[119] Cited in A. J. Hanna, *Rhodesias and Nyasaland*, 187.
[120] Gray, *The Two Nations*, 152.
[121] Gray, *The Two Nations*, 104.

sold their maize, and Africans being able to undercut white farmers in the domestic market because of their lower production costs and, therefore, lower prices, it was felt urgent to protect the white producers. This was done by the Act ruling that the Maize Control Board would buy maize in the domestic market but doing so in a discriminatory manner which paid African farmers lower prices than those paid to white farmers or by compelling Africans to sell their maize to white farmers who would then resell the maize to the Board at a the higher price. They were expressly barred from selling directly to the mines and towns at prevailing market prices.[122]

Other pieces of legislation that advantaged white farmers at the expense of Africans were the Cattle levy Acts of 1931 and 1934, which 'imposed a 2s 6d levy on the slaughter of all cattle for domestic consumption in order to pay a bounty subsidizing export stock almost exclusively owned by whites'. In 1934, an additional 3d tax per head of cattle was introduced. White farmers easily evaded paying this tax, while Africans could not, as their contribution was deducted from the Native Development account by Treasury. Later, government imposed a 10 shillings laughter levy which, again, fell most heavily on African farmers.[123]

Meanwhile, government did its best to ensure the prosperity of the white agricultural sector by providing the sector with good communication and transportation networks to facilitate the marketing of products and by supporting it with research and extension services, in what has been described as 'web of political, legal, institutional, and infrastructural arrangements which strengthened its dominance as the leading sector and driving force of agriculture'.[124] Under the circumstances, not surprisingly, African agriculture languished while white agriculture thrived.

When Africans living near urban centres turned to market gardening as an alternative, they soon ran afoul of the law in the form of the 1936 Native Registration Act passed by the Huggins administration which sought to control the African people's movement into and within urban areas. For instance, the Act 'barred Africans from trading select commodities, including vegetables, chickens, eggs, butter and other foodstuffs' in

---

[122] For discussions of the Maize control Act, see Phimister, *Economic and Social History*; Gray, *The Two Nations*; and Schmidt, *Peasants, Traders and Wives*.

[123] Phimister, *Economic and Social History*, 184.

[124] [O. Sichone], 'Zimbabwe's Economic Policies 1980 to 2002', *DPMN Bulletin*, 10, 2 (April, 2003), http://www.dpmf.org/images/zimbabwe-economic-policy-sichone.html (accessed 20 November 2013).

the European areas of Salisbury.[125] The Act also regulated the movement of African males into the urban centres by requiring that, in addition to the registration certificate introduced before the First World War, one had to have either 'a pass authorising him to seek work in town, a certificate to prove that he was employed in the town, a certificate signed by a native commissioner' testifying that he was 'earning a living in the town by lawful means' or a visiting pass from his employer if employed outside town.[126]

By the 1930s, economic marginalisation, racial segregation and paternalism had become established elements in the socio-economic and political fibre of the country. The system was clearly loaded against the African, as the Chief Native Commissioner, C. L. Carbutt, admitted in the 1930s: '[F]rom the Natives' personal point of view, the situation is very harassing: he cannot sell cattle: he cannot get cash for his maize ... and he has great difficulty in obtaining employment, and when he does get it, it is at a reduced rate of pay'.[127] In addition, over time, the settlers developed a distinctly condescending paternalist attitude towards the African majority whom most regarded as children to be mentored by the white population on whom they depended. This was clearly reflected in the fact that African males were generically referred as 'boys', regardless of their age, and were expected, like children, to behave respectfully towards their elders, the whites. Consequently, insolent behaviour against whites in general and against white officialdom in particular was highly criminalised throughout the colonial period. Thus, behaviour which ranged from speaking in a loud voice, using gestures, appearing angry towards an authority figure, 'laughing outright and grinning when being interrogated by the police' and/or behaving in any manner that was likely to undermine the dignity of the colonial establishment were listed as prosecutable behaviour.[128]

Indeed, there developed a certain Rhodesian culture of handling Africans into which every new immigrant was socialised. As Doris Lessing's novel *The Grass Is Singing* shows, there was a pervasive notion

---

[125] Elizabeth Schmidt, 'Farmers, Hunters, and Gold-Washers: A Re-Evaluation of Women's Roles in Pre-colonial and Colonial Zimbabwe', *African Economic History*, 17 (1988), 45–80.

[126] Phimister, *Economic and Social History*, 202.

[127] Schmidt, *Peasants, Traders, and Wives*, 77.

[128] Allison Shutt, '"The Natives Are Getting Out of Hand": Legislating Manners, Insolence and Contemptuous Behaviour in Southern Rhodesia, c. 1910–1963', *Journal of Southern African Studies*, 33, 3 (September 2007), 653–72.

in the country that, for one to be considered a true Rhodesian, one had to adopt a 'Rhodesian attitude towards Africans'. In the novel's words,

When old settlers say 'One has to understand the country,' what they mean is, 'You have to get used to our ideas about the native.' They are saying, in effect, 'Learn our ideas, or otherwise get out: we don't want you.' Most of these young men [from England] were brought up with vague ideas about equality. They were shocked, for the first week or so, by the way natives were treated. They were revolted a hundred times a day by the casual way they were spoken of, as if they were so many cattle; or by a blow or a look. They had been prepared to treat them as human beings. But they could not stand out against the society they were joining. It did not take them long to change.... When it came to the point, one never had contact with natives, except in the master-servant relationship. One never knew them in their own lives, as human beings.[129]

Huggins, however, gradually moved away from his two-pyramid policy in the post–Second World War period towards the 'partnership' policy. Probably contributing to this change of approach was the victory of the Nationalist Party in South Africa and the introduction of its rabidly racist apartheid segregationist policy which the leading white Rhodesian politicians found somewhat excessive. For Huggins, however, the partnership was not of equals but akin to that of a rider and a horse, while for Roy Welensky, the federal prime minister, partnership meant allowing Africans greater participation in the running of the country,

as and when he [the African] shows his ability to contribute more to the general good, but we must make it clear that even when that day comes, in a hundred or two hundred years time, he can never hope to dominate the partnership. He can achieve equal standing but not go beyond it.[130]

It is important to note, however, that while such views were common among the ruling white elites, the white population was not homogenous in its views about and attitudes towards Africans. After the Second World War, in particular, an identifiable group of whites regarding themselves as liberals in terms of race emerged and coalesced around the partnership campaign. Prominent among such individuals were members of the Capricorn Society, a multiracial organisation founded in Southern Rhodesia in 1949 by Colonel David Stirling. Under mostly post–Second World War white immigrant leadership, this organisation was a pressure

---

[129] Doris Lessing, *The Grass Is Singing* (London, Ibadan, Nairobi: Heinemann, 1950), 20–1.

[130] Martin Meredith, *The Past Is Another Country: Rhodesia UDI to Zimbabwe*, (London: Pan Books, 1980), 24.

group which promoted the idea of a common nationality based on the principle of 'equal rights for civilised' men. Members of the Society believed that educated Africans should be allowed into the country's political elite. Its philosophy was contained in the Capricorn Manifesto of 1954 which called for individuals' 'standing and ability to share in the government of the country ... (to be) determined by his personal qualities and not by the colour of his skin'.[131] Also important was the Interracial Association of Southern Rhodesia launched in 1953 to promote partnership. Several individual whites publicly opposed colonial racial policies and risked their own freedom by supporting the African people's struggle for justice and self-determination, as shown in the discussion that follows.

Gender Relations

In early historical studies of the colonial period's impact on the African population, the general tendency was to focus on the experiences and responses of African males and to render African women invisible or, at best, to treat them only as inconsequential appendages to the men. Thus, historical accounts narrated the experiences of men as taxpayers, as workers on the mines and the farms, as migrant labourers and as resisters to colonialism, and mentioned women only in passing in so far as their activities were seen as supportive to the men's struggles. Recent studies have, however, demonstrated that it is impossible to understand colonialism fully without acknowledging the central role that women played in the country's history, for the measures that were imposed on the men also directly influenced women as mothers, wives and daughters and as individuals, eliciting individual responses, some of which were at direct odds with what the African men either expected or wanted.[132]

Scholars are not fully agreed on the role of women in precolonial Zimbabwean African society, with some regarding them as largely subordinate and marginal in a predominantly patriarchal society where they had no meaningful presence in public political life or access to land and

---

[131] Bizeck Jube Phiri, 'The Capricorn Africa Society Revisited: The Impact of Liberalism in Zambia's Colonial History, 1949–1963', *The International Journal of African Historical Studies*, 24, 1 (1991), 65–83.

[132] See, for instance, Teresa Barnes, *We Women Worked So Hard* (Oxford: James Currey; Harare: Baobab; Cape Town: David Philip, 1999); Schmidt, *Peasants, Traders and Wives*; Angela Cheater, 'The Role and Position of Women in Pre-Colonial and Colonial Zimbabwe', *Zambezia*, 13, 2 (1986), 65–79, among others.

other property. Others argue that, while precolonial Zimbabwean society was clearly patriarchal, women were not as powerless as their absence from public political activities and structures might suggest. Absence from the visible corridors of power did not necessarily mean lack of influence and power, as women, at least among the majority Shona people, 'had more say in Shona society than was formally admitted'.[133] In any case, in a few precolonial communities, for instance in Manicaland in the east and Mutoko in the north-west, women could, and did, become headwomen of their communities, exercising the same political power as their male counterparts in other parts of the country.[134]

Even where they were not visible in the public sphere, women were not always entirely powerless or marginalised. As Cheater argues,

Shona women did exercise authority in other roles: as mothers, especially over their daughters; as *vatete* [sisters-in-law], particularly over the education of their brothers' children; as ancestors, over the reproductive capacity of their female descendants (although the degree to which women were able to control their own fecundity is less certain); as producers or service-workers possessing special skills (in pottery or healing, for example), over the proceeds of their own work; as mothers of married daughters for whom *roora* [bride wealth] had been paid, over property.... [Moreover] Female authority grew over time, in much the same way as did that of men ... by the time she had acquired grandchildren, she had normally become a force to be reckoned with in most if not all matters affecting both her natal family (as *tete* – i.e. sister-in-law) and her husband's family (as mother-in-law). Commonly, post-menopausal women became a type of 'honorary male' in village society, having lost the mystical influence associated with menstruation, abandoned domestic responsibilities to the work of younger women, and acquired personal property.[135]

In addition, women could become very powerful if they were spirit mediums (*Masvikiro*), individuals traditionally respected and valued for their capacity to relay messages from the spirit world to the living. A good example of such a powerful woman was Nehanda, the spirit medium who played a central role in mobilizing against colonial rule during the First Chimurenga of 1896 and who was executed by the colonial administration for her activities.

While it is customary to consider precolonial women's economic roles as being mostly restricted to agricultural cultivation and the home, recent work suggests that women were involved in other economic activities,

---

[133] Bourdillon, 1976, 72, cited in Cheater, 'Women in Pre-Colonial and Colonial Zimbabwe'.

[134] Cheater, 'Women in Pre-Colonial and Colonial Zimbabwe'.

[135] Cheater, 'Women in Pre-Colonial and Colonial Zimbabwe'.

hitherto considered to be the preserve of men, more than has been appreciated. Women participated in hunting, working hand in hand with their male counterparts in trapping animals in 'long nets made from the bark of certain trees' and helping to drive animals into these nets by shouting and making noise. They were also active in gold mining in the agricultural off-season and made up the majority of the gold panners, while men dug up the ore from the mine shafts. Thus, given their role as key producers of gold, they contributed to their society's economy through trade and the acquisition of firearms and other goods. In addition, they were also 'highly respected artisans and skilled workers, predominating in such trades as the moulding and burning of pots, beer brewing, midwifery, salt production, and herbalism'.[136]

Notwithstanding this, it is clear that women did not have as much political or economic power as their male counterparts did and that, while they played a key role in agricultural production and controlled some of the production, 'they did not control the means of production', even though they often 'provided much of the labour'.[137] Summing up the status of Shona women in precolonial Zimbabwe, Cheater writes:

[I]t would appear that – in at least some situations in pre-colonial Zimbabwe, which extended into colonial times – women's roles were not only differentiated but included those of religious and political authority, notwithstanding their general exclusion from areas of secular decision-making reserved for men.[138]

Similarly, in Ndebele society, while women 'were perpetually considered to be minors (*abesintwana*)' who were not allowed to participate 'in national issues such as war and were not represented in public forums ... where national issues were debated and discussed', they did wield influence, albeit indirectly, 'through their husbands, brothers and sons who were prominent in the Ndebele state'. Here, too, women's roles were not monolithic and differed depending on their status in society by birth and as wives, daughters or sisters.[139]

Colonial rule entrenched the position of women as subservient to men and even worsened their situation in a variety of ways, including by legislating the status of women as minors, unable to enter into any

---

[136] Schmidt, 'Farmers, Hunters and Gold-Washers', 45–80.
[137] Cheater, 'Women in Pre-Colonial and Colonial Zimbabwe'.
[138] Cheater, 'Women in Pre-Colonial and Colonial Zimbabwe'.
[139] Sabelo J. Ndlovu-Gatsheni, 'Who Ruled by the Spear? Rethinking the Form of Governance in the Ndebele State', *African Studies Quarterly*, 10, 2–3 (2008), online at http://www.africa.ufl.edu/asq/v10/v10i2a4.htm (accessed 20 November 2013).

contractual agreement without the permission of a husband or guardian. Their workload also increased, as the men left the villages to work
in the emerging capitalist sector whose wages were very low and, therefore, necessitating income subsidies from agricultural produce from the
women left in the villages. Because of the absence of men from the villages, women were forced to take over duties and activities that used to be
fulfilled by men, such as threshing grain, tending cattle and clearing and
ploughing the land. Moreover, as overcrowding became a major problem
in the African Reserves with the intensified colonial appropriation of land
and yields declined due to soil degradation, women who remained on the
land had to work even harder 'for diminishing returns'.[140]

Not surprisingly, with time, some women also left the countryside to
fend for themselves in the urban areas in various ways, including by joining the capitalist labour market, working as domestics in white homes
or as farm and factory hands, generally taking the jobs that commanded
very low wages. Some became prostitutes and brewers of illicit alcohol
for sale or entered into informal and temporary co-habitation arrangements with males as *mapoto* wives. *Mapoto* marriages (literary cooking-
pot marriages) were

gender relationship(s) free of the ties (and obligations) of formal marriage, in
which bride wealth was not paid to the woman's relatives. Once she moved in
with a man and started to work for him (i.e., cooking food in pots) she was his
'wife'.[141]

As they became more self-reliant, they also progressively asserted their
independence from traditional patriarchal control.

The increased entry of women in the capitalist labour market and into
urban spaces away from the traditional control of the patriarchs in the
villages in the 1930s and beyond posed challenges to both the African
males and colonial administrators. For African patriarchs, the loss of
control was unacceptable, especially since they regarded urban centres
as havens of iniquity that were corrupting their wives and daughters.
In addition, they objected to the loss of access to the wages of junior
men working in the urban centres, who would normally send money to
their wives who remained in the rural areas and under the control of
senior African males. This income was drying up with the relocation of

[140] Schmidt, 'Farmer, Hunters and Gold-Washers', 48.
[141] Teresa A. Barnes, 'The Fight for Control of African Women's Mobility in Colonial
Zimbabwe, 1900–1939', *Signs*, 17, 3 (Spring 1992), 586–608.

women to the urban areas. African rural leaders and elderly men thus solicited government support in restricting female mobility.[142] This resonated well with the colonial administrators who were also not keen, for economic reasons, on African women moving into the towns in large numbers.

Thus, at the heart of the state legislation on women was the desire of African patriarchs and the colonial authorities to control women's mobility through manipulating and manufacturing 'tradition' by, for example, making 'African women into permanent legal minors' and codifying 'polygamy and the system of bride-wealth payments known as lobola'.[143] This was necessitated by the fact that women were increasingly rebelling against their newly assigned roles of being essentially a supporting act for their men who were now absorbed by the capitalist economy as underpaid labourers, and against other practices, such as arranged marriages, that they found increasingly unacceptable. They were doing this through increased mobility from the confines of the rural areas into the urban spaces in search of economic sustenance and independence. Consequently, the state responded with a range of laws, including the 1916 Native Adultery Punishment Ordinance to control women's 'promiscuity', as this was said to deter 'men from leaving their homes to seek employment out of fear that their wives will misconduct themselves during the husband's absences'.[144]

Thus, behind the state's moral 'rhetoric' used to justify control over African women's mobility, ostensibly for their own good, was the fact that the state stood to gain considerably from African women's agricultural produce subsidizing the meagre wages of African male workers in the mines and towns. This was because

[t]he control of women and children's labour by senior African men was central to the establishment and consolidation of colonial rule in S[outhern] R[hodesia]. The creation of 'native' reserves not only served the interests of capital, by forcing women and children to subsidize male wages through agricultural production; it also served those older men, by facilitating their control over women and children. By forcing women to submit to male authority, the colonial regime both advanced its own project and mollified potentially powerful opposition force – that of chiefs, headmen and other senior men. Thus the origins of female subordination in S[outhern] R[hodesia] were not solely the result of policies imposed by foreign capital and the colonial state. Rather, indigenous and European structures

---

[142] Schmidt, *Peasants, Traders and Wives*, 99.
[143] Barnes, 'African Women's Mobility', 9.
[144] Barnes, 'African Women's Mobility', 16.

of patriarchal control reinforced and transformed one another, evolving into new structures and forms of domination.[145]

The situation was further compounded by the racist white settlers' view of African women as promiscuous and vectors of sexually transmitted diseases.

This notwithstanding, the colonial state was ambivalent in its attitudes towards female mobility and independence, as it allowed some women to become independent economic actors, working in various capacities in the urban spaces at

the myriad tasks of domestic labour cooking, cleaning, sewing, child rearing, supplementing male incomes and providing sexual services ... [which was] vital for the reproduction of the migrant male labour force and for the development of colonial capitalism that was predicated on that labour.[146]

Also important in this early period was the ever-present white fear of the so-called black peril; the threat to white womanhood by African men who, in the white male's imagination, were always lusting after white women. Because of this pervading fear, there were numerous 'black peril' scares between 1902 and 1932, some of which resulted in attempted lynchings of blacks suspected of molesting white women. This widespread fear was well captured in Doris Lessing's *The Grass Is Singing* in which the main female character, Mary Turner, is murdered by her African male servant under circumstances that hint at sexual intimacy between them. Because sexual liaisons between black men and white women were inconceivable in this racially constructed colonial setting, Mary Turner's murder seemed merely to confirm what was thought to be the inevitable tragic outcome of such a relationship. Hence the novel open with the words:

Mary Turner, wife of Richard Turner, a farmer at Ngesi, was found murdered on the front verandah of their homestead yesterday morning. The houseboy, who has been arrested, has confessed to the crime. No motive has been discovered. It is thought he was in search of valuables. The newspaper did not say much. People all over the country must have glanced at the paragraph with its sensational heading and felt a little spurt of anger mingled with what was almost satisfaction, as if some belief had been confirmed, as if something had happened which could only have been expected.[147]

[145] Schmidt, *Peasants, Traders and Wives*, 99; Schmidt, 'Farmers, Hunters and Gold-Washers'.
[146] Barnes, 'African Women's Mobility'.
[147] Lessing, *The Grass Is Singing*, 9.

It was in response to white fears of the black peril that, in 1903 and 1916, the British South Africa Company passed laws to suppress immorality in general and black-white sexual relations in particular. Under this legislation, a white woman convicted of inter-racial sexual relations could be sentenced to two years hard labour, while the African was liable to five years imprisonment for the same offence. The death penalty was imposed for rape or attempted rape. As a result, approximately thirty black men were hanged for this crime in the subsequent thirty years. Tellingly, not a single white male was ever hanged for raping a black woman throughout the colonial period.[148] The hypocrisy of white males regarding inter-racial sexual relations is evident in the growing population of the country's coloured (mixed-race) population throughout the colonial period, testimony to widespread white male sexual relations with African women. African men, thus, had every reason also to be worried about the white peril, namely white man abusing African women.[149] Thus, denunciations of the black peril were, in fact, a diversionary tactic, because

by encouraging white rage against black sexual offenders, settler men were able to hide their own far more widespread and often violent sexual relations with black women. This was the real sexual 'peril' in colonial society, but it can only be discovered by reading between the lines of the tirades against [Africans accused of such crimes].[150]

The white people's fears of the black peril persisted well into the 1950s, as shown by the fact that new female immigrants into the Federation of Rhodesias and Nyasaland were enjoined by federal authorities 'never to allow their female children to exhibit any degree of nakedness and for themselves to make their owns beds, wash their own underwear and avoid appearing in a state of casual undress ... [as this would put them] at risk at the hands of males servants'.[151]

Another controversial gender-related issue in the colonial era was the campaign by the authorities to promote family planning among the African population in order to curb the African population that was said to be growing too fast. Work by Amy Kaler[152] has traced the history of

[148] Vambe, *From Rhodesia to Zimbabwe*, 107–8, 112.

[149] Schmidt, *Peasants, Traders and Wives*, 172.

[150] John Pape, 'Black and White: The "Perils of Sex" in Colonial Zimbabwe', *Journal of Southern African Studies*, 16, 4 (December 1990), 699–720.

[151] Peter Baxter, 'White Man's Burden', at http://peterbaxterafrica.com/index.php/2012/04/04/the-white-mns-burden (accessed 3 December 2012).

[152] Amy Kaler, *Running after Pills: Politics, Gender and Contraception in Colonial Zimbabwe* (Portsmouth, NH: Heinemann, 2003); Amy Kaler, 'A Threat to the Nation

family planning in Rhodesia and Zimbabwe from the 1950s onwards and demonstrated how the promotion of contraception among African women by the colonial authorities became a site of struggle, especially since Africans were suspicious of the government's motives in pushing this agenda. Given the fact that the colonial government was constantly promoting white immigration into the country, Africans could not understand why the Family Planning Association of Rhodesia was pushing contraceptive methods on the African women in the name of curbing population growth. Furthermore, contraceptive methods, such as the Pill, challenged traditional notions of family values, leading to fears by African males that the availability of contraception pills would undermine their control and encourage female immorality. Kaler's studies thus suggest that modern contraceptive methods, as introduced under colonial rule, were controversial because they gave a great deal of power to women to control their fertility and also because 'these contraceptive technologies also raised questions about who should have the power to dictate respectful behavior, to define patriotism, and to incorporate new ideas and means into cultural tradition'.[153]

and a Threat to the Men: The Banning of Depo-Provera in Zimbabwe, 1981', *Journal of Southern African Studies*, 24, 2 (June 1998), 347–76; Amy Kaler, 'Who Has Told You This Thing? Toward a Feminist Interpretation of Contraceptive Diffusion in Rhodesia, 1970–1980', *Signs*, 25, 3 (Spring 2000), 677–708.

[153] Leslie Bessant, 'Review of Amy Kaler, *Running after Pills: Politics, Gender, and Contraception in Colonial Zimbabwe*', *Canadian Journal of African Studies / Revue Canadienne des Études Africaines*, 39, 1 (2005), 181–3.

5

The Federation Years, 1953–1963

Introduction

In 1953, Southern Rhodesia joined two other Central African countries, Northern Rhodesia (Zambia) and Nyasaland (Malawi), in a three-nation political and economic unit known as the Central African Federation (CAF). Also known as the Federation of Rhodesia and Nyasaland, it collapsed in 1963 because of the impending independence of Northern Rhodesia and Nyasaland in 1964, as well as because of mounting African hostility to it in all the three territories. Only two prime ministers led the Federation before its collapse, the first one being the hitherto long-serving prime minister of Southern Rhodesia, Godfrey Huggins, from 1953 to 1956. The second and last prime minister was Northern Rhodesian political leader Roy Welensky who presided over the union from 1956 until its dissolution.

The Federation was a product of geopolitical, economic and political considerations on the part of both the white inhabitants of the three territories and the colonial power, Britain, which encouraged political and economic amalgamation of its central African territories for reasons that had to do with the opportunity a large economic and political entity would provide in terms of markets as well as its role as a buffer against possible Apartheid South Africa's influence in the region. The origins and development of the Central African Federation are discussed in the following sections.

The Federation of Rhodesia and Nyasaland
First mooted by officials of the British South Africa Company in 1915 as a way to minimise administration costs of its territories, the idea of

amalgamating Northern and Southern Rhodesia was strongly opposed by the whites of Southern Rhodesia who were still hopeful of obtaining self-government and feared that the amalgamation would only complicate matters and delay the realisation of their objective.

The Hilton Young Commission of 1927–1929, set up to enquire into the possibility of a federation between the east African and central African colonies of Tanganyika, Kenya, Uganda, Southern and Northern Rhodesia and Nyasaland, did not find enough common interests between the two groups of countries to justify any formal union among them, but suggested the possibility of a federation of the Rhodesia and Nyasaland, instead. By this time, Southern Rhodesia was more favourably disposed to the idea of a federation, having successfully secured self-government status in 1923 and also particularly attracted by the discovery of considerable mineral wealth on the Northern Rhodesian Copperbelt in the 1920s. The suggestion came to naught as Northern Rhodesian and Nyasaland settlers were rather unenthusiastic about the idea, with the latter particularly unhappy about Southern Rhodesia's policy of racial segregation.[1] Other attempts in 1933 and 1936 also failed as a result of African opposition in Northern Rhodesia.

The first real breakthrough came in January 1936, when members of the Northern Rhodesian Legislative council and representatives of the major white political parties in Southern Rhodesia met at the Victoria Falls Conference and recommended amalgamation of the two countries. On the basis of the recommendation, the British government set up a Royal Commission, under the chairmanship of Viscount Bledisloe, to enquire

> whether any, and if so what, form of closer co-operation or association between Southern Rhodesia, Northern Rhodesia and Nyasaland is desirable and feasible, with due regard to the interests of all the inhabitants, irrespective of race, of the Territories concerned and to the special responsibility of Our Government in the United Kingdom of Great Britain and Northern Ireland for the interests of the Native inhabitants.[2]

In its March 1939 report, the Commission noted that both territories stood to gain from some form of closer cooperation, but recommended postponement of any efforts at amalgamation until it was ascertained whether the Southern Rhodesian native policy of parallel development,

---

[1] D.O 35/424/11969/24, SS to Gov SR, 1 July 1931, cable, cited in I. Wetherell, 'Settler Expansionism', 222.
[2] Bledisloe Commission Report.

otherwise known as the two-pyramid, 'was in the best interests of the Africans'. It also reported on the 'striking unanimity' of African opposition to the withdrawal of the British government's protection as a result of amalgamation.[3] Africans in the northern territories were particularly concerned at the possibility of Southern Rhodesia's racial policy, which placed severe limitations on Africans with regard to land tenure and residential and employment opportunities, being extend to them, thus curtailing their comparatively less confining regime under British rule.[4] Because of these misgivings, the Commission suggested instead the creation of an Inter-Territorial Council to be made up of the prime minister of Southern Rhodesia and the governors of the Northern Territories to coordinate services and to promote regional economic development.

The amalgamation debate was muted during the Second World War, the only notable development being a statement by the Secretary of State for Colonies in 1944 to the effect that 'after careful consideration, [his government had] come to the conclusion that the amalgamation of the Territories under existing circumstances cannot be regarded as practicable'. A Central African Council should, however, be set up to coordinate the actions of the three governments regarding communications, economic relations, industrial development, labour education, agriculture and health as a transition measure.

The economic prosperity of the three territories after the war, marked by rapid industrialization in Southern Rhodesia and marked growth in Northern Rhodesia's mineral and Nyasaland's agricultural economies, and the considerable influx of white immigrants into Southern Rhodesia in particular, made the climate more auspicious for the revival of the amalgamation project, more so since the economies of the three territories were increasingly interdependent. For Britain, the amalgamation of the Central African territories would bring the advantages of a larger market for British goods, a counter to the rising Afrikaner political influence in the post-1948 South Africa and a possible check on the growing threat of African nationalism.[5] Consequently, in 1951, the British government hosted a conference for officials from Southern Rhodesia,

[3] Bledisloe Commission Report.
[4] S. Albinski, 'The Concept of Partnership in the Central African Federation', *The Review of Politics*, 19, 2 (April 1957), 186–204.
[5] R. Hyam, 'The Geopolitical Origins of the Central African Federation: Britain, Rhodesia and South Africa, 1948–1953', *The Historical Journal*, 30, 1 (March 1987), 145–72.

Northern Rhodesia, Nyasaland and representatives of the Colonial Office to revisit the amalgamation issue. The conference supported closer association of the countries because of the 'economic inter-dependence of the whole area' and pointed out that 'a single economic system would provide a more attractive field for investment than the three small territories'. The conference also noted that 'strategic problems, communication and other basic services could be more easily handled on a federal scale'.[6] As a result, on 3 September 1953, the Federation of Rhodesia and Nyasaland came into being, even though there was strong opposition from the Africans, particularly those in the northern territories. For instance, in 1951, African representatives from the three territories denounced the Federation. Southern Rhodesia African opinion was represented by three organisations: the African Voice Association (the Voice), founded by Benjamin Burombo in 1947; the Reformed Industrial and Commercial Workers' Union (RICU), under Charles Mzingeli, and the Southern Rhodesian African National Congress (SRANC). Thereafter, Africans set up the All-African Convention to mobilise African opposition to federation.[7]

Not all Africans leaders in Southern Rhodesia were opposed to the Federation at the start, however. Whereas Robert Mugabe denounced the Federation as little more than 'an instrument that will be wielded to suppress our self determination and progress',[8] some Southern Rhodesian nationalist leaders, such as Joshua Nkomo and Jasper Savanhu, went to the 1952 London talks that paved the way for the Federation, while others also participated in the Federal government structures through their membership of the white-led United Rhodesia Party and the Federal Party. Explaining why the Southern Rhodesian African elite accepted federation, Nathan Shamuyarira wrote that the establishment of the Federation was regarded by Southern Rhodesian Africans as full of promise:

[T]he new policy of partnership, which was to be inscribed in the federal constitution, would bring to a speedy end the segregation, humiliation and indignation which we had suffered for 40 years … the Northern territories would help to break down the racial barriers and the southern Rhodesian whites would even

---

[6] J. J. B. Sommerville, 'The Central African Federation', *International Affairs (Royal Institute of International Affairs 1944–)*, 39, 3 (July 1963), 386–402.
[7] *Keesing's Contemporary Archives*, 8 (Cambridge: Keesings Worldwide, 1950–52, June 30–July 7, 1951), 11770.
[8] *Bantu Mirror*, 27 June, 1953.

of their own accord, inspired by partnership, pass laws which would let us share political power and economic privileges and enjoys social justice.[9]

Under the federal arrangement, legislative powers were divided between the federal and territorial governments, while the federal governments assumed responsibility for external affairs, defence, European education, agriculture and health services, African affairs were retained by the territorial governments. On its part, the British government retained ultimate responsibility for foreign affairs and certain types of legislation pertaining to the franchise and constitutional matters. Partially in response to the criticism of the parallel development racial policies of Southern Rhodesia, which had stalled earlier attempts at promoting regional union, proponents of the amalgamation idea had developed the concept of partnership to provide the guiding principle for future white and African relations. Thus, the Preamble to the Federal Constitution expressed the hope that the federation would promote racial partnership in all three territories. This turned out to be more rhetoric than substance, as racial discrimination continued as in the past. Indeed, although it was supposedly a policy to promote harmonious co-operation between the races, Africans had, in fact, not been consulted about the need for or even the form of the proposed partnership policy. Moreover, partnership was not envisaged as between Europeans and Africans as a whole, but only with selected African individuals, namely those who were adjudged to have acquired the rudiments of 'civilization'.[10]

By the end of the decade, even those African elites that had bought into the idea at the beginning of the federation had become disillusioned. As one of them, Nathan Shamuyarira, wrote in 1961,

The first major failure was in the implementation of the policy of partnership or multi-racialism on which the Federation was founded. After seven years, senior positions in the Federal Civil Service are still occupied exclusively by whites; there is only one African Parliamentary Secretary in a Cabinet of nine men; the Federation's government-owned airline employs Africans only as janitors, drivers and the like; and, with the exception of doctors and some nurses, the principle of equal pay for equal work is by no means honored, even by the Government. In matters for which the territorial governments are responsible, discrimination is still extreme, especially in Southern Rhodesia, aptly referred to as the 'nigger

[9] Nathan Shamuyarira, *Crisis in Rhodesia* (London: Andre Deutsch, 1965), 15–16.
[10] Abinski, 'The Concept of Partnership in the Central African Federation'.

in the woodpile' of Federation. There the Civil Service can be entered only by Europeans (an amendment has been promised); residential segregation is so sharp that even the African Cabinet Minister could not be accommodated in the white suburbs where other Ministers live; African businessmen cannot trade in the center of the main towns; passes are still enforced; wages are disproportionate; cafes and restaurants are closed to non-whites. Several breaches in the color bar have been made in respect of common services in post offices, in trains and at airports, and at the University College at Salisbury. But the fundamental issues of the land and the vote have not been tackled.[11]

The federation justified its creators' expectations that it would enhance economic development, at least for the first few years of its existence, when the region experienced rapid economic growth and became the second-most industrialized bloc in Africa after South Africa. Other economic sectors, including mining, agriculture, transport, tourism and the service industries, also prospered. Investment increased notably in the federation years, amounting to £805 million between 1954 and 1959, £224 million of which came from overseas. National income rose from £303 million in 1954 to £440 million in 1959, while exports increased by 74 per cent in the first six years of federation, as compared to 56 per cent in the six years immediately preceding its establishment.[12] The region also witnessed impressive infrastructural improvements epitomised by the construction of the Kariba hydroelectric plant and the establishment and commissioning of the University College of Rhodesia and Nyasaland in 1957. Meanwhile, the federation's cities and towns grew rapidly because of increasing rural-to-urban African migration as Africans sought employment in the emerging industries. Figure 5.1 shows the Kariba Dam under construction.

Southern Rhodesia benefitted most economically from the federation. This was because of its more diversified economy and more developed industrial sector which were able to take advantage of the larger domestic market and abundance of cheap labour from its partners, especially the relatively poorer Nyasaland, for its own benefit. Southern Rhodesia also benefitted from Northern Rhodesia's copper exports earnings and federal infrastructural development. By the end of the decade, however,

[11] N. M. Shamuyarira, 'The Coming Showdown in Central Africa', *Foreign Affairs*, 39, 2 (January 1961), 291–8.
[12] 'Federation of Rhodesia and Nyasaland: Report of the Monckton Commission', in *Commonwealth Survey*, 6, 22 (25 October 1960), 997–1006 (Hereafter the Monckton Commission Report).

ORAFs

FIGURE 5.1. Kariba Dam nearing completion in 1960.
Source: Gale, D., *Rhodesia: The Years between 1923–1973: Half a Century of Responsible Government in Rhodesia* (Salisbury: H. C. P. Andersen, 1973).

the economy slowed down as a result of falling world demand for copper and declining foreign investment inflows.[13]

Meanwhile, in 1959, accumulated African resentment against federation, especially in Nyasaland, exploded into violence which eventually engulfed the entire region. Having recently returned from many years of residence abroad to take up the leadership of the Malawi National Congress, an African nationalist party, Dr Hastings Kamuzu Banda vehemently opposed the federation and issued a call in January 1959 for immediate independence for Malawi. The call was followed by widespread disturbances which ended with 52 African deaths and 1,300 arrests of Congress supporters and leaders. In response, the federal state deployed soldiers in Malawi to quell the disturbances and also declared a state of emergency. A state of emergency was also declared in Southern Rhodesia, followed by the arrest and detention of approximately 500 Southern Rhodesia Congress members. These disturbances

---

[13] T. H. Mothibe, 'Zimbabwe: African Working Class Nationalism, 1957, 1963', *Zambesia*, 23, 2 (1996), 160.

contributed to the establishment of the a Royal Commission led by Walter Monckton (the Moncton Commission) to advise on the future of the federation.

The Monckton Commission reported the existence of strong African opposition to federation that it characterised as 'widespread, sincere and of long standing. It is almost pathological', especially among those in the northern territories who regarded the existing political arrangements as tumbling blocs to their independence from colonial rule. In the words of the Commission,

It now appears to many Africans that only the presence of the European community politically entrenched behind the Federal constitution stands between them and the form of freedom already granted to their fellow Africans in most other parts of the continent. So long as Federation seems to them to block their way to rapid political progress, so long will their hostility to it continue to grow.

In the Commission's opinion, 'the strength of African opposition in the Northern Territories is such that Federation can not ... be maintained in the present form'.[14]

Meanwhile, the federation also came under attack from Southern Rhodesian settler right-wing elements who were worried that Britain might be stampeded by rising African nationalism to grant independence to the country under majority rule, as was happening elsewhere in Africa. This fear was not entirely unjustified, for Africans in Southern Rhodesia were indeed inspired by the steady march towards independence in the rest of Africa. In the words of Nathan Shamuyarira, Africans could not submissively accept their subjugation

when all around them they can see their fellowmen governing themselves. The advent of Ghana, Nigeria and other states as free and independent nations, represented at the United Nations, and of Tanganyika as a self-governing state, is obviously an exciting idea to every African. Southern Rhodesia boasts of the highest literacy rate south of the Sahara; it has more than 100 university trained Africans. But, paradoxically, it has not a single African in its 30-member legislature, and not one has entered the Territory's Civil Service in the 37 years since self-government was granted to Southern Rhodesia. This applies even to the Department of Native Affairs which looks primarily after African interests.[15]

In the light of rising domestic African nationalism, some white settlers, under the banner of the newly established Rhodesian Front Party, wrested

[14] The Monckton Commission Report.
[15] Shamuyarira, 'The Coming Showdown in Central Africa'.

power in Southern Rhodesia in 1962 and campaigned for an end to the federation. Under attack from both ends of the racial divide, the federation collapsed in 1963, as Northern Rhodesia and Nyasaland became independent as Zambia and Malawi, respectively, while Southern Rhodesia drifted irrevocably towards the unilateral declaration of Independence (UDI) under Ian Smith in 1965.

6

Nationalist Movements to 1965

Introduction

African organisations and protest went through a process of evolution which began with what Michael West has labelled the proto-nationalist period between the two world wars, and went through the national moment from 1945 to 1948 to end with the nationalist moment from the late 1950s onwards.[1] The first phase can be said to have started after the defeat of the Mapondera military uprising in 1900. Mapondera was a Shona chief who tried, unsuccessfully, to regain control of his territory in Eastern Zimbabwe by attacking colonial installations and personnel in the area. Thereafter, it was not until the 1960s that Africans took up arms again to try and dislodge colonial rule. Until then, they employed less confrontational ways of challenging the status quo. In this phase, a sense of nationalism was yet to develop, even though anti-colonial resentment simmered under the surface, and Africans took various initiatives to mobilise and organise themselves around specific interests.

For the emerging small mission-educated African elite, the focus was more on promoting their group interests, such as the right to vote, than on speaking on behalf of the African population as a whole on political matters. Because they had little mass support, they had no bargaining power. Therefore, the colonial authorities could easily ignore their demands. In any case, as has been argued, at this time, the African elite were not really interested in the destruction of colonialism, but were, rather, requesting that they also be accommodated among the colonial

[1] See M. O. West, *The Rise of an African Middle Class: Colonial Zimbabwe 1898–1965* (Bloomington: Indiana University Press, 2002).

elite, as educated Africans. Thus, they were not demanding self-rule but only that they be governed well. It was the failure of the colonial system to respond positively to their requests, combined with the impact of the Second World War on African political consciousness, which eventually radicalised the African political leadership. The immediate post–Second World War period saw a quickening of African protest, dominated by two major workers' strikes, followed thereafter by the rise of radical mass African nationalism now demanding 'one man, one vote' and an end to colonialism. This chapter traces the development of African political consciousness from conquest to the nationalist struggles of the post–Second World War era to analyse the factors that influenced growing African political awareness and the various forms African organisations took.

The Early Phase

The first phase of post-conquest African mobilisation in Zimbabwe was characterised by the emergence of a variety of self-help, mutual help and solidarity organisations and associations such as burial societies and ethnic cultural associations which articulated and/or promoted specific group interests that were not necessarily anti-colonial.[2] Africans also established proto-nationalist organisations in the form of trade unions, voters' associations and independent churches which allowed them the opportunity to run their own affairs, independent of white tutelage – arguably a good preparation for later nationalist party organisation. There were also a number of small African workers' strikes in the immediate post–First World War period, including the Globe & Phoenix Mine workers' strike of November 1918 and the strike by Wankie Colliery sanitations workers in March 1919. Another significant action was the July 1919 strike by African railway employees in Bulawayo, which involved some 570 workers and lasted for three days.[3] Until the Second World War, however, African protest, in Southern Rhodesia and elsewhere on the African continent, was generally mild and based on efforts to persuade the colonial authorities to reform through petitions and delegations to the local and overseas colonial authorities requesting select reforms.

Early African organisations in Zimbabwe were clearly elitist in composition and in their concerns and objectives. Established and led by

[2] T. Yoshikuni, 'Strike Action and Self-Help Associations: Zimbabwean Worker Protest and Culture after World War I', *Journal of Southern African Studies*, 15, 3 (1989), 440–68.
[3] Yoshikuni, 'Strike Action', 440–68.

black South Africans who had come up with the Pioneer Column, they
petitioned for exemption of the 'superior' or 'advanced' Africans from
segregation in public spaces and humiliating requirements such as removing their hats when in the presence of white people. They were not particularly concerned about the general mass of the African people, whom
they looked down upon. In 1919, for instance, Africans employed as mes-
sengers and boss boys who had had some education at the country's mission schools and regarded themselves as the African elite established the
Rhodesian Native Association (RNA) whose aims were, among others,
to keep the colonial government 'informed of Native Public Opinion'.
This was followed in 1921 by the Union Bantu Vigilance Association
(UBVA),[4] as well as the Rhodesia Bantu Voters Association (RBVA), a
Matebeleland-based organisation which 'advocated cooperation with
settler politicians in return for concessions and privileges for "civilised
Bantu"' and exemption of 'advanced' Africans from pass laws, lowering
of franchise qualifications to enable 'superior' Africans to vote, as well as
some educational reforms. Under its secretary Martha Ngano, the RBVA
attempted to extend its influence into the surrounding countryside, with
little success.[5]

Later, indigenous Africans established their own organisations, such
as the Amandebele Patriotic Society (also known as the Loyal Mandebele
Patriotic Society), Gwelo Native Welfare Association, Rhodesia Native
Association and the Ndebele National Home Movement (later called the
Matabele Home Society). The Amandebele Patriotic Society was concerned mainly with the African people's moral betterment in the face of
growing incidences of sexually transmitted diseases, while the Matabele
Home Society, under Lobengula's chosen successor Nyamanda Khumalo,
was essentially an ethnic organisation which agitated for the creation of
a Ndebele homeland, in the wake of the destruction of the Ndebele state
in the Anglo-Ndebele War.[6] Another elitist organisation was the Rhodesia
Native Association (RNA), later renamed the Southern Rhodesia Native
Association (SRNA), whose concerns were similar to those of the RBVA,
namely the franchise for the elite Africans, exemption from pass laws
and access to European liquor. It also promoted a determined agenda
to control 'loose' African women whom it sought to have expelled from

---

[4] M. O. West, *The Rise of an African Middle Class: Colonial Zimbabwe 1898–1965*
(Bloomington and Indianapolis: Indiana University Press, 2002), 122–3; Yoshikuni,
'Strike Action', 440–68.
[5] Phimister, *Social and Economic History*, 152.
[6] West, *African Middle Class*, 129.

the country's urban centres.[7] None of these early organisations and movements succeeded in their objectives, as they had a narrow support base and could, therefore, be easily ignored by the colonial authorities.

More effective was the Industrial Commercial Workers Union (ICU) established by Robert Sambo in 1926. Inspired by the Clement Kadalie-led South African Industrial and Commercial Workers Union, which was founded in 1919 and grew to become 'one of the largest organizations ever to operate in Africa, and [which] mobilized rural blacks in a way no South African movement has accomplished before or since',[8] the Rhodesian ICU differed from earlier organisations in its efforts to unite all African workers regardless of class or origins and to address issues that were of concern to all Africans, including those who were not strictly workers. Discarding the petition politics of the earlier organisations, the ICU mobilised mass support through 'mass meetings and public denunciations of the government'.[9] It also 'agitated for better wages, condemned the neglect of the township by the white city fathers, condemned police harassment and denounced police campaigns against pass violators and tax defaulters' and challenged the Land Apportionment Act. The state considered the ICU to be such a subversive organisation that it deported Sambo to Malawi, his home country, and then proceeded to target remaining ICU leaders, such as Masocha Ndlovu and Charles Mzingeli, for periodic arrests and general harassment.

The early years of ICU coincided with increased worker protests on the country's mines in reaction to wage cuts and other unsatisfactory working conditions. The most notable workers' strike occurred at Shamva Gold Mine near Salisbury where, from 12 to 17 September 1927, approximately 3,500 African workers went on strike in protest against, inter alia, a debt peonage system that tied workers to the mine through endless debt and for higher wages. It was only when the army intervened that the strike ended.[10]

Also important at the time were independent African churches which emerged soon after colonisation as newly converted Africans realised that there was a close working relationship between the established churches

---

[7] West, *African Middle Class*, 130–1.
[8] Bradford, 'Class Contradictions and Class Alliances: The Social Nature of ICU Leadership, 1924–1929', African Studies Seminar Paper, Wits University (1983), 3, http://wiredspace. wits.ac.za/bitstream/handle/10539/8443/ISS-50.pdf?sequence=1 (accessed 26 May 2012).
[9] West, *African Middle Class*, 136.
[10] Phimister, *Social and Economic History*, 160–5.

and the colonial authorities. Just as they rejected white domination in politics, Africans in white-led denominations also rejected white domination in matters of religion and opted to set up their own denominations that they could lead independently. Known as Ethiopianism or the Ethiopian Church Movement, independent African churches preached a black theology and were generally anti-colonial. Examples elsewhere on the continent include Kimbanguism in the Belgian Congo in the 1960s or the church led by John Chilembwe in 1915 in Nyasaland, which organised a revolt against the colonial regime in protest at the shedding of African blood in the First World War. In Zimbabwe, the leading independent churches between the two world wars were the Watch Tower Movement and the Zionist and Apostolic Churches. Some of these churches did not limit their activities only to spiritual matters; they also organised political protests against the colonial administration. An example was the heavy involvement of the Watch Tower Movement in the organisation of the first African workers' industrial action in the Shamva Mine strike of 1927. This religious movement, originating in the United States at the turn of the twentieth century and brought into Southern Rhodesia by Malawi migrant labourers, became strongly rooted in the country's mining centres, mainly because of its denunciation of pass laws and taxation, as well as its claim that the departure of all white people from the country was imminent.[11]

Ethiopianism in Zimbabwe was inspired partly by Black Nationalist ideas filtering in from the African diaspora across the Atlantic Ocean, especially those associated with Marcus Garvey and his United Negro Improvement Association (UNIA), an organisation that flourished in the United States in the 1920s and which preached African pride and self-sufficiency and the doctrine of 'Africa for the Africans'. Also influential was the American Methodist Episcopal Church (AME), founded by a black American Richard Allen in protest against white racism in the church in the nineteenth century and brought to southern Africa by AME missionaries in the 1890s.[12]

The economic hardships of the Great Depression in the 1930s led increasingly to Ethiopian churches preaching an anti-state theology that denounced white rule. Not surprisingly, such politically charged

---

[11] Phimister, *Social and Economic History*, 155.
[12] West, *African Middle Class*, 142. For the history of Marcus Garvey and UNIA, see Marcus Garvey and Amy Jacques-Garvey, *The Philosophy and Opinions of Marcus Garvey or Africa for the Africans* (Dover, MA: Majority Press, 1986); Robert A. Hill (ed.), *Marcus Garvey: Life and Lessons* (Berkeley: University of California Press, 1987).

church pronouncements worried the colonial government enough to lead it to legislate against some of their activities. Thus, the state banned the Apostolic Church in the 1930s and passed the 1936 Sedition Act, aimed partly at combating activities of the Watch Tower Movement and Ethiopian churches which were accused of spreading 'subversive and seditious propaganda and literature in the colony'. The Act made it an offence 'to engender feelings of hostility between Europeans and others'.[13] Also in 1936 came the Native Registration Act compelling every African male in the towns to have, in addition to the already required registration certificate (*situpa*), either a pass to week work in the town, a certificate signed by a native Commissioner certifying that the individual was gainfully employed in town, or a visiting pass if only temporarily in town.[14] This act was a follow-up to legislation passed before the First World War requiring every African male of fourteen years and older to register and always carry with him a *situpa* (registration certificate) which identified who he was and whether or not he had a contract of service.

As shown, Africans organised themselves and mobilised around issues that were of concern to their particular groups in the decades after the establishment of colonial rule. Because of their rather parochial composition and scope, they remained largely ineffective. The one exception was the ICU which introduced a degree of militancy hitherto absent in African protest. Even then, however, African protest, which the aforementioned state legislation was designed to stamp out, was still very mild and aimed primarily at getting the colonial authorities to reform the system rather than to overthrow white rule. The days of the African cry for one-man-one-vote or 'freedom' were still far into the future mainly because, as Zimbabwean writer and commentator Lawrence Vambe observed,

[i]n the early 1930s majority rule was a concept that neither the Africans nor the settlers entertained as a remote possibility.... The bulk of the African people were prepared to submit to white rule; it seemed so entrenched at that point that few could doubt it as a fixed element of the natural order of creation.[15]

---

[13] Phimister, *Political Economy*, 197–8. According to Phimister, 'Garveyite tracts and *Umsebenzi*, the South African Communist Party newspaper, had circulated in the country ... [while] copies of Garvey's *Black Man* were sold for 8d. each in Bulawayo ... Watch Tower literature also appeared at this time which identified the British Empire as the work of Satan'. Phimister, *Social and Economic History*, 198.

[14] Phimister, *Social and Economic History*, 202.

[15] Vambe, *From Rhodesia to Zimbabwe*, 101.

Impact of the Second World War

The nature and tone of African nationalism throughout the continent changed dramatically after the Second World War, mainly because the war acted as a catalyst in transforming the mild interwar petition politics into the increasingly confrontationist mass nationalism of the post-war years. As argued, in the interwar period, the educated African elite which led protest movements was not seeking an end to European rule; rather they were demanding to be governed well and to be co-opted into the colonial project. The guiding belief then was that all that was needed was for them to point out injustices to the colonial authorities and the authorities would, of their own volition, undertake the necessary reforms. Thus, they sent delegations and petitions to local legislatures or governors and to the capitals in Europe pleading the case of the Africans' desire to vote and to be represented in the local legislatures by their own representatives – to no avail. A good example is the petition sent to the British monarch by the South African Native National Congress in 1918 protesting the 1913 Land Act which expropriated African land in favour of the whites, and which avers 'our affectionate loyalty and devotion to Your Majesty's person and Throne and the sincerity of our desire that Divine Blessing and prosperity may attend Your Majesty and all Your Majesty's Dominions in the dawn of a better age' and expresses 'the hope and wish that during Your majesty's Reign all races and Nations will be treated fairly and with justice, and there will be no discrimination on account of colour or creed; and will enjoy the right of citizenship and liberty under your flag'. The petition ends with an expression of the confidence that the king's intervention will ensure that 'the position of Your Majesty's subjects under the sun will be improved and be readjusted in terms of this Memorial'.[16]

The tone of this petition was in direct contrast to the following document drawn up by the Fifth pan-African Congress in Manchester, England, where black leaders from the African diaspora and from the African continent issued what was, in fact, a call to arms in the anticolonial struggle. The declaration written by emerging African nationalist leader Kwame Nkrumah stated:

---

[16] Sefako Makgatho, 'Petition to King George V, from the South African National Congress, 16 December 1918', www.anc.org.za/show.php?id=4401 (accessed 1 November 2012).

We believe in the rights of all peoples to govern themselves. We affirm the right of all colonial peoples to control their own destiny. All colonies must be free from foreign imperialist control, whether political or economic. The peoples of the colonies must have the right to elect their own government, a government without restrictions form a foreign power. We say to the peoples of the colonies that they must strive for these ends by all means at their disposal.

The object of imperialist powers is to exploit. By granting the right to the colonial peoples to govern themselves, they are defeating that objective. Therefore, the struggle for political power by colonial and subject peoples is the first step towards, and the necessary pre-requisite to, complete social, economic and political emancipation.

The Fifth Pan-African Congress, therefore, calls on the workers and farmers of the colonies to organize effectively. Colonial workers must be in the front lines of the battle against imperialism.

This Fifth Pan-African Congress calls on the intellectuals and professional classes of the colonies to awaken to their responsibilities. The long, long night is over. By fighting for trade union rights, the right to form co-operatives, freedom of the press, assembly, demonstration and strike; freedom to print and read the literature which is necessary for the education of the masses, you will be using the only means by which your liberties will be won and maintained. Today there is only one road to effective action – the organization of the masses.

Colonial and Subject Peoples of the World – Unite![17]

The change of tone reflected in the Fifth Pan-African Congress declaration has to be seen in the context of how, first, the invasion of Ethiopia by Mussolini in 1935 and, then, the Second World War heightened African political consciousness and changed the power relations between white and black on the continent. The first outraged Africans by attacking the symbol of African independence, given the fact that Ethiopia had never been colonized, while the second helped to destroy the prevailing myth of white invincibility which had taken root as a result of European conquest at the turn of the century.

In 1935, Italian dictator Benito Mussolini invaded Ethiopia as part of his campaign to aggrandize Italy's power. As a country which had escaped

---

[17] Fifth Pan-African Congress, *Declaration to the Colonial Peoples of the World* (Manchester, England, 1945).

European colonisation, Ethiopia was a symbol of black independence whose continued freedom black people everywhere cherished. When Mussolini overran it, black people were outraged and hundreds of them from the diaspora and from the African continent volunteered to fight in defence of Emperor Haile Selassie and his country until the Italians were forced to withdraw. Then with the outbreak of the Second World War, Africans participated in the war in large numbers, with an estimated 80,000 or more Africans fighting in the French and 370,000 in the British Army. Moreover, when France fell to the Germans in 1940, Brazzaville (French Congo) became, for a while, the capital city of Free France in exile. In the case of Zimbabwe, thousands of Africans actively participated in the war at the various fronts, while those left at home contributed to the Allied war effort through the production of foodstuffs and various minerals, such as chrome, plutonium, and other base metals that were essential to the Allies and by 'building military bases for use by the British Air Forces'.[18]

While Africans fought in defence of their colonizers for a variety of reasons, including conscription and the power of European anti-German propaganda, many also fought because of a rational appreciation that they were better off under the devil they knew than have the Nazis, who were even more rabidly racist than their colonisers, become their masters should they win the war. Still, at home, resources for the front were often produced under duress, as colonial authorities forced Africans to contribute to the war effort. Groundnuts, cotton, palm oil, tin, wild rubber and food crops were produced for the Allied war effort across the African continent. Because Africans contributed so much to the war effort, Britain and France could no longer continue to treat them as they have in the past. On their part, Africans expected to be accorded more respect and rights by their colonizers after the war, given their immense sacrifice during the war years. Anti-colonial feelings increased when their expectations were not fulfilled.

The psychological impact of the Second World War on African soldiers was also significant. For instance, in their efforts to get Africans to enlist, representatives of European powers emphasised the crucial importance of saving the world for democracy from tyranny and the sanctity of self-determination, leading Africans to wonder why they should fight in defence of these benefits for their rulers when they themselves were denied the right to determine their own future and democratic political

[18] West, *African Middle Class*, 155.

participation and governance. This was brought out clearly in the following imaginary conversation that was presented in a publication by one Waruhiu Itote, a Kenyan African veteran of the Second World War and later a leader of the anti-colonial Mau Mau uprising in Kenya.

> **British Soldier:** *'You know, sometimes, I don't understand you Africans who are out here fighting. What do you think you are fighting for?'*
> African soldier: 'I am fighting for the same thing that you are fighting for, of course'.
> **British soldier:** *'In a funny way, I think you are right ... and I'm not sure that's such a good idea'.*
> African soldier: 'Please explain what you mean.'
> **British soldier:** *'Look. I'm fighting for England, to preserve my country, my culture, all those things which we Englishmen have built up over the centuries as a nation; it's really my national independence that I am fighting to preserve. And, I suppose, all that goes with it, including the British Empire. Does it seem right to you that you should be fighting for the same things as I?'*
> African soldier: 'I doubt it, I don't think so.'
> **British soldier:** *'I can't see why you Africans should fight to protect the Empire instead of fighting to free yourselves. Years from now, maybe, your children will fight a war to preserve the national independence of your country, but before that, it's up to you to see that they get independence in the first place, so they can preserve it later! At least if I die in this war, I know it will be for my country. But if you are killed here, what will your country have gained?'*[19]

Africans thus began to question the sense in defending democracy for their oppressors while they were denied democracy in their home countries. They concluded that 'what was good for the goose was also good for the gander' – they too deserved to enjoy democracy.

Another development upsetting Africans was the treatment of the Atlantic Charter by its drafters, U.S. President Franklin D. Roosevelt and British Prime Minister Winston Churchill, created in 1941 to clarify the Allies' war aims. Clause 3 of the Charter stated that the Allies 'respect the right of all peoples to choose the form of government under which they will live; and they wish to see sovereign rights and self-government restored to those who have been forcibly deprived of them'. When the two leaders realised the implications of this statement to the colonised peoples of Africa, however, they were quick to issue a disclaimer that these principles were not applicable to Africa. Not surprisingly, Africans were incensed. Without realising it, Roosevelt and Churchill had signed

[19] Waruhui Itote, *Mau Mau General* (Nairobi, 1967), 9–15.

the death warrant of colonialism, for the very struggle against German, Italian, and Japanese tyranny and conquest was incompatible with colonialism, which Africans regarded as also tyrannical. Indeed, it became increasingly clear that one could not logically condemn the one without also condemning the other. After the Second World War, it became increasingly difficult to justify colonialism morally.

Highlighting the contradiction between the Allies' war objectives, as espoused in the Atlantic Charter, and the subsequent exclusion of the colonised people from its provisions, Rhodesian African soldier, Lance Corporal Masiye, commented on the ongoing debate in the local African press on whether Africans should be included in the provisions of the Atlantic Charter:

A denial was published in the *Bantu Mirror* as to whether Africans should be included in the New World Order through the Atlantic Charter. This did not only surprise me, but I took it for granted that whatsoever faithfulness and devotedness [sic] we might show the Europeans, we must never dream of comparative human rights.... It must be a very shameless sort of ruler who exploits people under his thraldom at ease and yet he never dreams of their release nor allows them to have privileges to race for comparative human rights. The African has served his rulers with admirable devotedness. What is he to receive for this? A continual exclusion from human rights? If so, our rulers must be quite shameless to blame the enemy for his brutality and assumed racial superiority.[20]

Moreover, the war brought Africans into contact with other colonised peoples, notably the Indians, who had already made some headway in the struggle for their independence from Britain and learnt that it was possible to demand the right to self-determination from the colonial masters. The war also shattered whatever remained of the African people's awe of the Europeans and belief in their invincibility. Not only did they see white soldiers kill each other at the front; they were, in fact, required to kill enemy whites! They also realised that the whites were relying on them to help to save their way of life and were, as a result, forced to treat the Africans as comrades in arms and equals. This changed the African people's perception of Europeans and undermined white authority in the colonies. The effect of facing common danger was described by Waruhiu Itote:

In 1944, we returned to India from the Kalewa battlefront [Burma]. I took back with me many lasting memories. Among the shells and bullets, there had been no pride, no air of superiority from our European comrades-in-arms. We drank the

[20] *Bantu Mirror*, 17 June 1944.

same tea, used the same water and lavatories and shared the same jokes. There were no racial insults, no references to derogatory names. The white heat of battle had blistered all that away and left only our common humanity and our common fate, either death or survival.[21]

In addition, while before the war, Africans saw only powerful Europeans in the form of colonial administrators, soldiers and wealthy individuals, at the front they intermingled with working-class Europeans and found them no different from themselves. They had also seen European poverty in Europe and savagery in warfare. They could never again accept colonial domination without question.

Lastly, African anger increased when, after the war, returning white soldiers were rewarded with farms, whereas Africans received a pat on the back and were shoved back into the crowded African reserves in which they had lived before the war. Returning white soldiers were rewarded with free land and cheap loans under a government-sponsored land resettlement scheme, with the state sometimes developing the farms first 'before handing them over to White ex-servicemen'. Government also provided other support to these ex-servicemen, including helping the new farmers to stock their farms with livestock and establish irrigation schemes.[22] In contrast, African expectations of recognition and material reward for their sacrifices and the hope that they would be accorded greater political participation and enjoyment of democracy were dashed. They had to contend with the same racial discrimination and marginalisation they had experienced before enlisting, the more galling now that they had given so much in defence of their colonial rulers. That their sacrifices counted for naught was evident in an incident recounted by Lawrence Vambe of one of his relatives' attempt to assert his rights by claiming that 'as someone who had risked his life in the last war for the freedom of white men in Rhodesia, he deserved a little courtesy' and who received a beating by a white policeman instead, for his 'cheek'. To add insult to injury, he was also told: 'You joined the army of your own accord.... We paid you ... and owe you nothing now.... You are a native and always will be.... Don't you ever forget that when you talk to a white man, especially a police officer'.[23]

[21] Itote, *Mau Mau General*, 9–15.
[22] David Johnson, *World War II and the Scramble for Labour in Colonial Zimbabwe, 1939–1948* (Harare: University of Zimbabwe Publications, 2000), 26–7.
[23] Cited in Johnson, *Scramble for Labour*, 27.

Such grievances increased the anti-colonial sentiment among Zimbabwe's African population. There is, however, no evidence that war veterans played a special leading role in the anti-colonial struggle in Zimbabwe, for as Johnson has pointed out, the number of ex-combatants was very small. Nevertheless, the unfair treatment veterans received after the war was used by nationalist leaders to challenge white rule.[24]

Further adding to African grievances in Southern Rhodesia were the post–Second World War removals that saw black Africans being moved to the remote and malarial parts of the country to make room for the thousands of white immigrants from Britain and other European countries. Taking advantage of the Southern Rhodesian government's post-war resettlement scheme and escaping Europe's post-war economic hardships, white immigrants, including many who had been stationed in the country as Royal Air Force trainees and who had taken a liking to it, entered the country in large numbers.[25] The volume of the influx can be seen from the fact that the country's white population increased from 82,000 in 1946 to 135,000 in 1961, with a record 17,000 immigrants entering the country in 1948 alone.[26] As a result, more than 100,000 Africans were evicted from their lands, now reclassified as European areas, and dumped in the already overcrowded African reserves or in the remote and malarial lands of the Zambezi Valley.[27] As in the past, no compensation was paid, either for the land or for the property destroyed as a result of the forced removals.

Other factors contributing to the radicalisation of African nationalism include the establishment of the United Nations in 1945 and the subsequent growing representation of developing nations in the UN Assembly

---

[24] Johnson, *Scramble for Labour*, 27.

[25] Frank Clements, *Rhodesia: The Course to Collision* (London: Pall Mall, 1969), 78.

[26] Julius Isaac, *British Postwar Migration* (Cambridge: Cambridge University Press, 1954), 132–4; Harold D. Nelson et al., *Area Handbook for Southern Rhodesia* (Washington, DC: American University, Foreign Area Studies, 1975), 73.

[27] An example of the late colonial forced removals is the relocation of the Gwebo Chieftaincy from the Charter Estates in Gweru to the malaria-infested and arid area of Gokwe. See P. S. Nyambara, 'Madheruka and Shangwe: Ethnic Identities and the Culture of Modernity in Gokwe, Northwestern Zimbabwe, 1963', *Journal of African History*, 42 (2002), 287–306; Nyambara, 'Immigrants, "Traditional" Leaders and the Rhodesian State: The Power of "Communal" Land Tenure and the Politics of Land Acquisition in Gokwe, Zimbabwe, 1963-1979', *Journal of Southern African Studies*, 27, 4 (2001), 771–91; Nyambara, 'The Politics of Land Acquisition and Struggles over Land in the "Communal" Areas of Zimbabwe: The Gokwe Region in the 1980s and 1990s', *Africa*, 71, 2 (2001), 54–108. See also Robin Palmer and I. Birch, *Zimbabwe: A Land Divided* (Oxford: Oxfam, 1992), 8.

as Latin American and Asian country membership increased, and the influence of the Cold War, as the Socialist bloc fished in Africa's troubled waters in order to win allies against the West. Also important in a number of countries, including Zimbabwe, were the ideas of black leaders in the diaspora, such as Marcus Garvey and W. E. B. Dubois, which asserted black pride and called for black solidarity. It is significant, for instance, that the leaders of the Gwelo Native Welfare Association and, subsequently, the Southern Rhodesia Native Welfare Association, some of whom, such as Sambo and Masotsha Ndlovu, then went on to lead the ICU, were subscribers to Garvey's ideas and connected to the Universal Negro Improvement Association (UNIA), an organisation pushing for black self-reliance that Garvey had set up in the diaspora.[28]

Added to all this was the rapid increase in the urban African industrial workforce in response to the country's expanding industrial economy and the poverty and housing problems that accompanied these changes. Between 1939 and 1953, manufacturing production increased by an average 11.7 per cent annually, while the African industrial workforce increased threefold to 469,000.[29] According to historian Richard Gray,

By the end of the Second World War ... the experiences of urban poverty and frustration were creating a new unity in which class became one with colour, and at the same time the African initiative was passing to those leaders who made clear the new demands and awareness of African labourers.[30]

The new forms and character of African protest became evident in the 1945 railway workers' strike in Bulawayo. Organised by the Rhodesian Railways African Employees Association (RRAEA) founded in 1944, the strike involved 2,708 African workers employed in Southern Rhodesia's second-largest town of Bulawayo but spread throughout the country to the towns of Gwelo, Selukwe, Fort Victoria, Salisbury, Umtali and Wankie Colliery, and also into Northern Rhodesia (Zambia) in a matter of days. By the end of the strike, no less than 80 per cent of the black employees of the Southern Rhodesia Railways network amounting to 10,000 workers had downed tools.[31] By then, both management and the

---

[28] West, *African Middle Class.*
[29] EISA, 'Zimbabwe: Self-government and Federation (1923–1963)', http://www.eisa.org.za/WEP/zimoverview2.htm (accessed 12 October 2012).
[30] Gray, *The Two Nations*, 316.
[31] Ken Vickery, 'The Rhodesia Railways African Strike of 1945, Part I: A Narrative Account', *Journal of Southern African Studies*, 24, 3 (September 1998), 545.

colonial administrators were worried that this action might trigger a general strike in the country's industries.

The workers were resisting management's announced plans to reduce overtime payments and to pay part of the wages in rations, among other grievances, including unhappiness with poor accommodation. The strike was partly caused by management's refusal to attend to the workers' grievances. Since its formation, the RRAEA had sent many written requests to management for their grievances to be attended to, without getting any response. Workers were galvanised into action when management decided to change the company's overtime policy for black employees in September 1945 in a manner which workers regarded as prejudicial to them.

Insert

List of demands submitted by strikers in Bulawayo to the General Manager of Rhodesia Railways:

'Sir,
With most respectful [sic] we beg to inform you and your Administration that the strike of the African employees here in Bulawayo is due to the fact that the African employees submitted their requests to the General Manager, but however met with no satisfactory results.

Wages as No. I
... they should be paid according to their grades or a class of work they perform. That no man shall have to work for less than 5/- to 7/6 per day which is due to the fact that no man can ever live with the money paid to Africans by the Railways....

Overtime
That the overtime should be paid just as it has been paid before ... he must get what he usually gets that is his daily pay instead of 3d per hour which is regarded as an increase and yet it is not.

Ration
That every African here is prepared not to receive any ration from the Railways... [Namely, to paid in cash, rather than food rations.]

Office of the Supervisor of Natives
One of the things which causes much misunderstanding ... is the Office of Supervisor of Natives, because of what it does, it never do anything

for the Africans, which is quite clear that since this Office came into existence nothing has been done for the good of the Africans.
... We assure you that we are prepared to go back to our work at any time provided our requests being granted.

We are Sir,
Your most humble servants.
Rhodesia Railway Native Employees.'[32]

The strike lasted two weeks and only ended when the government promised to set up a commission to look into the workers' grievances. The commission recommended a 25–30 per cent wage increase, far less than workers had hoped for, and weakened the power of the Supervisor of Natives, which had caused some of the workers' unhappiness. It did not address the issue of rations in lieu of cash wages. The militancy of the railway workers during this strike heralded a change in the tone and character of African protest.

In 1948 came the first 'general strike'. The strike began on 13 April as Bulawayo municipal workers protested the 10 per cent wage increment that management had offered them following protracted negotiations with their union, the Bulawayo Municipal African Employees Association (BMAEA), and management's refusal to set up a Labour Board that the workers wanted. In a matter of days, workers in other centres across the country, including Umtali, Salisbury, Gwelo, Gatooma and Selukwe, also downed tools. The strike in Bulawayo soon collapsed when workers were falsely informed by Benjamin Burombo, a leading African political figure at the time, that government had agreed to a substantial wage increase for all the workers. This was, in fact, not true, and scholars are still debating Burombo's motives, with some regarding his action as a betrayal of the workers and others claiming that this was a tactical move on his part designed to avert a police crackdown.[33]

[32] Available at http://nvdatabase.swarthmore.edu/content/black-rhodesian-railroad-workers-strike-better-pay-1945
[33] O. Pollak, 'The Impact of the Second World War on African Labour Organisation in Rhodesia', *Rhodesian Journal of Economics*, 7, 3 (1973); S. Thornton, 'The Patterning of Industrial Conflict: African Working Class Assertion and a Collective Employer Response' (Unpublished, 1979); J. Lunn, 'The Political Economy of Protest: The Strikes and Unrest of 1948 in Southern Rhodesia', B.A. Honors thesis, University of Manchester (1982); N. Bhebe, *Benjamin Burombo*; E. Dumbutshena, *Zimbabwe Tragedy* (Nairobi, East African Publishing House, 1975); West, *African Middle Class*, 174–6.

Scholars are not agreed on whether or not the series of workers' actions that occurred across the country in that year constituted a general strike. For instance, some have argued that there was, as yet, no industrial working class in the country with a common working-class consciousness that was capable of mobilising on a countrywide scale, as the manufacturing sector was still in its infancy. After all, it is argued, there were only 382 industrial establishments in the country by 1945 with a small black workforce of 30,439, some of whom were migrant workers from neighbouring countries. Rather than being one massive countrywide general strike, what occurred in 1948 was a series of unconnected workers' actions.[34] Other scholars insist that this was a radical industrial workers' strike which might have achieved its goals had it not been betrayed by the African elite.[35]

Both the 1945 and 1948 strikes had taken place in a legal climate that was still governed by the 1902 Masters and Servants Act which did not permit them either to form trade unions or to engage in collective bargaining with their employers, since the 1934 Industrial Conciliation Act had excluded Africans in its definition of workers. Because of the two major strikes in the 1940s and workers' determination to get organised, government passed the revised Industrial Conciliation Act of 1959, permitting African workers, except agricultural and domestic workers, public servants and Railways employees, to form and join trade unions.[36] The Act's recognition of only skills-based workers' unions meant that the majority workers were excluded, and also ensured that white unions continued to be dominant because Africans had been excluded from apprenticeships by the 1934 Act. Nevertheless, the 1959 Act did provide some room for African unions to operate.

The post–Second World War years also witnessed the emergence of militant mass African political organisations and nationalist parties marking what historian Michael West has identified as the 'nationalism moment'.[37] Among the organisations that surfaced at this time were the revived ICU, now renamed the Reformed Industrial and Commercial

---

[34] I. Phimister and B. Raftopoulos, '"Kana Sora Rikatsva Ngaritsve": African Nationalists and Black Workers. The 1948 General Strike in Colonial Zimbabwe', *Journal of Historical Sociology*, 13, 3 (2000), 289–324.

[35] O. Pollak, 'The Impact of the Second World War on African Labour Organisation in Rhodesia', *Rhodesian Journal of Economics*, 7, 3 (1973), 121–137; Thornton, 'The Patterning of Industrial Conflict'; Lunn, 'The Political Economy of Protest'.

[36] Peter Harris, 'Industrial Workers in Rhodesia 1946–1972: Working Class Elites or Lumpenproletariat?' *Journal of Southern African Studies*, 1, 2 (April 1975), 139–61.

[37] West, *African Middle Class*.

Workers Union (RICWU) under Charles Mzingeli, Benjamin Burombo's British African Voice Association and the City Youth League (CYL). The CYL was formed in Salisbury in 1955 by George Nyandoro, James Chikerema, Edson Sithole and Duduza Chisiza from Malawi. Its members believed in confrontational politics and sought to radicalise African protest activities through taking the state head on. For instance, it organised a three-day boycott of Salisbury's bus service in protest against increased bus fares by the town's United Transport Company. Unfortunately, the boycott became violent and several women were raped at Carter House in Harari Township, ostensibly as a form of punishment for breaking the boycott by using the buses, suggesting underlying gender tensions in the African community of Salisbury. There is no evidence, however, that this action was sanctioned by the leaders of the boycott campaign.[38]

Out of the CYL and a Bulawayo-based political grouping, the African National Council, came the first African national political party in the country, the Southern Rhodesian African National Congress (SRANC). Joshua Nkomo was elected leader of the party, the membership of which was estimated at 6,000 by May 1958 and which popularly became known as simply the ANC.[39] The ANC gained rapid popularity throughout the country by mobilising the Africans against the recently established Native Land Husbandry Act, de-stocking, unpopular government-sponsored soil conservation policies, the Native Affairs Department and its Native Commissioners and government-appointed chiefs.[40] Alarmed at the ANC actions which, according to the then-prime minister, threatened to make colonial administration of the 'Native Areas' impossible, government banned the party in 1959 and declared a state of emergency under which 500 leaders and members of the ANC were detained, some for as long as four years. African nationalists responded by forming another political party, the National Democratic Party (NDP), in January 1960. For the first time in the history of African protest in the country, the new party openly demanded majority rule under universal suffrage or a one-man-one-vote system. The NDP's popularity and confrontational tactics that sometimes escalated into riots, destruction of property and loss of lives led to its banning in December 1961.[41]

[38] West, *African Middle Class*, 206.
[39] Eshmael Mlambo, *Struggle for a Birthright*, 117; Ngwabi Bhebe, 'The Nationalist Struggle, 1957–1962', in C. Banana (ed.), *Turmoil and Tenacity* (Harare: College Press, 1989), 66–7.
[40] For a discussion of the ANC's influence in the rural area of Matopos, see T. Ranger, *Voices From the Rocks* (Harare: Baobab, 1999), chapter 6.
[41] Mothibe, 'Zimbabwe: African Working Class Nationalism', 172.

While there was a clear radicalisation process of African protest in the post–Second World War period as shown earlier, not everyone believed in the politics of confrontation and opposition to the colonial system. Naively believing that closer interaction with the dominant white population would lead the white rulers to accept the Africans more and encourage them to reform their policies, African elites decided to participate in the multiracial experiment championed by some white liberals at the time. Preferring to hobnob with the white liberals and socialise with them at regular tea parties, the African educated elite, comprising mainly 'clerks, teachers, preachers, social workers, journalists, nurses, lawyers and doctors', turned their backs on the African majority whom they regarded as backward, poor and uneducated. [42] Their quest for 'respectability' thus alienated them from the African majority and delayed their entry into the anti-colonial struggle which they were later to lead.[43]

Rather than join the ANC activists in mobilising people against the colonial system, the educated elites preferred to become members of the white-led multiracial organisations, such as the Inter-Racial Association (IRA) and the Capricorn Africa Society (CAS), which were really intended to prevent the rise of radical African nationalism. Promoting Cecil John Rhodes's call for 'equal rights for all civilised men', white liberals denounced racial segregation and African nationalism as racist, while championing the extension of the vote to the educated Africans who were also to be allowed to own property in the towns, among other privileges suitable for 'civilised' people, provided that the Africans, so favoured, demonstrated their responsibility. In this paternalistic relationship, there was, of course, never any doubt that Africans were the junior partners.[44] Leading African multiracialists, who were later to become prominent anti-colonial nationalist leaders, included Nathan Shamuyarira, Herbert Chitepo, Joshua Nkomo and Enoch Dumbutshena.[45] With time, however, the Africans realised that multiracialism or partnership was not leading anywhere and that the colonial system could not be changed by attending white liberals' tea parties, especially when the one prime minister who seemed to be sympathetic to African aspirations, Garfield Todd,

---

[42] T. Scarnechia, 'The Mapping of Respectability and the Transformation of African Residential Space', in B. Raftopoulos and T. Yoshikuni (eds.), *Sites of Struggle*, 161; West, *African Middle Class*, 2.

[43] Eshmael Mlambo, *Struggle for a Birthright*, 123.

[44] H. Holderness, *Lost Chance: Southern Rhodesia 1945–58* (Harare: Zimbabwe Publishing House, 1985), 107.

[45] Eshmael Mlambo, *Struggle for a Birthright*, 123–4.

was removed from power precisely because of his perceived sympathies towards African advancement. Increasingly, thereafter, the multiracialists joined the masses in the anti-colonial struggle, providing the needed leadership in the fight for 'one man, one vote'.

Also contributing to the radicalisation of the African protest movement in general and of the educated African elite in particular were the 'winds of change' that were sweeping across the continent and ushering in the decolonisation process. Southern Rhodesian Africans were aware of the Mau Mau uprising in Kenya in the 1950s, which saw the Kikuyu people waging war against white settlers in the Kenyan Highlands in a bid to recover their ancestral land that had been expropriated under British colonial rule. Meanwhile Ghana attained its independence in 1957 under Kwame Nkrumah as its first prime minister. Francophone African countries became independent in 1960, while neighbours such as Northern Rhodesia and Nyasaland gained independence as Zambia and Malawi, respectively. All this made Africans in Southern Rhodesia more resolved to attain self-determination.

Meanwhile, ten days after the banning of the NDP, a new African political party, the Zimbabwe African People's Union (ZAPU), was formed. Organised on a mass scale hitherto unknown in the country, its political rallies were often attended by thousands of Africans from all walks of life. It also adopted a confrontational approach to the colonial administration, with its members undertaking many demonstrations, often violent, and destructive of government installations and perceived sympathisers.

In the light of growing African radicalism and violent demonstrations, in 1960 the state passed the Law and Order (Maintenance) Act giving wide powers of arrest and detention to the security agencies in a bid to contain African nationalist activities. Not surprisingly, ZAPU was banned in September 1962. By then, however, its leaders had made two important decisions, namely to smuggle arms into the country and to recruit cadres for military training abroad so as to fight colonial rule through acts of sabotage and, eventually, armed confrontation. It was also decided that if the party was banned, it would go underground and no other party would be formed. At this point, unfortunately for the nationalist anti-colonial struggle, ZAPU split into two, with the splinter group expressing dissatisfaction with ZAPU president Joshua Nkomo's leadership style and forming a new party, the Zimbabwe African National Union (ZANU), in August 1963. The leader of the new party was former deputy president of ZAPU, Reverend Ndabaningi Sithole. The future president of independent Zimbabwe, Robert Gabriel Mugabe, was the new party's secretary general.

The split threw African nationalism into turmoil, as rival supporters fought running battles in the streets and Africans turned against each other in a senseless orgy of violence that diverted attention from the struggle for independence. The political intolerance reflected in the inter-party violent clashes of the 1960s presaged the virulent political hostility of the ruling party in the independence period after 1980, which will be discussed in detail later. The clashes between ZANU supporters and those belonging to a caretaker organisation that fronted for the banned ZAPU called the People's Caretaker Council (PCC) gave the colonial government a convenient excuse to ban both movements in August 1964. Several political leaders, including Nkomo, Sithole and Mugabe, were arrested and detained, while those who managed to escape went into the neighbouring countries and spearheaded the campaign to overthrow the colonial regime through the armed struggle. The determination to remove the colonial system through military means became stronger when the Rhodesian prime minister, Ian Douglas Smith, issued a unilateral declaration of independence (UDI) in 1965.

7

Unilateral Declaration of Independence
and African Response

After Todd was forced out of office because of his perceived sympathy for African advancement, Edgar Whitehead took over as leader of the ruling United Federal Party and prime minister. He was keen to negotiate with Britain for Southern Rhodesia's independence under white rule. His government's strategy included reforming the country's constitution in order to allow more Africans to vote in national elections by creating a lower voters' roll, to be known as the 'B' Roll, with lower eligibility qualifications. Voters on this roll would vote for fifteen of the sixty members of parliament, with the 'A' Roll voters voting for the rest. These proposals were accepted by the 1961 London Constitutional Conference attended by members of the Southern Rhodesian Government, African nationalist leaders, including Joshua Nkomo, and representatives of the British government. African leaders were later to change their minds and denounce the constitution as not likely to promote African political advancement sufficiently to bring about any meaningful change for a long time.

Meanwhile white right-wingers, grouped under the opposition Dominion Party (later renamed the Rhodesian Front), felt that Whitehead had gone too far in the opposite direction and had made unacceptable concessions to African nationalism.[1] On this ticket, the Rhodesian Front (RF) won the December 1962 general elections, and its leader, Winston Field, became prime minister, while Ian Smith served as deputy prime minister and minister of treasury. Failing to make any headway in the quest to obtain independence from Britain, Winston resigned in April

[1] Patrick Bond, *Uneven Zimbabwe: A Study of Finance, Development, and Underdevelopment* (Trenton, NJ: Africa World Press, 1998), 111.

149

1964, to be succeeded by Ian Smith[2] who was determined to gain the
country's independence under white rule at all costs. Driving this agenda
was, of course, the long-established racial chauvinism that had fuelled the
segregationist laws of the 1930s and which had, throughout the colonial
period, nurtured the sense of paternalism which regarded whites as men-
tors and guardians of the African people who could not be trusted to run
things on their own. The clarion call for Ian Smith and his supporters,
thus, became the need to keep power in 'responsible hands', namely white
hands. This resolve was strengthened by the civil war in the Congo at its
independence in 1960 which saw many whites killed or forced to leave
in the wave of riots and lawlessness that swept the country as the Belgian
colonial rulers withdrew. This made Southern Rhodesians to fear black
majority rule even more and informed their determination to pre-empt
black majority rule by seizing power themselves. In Ian Smith's words:

> Meanwhile, to the north of us, things were not going all that smoothly. In
> the spirit of Macmillan's 'Winds of Change' speech, the Belgian government
> decided that the time had come for them to pull out of the Congo. Tragically,
> instead of an organised plan for withdrawal and transfer of power, they allowed
> a state of panic to develop, leading to chaos and a stampede, with the white
> people being caught up in the usual pillage, murder and rape associated with
> such events. The responsible authority took the first plane back home, and sim-
> ply abandoned all commitments. The refugees poured down through the two
> Rhodesias, where emergency committees were set up to provide accommoda-
> tion, food and medical facilities. It was the latter half of 1960. The event had a
> profound effect on our people, making them realise all the more positively the
> danger of capitulating to the metropolitan powers, who were ready to cut and
> run at the drop of a hat.[3]

Consequently, the Rhodesian Front Party campaigned for independence
under white rule during the 1965 general elections. Its decisive victory
suggested overwhelming support for the independence platform and
emboldened the party to call for negotiations with Britain over the matter.
The British government would not hear of independence before majority rule, however. Its no-independence-before-majority-rule (NIBMAR)
stance was that independence would only be considered on condition
that 'the principle and intention of unimpeded progress to majority
rule' was guaranteed. Racial segregation was to end and there should

---

[2] W. Gale, *The Years between, 1923–1973: Half a Century of Responsible Government in
Rhodesia* (Salisbury: H. C. P. Andersen, 1973), 49. The story of Field's ouster is told in
detail in Ian Smith, *The Great Betrayal* (London: Blake Publishers, 1997).
[3] Smith, *Great Betrayal*, 44.

FIGURE 7.1. Ian Smith signing the UDI Proclamation on 11 November 1965.
Source: http://www.corbisimages.com/stock-photo/rights-managed/U1494684/
ian-smith-signing-rhodesian-declaration?popup=1

be immediate improvement in the political status of the Africans. Failure
to reach agreement on these issues led the Rhodesian Front government
to issue a unilateral declaration of independence (UDI) from Britain on
November 11, 1965. (Figure 7.1 shows Rhodesian prime minister signing
the Unilateral Declaration of Independence document in 1965.)

Cast in the mode of the American Declaration of Independence, the
UDI proclamation document highlighted the fact that Southern Rhodesia
had been self-governing since 1923, that Rhodesians had always been
loyal to the Crown and 'to their kith and kin in the United Kingdom and
elsewhere through two world wars' only to discover that 'all that they
have cherished' was about 'to be shattered on the rocks of expediency'.
It further declared that 'the people of Rhodesia fully support the requests
of their Government for sovereign independence' and concluded by proclaiming its independent constitution in the name of, ironically, the 'dignity and freedom of all men'. All twelve members of the Cabinet signed
the Proclamation.

International Economic Sanctions

The decision to declare unilateral independence plunged the country into a crisis that was to see African nationalists under ZAPU and ZANU pitted in a bitter armed conflict against Rhodesian government forces until the end of 1979. The British government reacted to UDI immediately by throwing Rhodesia out of the Sterling Area, freezing Rhodesian assets in the United Kingdom, banning trade in arms and any further British investment in Rhodesia, suspending the country from the Commonwealth Preference Area, banning any purchases of tobacco from Rhodesia and decreeing that Rhodesian passports would, henceforth, not be recognised in Britain. This was soon followed by UN Security Council Resolution 217 recommending that all states 'break off all economic relations' with Rhodesia.

In December 1966, the Security Council imposed selective mandatory sanctions against Rhodesia, including a prohibition on exports to Rhodesia of petroleum, armaments, vehicles and aircraft and a ban on imports of Rhodesian agricultural products and minerals. Finally, in May 1968, the Security Council passed Resolution 253 imposing a ban on all exports to and imports from Rhodesia, prohibiting the transfer of funds to Rhodesia for investment and severing all air links with the country.

For British Prime Minister Harold Wilson, these measures would be more than sufficient to end the Rhodesian crisis quickly and would thus obviate the need to send British troops into the country, as was being demanded by many countries of the Afro-Asian block in the United Nations. A landlocked country with a small and heavily dependent economy such as Rhodesia, it was argued, could not survive international isolation for long, particularly in the light of the oil embargo that the international community had imposed. Without oil and other essential imports and deprived of foreign currency earnings because of the ban on Rhodesian exports, how could such a small country like Rhodesia survive?

Yet survive it did. Sanctions were not very effective in the first few years, partly because the Rhodesian government had started preparing to weather sanctions almost a year before UDI, having been forewarned that economic sanctions were likely to be imposed as a reprisal, and also partly because of the decision by South Africa and Portugal not to enforce sanctions against Rhodesia. Also crucial was the hypocrisy of various nations which espoused the sanctions cause by day but nicodemously broke them by night, more so since there was no mechanism to enforce sanctions or to penalise countries that ignored them. It was left to each member nation of the Security Council to police its own trade with Rhodesia. Not surprisingly, many countries continued to trade with Rhodesia, their public statements supporting the sanctions notwithstanding.[4] Among these were France, Belgium, Italy, Greece, various North and West African countries, Brazil, Mauritius, West Germany, and Taiwan. Even the Soviet Union, which claimed to be a staunch supporter of the liberation struggle in Rhodesia, 'continued to import Rhodesian chrome through Mozambique', while the Japanese 'took advantage of the vacuum created by the withdrawal of British products to flood the Rhodesian market with cars, motorbikes and electronic gadgets of all kinds'.[5] According to John Handford, German, Japanese, French and Dutch exports to Rhodesia actually increased by 62 per cent, 62 per cent, 22 per cent and 24 per cent, respectively, while Swiss imports from Rhodesia increased by 107 per cent in the two years following UDI.[6] Indeed, as late as October 1968, reports documented the continued export of Rhodesian pig iron to Argentina and Rhodesian beef and maize to Greece and Europe, respectively.

The United States equally disregarded international sanctions against Rhodesia when, in January 1972, the U.S. Senate passed the Byrd Amendment, allowing the United States to import chrome from Rhodesia. The excuse was that the United States had no option, as the only other alternative source of chrome was its Cold War rival, the Soviet Union. Apart from this reason, as Gerald Horne shows, there were other factors accounting for some Americans' support for the Rhodesian cause. Among these was the perception of Rhodesia as a valuable Cold War ally in the fight against communism, in addition to the fact that some Americans held similar racist attitudes to non-whites as those upheld by Rhodesian whites and, therefore, sought to preserve in Rhodesia the segregationist regime that desegregation laws had made illegal at home. In

---

4 *Time Magazine*, 23 December 1966.

5 Ken Flower, *Serving Secretly: Rhodesia to Zimbabwe 1964–1981* (London: John Murray, 1987), chapter 4. This section on international sanctions was previously published in the following two articles: A. S. Mlambo, '"We Have Blood Relations over the Border": South Africa and Rhodesian Sanctions, 1965–1975', *African Historical Review*, 40, 1 (2008), 1–29 and A. S. Mlambo, 'Prelude to the 1979 Lancaster House Constitutional Conference on Rhodesia: The Role of International Economic Sanctions Reconsidered', *Historia*, 50, 1 (2005), 147–72.

6 John Handford, *A Portrait of an Economy under Sanctions, 1965–1975* (Salisbury: Mercury Press, 1976), 21.

addition, some had family ties in Rhodesia, while others were outright mercenaries.[7]

Sanctions evasion was so widespread that the UN Security Council Sanctions Committee, established in May 1968 to monitor the implementation of sanctions, was receiving an average of fifty new cases in each year of its eleven-year existence.[8] In 1969, the UN Sanctions Committee learnt that there were $100 million worth of Rhodesian exports in 1968 that were unaccounted for, suggesting that these exports were smuggled out despite sanctions.[9] Indeed, as late as 1973, West Germany was reportedly investigating forty national companies for violating international sanctions. One of the clearest indications of the porous nature of the international boycott was the fact that, eight years after Britain first imposed sanctions on Rhodesia, the country was able to purchase three Boeing 707 and 720 aircraft.

Even British petroleum companies were involved in sanctions busting.[10] This became evident in April 1966, when, irked by continuous British charges that Portugal was engaged in sanctions busting, the Portuguese Ministry of Foreign Affairs revealed that 'between April 1966 and may 1967, 169 [oil] tankers entered Lourenco Marques Port, 58 (fifty eight) of which were of British nationality and in the service of British companies'.[11] Furthermore, Rhodesia continued to receive petroleum and petroleum products through an intricate international network in which

Shell's Middle East Organisation sold crude oil to the refinery at Durban in South Africa, jointly owned and controlled in London by Shell and B.P, the British government's oil company. The refinery company sold oil and petrol to Shell/B.P. Marketing (South Africa).... In turn, it sold to independent dealers, many of whom drove the oil across the Rhodesian border in tankers. In Rhodesia, the petrol was bought by GENTA, the Rhodesian government purchasing agency. GENTA re-sold it to Shell/B.P. Marketing (Rhodesia) who retailed it.[12]

---

[7] Gerald Horne, *From the Barrel of a Gun: The United States and the War against Zimbabwe* (Chapel Hill: University of North Carolina Press, 2001).

[8] Margaret P. Doxey, *International Sanctions in Contemporary Perspective*, 2nd edition (London: Macmillan Press, 1996), 86–8.

[9] NASA-DFA, 1/156/2, No. 11 – Rhodesia: Economic and Financial Situation, 1/11/67–27/10/69, 'Rhodesia: Sanctions-Wilhelm Report on New Loading Terminal in South Africa'.

[10] Jorge Jardim, *Sanctions Double-Cross*, 87–99; Handford, *A Portrait of an Economy*, 21.

[11] National Archives of South Africa, Department of Foreign Affairs, Pretoria, [Hereafter, NASA-DFA] 1/156/1/18/10, Vol. 1: Petroleum-British Action in Mocambique Channel.

[12] Handford, *Portrait of an Economy*, 23. A 1978 report by the Centre for Social Action of the United Church of Christ to the United Nations Special Committee on the Situation

'Some Observations within Rhodesia' (Personal comments of a recent visitor to Rhodesia)

For those of you who feel that oil sanctions evoked against the rebellious colony will stymie power and transportation thus bringing industry to a standstill, hitch your hopes to another star. First of all, let us look at the facts. White Rhodesia is getting petrol. Make no mistake about that. To begin with, the Republic of South Africa is definitely a source of refined oil products ... I watched the oil being brought in daily to Salisbury via road tankers. And last Friday, trucks rumbled through the streets of the capital amid cheering bystanders carrying their thousands of gallons of petrol that were the gift of people in the Northern Transvaal.... The next thing that needs to be demythologized is the official British policy belief that general sanctions will bring Smith's apartheid regime to its knees.... One man in Salisbury summed it up well when he said, 'the only thing we are short of is breakfast cereal, so we will shortly begin to produce it ourselves'.... It is those staunch advocates of 'democracy', the West Germans, French and Americans who are surreptitiously keeping this racist government economically viable.... The Almighty dollar, mark, franc, or yen commands much more worship than any multi-nation attempt to punish a treasonous police state where four million Africans are subjected to a living death of psychological and oft times physical harassment by 220,000 whites.'[13]

As for the African countries which had pressured Britain to impose punitive measures on Rhodesia and which continued to denounce South Africa for maintaining trade with Rhodesia, it proved difficult for some of them to break economic ties with the white-ruled regimes of Southern Africa. For example, hostage states such as Botswana, Swaziland and Lesotho had no choice but to continue to trade with apartheid South

with regard to the implementation of the declaration of the Granting of Independence to Colonial Countries and Peoples listed more than thirty transnational oil companies and subsidiaries which were involved in a conspiracy to supply Rhodesia with oil through bogus companies registered in South Africa. The list included oil giants like Mobil, Texaco, Caltex, Standard Oil, Shell, British Petroleum and Total. See NASA-DFA, 1/156/1/19, Vol. 26 – Zimbabwe UDI: Events at the UN, Declared Measures by Particular States, 24/11/76 – 31/7/78.

[13] 'Rhodesia News Summary Mar. 24 1966', in Aluka, http://www.aluka.org/action/showText?doi=10.5555%2FAL.SFF.DOCUMENT.nusa19660324&p=1

Africa, on which they were completely economically dependent, while
Malawi, under Kamuzu Banda, defied the rest of the continent to continue to trade with Salisbury and Pretoria openly under the pretext that
this was in its economic interests. In addition, reportedly, Rhodesian
products continued to be sold in various African capitals, while African
countries maintained normal trade with well-known sanction violators
like Portugal and South Africa despite their constant resolutions denouncing UDI and apartheid in Organisation of African Unity summits and in
the UN General Assembly and Commonwealth conferences.[14]

One country that was completely out of step with the rest of the
African continent regarding Rhodesian sanctions and the African people's
struggle for freedom was Gabon under President Omar Bongo. While the
Organisation of African Unity was denouncing UDI and calling for a
global economic boycott of Rhodesia, Bongo was actively violating international sanctions against Rhodesia by aiding the sanctions-busting efforts
of the Smith regime. He did this by collaborating with leading Rhodesian
sanctions buster Jack Malloch in circumventing international sanctions
by allowing Malloch to register his Trans Africa Airline, established in
1964 in order to carry out various sanctions-busting operations on behalf
of Rhodesia, as a Gabonese company. This allowed Malloch's planes to
fly freely to European and other destinations. Also with Bongo's support,
Malloch used his many dummy companies registered in Switzerland and
Lichtenstein and other European countries to smuggle Rhodesian goods
into Europe and Rhodesia. When Air Trans Africa folded, Malloch set up
Affretair, an airline registered in Lichtenstein, which, by all accounts, conducted a very successful smuggling operation, often smuggling Rhodesian
beef, disguised as Gabonese, into European markets, even though Gabon
did not produce export beef at all.[15] This, in addition to the fact that
Rhodesians operated an efficient worldwide sanctions-busting network
that worked closely with Rhodesia's diplomatic missions abroad, allowed
the country to continue to trade internationally.

Moreover, as noted, Rhodesia's immediate neighbours, South Africa
and Mozambique, refused to enforce international sanctions.[16] With

---

[14] Anthony Lake, *The 'Tar Baby' Option: American Policy toward Southern Rhodesia*
(New York: Columbia University Press, 1976), 37–8; 46–53.

[15] J. Makuwire, 'Omar Bongo Rescued Ian Smith', *The Zimbabwe Times*, 11 June 2009.

[16] NASA-DFA, 1/156/1/17, South Africa's Attitude (as set out in Public Statements) to the
Declaration of Independence of Rhodesia and in particular South Africa's Attitude to UN
Action as Reflected in Resolutions of the Security Council.

regard to the former, it was well aware that the success of sanctions against Rhodesia would be only a prelude to their being deployed against itself because of its policies of apartheid. It was, thus, in South Africa's interest to undermine this potentially dangerous international instrument.[17] Moreover, there was sympathy by South Africans for their kith and kin in Rhodesia who were regarded, like South Africans, as fighting the same battle to defend white privilege and power against African nationalist demands. Rhodesian leader Ian Smith was well aware of this fact as revealed in his June 1964 speech when stated:

If we have any better friends than the people who live south of the Limpopo, I don't know who they are. The survival of Southern Rhodesia is vital to the Republic. Once it is proved that there is going to be no handover here [presumably of political power to whites], we will get so much help from them that even Southern Rhodesians will be surprised.[18]

On his part, then-South African leader Verwoerd confirmed in January 1966 that '[w]e have blood relations over the border. However others may feel or act towards their kith and kin when their international interests are at stake, South Africa, on the whole, cannot cold shoulder theirs'.[19] Emphasising the same point, Robert Kirsten, a former South African High Commissioner to the Federation of Rhodesia and Nyasaland, was reported in January 1966 as saying that many South Africans were keen to 'go to the aid of the Rhodesians, who were, after all, fighting for the same principles as we are ... and 60 per cent of whom had blood ties there'. For this reason, he continued, 'trade would continue whether Britain liked it or not and businessmen ... [would] ... go ahead and deal with the Rhodesians. Their deals would not be affected by any form of sanctions'.[20]

For these and other reasons, therefore, in the first ten years of UDI, South Africa did everything in its power to undermine international economic sanctions against Rhodesia. It facilitated Rhodesian oil imports through its northern border at Messina and disguised Rhodesian exports and imports as its own, among other measures.[21] Indeed, a 1974 South African Special Committee set up to recommend policies that the South

---

[17] As is well documented, South Africa's fear became reality in the late 1970s, when international sanctions were imposed on it because of its apartheid policy.
[18] The *Star*, 23 June 1964.
[19] The *Rand Daily Mail*, 1 January 1966.
[20] *Pretoria News*, 1 October 1966.
[21] Mlambo, 'We Have Blood Relations over the Border'.

African government should follow with regard to Rhodesia confirmed that South Africa had participated in schemes to disguise the Rhodesian origins of goods exported overseas through the use of South African certificates of origin issued by South African Chambers of Commerce as a means of disguising the nationality of Rhodesian goods exported to overseas markets'. It confirmed that the

maintenance of Rhodesia's imports from overseas countries has thus far been achieved mainly by means of the establishment of various 'fronts' in South Africa ... which placed orders on behalf of Rhodesian firms or the Rhodesian Government.... The goods thus ordered were then shipped to Mozambique and consigned to one of the Rhodesian 'fronts' in South Africa or elsewhere. On arrival at Lourenco Marques [a Mozambican port city], the names and addresses of the consignee were obliterated from the packages. The packages were then re-marked and railed direct to Rhodesia.[22]

By 1975, however, South Africa's policy towards Rhodesia begun to change as geopolitical circumstances in the region also changed and South Africa became increasingly more concerned about its own national security interests rather than propping up its northern neighbour. Changes were marked mostly by the collapse of Portuguese rule in Mozambique and Angola and the widening of the frontier of black rule and it became necessary for South Africa to reach out to black Africa in what became known as its outward policy or détente, in addition to increasing international pressure on South Africa to help to find a solution to the Rhodesian impasse, that national interests dictated a modification of policy. This resulted in South Africa putting economic pressure on Rhodesia to persuade the Smith regime to negotiate with its African Nationalist opponents.

Despite the earlier observation that sanctions were generally not effective in the first ten years following their imposition, they did hit the Rhodesian economy hard, at least in the first two years. For example, in 1966, Rhodesian exports fell by 39 per cent, while in 1968 total Rhodesian exports were worth only slightly more than half their 1965 value.[23] Also hard-hit was the automotive industry which suffered directly from the introduction of petrol rationing in the period before Rhodesia

---

[22] NASA-MFA, 1/156/1/2, Vol. 6, Rhodesia: UDI – Special Committee on Short Term Problems: Meetings and Recommendations, 'Problems Connected with the Maintenance of Rhodesia's Exports to Overseas Countries – Certificates of Origin'.
[23] J. Hanlon and R. Ormond, *The Sanctions Handbook* (London: Penguin, 1987), 205; R. B. Sutcliffe, 'Rhodesia Trade since UDI', *The World Today*, 23 (1967), 420; Minter and Schmidt, 'When Sanctions Worked', 221.

found a way to circumvent the oil embargo. The immediate result was the collapse of the country's two car-assembling plants. [24] Similarly, the agricultural economy suffered considerable setbacks, with tobacco exports, which were responsible for 44 per cent of total white settler agricultural output and 30 per cent of the country's total exports in 1965, dropping significantly under sanctions, forcing reduction of production from 110 million kilograms in the 1965–6 agricultural year to only 60 million kilograms in 1969–70. Even then the country could not sell a great deal of its tobacco so that as much as £300 million worth of tobacco was stockpiled in the country by 1969.[25] Thereafter, the country's economy performed well, sanctions notwithstanding.

Eventually, however, a number of factors also contributed to the effectiveness of sanctions. For example, the global economic recession of the 1970s, triggered by the Organization of the Petroleum Exporting Countries' (OPEC) oil price hike of 1973, impacted negatively on the Rhodesian economy, as Rhodesia's overseas markets contracted and it had to contend with high oil import costs, especially given the fact that it had to pay extra costs for middlemen who smuggled oil into the country. Secondly, the enforcement of sanctions improved, while the U.S. government under President Carter repealed the Byrd Amendment which had permitted the United States to import chrome from Rhodesia in violation of international sanctions for strategic reasons. Thirdly, the long-term effects of sanctions were beginning to bite. These included the shortage of capital, technology and machinery, which meant that no new projects could be initiated and that the maintenance of existing plants became more difficult. Fourth, the escalating guerrilla war meant not only that normal economic activities were constantly disrupted but also that resources were increasingly diverted to the war effort, thus starving the productive sector. Finally, South Africa started to apply its own pressure on Rhodesia to resolve its political crisis through negotiations. This was partly because South Africa was now itself a target of international economic sanctions designed to end apartheid. It could no longer afford to support Rhodesia materially and otherwise as in the past. Thus, when the Arab countries imposed an oil embargo on South Africa, it reduced its oil supplies to Rhodesia, in turn, resulting in the reimposition of petrol rationing in 1974 by the Salisbury regime.[26]

---

[24] *Financial Mail*, 14 October 1966.
[25] A. F. Hunt, 'European Agriculture', in G. M. E. Leistner (ed.), *Rhodesia: Economic Structure and Change* (Pretoria: Africa Institute, 1976), 80; *Financial Mail*, 14 October 1966.
[26] Hanlon and Ormond, *Sanctions Handbook*, 206.

In addition, the changes in the regional political dynamics worked to
Rhodesia's disadvantage. Changes included Zambia's decision to close its
border with Rhodesia in 1973 and the independence of Mozambique in
1975, followed by its decision to also close its border soon after. These and
other pressures began to tell on the country's economy. Consequently,

[b]etween 1975 and 1978, the [Rhodesian] economy registered an average annual
decline in GDP of 2.3% in real terms, compared to an annual average growth of
almost 7% between 1971 and 1974. Real per capita GDP (market prices) fell at
an annual average of 6.9% from 1975 to 1978.[27]

Thus, despite numerous weaknesses, sanctions did work in the end, especially in the context of Rhodesia's deteriorating security situation because
of the liberation movements' armed struggle, as will be shown. Factors
accounting for the decline of the Rhodesian economy in the mid-1970s
include the global economic recession of the 1970s, triggered off by the
1973 oil crisis stemming from the sharp oil price increases by the OPEC.
The crisis resulted in Rhodesia's loss of markets in the developed countries that had helped sustain its economy.

Guerrilla Insurgency

The role of sanctions must be seen within the context of Rhodesia's escalating human and financial costs, especially from 1972 onwards, when the
guerrilla campaign, which had begun in the wake of the UDI declaration
as African nationalists took up arms to overthrow white rule, entered a
new and more intense phase. This meant that the Rhodesian government
had to contend not only with heavier military expenditure, but also with
the increasing disruption of economic activity, as it became necessary to
call upon even more men for the military effort. Thus the escalation of
the war, with the consequent direct and indirect costs to the economy in
the form of destroyed assets, reduced incomes, unemployment effects, the
diversion of money to non-productive military outlays and skill realloca-
tion as productive men were called up for military service, compounded
the negative effects of sanctions, forcing the Rhodesian regime to the
negotiation table.

What later became a serious military threat to the Rhodesian regime
had started very modestly in the early 1960s as a generally undistinguished

---

[27] Ministry of Finance, Economic Planning and Development, *Socio-Economic
Review*, 13.

sabotage campaign involving a few cadres trained abroad.[28] At this early stage of the struggle, nationalist leaders were convinced that it would only take a few incidences of sabotage and military action to convince the whites of the folly of their ways and to persuade them to change their minds and grant majority rule to the Zimbabwean people. When the expected results did not materialise, both ZAPU and the ZANU were forced to reconsider their strategies and to prepare for a longer and more sustained war of attrition against the Rhodesian government before victory could be achieved. [29] By this time, ZANU had secured China's military support from where the party obtained most of its arms, while ZAPU received military support from the Soviet Union. Throughout the late 1960s, both parties infiltrated armed groups into the country, which were involved in numerous military clashes with the Rhodesian security forces in various parts of the country. In April 1966, seven guerrillas of ZANU's military wing, the Zimbabwe African National Liberation Army (ZANLA), engaged the Rhodesian army in a long battle outside the town of Chinhoyi, north of Salisbury, marking the beginning of ZANLA's military campaign.

At about the same time, ZAPU's military wing, the Zimbabwe People's Revolutionary Army (ZIPRA), also intensified its military campaign. In 1967, ZIPRA entered an alliance with the South African National Congress (ANC) which was looking for a route for its Umkonto we Sizwe (MK) guerrillas through Rhodesia to South Africa. In June 1967, a combined force of ZIPRA and MK guerrillas crossed from Zambia and clashed with the Rhodesian armed forces in the northwest of the country. More ZIPRA/MK groups entered the country in December 1967 and July 1968, but proved to be no match for the well-equipped and well-trained Rhodesian armed forces that also enjoyed the advantage of air support. Meanwhile, the involvement of the MK gave South Africa the excuse to send in its soldiers to support Rhodesia's counter-insurgency operations.

Meanwhile, in 1969, the Rhodesian government introduced the Republican Constitution which purported to offer equal partnership between black and white – an arrangement which it found preferable to majority rule. It provided for blacks and whites to vote on separate

---

[28] For the history of the early guerrilla campaigns, see K. Maxey, *The Fight for Zimbabwe: The Armed Conflict in Southern Rhodesia since UDI* (London: Rex Collings, 1975); A. Seegers, 'Revolution in Africa: The Case of Zimbabwe 1965–1980', Ph.D. dissertation, Loyola University, Chicago (1984); and J. K. Cilliers, *Counter-Insurgency in Rhodesia* (London: Croom Helm, 1985).

[29] D. Martin and P. Johnson, *The Struggle for Zimbabwe* (Harare: ZPH, 1981), 11.

rolls in general elections for a given number of parliamentary members depending on the income tax paid by each racial group. Initially, parliamentary representation would be fifty whites and sixteen Africans, with the African representation to rise until parity with white representations was reached as Africans contributed more to the national treasury in taxes. Given the low level of African economic advancement, however, parity was not likely to be reached for a very long time, or in Ian Smith's terms, 'not in a thousand years'. This new constitution merely fuelled African anger even further.

Until 1972, however, guerrilla incursions were little more than an irritation to the Rhodesian government. Poor strategy and tactical errors, among other problems, made the guerrillas easy prey to the Rhodesians. According to Evans:

The Zimbabwean guerrillas who infiltrated Rhodesia from 1966 to 1971 were annihilated by the Rhodesian army. They made the elementary errors which, in insurgency, led to death. Instead of dispersing, the guerrillas moved in columns, wore green fatigues and a standardised boot that made tracking easy.[30]

Evans noted that the guerrillas' Che Guevaran approach, which was based on the concept of 'detonating' a revolutionary situation by means of an insurgent vanguard, was not likely to succeed. Not only were the African masses in the country not ready to erupt in an all-consuming revolution against the Rhodesian regime, but also the Rhodesian Security Forces enjoyed the advantages of superior training and tactics, firepower and mobility, as well as the command of the air. In any case, the Rhodesian forces had to contend with nationalist infiltration from only one direction, namely from Zambia, whose border presented severe challenges to incoming guerrillas. Guerrillas had to not only cross the Zambezi River, but also traverse dense jungles of sparsely inhabited areas where they could easily be detected and liquidated. By the 1970s, the nationalist leaders had realised the weaknesses in their approach and revised their strategy accordingly. The new strategy was clearly spelt out by ZANU Chairman Herbert Chitepo when he observed that ZANU had, in the past, emphasised military attack at the expense of political struggle, but

have since tried to correct this tragic error by politicising and mobilising the people before mounting attacks against the enemy. After politicising our people, it became easier for them to cooperate with us and identify with our programme....

[30] M. Evans, 'Fighting against Chimurenga: An Analysis of Counter-Insurgency in Rhodesia, 1972–1979'. Paper presented at the University of Zimbabwe, Zimbabwe, 1981, p. 5.

[In the coming struggle,] ... The strategical aim ... is to attenuate the enemy forces by causing their deployment over the whole country. The subsequent mobilisation of a large number of civilians from industry, business and agriculture would cause serious economic problems. This would have a psychologically devastating effect on the morale of the whites.[31]

ZAPU also adopted a similar strategy. According to one its leaders, James Chikerema,

We do not intend to finish in a matter or two, three, four or five years ... this is a protracted struggle. The type of war we fight depends on changes of tactics and I can tell you that we have changed our tactics.[32]

As a result of this revised strategy, both ZIPRA and ZANLA guerrillas presented a more formidable military challenge to the Rhodesian forces in the 1970s. In ZANLA's case, following a long period of mobilising the peasants in the north-east of the country, it embarked upon the second and more intensive phase of the armed struggle in December 1972. Throughout the decade, both liberation movements infiltrated increasing numbers of guerrillas into the country as the war escalated and Rhodesian security forces were stretched from the western, northern and north-eastern to the south-eastern fronts. The guerrillas also began to use landmines, which made most of Rhodesia's roads unsafe and claimed many lives.

The colonial regime became increasingly repressive in response. It sometimes imprisoned or detained entire villages for supporting the guerrillas and forced communities into security-fenced and patrolled 'protected villages', while it resorted to displaying corpses publicly to drive home to the Africans the consequences of supporting the 'terrorists'. A massive propaganda through radio, the press and pamphlets was mounted to dissuade the African population from supporting the guerrillas. Military sorties were undertaken into the neighbouring countries, resulting in massacres of people in refugee camps such as Nyadzonia in 1976, Chimoio in Mozambique in 1977, and Mkushi and Freedom Camp in Zambia in 1978, which the colonial regime claimed were terrorist training camps. Despite all this, ZANLA and ZIPRA campaigns continued, although lack of unity between and within the two liberation movements sometimes threatened to derail the liberation campaign.

Several attempts were made from time to time to unite the two liberation movements, but unity never materialised for much of the war period.

---

[31] Quoted in Flower, *Rhodesia to Zimbabwe*, 135.
[32] Martin and Johnson, *The Struggle for Zimbabwe*, 13.

For instance, in 1971, both parties announced that they had agreed to unite under the banner of the Front for the Liberation of Zimbabwe (FROLIZI) led by Shelton Siwela, but this led nowhere. In 1972, another attempt was made to unite the military wings of the two parties through the establishment of the Joint Military Command (JMC), led by Herbert Chitepo from ZANU and with Jason Ziyapapa Moyo from ZAPU as the secretary. Differences between the two groups led to the demise of the JMC by 1974. The Frontline States (FLS), then comprising Zambia, Tanzania and Botswana, made yet another attempt to unite the two parties by creating what was known as the 'third force' or the Zimbabwe Independence People's Army (ZIPA). This also came to grief when differences between the two armed forces led to fighting and loss of life in the training camps.[33] These tensions and conflicts demonstrate that there were many ethnic, personality and class differences among and within the liberation movements just as much as the motives for participating in the struggle were also different. Some semblance of unity came at last in October 1976 when the leaders of ZAPU and ZANU agreed to establish the Patriotic Front in order to coordinate their opposition to the recent peace proposals tabled by U.S. Secretary of State Henry Kissinger. The Front was, however, merely an umbrella for the two parties that remained separate and distinct. Clearly, the liberation struggle had its contradictions.

Other ambiguities and contradictions of the liberation struggle were in regard to the role and significance of African traditionalism and spirituality, particularly the place of ancestors and spirit mediums in the struggle for independence, the place and role of Christianity and Christian missions, and traditional leaders, such as chiefs, as well as the role and treatment of women in the struggle, as mothers, collaborators, refugees or combatants. Participants in the armed struggle were not always in agreement over these issues or the correct way to treat women involved in the struggle. Several studies have shown that women were often abused and not accorded the same status as their male counterparts, the liberation rhetoric of fighting for freedom and egalitarianism notwithstanding.[34]

---

[33] For an insider's account of this phase in the history of ZANLA's liberation struggle, see Dzinashe Machingura, *Dzino: Memories of a Freedom Fighter* (Harare: Weaver Press, 2011).

[34] J. Simbanegavi Nhongo, *For Better or Worse? Women and ZANLA in Zimbabwe's Liberation Struggle* (Harare: Weaver Press, 2000); T. Lyons, *Guns and Guerrilla Girls: Women in Zimbabwe's Liberation Struggle* (Trenton, NJ: Africa World Press, 2004); D. Lan, *Guns and Rain: Guerrillas and Spirit Mediums in Zimbabwe* (Harare: Zimbabwe

TABLE 7.1. *Rhodesia: White Migration Trends, 1972–1979*

Year	Immigrants	Emigrants	Net Migration
1972	13,966	5,150	+ 8,816
1973	9,433	7,750	+ 1,683
1974	9,649	9,050	+ 599
1975	12,425	10,500	+ 1,925
1976	7,782	14,854	− 7,072
1977	5,730	16,638	− 10,908
1978	4,360	18,069	− 13,709
1979	3,416	12,973	− 9,557

Sources: Monthly Migration and Tourist Statistics (Central Statistical Office, Salisbury, 1972–1979); Annual Reports of the Commissioner of the British South Africa Police, 1972–1979.

Meanwhile, as the guerrilla war intensified and sanctions began to bite, Rhodesian society and economy felt the strain, and white emigration increased dramatically, as documented in Table 7.1.

Escalating white outmigration put a heavier economic and military burden on the whites that remained in the country, fuelling more emigration. Meanwhile, the Rhodesian government was forced to increase the size of its army and to spend more on defence than it has previously. The independence of Mozambique in 1975 opened Rhodesia's longer, more vulnerable and more easily accessible eastern border to ZANLA guerrilla infiltration.

By 1976, guerrillas had penetrated deep into the southern, western and central areas of the country. By 1979, the security situation had deteriorated so much that more than 90 per cent of the country had been placed under martial law. At that point, it was estimated that ZANLA alone had more than 10,000 guerrillas operating in the country, while thousands of others were ready for deployment. More than 12,000 were also undergoing military training in various countries. More than 15,000 were available for training in Mozambique.[35] According to J. Tungamirai, a total of 66,367 people 'were registered in the categories of refugees,

Publishing House, 1985), J. MacLaughlin, *On the Frontline: Catholic Missions in Zimbabwe's Liberation War* (Harare: Baobab Books, 1996); Fay Chung, *Re-Living the Second Chimurenga: Memories from the Liberation Struggle in Zimbabwe* (Harare: Weaver Press, 2005).

[35] Cilliers, *Counter-Insurgency*, 239; A. R. Wilkinson, 'The Impact of the War', in W. H. Morris Jones and D. Austin (eds.), *From Rhodesia to Zimbabwe* (London: Cass, 1980), 110–23.

recruits [sic] undergoing military training and combatants in the field by 1979'.[36] ZAPU's ZIPRA had about 20,000 trained guerrillas of whom about 3,000 were deployed in the country. The remainder were in camps in Zambia, while an additional 5,000 were undergoing training in Angola and Zambia. To these forces arrayed against the Smith regime should be added the countless thousands of *Mujibas* inside the country.[37]

Financially, the escalating war was taking a heavy toll on the Rhodesian treasury. By 1979, Rhodesia was spending no less than R$1 million per day on defence. To meet the rising war costs, the Rhodesian regime was forced to increase taxes in 1978 and to introduce a National Defence Levy of 12.5 per cent in the same year.[38] Total defence-related spending rose from R$77 million in 1975 to R$197 million in 1978, representing an increase from 25 per cent to 40 per cent of the country's total budget. The rise in defence expenses was combined with a declining growth rate as the gross domestic product (GDP), in real terms, fell by 3 per cent and 7 per cent, respectively, in 1976 and 1977.[39] As more and more guerrillas infiltrated the country, the Rhodesian defence capabilities were stretched to the limit, making it necessary for the country to dig even deeper into its manpower resources to try to meet the onslaught. Consequently, in 1978, the military call-up was extended to cover various categories of white males who were required to spend a specified number of days per year on military duty. All white males between the ages of eighteen and thirty-eight were required to spend up to six months on operational duty, while those between thirty-eight and fifty spent seventy days, and those older than fifty up to forty days a year on military and police reserve duties.[40]

In 1979, the call-up was extended to Africans in a bid to beef up the country's defence. The impact of the extended call-up duty on the national economy was critical as able-bodied and economically productive men were withdrawn from civilian production to serve the war machine. Military call-ups, together with the deteriorating security and economic situation, sparked a growing emigration wave as whites took what was contemptuously known by those who stayed in the country as the 'yellow

---

[36] J. Tungamirai, 'The Qualitative and Quantitative Change in Recruitment by Zimbabwe African National Liberation Army, ZANLA'. Paper presented to the Darwendale ZANU History Project Seminar, Darwendale, 1994, p. 9.
[37] Wilkinson, 'The Impact of the War', 113–14. *Mujibas* were young boys (often herd boys) who acted as the guerrillas' eyes and ears, some of whom were later trained in sabotage techniques and the use of firearms.
[38] Wilkinson, 'The Impact of the War', 113–14.
[39] Wilkinson, 'The Impact of the War', 113–14.
[40] Wilkinson, 'The Impact of the War', 113.

route'. Contemporary statistics reveal that total net negative migration amounted to 13,709 in 1978.[41] The seriousness of the situation becomes evident when one considers that the thousands of emigrants included skilled professionals whose services were vital to the efficient operation of the economy. In his 1979 New Year broadcast to the nation, Prime Minister Ian Smith acknowledged the danger which such high levels of emigration posed to the economy:

The main effect of the emigration of skilled personnel, which accelerated in 1978, will be felt in 1979 and become more severe unless the trend is stopped. This will be the main difference between 1978 and 1979. A growing shortage of skilled personnel will reduce rather than create employment.[42]

Another major casualty of the war was the country's tourist industry, one of its major income earners. From the beginning of the escalation of the guerrilla campaign in 1972 to the end of 1978, the number of tourist visitors to Rhodesia dropped from the high figure of 339,210 to a mere 87,943. It was the result of Rhodesia being increasingly perceived as an unsafe place to visit because of the war.[43] In the meantime, normal colonial administration had virtually ground to a halt in the countryside on account of guerrilla attacks on government installations, institutions and representatives. As evidence of the negative impact of the war on government institutions and infrastructure, the reports of the Secretary for African Education in the late 1970s noted that 'terrorism' was resulting in the closure of some schools and 'hot-seating' of pupils in the urban areas. It addition it was disrupting the examination process, in-service training programmes for teachers and the distribution of educational materials. The war was also reportedly preventing school inspectors from carrying out their duties while, in some areas, schoolchildren had to be transported in armed convoys because of the bad security situation.[44] (Table 7.2 documents the impact of the guerrilla war by 1979.)

In a desperate bid to arrest the deteriorating situation, the Rhodesian government withheld food supplies from certain areas that were considered to be a security risk and bundled thousands of peasants into militarised camps known as Protected Villages (PVs). By late 1977, there was a

---

[41] *Monthly Migration and Tourist Statistics*, Central Statistical Office, Salisbury, 1972–9.

[42] Smith, *The Great Betrayal*, 286.

[43] *Monthly Migration and Tourist Statistics*, Central Statistical Office, Salisbury, 1972–9.

[44] See *Annual Reports* of the Secretary for African Education, 1976–9. 'Hotseating' refers to the use of the same classrooms for two streams of students because of a shortage of classrooms or schools. Thus one group would attend classes in the morning, while another group, from the same class/grade, would attend classes in the afternoon.

TABLE 7.2. *Impact of the Guerrilla War by 1979*

Number of Schools Closed	1,000
Schoolchildren displaced from schools	483,000
Secondary school teachers unemployed due to school closures	2,000
Rural hospitals closed	155 (out of a national total of 450)
Cattle dips closed	6,500 (out of 8,000)
Total number of people killed since the beginning of the war	30,000
People maimed/crippled	10,000
Refugees in Botswana, Zambia and Mozambique	250,000
Total rural-urban migration as a result of the war	500,000

Sources: Compiled from *Annual Reports of the Secretary for African Education, 1977–79*; M. Bratton, *Beyond Community Development: The Political Economy of Rural Administration in Zimbabwe* (London: Catholic Institute for International Relations, 1978), pp. 34–5; A. R. Wilkinson, 'The Impact of the War,' W.H. Morris Jones and D. Austin (eds.), *From Rhodesia to Zimbabwe* (London: Cass, 1980), pp. 119–20; J. K. Cilliers, *Counter-Insurgency in Rhodesia* (London: Croom Helm, 1985), p. 241.

total of 203 PVs with a population of 580,832. By 1980, the number of PV inhabitants had risen to 750,000. Meanwhile, collective punishments were meted out to whole villages for abetting 'terrorists', while villagers were sometimes relocated far away from their traditional home areas once they were suspected of being sympathetic to the guerrillas.[45] Increasingly, the Rhodesians launched raids on refugee camps in Mozambique and Zambia. Such measures only made the regime more unpopular among the African masses. By 1979, the military balance had arguably tilted in favour of the guerrillas.

Meanwhile, by 1980, there were thousands of Zimbabweans who had fled the war and were living in exile in the neighbouring countries. It is estimated that up to 20 per cent of the country's population (1.4 million people) had been displaced by the war and were living in refugee camps in Botswana, Mozambique and Zambia, among other countries in Africa and abroad. An estimated 400,000 peasants had fled the countryside into the cities and were crowded in makeshift shanty settlements in the country's major urban areas.

---

[45] *Africa Research Bulletin* (1–30 April 1974), 3212, reports, for instance, that 200 members of Madziwa Tribal Land were relocated all the way across the country to the Beit Bridge area 'as punishment for assisting terrorists' in 1974.

To undermine the armed opposition, in 1978, the Rhodesian government initiated negotiations with two internally based political parties, the United African National Council (UANC) led by Bishop Abel Muzorewa and Zimbabwe African National Union (Ndonga), led by Reverend Ndabaningi Sithole and Chiefs Chirau and Ndiweni. It was hoped that an agreement with them might persuade the armed freedom fighters of the two liberation movements, ZAPU, under Joshua Nkomo, and ZANU, now under Robert Mugabe, to lay down their arms and, hopefully, join the internal negotiating process. The government and the internal leaders signed the Internal Settlement Agreement in 1978 and, on the basis of the general elections held thereafter, in April 1979, Muzorewa became the first black prime minister of the country, now renamed Zimbabwe-Rhodesia. Under the agreement, whites kept control the country's judiciary, civil service, police and armed forces and were allocated a quarter of the seats in parliament, which were reserved for them. This was insufficient to convince the other nationalist leaders that there had been any substantive change in the status quo, the new black leadership notwithstanding. Consequently, the liberation movements refused to recognise the Internal Settlement government and continued the armed struggle. At the same time, despite a concerted diplomatic campaign to gain international recognition, the Internal Settlement government of Zimbabwe-Rhodesia failed to secure international recognition.

With the economy fast deteriorating and the guerrilla campaign escalating, it became imperative for the Smith government to negotiate with the leaders of the liberation movements. Moreover, international sanctions were, by this time, affecting the country's ability to continue to procure the necessary arms with which to wage war against the guerrillas, especially after South Africa changed its position on continuing to support Rhodesia. While by the mid-1970s Rhodesia had developed the capacity to manufacture aircraft bombs and small arms, it still relied heavily on imported weapons and ammunition, now increasingly difficult to procure because of shortages of foreign currency.[46]

Aware that both ZANU and ZAPU had large reserves of people and materials outside the country and were preparing for a final onslaught in the rainy season of 1979 to 1980, when conditions would be ideal for guerrilla activity, Rhodesian political leaders had to acknowledge that the future was bleak. Consequently, on the recommendation of both

---

[46] N. Downie, 'Rhodesia: A Study in Military Incompetence', at http://www.rhodesiaforces. org (accessed 2 February 2012).

his intelligence advisers and Combined Operations (COMOPS) command, Smith went along with the British proposals to end the Rhodesian conflict.[47] He was later to write that, given the forces arrayed against Rhodesia, it had become 'difficult to avoid the conclusion that we were in a no-win situation'. He had realised that there was no alternative but to negotiate with the nationalist leaders. In his words, 'while I had previously resisted any thought of an all-party conference ... I was reconciling myself to a change of thought and my colleagues in the Rhodesian Front agreed'.

He cited two reasons for this change of heart, namely the fact that guerrillas 'were gaining support among the indigenous population', as well as the Western powers' unwillingness to antagonise African countries by recognising Rhodesia's independence.[48] It is clear, therefore, that escalating guerrilla pressure reinforced the growing negative impact of international sanctions to persuade the Rhodesian regime of the need to negotiate a peaceful end to the conflict. Added to these pressures was the changing geopolitical situation, which left the Rhodesian regime in an increasingly precarious position.

Protest Literature and Music

A noticeable development during the Zimbabwean anti-colonial struggle was growing anti-colonial protest through literature and music. Protest literature encompassed novels in vernacular languages and in English. The best-known anti-colonial Shona novel was *Feso* (1956) by Solomon Mutsvairo. A response to colonial political oppression, Mutsvairo's book was an allegorical romance which looked nostalgically at the halcyon days of the precolonial era when, ostensibly, all was harmonious and peaceful, and which denounced colonial rule and 'its attendant problems of oppression and social injustice'. It represented the rise of African nationalism and its denunciation of the colonial dispensation, casting the precolonial communalistic period of 'innocence, harmony, plenty, security, peace and tranquility' as contrasted to 'the colonial period of starvation, apathy, insecurity, social and psychological alienation'. Among the aspects of colonial rule that *Feso* denounced was land expropriation by the white settlers. In a poem in the book entitled '*Nehanda Nyakasikana*', Mutsvairo explicitly protests the dispossession of the 'land of the *vanyai*

---

[47] This interpretation is based on Ellert, *The Rhodesian Front*, 53.
[48] Smith, *The Great Betrayal*, 313.

[Shona people] by the despotic Pfumojena [a character representing the whites]'. In raising the question '*Kunozove riiniko isu vanyai tichitam-budzika?* (How long shall we, the Vanyai continue to suffer?)', the poem is, thus, a call to arms in the struggle against colonial oppression.[49]

Denunciation of and protest against colonial rule are also features in Zimbabwean African literature in English published at the time. Examples include Stanlake Samkange's *On Trial for My Country* (1965) and his *Year of the Uprising* (1978), both of which are preoccupied with the injustices of colonial rule and the manner in which Africans were dispossessed of their heritage, especially their land. These are also the concerns of Solomon Mutsvairo's *Mapondera: Soldier of Zimbabwe* (1978), while culture conflict and protest are the themes of Stanlake Samkange's *The Mourned One* (1975), Wilson Katiyo's *A Son of the Soil* (1976) and Charles Mungoshi's *Waiting for the Rain* (1975) and *Coming of the Dry Season* (1972).[50] In these and other novels,

African characters are glorified as heroes with pride and dignity fighting against the arrogance of white oppressors who are portrayed as outrageously racist, murderous and hungry land grabbers. These writings also glorify the African past as a way of rediscovering their cultural identity ravaged by colonisation. This was a kind of cultural nationalism which was a reaction to the distortions brought by cultural imperialism.[51]

Thus, as well as being a call to arms in the fight against colonialism, these novels also sought to 'refute the White man's fraudulent claims that the Black man had no history and no culture to speak of (and) to re-establish a meaningful relationship with the African past (which had been deliberately distorted by the settlers) in order to enable the Black man to shape his future'.[52] Meanwhile, Charles Dambudzo Marechera's *House of Hunger* (1978) expresses a very pessimistic sense of disillusionment with the human condition generally and catalogues 'the horrors which beset the African community well after the onset of colonialism'.[53]

Paralleling developments in literature was the rise of a new genre of popular African protest music known as Chimurenga music which was spearheaded by a handful of musicians, the most prominent of whom

---

49 Mickson Mazuruse, 'The Theme of Protest in the Post Independence Shona Novel', M.A. thesis, University of South Africa (2010), 25–7.
50 R. Zhuwarara, 'Zimbabwean Fiction in English', *Zambezia*, 14, 2 (1987), 132.
51 Mazuruse, 'Protest in the Post Independence Shona Novel', 27.
52 Zhuwarara, 'Zimbabwean Fiction in English', 132–3.
53 Zhuwarara, 'Zimbabwean Fiction in English', 133.

was Thomas Mapfumo. Traditional music had always played a central role in the lives of Zimbabwean Africans, regardless of their ethnic origins and/or location in the country, although the instruments and the rhythms might differ from one part of the country to the other. However, traditional African music came under heavy and sustained attack from colonial forces and influences, including the missionaries, who regarded African music as pagan and sought to change it, or at least to harness it for Christian purposes.[54] Scholars have commented on the concerted efforts by the colonial system to eradicate African cultural practices and traditions, including traditional music, in order to replace them with Western cultural norms and practices.[55] Thus, for instance, 'The *mbira* and the drum which had carried the tradition of the Shona people's music for a long time were often dismissed as unholy'.[56] The constant subversion of African traditional music and its increasing commodification by record companies or white music promoters led to the development of an entertaining but shallow type of music that went by the generic term of 'township music', reflecting the new 'township culture' of a rapidly urbanising or urbanised African population in the country's emerging urban centres.[57] Such music was largely influenced by external trends, such as jazz in the 1930s and 1940s, South African and Congolese music and Western pop music in the 1960s. During these years, the most popular local musicians were those who best imitated Western bands, such as the Rolling Stones and the Beatles, so that local bands sang mostly copyright versions of music chart toppers in the North. Among such artists were the future stars of Chimurenga music, namely Thomas Mapfumo and Oliver Mutukudzi (see the latter in Figure 7.2).

With the escalation of the armed liberation struggle in the 1970s, however, there was a noticeable change in both the style and the messages of the increasingly popular local music as some of the already

---

[54] M. B. Zimunya, 'Music in Zimbabwean History; Music as Historical Communication', in M. B. Zimunya (ed.), *Media, Culture and Development* (Oslo: Department of Media & Communication, 1993), 129–35.

[55] See, for instance, C. Dube, 'The Changing Context of African Music Performance in Zimbabwe', *Zambezia*, 23, 2 (1996), 99–120; A. D. Kwaramba, *Popular Music and Society: The Language of Chimurenga Music: The Case of Thomas Mapfumo in Zimbabwe* (Oslo: University of Oslo, 1997), 3–4; M. B. Zimunya, 'Music in Zimbabwean History', 129–35.

[56] Kwaramba, *Popular Music*, 3.

[57] Joyce Jenje Makwenda, *Zimbabwe Township Music* (Harare: Storytime Promotions, 2005), 16–18.

FIGURE 7.2. Oliver Mutukudzi, a prominent Chimurenga music singer.
Source:http://www.corbisimages.com/stock-photo/rights-managed/42–36081026/
oliver-tuku-mtukudzi-graces-the-hoza-festival?popup=1

established artists dumped copyright Western tunes for traditional songs that were now imbued with anti-colonial lyrics. As noted earlier, the term 'Chimurenga' was first used to describe the 1986–7 anti-colonial uprisings and was adopted again in the anti-colonial armed struggle of the 1960s and beyond. It is fitting therefore that the anti-colonial type of music of the 1970s, with its overt support for the guerrilla armed struggle, should also be known by the same name. According to M. T. Vambe,

The word *chimurenga* refers to war or the struggle against any form of tyranny, and songs that capture the sentiment of war and the longing for freedom became *chimurenga* music … *Chimurenga* (Music) protested the colonial exploitation of Africans and also criticized the oppression of women in African society.[58]

Indeed, ZANLA liberation fighters in the camps in Tanzania and Mozambique sang Chimurenga songs to boost their morale in the ongoing anti-colonial struggle, as evident in the rise to prominence of one Dickson Chingaira, otherwise known as Comrade Chinx, who became

---

[58] M. T. Vambe, 'Versions and Sub-Versions: Trends in Chimurenga Musical Discourses of Post-Independence Zimbabwe', *African Study Monographs*, 25, 4 (2004), 167–93.

the official choirmaster of the ZANU-PF liberation struggle. During the liberation war,

Chinx composed political songs urging the African masses to reclaim their country that had been colonized by the British. Songs such as 'Maruza Imi (You Have Lost)' (1975) recount the history of Zimbabwe, beginning with the colonization of the country in 1890, and the countless acts of white arrogance that culminated in Africans taking up arms.[59]

Chimurenga songs were also sung at the all-night gatherings called Pungwes (all-nighters) which were conducted by ZANLA guerrillas in order to mobilize the rural people in support of the liberation war.[60] Chimurenga or Liberation war songs 'raised consciousness in the masses about the need to fight the war, clarified the goals of the struggle, and encouraged Africans to fight' and, arguably, had the 'capacity to shape, direct, and transform the political consciousness of Africans towards the goal of political independence'.[61] Meanwhile, in the popular music industry, the music of Mapfumo, Mutukudzi and others, now fusing traditional musical instruments, such as the Mbira, with Western guitars and other instruments and often couched in subtle language to avoid trouble with the colonial police, promoted the struggle and denounced colonialism. As will be shown, Chimurenga music did not die with the attainment of independence but also featured strongly in the postcolonial period when they were now deployed as a critique of the postcolonial dispensation.

Complexity and Diversity in Inter- and Intra-Racial Attitudes to the African Struggle

While Zimbabwe's colonial history is often discussed in terms of black and white, it is important to recognise that neither the black nor white population groups were homogenous. As shown in the section on white immigration, there were differences among the country's white population with the dominant English-speaking group regarding themselves as the elite while other white groups such as Poles, Greeks, Afrikaners and Jews were regarded as of a lesser breed.[62] In addition, whites who had

---

[59] Vambe, 'Versions and Sub-Versions'.

[60] A. J. C. Pongweni, *Songs That Won the Liberation War* (Harare: The College Press, 1982).

[61] Vambe, 'Versions and Sub-Versions'.

[62] A. S. Mlambo, "Some Are More White Than Others": Racial Chauvinism as a Factor in Rhodesian Immigration Policy, 1890 To 1963', *Zambezia*, 2 (2001), 139–60.

been in the country longer tended to look down upon the more recent arrivals. Indeed, at the very height of Rhodesian racial supremacy during the UDI years, many whites supported the principle of white superiority, but a significant number sympathized with African aspirations for self-rule. Still others were not entirely opposed to African majority rule, but only in the long run.[63]

Similarly, it should be noted that among the colonial regimes' defenders were numerous African policemen and women, soldiers, informers and the notorious counter-insurgency unit known as the Selous Scouts. As Mtisi and colleagues point out, the Africans who fought on the Rhodesian side, unlike their white counterparts, were not conscripted but volunteers and served dutifully under white officers in such units as the Rhodesian African Rifles. T. Stapleton highlights the fact that, while colonial society in Southern Rhodesia 'was dominated by a white settler minority, from World War II onward, the vast majority of police were black', and that 'by the mid-1970s, at the height of Zimbabwe's War of Independence, there were approximately 2,000 white and 6,000 black full-time police'.[64] Moreover, during the UDI years,

[b]esides their usual law enforcement activities, African policemen became involved in paramilitary operations as members of the rapidly expanding support Unit and Police Anti-Terrorist Unit (PATU). Involved in counter-insurgency operations throughout the conflict, the RAR [Rhodesia African Rifles] expanded from one to three battalions in the 1970s. The RAR also provided the nucleus of personnel for the formation of new units such as the Guard Force, which secured 'protected villages' ... and the controversial Selous Scouts, which infiltrated and eliminated insurgent groups.[65]

Motives for Africans to serve in the police, the military and related security organisations were complex, ranging from the desire for material gain in the form of employment, association of policing with masculinity, desire to combat crime or to repel the insurgents based on the persuasive power of the regime's propaganda, to reasons of prestige. With regard to the latter, the following passage by veteran journalist Lawrence Vambe is revealing:

---

[63] Godwin and Hancock, *Rhodesians Never Die*, 46, cited in J. Mtisi et al., 'Social and Economic Developments during the UDI Period', in Raftopoulos and Mlambo (eds.), *Becoming Zimbabwe*, 20–1.

[64] T. Stapleton, *African Police and Soldiers in Colonial Zimbabwe, 1923–80* (New York: Rochester Press, 2011), 5.

[65] Stapleton, *African Police and Soldiers*, 10.

The Rhodesian authorities did not lack black recruits for their police force. The lure of the uniform, the handcuffs, the sjambok and personal power which went with this position made the police force the only form of employment that black men did not shy away from. It gave its members a superior status and a share of the spoils of power which they would not otherwise have had.[66]

Equally, while it has become customary to regard all white farmers as implacable enemies of the African liberation fighters and staunch defenders of the colonial regime, the situation was more complex than this. Mtisi and colleagues, for instance, argue that some white farmers entered into protection 'arrangements' with guerrillas during the liberation war years in which their safety was guaranteed in return for food, clothing and medicines. Others, such as former Prime Minister Garfield Todd, supported the liberation fighters out of conviction.[67] Apart from the aforementioned examples, there were many other whites who opposed the colonial regime and its policies towards Africans, some of them at great personal cost of imprisonment and/or deportation. A few examples are examined in the following sections.

Guy Clutton-Brock

A major critic of the colonial dispensation was Guy Clutton-Brock, who was born in England in 1906 and subsequently went to Southern Rhodesia in 1949 as an agricultural instructor and missionary and established a thriving non-racial agricultural cooperative at St. Faiths Mission in Rusape, a small town in the eastern part of the country. He became one of the advisers of the founders of the Southern Rhodesian African National Congress and helped to craft its 1957 constitution calling for a true partnership of all the country's inhabitants and equal opportunities for all. When the SRANC was banned in 1959, Clutton-Brock was detained without trial for a month. Later, with the help of his wife Molly and other white liberals, he established another non-racial cooperative farm, Cold Comfort Farm, just outside Salisbury. This was greatly resented by the very race-conscious Rhodesian ruling elite, as shown in the fact that the government subsequently declared it an unlawful organisation. The Rhodesian government stripped Clutton-Brock of his citizenship and deported him in 1971 because of his opposition to Rhodesian racist policies. He was able to return to Zimbabwe

---

[66] Cited in Stapleton, *African Police and Soldiers*, 17.
[67] Mtisi et al., 'Social and Economic Developments', 129–30.

when it became independent in 1980. He was given a hero's burial in Zimbabwe by the ruling ZANU-PF government when he died.

Garfield and Judith Todd

An integral part of the Zimbabwean political struggle for justice and non-racialism were the father-and-daughter team of Garfield and Judith Todd. Born in New Zealand in 1908, Todd emigrated to Southern Rhodesia in 1934 as a missionary and ran the Dadaya New Zealand Churches of Christ Mission School in the Zimbabwean Midlands where he worked with future nationalist leaders Robert Mugabe and Ndabaningi Sithole who were then young teachers. He later entered politics, rising to become the country's prime minister in 1953. Todd introduced modest reforms in African education, including increasing the number of primary schools and providing grants to schools to enable them to introduce secondary school courses, as well as making preparations to introduce universal primary school education for African children. Not surprisingly, this policy alienated most of the Rhodesian whites and, as a result, he was forced to step down when his cabinet colleagues revolted against his leadership in 1958. While generally regarded as a liberal whose sympathies were with the African majority in the colonial period, Todd has been criticised for some of his actions, both as head of school at Dadaya Mission and as prime minister, which were rather authoritarian, such as his widespread use of corporal punishment at his school, the sacking of teachers, including future nationalist leader Ndabaningi Sithole, for protesting such practices and his rather brutal suppression of the 1954 African workers' strike at Wankie Colliery.

After UDI, he remained one of the Smith government's staunchest critics and was at first placed under house arrest for a year in 1965, and then imprisoned, together with his daughter, Judith, in 1972. Thereafter, he was confined to his Hokonui Ranch at Dadaya where he continued to be treated as a pariah by his white compatriots for his sympathies for the African liberation struggle. At independence, he served in the Zimbabwean Senate until his retirement in 1985. He fell out with the Mugabe government when he became increasingly critical of its human rights violations and abuse of political opponents. For this he was stripped of his Zimbabwean citizenship in 2002, the year he died at the age of ninety-four.

An instantly recognizable white campaigner for African rights and freedom was Judith Todd. Born in 1943, Judith became a prominent political activist against the racist policies of the Smith government from the early 1960s, 'working first as a student activist and later as a writer, organiser, public speaker and journalist in the cause of Zimbabwe's liberation'.[68] She joined the NDP at its formation and, after it was banned, became a member of the successor nationalist party, ZAPU, which, as noted, was also banned. She was actively involved in the campaign to reject the Pearce Proposals of 1971–2. Her two books[69] which were critical of the Rhodesian regime were banned in the country but widely read abroad. Judith was arrested and fined in October 1964 for leading a demonstration by students of the University College of Rhodesia outside parliament against the recent banning of the *Daily News* newspaper that gave voice to African political views. Arrested in 1972 and declared a prohibited immigrant, she moved to London where she continued her campaign against the UDI regime. In 1978, she helped to establish the Zimbabwe Project Trust, an organisation committed to helping Zimbabwean refugees. She was only able to return to Zimbabwe in 1980 when the country obtained independence. The Trust was relocated to Zimbabwe, with Judith remaining active in its programmes until 1987. Ever the champion for the downtrodden, Judith eventually ran afoul of the independence government of Robert Mugabe and was stripped of her Zimbabwean citizenship in 2003.[70]

Fr. Michael Traber

Another prominent white supporter of the African struggle was Roman Catholic Priest and journalist, Fr. Michael Traber, who was the executive director of Mambo Press, a Catholic Church–owned enterprise that published *Moto Magazine* which was very popular with African readers. He was deported in 1970 for publishing a cartoon in the magazine showing a pair of white hands squeezing Africans to death to lampoon the Smith regime's constant claim that the whites were safeguarding civilisation by keeping government in responsible white hands. He received a hero's send-off at Salisbury Airport from large crowds of black and white well-wishers on the day that he left the country.

---

[68] Richard Saunders, 'Judith Todd – Zimbabwean Nationalist and Writer, Born 1943', at http://www.davidkrutpublishing.com/8478/judith-garfield-todd-biography (accessed 10 February 2012).
[69] Judith Todd, *An Act of Treason: Rhodesia 1965* (London: Longman, 1965); Judith Todd, *The Right to Say No* (London: Sidgwick & Jackson, 1972).
[70] For her life story, see her autobiography, Judith Todd, *Through the Darkness: A Life in Zimbabwe* (Cape Town: Zebra Press, 2007).

Insert

Catholic Herald

6 March 1970

'Priest Editor expelled from Rhodesia'

From a Special Correspondent

The editor of the Rhodesian Catholic newspaper Moto, Fr. Michael Traber, has been ordered to leave the country by Monday. So also has Mr. Anthony Schmitz, assistant editor. Under Fr. Traber's editorship since 1962, the circulation of Moto has soared from 7,000 to 35,000 copies. It has come to be regarded as the principal voice of Africans in the country.

Swiss-born Fr. Traber was sentenced to six months' imprisonment with hard labour last December for publishing a 'subversive statement,' although the sentence was later suspended conditionally for three years. The 'subversive statement' was a cartoon published in Moto last June. It depicted a pair of white hands crushing black African bodies. The caption was a quotation from the Government's White Paper on the new Constitution, reading: 'The proposed new Constitution will ensure that Government will be retained in responsible hands'.

....

The apartheid-style Constitution, with which Rhodesia declared herself a Republic on Sunday, has been 'publicly condemned' by the country's five Catholic bishops. They have declared it to be 'irreconcilable with God's law,'

Protestant church leaders have described it as 'a potential tool of tyranny.'[71]

Bishop Donal Lamont

Equally undesirable to the Rhodesian regime was Irish-born Catholic Bishop Donal Lamont who became the Bishop of Mutare in eastern Zimbabwe in 1957. As early as 1959, he had expressed strong criticism

---

[71] http://archive.catholicherald.co.uk/article/6th-march-1970/1/priest-editor-expelled-from-rhodesia

of colonialism, publicly stating: 'Any violent seizure of territory which was at the time inhabited and cultivated by a native tribe and subject to the authority of its rulers constitutes unjust aggression'. In 1976, he was tried for allowing nuns in his diocese to give medical attention to liberation war fighters and failing to report their presence to the security forces and was sentenced to ten years in prison, later reduced to three years. Then, in an open letter to the prime minister, Lamont wrote: 'Far from your policies defending Christianity and Western civilisation, as you claim, they mock the law of Christ and make Communism attractive to the African people'. In 1977, he was stripped of his Rhodesian citizenship and deported.[72]

Others

Many other whites condemned the racial policies of the Smith regime and paid a heavy price for it. For example, some expatriate lecturers at the University of Rhodesia got into trouble for supporting an African students demonstration in March 1966. When the police were deployed on campus against the demonstrators, twenty-five lecturers went on strike in protest. After a short lull, following an official enquiry behind the student demonstrations, trouble re-emerged when the University principal, Dr. Adams, refused to allow an African student who had returned to campus without government permission and in breach of the conditions of his detention for political reasons which confined him to a remote part of the country in Gonakudzingwa in the south-eastern corner of the country. Members of staff from the Faculties of Arts and Social Studies resigned in protest. On 16 July of the same year, African students heckled the guest of honour, principal of the University of Cape Town, Dr. J. Duminy, at the graduation ceremony denouncing South Africa' apartheid system. As a result, on 28 July, the police arrested nine Arts and Social Studies lecturers, comprising five British, one Canadian, an Italian, a Norwegian and a Rhodesian. Nine students (five Africans, two whites and one Asian) were placed in restriction. The discovery of weapons in the possession of one of the lecturers a few days later led to his arrest and the deportation of eight non-Rhodesian lecturers who were accused of subversive activities.

---

[72] Paul Lewis, 'Bishop Donal Lamont, 92, Africa Missionary', *New York Times*, 2 September 2003, available at http://www.nytimes.com/2003/09/02/world/bishop-donal-lamont-92-africa-missionary.html

Another case was the deportation of Dr. Terence Ranger by the federal government of Rhodesia and Nyasaland at the request of the Southern Rhodesia administration which was unhappy with his involvement in African party politics. Ranger had been a member of the banned NDP and was then an active member of ZAPU and was also involved in campaigns against the colour bar.[73] Yet another critic of the colonial dispensation was Eileen Haddon, journalist and co-founder of the Interracial Association of Southern Rhodesia and editor of *The Central Examiner* newspaper which was highly critical of UDI in 1965. Eileen and her husband Michael donated their small farm, Cold Comfort, outside Salisbury for the establishment of a multiracial cooperative operated by Guy Clutton-Brock and his African partner Didymus Mutasa. Following harassment by the Rhodesian government, the Haddons left the country in 1969 and only returned to independent Zimbabwe in 1981.

The Organisation of African Unity, UDI and the Armed Struggle[74]

The Organisation of African Unity (OAU) was established by the then-independent African countries in Addis Ababa in 1963 for the purposes of, among others, supporting the decolonisation of the rest of the continent. While the OAU arguably failed to realise many of the goals set for it when it was established, it did play a vital role in the liberation struggle in southern Africa in general and in the Zimbabwean struggle in particular. It is difficult to conceive of the Zimbabwean liberation struggle succeeding at all without the support of the OAU member countries known as the Front Line States (FLS), whose original membership included Zambia, Tanzania and Botswana, but to which was later added Mozambique and Angola when they gained their independence in 1975. Also critical to the success of the Zimbabwean struggle was the OAU's Coordinating Committee for the Liberation of Africa, otherwise known as the Liberation Committee, which was hosted by Tanzania and whose task was to source material

---

[73] http://www.springerlink.com/content/y56141u952077609/ (accessed 20 February 2012); Aluka – News clippings dealing with Terence Rangers deportation, http://www.aluka.org/action/showMetadata?doi=10.5555/AL.SFF.DOCUMENT.ranger00056 (accessed 20 February 2012).

[74] The section on the OAU was initially published as A. S. Mlambo, 'Voci discordanti: l'Organizzazione dell'Unita Africana e la Dichiarazione Unilaterate di Indipendenza, 1965–1979 [Discordant Voices: The Organization of African Unity's Responses to the Unilateral Declaration of Independence, 1965–1979]', *Afriche e Orienti*, Special Issue 2 (2011), 108–22.

and logistical support for the liberation movements and to lobby on their behalf internationally. Indeed, from UDI until the Lancaster House Conference in 1979, OAU member countries and structures worked tirelessly in support of Zimbabwe's two main liberation movements and their respective military wings.

Support for the Zimbabwean liberation struggle was first announced by the moving spirit behind pan-Africanism and the subsequent establishment of the OAU, Ghana's President Kwame Nkrumah during the 1958 All African People Conference that he hosted in Accra and which was also attended by African nationalist leaders, including Robert Mugabe, Reverend Ndabaningi Sithole and Joshua Nkomo. The conference openly declared independent Africa's support for the liberation struggles of colonised peoples of Africa.[75]

Then in 1964, the First OAU Ordinary Session of the Assembly of the Heads of State denounced the impending Southern Rhodesian declaration of independence and pledged 'to take appropriate measures, including the recognition and support of an African nationalist government-in-exile should such an eventuality arise'. The meeting demanded that the United Kingdom 'convene immediately a constitutional conference in which representatives of all political groups in Southern Rhodesia would participate with a view to preparing a new and democratic constitution ensuring majority rule on the basis of one man, one vote'. It also called for the immediate release of African nationalist leaders Joshua Nkomo and Ndabaningi Sithole and other political prisoners and detainees in Southern Rhodesia and urged the African nationalist movements in Southern Rhodesia to intensify their struggle for immediate independence[76]

Similarly, the Second Ordinary Session of the Assembly of Heads of State in Accra, Ghana, deplored the reluctance of the UK government to 'meet with firmness and resolution the threat of a Unilateral Declaration of Independence by a European minority Government'. Should the British government fail to take the necessary steps to quickly resolve the Rhodesian crisis, the meeting resolved to

reconsider all political, economic, diplomatic and financial relations between African countries and the United Kingdom Government; use all possible means,

---

[75] E. K. Dumor, *Ghana, OAU and Southern Africa: An African Response to Apartheid* (Accra: Ghana University Press, 1991), 78.

[76] OAU, AHG/Res. 1(1) – AHG/Res. 24(1). Resolutions adopted by the first Ordinary Session of the Assembly of Heads of State and Government held in Cairo, UAR, from 17 to 21 July 1964 (Addis Ababa: OAU, 1964).

including force to oppose a unilateral declaration of independence; and to give immediate assistance to the people of Zimbabwe with a view to establishing a majority government in the country.[77]

Following Ian Smith's declaration of UDI, the OAU Council of Ministers met in Addis Ababa on 3 December 1965 and unanimously agreed that, if the UDI revolt was not crushed by 15 December, the OAU would declare war on Rhodesia, cut all economic exchanges and communications and break off diplomatic relations with Britain. Ultimately, however, only ten out of the thirty-two countries that voted in support of the resolution, namely Guinea, Tanzania, Ghana, UAR, Mali, Mauritania, Congo-Brazzaville, Sudan, Algeria and Somalia, actually went on to sever diplomatic relations with Britain.[78]

In May 1963, the OAU created the Liberation Committee to be based in Dar-es-Salaam, Tanzania. The Committee provided logistical help, funding, publicity and diplomatic support to all the liberation movements recognized by the OAU.[79] For Zimbabwe, it 'coordinated moral and material support ... encouraged member states to offer bases, training and materials to the [Zimbabwean] guerrillas while it put up a strong diplomatic offensive in favour of independence for black Zimbabweans'.[80] The OAU vigorously supported liberation movements in Zimbabwe and other southern African countries from the late 1960s onwards, but left the door open for peaceful negotiation. Thus, in 1969, it issued the Lusaka Manifesto declaring that Africans preferred to achieve the liberation through peaceful negotiation 'if peaceful progress to emancipation were possible, or if changed circumstances were to make it possible for the future'; however, as long as the white regimes maintained their current policies and attitudes, they would continue to give to the peoples of

---

[77] OAU, AHG/RES. 25(II). Resolutions adopted by the Second Ordinary Session of the Assembly of Heads of State and Government held in Accra, Ghana, from 21 to 26 October 1965 (Addis Ababa: OAU, 1965)

[78] N. McKeon, 'The African States and the OAU', *International Affairs*, 42, 3 (1966), 390–409. The threat to declare war could not be followed because Africa did not have a standing army and also not all independent countries were willing to contribute their men to such an army were it to be established.

[79] M. Sahnoun, 'Nyerere: The Organisation of African Unity and Liberation', *Pambazuka News*, 452 (2009), at http://pamabzuka.org/en/category/features/59501 (accessed 25 February 2012); A. Tekle, 'A Tale of Three Cities: The OAU and the Dialectics of Decolonisation in Africa', *Africa Today*, 35, 3–4 (1988), 54.

[80] T. J. Fowale, 'The OAU's Liberation Committee in Zimbabwe's Struggle for Freedom' (2009), at http://tongkeh-joseph-fowale-suite101.com – www.Suite101.com (accessed 25 February 2012).

the colonised territories 'all the support of which we are capable in their struggle against their oppressors'.[81]

Finally, in 1977, the OAU's Council of Ministers reaffirmed the OAU's support for the Zimbabwean liberation struggle, noting that 'the armed liberation struggle is a legitimate, inevitable and decisive means for the liberation (of) Zimbabwe' and pledging 'increased material, diplomatic and financial assistance to the continuous armed liberation struggle in Zimbabwe'. The ministers also declared that any settlement 'must necessarily lead to the transfer of total power to the people of Zimbabwe'.[82] It is clear, therefore, that the OAU presented a generally united response to UDI and that most African countries supported the Zimbabwean liberation struggle. As ZANU activist and historian Nathan Shamuyarira argued in the 1970s,

The general idea of liberating the African continent from colonial rule has kept the OAU united, no matter how bitterly the Heads of States disagree on the best method and strategy to be employed. The liberation of Southern Africa evokes applause and deep emotions of solidarity among Heads of States at OAU Summit conferences, or bilateral talks between visiting dignitaries. Some OAU meetings in which deep divisions occurred among members over matters of borders or security, however found common ground when they moved to reports of organs concerned with liberation.[83]

Thus, the majority of OAU members supported the liberation struggle and gave moral and logistical support to southern African liberation movements. Many countries housed refugees from southern Africa and provided skills training in anticipation of independence. Representing the OAU at the war front in southern Africa and playing a vital role in the struggle were the FLS of Zambia, Tanzania and Botswana, and after their independence in 1975, Mozambique and Angola. These countries bore the brunt of the liberation struggles in the region, with Zambia, in particular, paying a very heavy price for its continued support of Zimbabwean, South African, Angolan and Namibian liberation movements. Not only did it suffer trade disruptions with and through Rhodesia and repeated military and air attacks on Zimbabwean Liberation Movements' bases in Zambian territory, but it also had to contend with the constant in-fighting among the liberation movements it hosted.

[81] A. Ajala, *Pan-Africanism: Evolution, Progress and Prospects* (London: Andre Deutsch, 1973), 230.
[82] OAU, CM/Res. 551 (XXIX), 1977.
[83] N. Shamuyarira, 'The Lusaka Manifesto Strategy of the OAU States and its Consequences for the Freedom Struggle in Southern Africa', *Utafiti*, 2, 2 (1977), 247–66.

Tanzania also hosted several liberation movements, provided military training facilities and took a leadership role among the FLS. As noted earlier, it also hosted the OAU Liberation Committee since 1963. After independence in 1975, Mozambique joined the FLS and aided the Zimbabwean liberation struggle by hosting ZANU military operational bases and providing logistical support. The opening of the Mozambican military front tipped the balance in favour of liberation forces and stretched the Rhodesian military forces' capacity to the limit. As to be expected, Mozambique also paid a heavy price through Rhodesian reprisals.

Not all FLS were in a position to provide military support, however. For example, a hostage state like Botswana, economically dependent on South Africa and Rhodesia, could not antagonise its neighbours by openly supporting the region's armed struggles or allowing liberation movements to use its territory to launch military attacks. However, this did not mean that Botswana was cowed into silence, for under its first independence president, Seretse Khama, and consistently thereafter, Botswana openly condemned racism and supported the liberation struggles in Zimbabwe and South Africa while remaining a full member of the OAU, the UN, the FLS and Southern African Development Coordinating Conference (SADCC).[84]

Lastly, FLS played a key role in facilitating the Lancaster House negotiations that eventually ended the Zimbabwean war. The crucial Commonwealth Heads of Government meeting that paved the way for the 1979 Lancaster House talks was, after all, held in Lusaka, Zambia. It was also pressure from the FLS presidents that persuaded the somewhat reluctant liberation movements to participate in the Lancaster House negotiations. In doing this, the FLS demonstrated that, while they had frequently declared their support for the armed struggle as the only method to end white rule in Zimbabwe, in reality they subscribed to the Clausewitzian view of war as a continuation of diplomacy by other means.[85] Thus, they supported the armed struggle only in so far as it pressured the Rhodesian government to agree to a negotiated settlement.

As is to be expected, not all African countries supported the liberation struggle approach. Some, such Gabon under Bongo, Ivory Coast under Huphouet Boigny and Malawi under Kamuzu Banda, preferred dialogue

---

[84] Predecessor of the Southern African Development Community (SADC).

[85] C. Bassford, *Clausewitz in English: The Reception of Clausewitz in Britain and America, 1815–1945* (New York: Oxford University Press, 1994).

with the white-ruled southern African regimes and continuously violated sanctions by trading with these countries.

Efforts at Peaceful Negotiations from UDI to Lancaster

Tiger and Fearless Talks

At UDI, most African nationalists believed that Britain would use force to end the illegal Smith regime. Not wanting to set British soldiers against their kith and kin in Rhodesia, Britain opted instead for the oil embargo and sanctions route and peaceful negotiations. Consequently, British government leaders engaged the Rhodesian regime on a number of occasions, the first being on board the HMS *Tiger* in December 1966 and the second on board HMS *Fearless* in October 1968. In the 1966 meeting, the British proposed that the Rhodesian authorities accept a political reform package that included the establishment of a broad-based government under a British governor; that the government include representatives of existing political parties, independent members and Africans, and that this government would remain in control for only four months during which a Royal Commission would test the acceptability of new constitutional proposals. An election would follow thereafter if the constitution was acceptable to the majority of the Rhodesian people. Ian Smith flatly rejected these proposals. He also rejected the slightly modified proposals tabled at the 1968 meeting.

Pearce Proposals

In 1971, the British made yet another attempt to end the impasse by proposing a package which came to be known as the Pearce Proposals. After secret negotiations with the Smith regime, the British government announced a reform package that contained the following five principles:

1. Unimpeded progress to majority rule.
2. Guarantees against retrogressive amendments to the constitution.
3. Immediate improvements in the political status of the African population.
4. Progress towards ending racial discrimination.
5. Any basis for independence must be acceptable to the people of Rhodesia as a whole.

Under these proposals, Africans would attain a majority in parliament in the very long run. It also included a new constitution and bill of rights. A major condition was that any basis for independence must be acceptable to the people of Rhodesia as a whole. To the pleasant surprise of the British authorities, the Rhodesian government accepted the Pearce Proposals. The British government then sent a Commission under Lord Pearce to conduct a test of acceptability of these proposals.

Led by the African National Congress (ANC) under Bishop Abel Muzorewa, Africans overwhelmingly rejected the Pearce Proposals which had been drawn up without any African participation and which they regarded as designed to maintain the status quo.[86] Moreover, there were no safeguards to prevent the Rhodesian government from changing the agreement at a later stage. More importantly, under the terms of the proposals, African progress towards full political participation was to be extremely slow.

The ANC had been created in December 1971 as a front for the two banned liberation movements, with Muzorewa chosen as a compromise by the movements to lead the campaign against the proposals. It was meant to be a temporary organisation which would disband soon after the rejection of the Pearce Proposals. As will be shown, it lived beyond the Pearce Proposal campaign to become one of the major players in African nationalist politics until the Lancaster House constitutional conference of 1979.

The next initiative to find a peaceful resolution to the Rhodesian crisis came during the détente period from December 1974 to January 1976, when attempts were made to ease the hostility between the FLS and the white-ruled Southern African countries. The main architects of détente were the South African Prime Minister John Vorster and President Kenneth Kaunda of Zambia. Each of them had an interest in lessening the hostilities between their respective constituencies. For South Africa, a peaceful Rhodesia would promote South Africa's own long-term security, especially given the collapse of Portuguese rule in Mozambique, while an unstable white government in Rhodesia was less desirable than a stable black one, especially a moderate one that South Africa could easily manipulate. For its part, Zambia also had an interest in détente because UDI had hit the Zambian economy hard. Zambia depended on Rhodesian routes for the transportation of more than 95 per cent of its

---

[86] Jonny Ryan, 'Principled Failure: British Policy Toward Rhodesia, 1971–1972', *The History Review* (2004), at http://johnnyryan.wordpress.com/2004/02/20/ (accessed 3 March 2012).

imports and copper exports, while all its oil came through Rhodesia. For these reasons, President Kaunda was desirous of finding a quick solution to the Rhodesian crisis.

South Africa put considerable pressure on Ian Smith to negotiate with the African nationalists. For instance, South African Prime Minister B. J. Vorster, withdrew his country's diplomatic support for the UDI government, demanded that Smith release black nationalist leaders in detention, suddenly withdrew South African policemen who had hitherto been fighting side by side with Rhodesian forces against the liberation fighters and limited the supply of fuel and military equipment that Rhodesia desperately needed to support its military activities. Under such circumstances, Ian Smith had no choice but to participate in Vorster's détente scheme. The deal the two leaders cut was that imprisoned and detained Rhodesian nationalist leaders, such as Mugabe, Nkomo and Sithole, would be released to enable them to attend a round-table conference with Smith and his team in a bid to find a peaceful solution to the Rhodesian problem. In return, the liberation movements would suspend their campaigns. The nationalist leaders subsequently met the Rhodesian authorities on a train over the Victoria Falls Bridge (linking Zambia with Rhodesia), but the talks soon collapsed. Meanwhile, ZANU Chairman Herbert Chitepo, who had been strongly opposed to détente, was assassinated by car bomb in Lusaka, Zambia. It is not clear whether he was the victim of internal party conflicts or of Rhodesian assassination squads. Following the collapse of the Victoria Falls talks, the Rhodesian prime minister entered into talks with Joshua Nkomo in an attempt to reach a separate peace agreement with his party so as to undermine the guerrilla war. Negotiations continued until March 1976 but then collapsed, especially in the context of Smith's 20 March 1976 statement: 'I don't believe in majority rule, black majority rule, ever in Rhodesia, not in a thousand years'.

In the same year, the Kissinger Proposals were tabled in yet another attempt to find a diplomatic solution to the country's conflict. Backed by the U.S., British and subsequently South African governments, this plan proposed a step-by-step transition process that would eventually lead to African majority rule. The Kissinger Plan provided for a two-year transition period to majority rule during which an interim government would run the country, while a Council of State, made up of three whites and three blacks under a white chairperson, would draw up a new constitution which would usher in majority rule. Under growing Western pressure and facing escalating guerrilla insurgency and deepening economic challenges stemming from international sanctions, Smith was forced to accept the proposals in September 1976.[87]

When the African nationalists rejected the Kissinger Proposals, Britain convened another round-table conference in Geneva, Switzerland, in October 1976 in the hope that the warring parties would reach a peaceful agreement. The conference broke down when ZAPU and ZANU, now united as the Patriotic Front for the purposes of presenting a common position at the conference, and the Rhodesian government team failed to find common ground. The conference was adjourned after seven weeks in December 1976, never to meet again.

Other efforts to achieve a peaceful settlement in Rhodesia followed, the most notable one being the Rhodesian government's attempt to reach a settlement with nationalists based in the country who the government regarded as moderate compared to the ZAPU and ZANU leaders. Smith hoped that an 'internal settlement', as it came to be known, would lead to international recognition of Rhodesia and the removal of sanctions and would successfully undermine the armed struggle. He thus initiated talks with Bishop Muzorewa, Ndabaningi Sithole – now deposed from the leadership of ZANU through a palace coup and replaced by Robert Mugabe – and one traditional leader, Chief Jeremiah Chirau. The negotiating parties signed an agreement on 3 March 1978. General elections were subsequently held on the basis of the internal settlement agreement and the head of the United African National Council (UANC), Bishop Abel Muzorewa, became prime minister of the now renamed Zimbabwe-Rhodesia in June 1979, while Smith became minister without portfolio in the new government. The internal arrangement did not, however, end the armed conflict because it did not include ZAPU and ZANU which commanded the guerrillas prosecuting the war.

The last diplomatic initiative came in August 1979, at the Commonwealth Heads of State Summit, in Lusaka, Zambia, where the participating states unanimously adopted a document calling upon Britain to convene a constitutional conference for all parties to the Rhodesian dispute in order to find a solution to the country's conflict. While the warring parties in Rhodesia initially publicly resisted the call to negotiate, the realities of the situation were not lost on them. They were aware that the costs of intransigence in the form of lost international goodwill and support would be high and disastrous for any side that

---

[87] Sue Onslow, 'We Must Gain Time: South Africa, Rhodesia and the Kissinger Initiative of 1976', *South African Historical Journal*, 56 (2006), 123–53.

FIGURE 7.3. The 1979 Lancaster House Conference: (left to right) Bishop Abel Muzorewa, Lord Carrington, Ian Smith, Joshua Nkomo and Robert Mugabe. Photo courtesy of Corbis.

was seen to be deliberately obstructive to international efforts to secure peace in the country. Because of the regional and international interest in the Rhodesian question, as well as the international pressures brought to bear on both sides of the Rhodesian political divide, the Lancaster House Conference turned out to be more than just a round-table conference for the Rhodesian belligerents. A multiplicity of interest groups participated either directly or indirectly in the negotiations. While the British played the role of 'honest broker', the FLS, South Africa, the United States, the OAU and other interested groups and countries advised, pressured, influenced and otherwise 'assisted' the negotiations, or followed the conference's proceedings with keen interest. (Figure 7.3 shows Rhodesian nationalist leaders Robert Mugabe and Joshua Nkomo, together with Abel Muzorewa and British officials at Lancaster House in 1979.)

As James Barber justly pointed out, participants at the Lancaster House Conference were more than those seated around the negotiating table:

Indeed, some of the delegates inside Lancaster House might have been excused had they sat with their heads half turned, straining to catch the advice, the admonitions or support of those outside. These 'outsiders' ranged from the London-based officials of states and organisations to fleeting visitors like President Kaunda of Zambia or Mr. Pik Botha of South Africa, and, in the case of the British Ministers, attention had to be given to the noises off [sic] from Washington and from their own party.[88]

The Lancaster House Conference finally broke the Rhodesian impasse on 21 December 1979, paving the way for national multiracial elections that would eventually end colonial rule and usher in the independence government of Robert Mugabe and the now renamed ZANU-Patriotic Front (PF) on 18 April 1980.

Lancaster House Agreement

The Lancaster House Conference which brokered an end to the Rhodesian imbroglio ran from 10 September to 15 December 1979. The Conference chair was the British Secretary of State for Foreign and Commonwealth Affairs, Lord Carrington. Its purpose was 'to discuss and reach agreement on the terms of an Independence Constitution, and that elections should be supervised under British authority to enable Rhodesia to proceed to legal independence and the parties to settle their differences by political means'.[89]

Represented were the following: the British government, the Patriotic Front (ZAPU and ZANU), led by Joshua Nkomo and Robert Mugabe, respectively, and the Zimbabwe-Rhodesia government under Bishop Muzorewa and Ian Smith. As noted, many other directly and indirectly involved parties followed the Lancaster House deliberations with keen interest.

The negotiating parties agreed on the Zimbabwe Independence Constitution, which provided, among other things, for twenty seats in the national parliament to be reserved for whites for a period of ten years, and for a cease fire, to be monitored by a Ceasefire Commission comprising 'commanders of the Rhodesian forces and of the Patriotic Front forces ... under the chairmanship of the [British] Governor's Military Adviser, and other arrangements for the holding of general elections to be supervised

---

[88] J. Barber, 'Zimbabwe's Southern African Setting', in Morris Jones and Dennis Austin (eds.), *From Rhodesia to Zimbabwe*, 28.

[89] Southern Rhodesia, Constitutional Conference held at Lancaster House, London September–December 1979: *Report*, Printed in England for Her Majesty's Stationery Office by Burrup, Mathieson & Co., Ltd. S661980/MP Dd. 593426 K40 1/80

by an international military force and international observers.[90] Most contentious during the negotiations was the issue of land reform. Only the offer by the British and U.S. governments to provide funding to the new government to enable it to purchase land from white landowners on the basis of 'willing buyer, willing seller' broke the impasse between the nationalist movements and the Rhodesian government, making it possible for the agreed political arrangements to be effected.

'US backed Zimbabwe land reform'

Martin Plaut

http://news.bbc.co.uk

The land issue has always been emotive in Zimbabwe.... And it was important to all parties in 1980 that signed the Lancaster House Agreement that led to the transformation of Rhodesia into Zimbabwe. The road to the agreement was not straight forward, and as an investigation by the BBC's The Westminster Hour programme has revealed, it was much bumpier than at first suspected.... Gradually progress was made. Until the question of who would own the land. It was the toughest of issues. Whites – 5% of the population – owned 80% of the arable land. Millions of black people scratched a living on the rest. For Mr. Mugabe and Mr. Nkomo this was critical. Yet when Lord Carrington finally presented the draft constitution it contained no reference to the land. Sir Shridath [then Commonwealth Secretary] says the conference came close to collapse. 'From the British government's point of view the constitution was preserving the status quo for a minimum of 10 years,' he says. 'When Nkomo and Mugabe saw it and understood the implications they blew up. They asked Carrington what he meant. The struggle was about land. 'Was he saying to them they must sign a constitution which says that they could not redistribute land because if that was the case they should go back to the bush ...' Sir Shridath believed the conference was doomed to failure and that Mr. Mugabe and Mr. Nkomo would walk out and the civil war would resume. 'I took an initiative of my own as secretary-general which isn't much known and talked about but can be now.'

[90] Southern Rhodesia, Constitutional conference held at Lancaster House, London September–December 1979: *Report*.

Secret Promise

He secretly contacted the US ambassador in London, Kingman Brewster, and asked him to get the then US President, Jimmy Carter, to promise money to pay white farmers for their land. 'Brewster was totally supportive. We were at a stage where Mugabe and Nkomo were packing their bags,' he explains. 'He came back to me within 24 hours. They had got hold of Jimmy Carter and Carter authorised Brewster to say to me that the United States would contribute a substantial amount for a process of land redistribution and they would undertake to encourage the British government to give similar assurances. That of course saved the conference.'

The Lancaster House Conference finally agreed on the following issues: an independence constitution, arrangements for the pre-independence period and a cease-fire agreement.[91] In addition, the participants committed themselves to:

- accept the authority of the British governor who was to supervise the transitional arrangements;
- abide by the Independence Constitution;
- comply with the pre-independence arrangements;
- abide by the cease-fire agreement;
- campaign peacefully and without intimidation;
- renounce the use of force for political ends; and
- accept the outcome of the elections and instruct any forces under their authority to do the same.

Under these arrangements, Rhodesia went to the polls in February 1980. Robert Mugabe's ZANU, now renamed ZANU-Patriotic Front (ZANU-PF), won overwhelmingly with 57 seats in 100-member parliament, with ZAPU garnering 20 and Muzorewa's UANC only 3 seats. The Rhodesian Front swept all 20 white seats.

---

[91] See Appendix 1 (Lancaster House Constitution), at http://www.zwnews.com/ Lancasterhouse.doc (accessed 20 October 2012).

8

Independent Zimbabwe, 1980–2000

Introduction

After years of bitter armed conflict, Zimbabwe became independent in 1980 full of promise and hope that the future would be one of economic prosperity, political freedom and a generally decent livelihood for all and that the nightmarish past of the colonial period was gone forever. For the first decade, with the exception of the people of Matebeleland who were subjected to the horrors of the Gukurahundi massacres which were hidden from the rest of the population through rigorous press censorship, it seemed as if the good times had, indeed, arrived. There were many pro-people policies that made a real positive difference in people's lives. The incoming government expanded the country's education facilities and provided free primary school education and free health services to the poor majority. It subsidised basic consumer products such as the main staple food mealie meal (corn meal), milk and cooking oil to lessen cost of food for the poorest, while at the same time decreeing a minimum wage law to ensure a decent standard of living for the hitherto marginalised segments of the population.

By the mid 1990s, however, the optimism of a good life for all was fast dissipating. In its place was a deepening sense of despair in the face of mounting inflation and unemployment, declining household incomes, the informalisation of the economy, growing poverty, particularly in the urban areas, and severe housing shortages for the urban poor.

Politics

Given the protracted hostilities of the past, there was fear that independence might usher in a period of recriminations and reprisals, as Africans, now in charge, sought to settle old scores with the white population. Apprehensive of their safety under the independence government, many whites emigrated to South Africa and other countries, so that by the end of the first year of independence, only 170,000 out of the 250 000 pre-independence white population remained in the country. To avert the possibility of reprisals and to reassure the white population, the new prime minister, Robert Mugabe, announced a policy of reconciliation:

If yesterday I fought you as an enemy, today you have become a friend and ally with the same national interest, loyalty, rights, and duties as myself. If yesterday you hated me, today you cannot avoid the love that binds you to me and me to you. If ever we look to the past, let us do so for the lesson the past has taught us, namely that oppression and racism are iniquities that must never again find scope in our political and social system. It could never be a correct justification that because the whites oppressed us yesterday when they had the power, the blacks must oppress them today because they have power. An evil remains an evil whether practised by white against blacks or by black against white.[1]

He demonstrated his government's commitment to reconciliation by appointing a number of former Rhodesian white politicians to positions of leadership in the government. For instance, General Peter Walls who had commanded the Rhodesian Security Forces (RSF) in their war against the liberation movement retained his position as the country military commander and was, in fact, given the task of integrating the three erstwhile hostile military formations of ZANLA, ZIPRA and the RSF. Similarly, David Smith, formerly Rhodesia's deputy prime minister, was appointed as minister of commerce and industry, whereas Denis Norman, hitherto leader of the whites-only Commercial Farmers Union (CFU), became the minister of agriculture. Leading ZAPU members also joined the government of national unity, being granted four cabinet posts and three junior ministerial posts. The spirit of reconciliation did not last long, however, as the country was soon mired in a fratricidal war that pitched former allies against each other in the so-called dissident war in Matebeleland from 1983 onwards.

[1] The *Chronicle* (Bulawayo), 18 April 1980.

Gukurahundi

In the euphoria that accompanied the coming of independence, a crisis was brewing that would plunge the country into a fratricidal war leading to an estimated 20,000 deaths by the time it was over.[2] Triggering the conflict were armed clashes between former ZANLA and ZIPRA combatants who were temporarily accommodated in holding camps or Assembly Points while awaiting either demobilisation or integration into the national army that was then being restructured to accommodate all erstwhile antagonistic military formations. The worst clash between the two groups occurred in Bulawayo between November 1980 and February 1981, resulting in more than 100 deaths. Tensions continued to mount thereafter, as Mugabe demoted Joshua Nkomo from his position as minister of home affairs in the government of national unity amidst charges by Mugabe that ZAPU was working to overthrow his government. The discovery by the police in 1982 of military arms caches on farms and other properties owned by ZAPU led to the arrest of ZIPRA's commanders, Lookout Masuku and Dumiso Dabengwa, government confiscation of the farms and properties and the expulsion from the Government of National Unity of ZAPU leader Joshua Nkomo and other members of his party.

Outraged by government actions, some former ZIPRA cadres took to the bush to wage a guerrilla campaign against government in protest. Although there was no evidence linking this small group of dissidents to ZAPU, government propaganda pushed the line that they were sponsored by both Nkomo's party and the apartheid government of South Africa. South Africa did take advantage of the situation to destabilise its northern neighbour by setting up and training a group of bandits calling itself Super ZAPU to join the fray in Matebeleland and generally cause mayhem. This was in line with South Africa's policy then of destabilising its neighbours partly in order to demonstrate to its own African population that black rule did not work, but also partly to keep neighbouring governments preoccupied with internal problems so that they would not have either the inclination or the resources to support anti-apartheid liberation movements.[3] In the face of mounting charges that he was 'the

---

[2] Catholic commission for Justice and Peace/Legal Resources Foundation, *Breaking the Silence, Building True Peace: A Report on the Disturbances in Matebeleland and the Midlands, 1980 to 1998* (Harare: CCJP/LRF, 1999).

[3] For a discussion of South Africa's destabilisation policies, see Joseph Hanlon, *Beggar Thy Neighbor* (Bloomington: Indiana University Press, 1986); John Dzimba, *South Africa's Destabilisation of Zimbabwe, 1980–89* (London: Palgrave Macmillan 1998).

father of dissidents', Nkomo was forced to flee the country in March 1983 in fear for his life. He returned only when government guaranteed his safety.

The ZAPU-ZANU tensions that led to the 1980s Matebeleland crisis have to be understood within the context of long-standing rivalries between the two political formations ever since the 1963 split that led to the establishment of the latter by Ndabaningi Sithole and others. Supporters of the two parties had engaged in numerous violent clashes at the time of the split that had led to the colonial government banning both parties and imprisoning or detaining most political leaders. Although never entirely tribal parties, as both parties had members and leaders from the two major ethnic groups, the Shona and Ndebele, each became increasingly associated mostly with one of the two ethnic groups, with ZANU being seen mostly as a party for the Shona, whereas ZAPU became widely regarded as mostly a Ndebele party. This perception was reinforced when the guerrilla war seriously got underway in the 1970s, with ZAPU operating mainly among the Ndebele-speakers of southwestern Zimbabwe, whereas ZANU cadres were concentrated in areas mostly occupied by Shona-speakers.

As noted earlier, another major difference was that whereas ZAPU received its military support and training from Russia, ZANU obtained its support mainly from China. The rivalry between them remained a constant source of friction throughout the period under study, sometimes spilling into armed clashes when cadres from the two parties met in the field, much to the glee of the common enemy, the Rhodesian government. The united front that the parties established in 1976 as the Patriotic Front in the run-up to the abortive Geneva Conference unravelled just before the 1980 independence elections when ZANU decided to run on a separate ticket from ZAPU as ZANU-Patriotic Front (ZANU-PF). Even the voting patterns reflected the ethnic delineation of the parties, as ZAPU received most of its support in Matebeleland and ZANU in the rest of the country, mostly from Shona-speakers. Given these long-standing rivalries and mutual suspicions, it is not surprising that the discovery of arms at ZAPU-owned properties led to such tragic national consequences.

Denouncing these fighters as dissidents and South Africa's puppets, the Mugabe regime unleashed its Korean-trained Fifth Brigade in Matebeleland in 1983 to put down the insurgency. According to Alexander and colleagues,

The deployment of the Fifth Brigade in early 1983 introduced terror and hardship on a scale civilians had known neither in the mounting insecurity of the 1980s nor at the height of the guerrilla war. The Fifth Brigade's exercise of violence was concentrated within a relatively short period – just under a year – ... [but] the death toll was high.[4]

Both the dissidents and government soldiers perpetrated serious human rights abuses that severely traumatised the local population, but evidence shows that most of those who perished or were maimed and tortured were the victims of the Fifth Brigade.[5] For example, a report by the Catholic Peace and Justice Commission noted the devastating impact of the Fifth Brigade in the Matebeleland North Region as follows:

The presence of the 5 Brigade in an area in 1983 meant an initial outburst of intense brutality, usually lasting a few days, followed by random incidents of beatings, burnings and murders in the ensuing weeks, months and years. It meant that any community which had once experienced 5 Brigade lived in a state of intense anxiety and fear, unsure where and when it might strike again, or who its next victims might be.... Many communities suffered massive material loss in the initial onslaught, losing huts and granaries. They also lost village members who had been killed or abducted, and were frequently forced to watch others close to them dying slowly from injuries sustained from beating, burning, shooting or bayoneting. Villagers were warned not to seek medical help, and risked being shot for curfew breaking if they did seek help. Many who were beaten were left with permanent disabilities, ranging from paralysis, blindness, deafness, miscarriage, impotence, infertility, and kidney damage, to partial lameness and recurring back and headaches.[6]

Similarly, Alexander reports on the brutal impact of the Fifth Brigade in Matebeleland as follows:

From its deployment in Matabeleland North in January 1983 until its withdrawal from Matabeleland South in late 1984, the brigade carried out a grotesquely violent campaign against civilians, civil servants, party chairmen and, occasionally, armed insurgents.... Reports compiled by Zimbabwean and international groups stressed the arbitrary and extreme use of violence. The Fifth Brigade introduced a qualitatively new and more horrific kind of war. For those civilians who bore its brunt, all preceding armies paled in comparison. Civilians stressed the explicitly tribal nature of the brigade's attacks, the forced use of Shona, the invoking of a mythical past of Ndebele raids against the Shona to justify the brigade's brutality. The brigade used Zanla mobilisation methods such as the all-night pungwe at

---

4 J. Alexander et al., *Violence and Memory: One Hundred Years in the 'Dark Forests' of Matabeleland*, (Oxford: James Currey, 2000), 217.
5 Catholic Commission for Justice and Peace, *Breaking the Silence*.
6 Catholic Commission for Justice and Peace, *Report on the 1980s Disturbances in Matabeleland and the Midlands*, 54.

which song and dance were accompanied by political education. But in this context the songs were in an unfamiliar language, the dance was forced, the slogans were anti-Zapu, and the 'festivities' were accompanied by beatings and killings.[7]

The Fifth Brigade's horrific activities in Matebeleland in this period have been described as genocide.[8] The fratricidal conflict in Matebeleland ended only when ZAPU and ZANU merged into one party after the 1987 Unity Agreement between the two parties. The combined political party took name of the Zimbabwe African National Union-Patriotic Front (ZANU-PF). This made Zimbabwe a de facto one-party state, even though smaller parties existed and it was nominally a multiparty democratic system.

War Veterans, Demobilisation and Disgruntlement

A major challenge facing the incoming independence government in 1980 was what to do with the bloated size of armed forces in the country, estimated at 100,000 soldiers, comprising former guerrillas of ZANLA and ZIPRA and the former RSF. Government decided to restructure the country's army by integrating all three formerly antagonistic military formations into one Zimbabwe National Army, commensurate with its size as a small nation. With the help of British military advisers, this was gradually achieved, with approximately 43,000 ex-combatants being absorbed in the government security and civil services.[9] Means had also to be found to help those not absorbed in the national army to find alternative ways of survival. Government's solution was to provide each of the discharged former guerrilla fighters with a demobilization grant of ZW$4,400 at the rate of ZW$185 a month for two years, as a stepping stone for them to find other occupations as civilians. This amount was inadequate to provide the ex-combatants with a meaningful foundation on which to build their new lives. Moreover, many beneficiaries of the grant lacked the requisite skills to maximise their financial resources, with the result

---

7 J. Alexander, 'Dissident Perspectives on Zimbabwe's Post-Independence', *Africa: Journal of the International African Institute*, 68, 2 (1998), 151–82.

8 John Simpson, 'Tracking Down a Massacre', BBC News, 7 May 2008.

9 Muchaparara Musemwa, 'The Ambiguities of Democracy: The Demobilisation of the Zimbabwean Ex-Combatants and the Ordeal of Rehabilitation, 1980–1993,' in Jakkie Cilliers (ed.), *Dismissed: Demobilisation and Reintegration of Former Combatants in Africa* (Cape Town: Halfway House: Institute for Defence Policy, 1996), 44–57.

that most of the money was soon squandered in unproductive activities. As G. Mazarire and M. Rupiya observe:

Given the impact of resources at the individual level, set at Z$185,00 per month over 24 months, the sums were generally far short of what was required to adequately assist former combatants to ease themselves back into the capitalist economy inherited from Rhodesia. Many lacked the necessary skills while those in command of the economy spurned the new entrants. Furthermore, serious government corruption was later unearthed in the selection and allocation of scholarships. As a result, these did not really benefit the intended beneficiaries – the ex-combatants.[10]

Nevertheless, 36,000 ex-combatants had been demobilised by 1985, but only 16,000 of these had secured meaningful alternative livelihoods, either through employment or skills training. Many were hampered by lack of education, as some had left for the liberation war before they had completed their primary education.[11]

In accordance with its espoused socialist objectives and as a way of addressing the question of ex-combatants' unemployment, the government encouraged demobilised war veterans to invest their grants in co-operatives. Consequently, co-operatives in poultry and livestock production, crop production and market gardening, retail and other economic activities mushroomed throughout the country in the early 1980s. Most soon collapsed, however, from poor management, undercapitalization, inability of members to borrow from financial institutions because of lack of collateral and the negative impact of the prolonged drought of 1982, among other factors. The Gukurahundi massacres in Matebeleland led to the collapse of co-operatives founded by ex-ZIPRA combatants in Matebeleland, as members were constantly harassed by the Fifth Brigade and abandoned their projects. As a result many demobilised liberation war veterans remained unemployed and destitute by the end of the first decade of independence. Significant also is the fact that while all unemployed war veterans found life difficult, female ex-combatants faced additional challenges of reintegration into society. This was because they were widely regarded by the ordinary male civilians as unmarriageable because of their perceived combativeness and a tendency towards insubordination to their male partners (unforgivable in a predominantly patriarchal society) and a rather unfounded and unsubstantiated suspicion of their morals.[12]

[10] G. Mazarire and R. M. Rupiya, 'Two Wrongs Do Not Make a Right: A Critical Assessment of Zimbabwe's Demobilisation and Reintegration Programmes, 1980–2000', *Journal of Peace, Conflict and Military Studies*, 1, 1 (March 2000), 3.

[11] Musemwa, 'Ambiguities of Democracy'.

[12] Musemwa, 'Ambiguities of Democracy'.

In response, war veterans established the Zimbabwe National Liberation War Veterans Association (ZNLWVA) in 1989 to champion their own interests which had been neglected by the government that they had helped to put into power. Under pressure from the Association, government enacted the War Veterans Act in 1992 to cater for the welfare of the former fighters by, inter alia, providing for the establishment of schemes to assist war veterans and their dependants, the creation of a fund for such a purpose and the establishment of a War Veterans Board. Despite these measures, little improved materially for the war veterans and they continued to agitate for their cause.

In 1996–7, the war veterans demanded compensation for their wartime sacrifices under the provisions of the War Victims Compensation Act (1993), which was based on the Rhodesian government's Victims of Terrorism (Compensation) Act of 1973, but now broadened to include anyone who had been negatively affected by the liberation war between 1962 and 1980. The War Victims Compensation Fund, which had been established at independence, was to disburse payments to those deserving compensation. High-ranking politicians had long benefited from this fund since 1980, but its existence remained largely unknown by the rank and file of the war veterans until a local newspaper publicised its existence in May 1996. Thereafter, there was a veritable stampede of war veterans applying for compensation. The result was chaotic and unregulated looting of the fund in 1997 with the help of the Association's new chairman, Dr. Chenjerai Hunzvi, who dished out medical certificates confirming disabilities to all and sundry to enable them to claim compensation. Payments were stopped in April 1997 following a public outcry.

Thereafter, war veterans began demanding pensions and other benefits enjoyed by civil servants. Under increasing pressure, President Mugabe promised to make lump-sum payments of ZW$50,000 (US$4,000) to all former fighters and to pay individual monthly pensions of ZW$2,000 (US$150) in addition to providing funding for the veterans' health care and education needs for their children. As these grants had not been budgeted for, the Zimbabwean economy paid a severe price as the national currency crashed on 13 November 1997 and its value dropped by 73 per cent in relation to the American dollar.[13] Thereafter, some members of

[13] *Wilfred Mhanda*, 'The Role of War Veterans in Zimbabwe's Political and Economic Processes', Paper presented to the SAPES Trust Policy Dialogue Forum in Harare on 7 April 2011. Available at http://www.solidaritypeacetrust.org/1063/the-role-of-war-veterans (accessed 03/04/2013).

the ZNLWVA increasingly became close to the ZANU-PF ruling party and became its foot soldiers in the farm invasions of 2000 and after and in the violent campaign against the Movement for Democratic Change (MDC) and other opposition groups.[14] In protest at what they regarded as unbecoming behaviour for liberation war veterans and against the ZNLWVA's increasing abuse of human rights, some war veterans, led by Dzinashe Machingura and others, founded the Zimbabwe Liberators' Platform (ZLP) in May 2000 and publicly distanced themselves from the ZNLWVA.[15]

Growth of Opposition Politics

Following its victory at the polls in 1980, ZANU-PF was determined to push for a one-party government system in Zimbabwe. The idea of a one-party state had been born during Africa's independence decade of the 1960s, when it was argued that, given the ethnic diversity of most African countries and the need to focus all energies on national building and development, it was not advisable to follow the Western multiparty democratic model which would only promote ethnic competition and conflict. Africa, it was argued, needed a one-party political system that would enable it to harness all its energies in a concerted and focused effort, since it could not afford the 'luxury' of multipartyism. Proponents of the one-party ideology maintained that democratic debate could be conducted within one party just as well as in a multiparty configuration. Many of the first independence leaders, such as Kwame Nkrumah, Julius Nyerere, Kenneth Kaunda, Jomo Kenyatta and others, fully subscribed to this political philosophy. However, the system was gradually discredited when it became clear that it had become a vehicle for stifling dissent and alternative political visions and the entire system became associated with a self-seeking presidentialism in which political leaders permanently clung on to power.

Throughout the first independence decade, the ruling ZANU-PF was determined to introduce a one-party system in the country, as shown

---

[14] For the role of war veterans in ZANU-PF post-independence political strategies and activities, see Norma Kriger, 'Political Constructions of War Veterans' *Review of African Political Economy*, 30, 96 (June 2003), 323–28; Norma Kriger, 'War Veterans: Continuities between the Past and the Present', *African Studies Quarterly* 7, 2–3, available at http://web.africa.ufl.edu/asq/v7/v7i2a7.htm (accessed 4 April 2013); Wilfred Mhanda, *Dzino: Memories of a Freedom Fighter* (Harare: Weaver Press, 2011).

[15] Mhanda, *Memories of a Freedom Fighter*.

by its 1984 Congress resolution to work towards a Marxist-Leninist one-party socialist state and the adoption of a new constitution which enlarged its Central Committee and established a fifteen-member politburo (a supreme governing party organ). Opposing this agenda were a few political parties that included the United African National Council (UANC) under Bishop Muzorewa; Zimbabwe African National Union (ZANU-Ndonga) under Ndabaningi Sithole; Zimbabwe African People's Union-Patriotic Front (ZAPU-PF), until the Unity Agreement of 1987, under Joshua Nkomo; and the Rhodesian Front (RF), later the Conservative Alliance of Zimbabwe (CAZ), under Ian Smith. While the white community was guaranteed twenty seats under the Lancaster House Constitution, the other opposition parties did not fare well at the polls. For instance, in the 1985 general elections, ZAPU-PF lost five of the twenty seats that it had won in 1980, while ZANU-Ndonga won only one seat. Muzorewa's UANC did not win a single seat. Meanwhile, ZANU-PF increased its parliamentary representation from fifty-seven to sixty-three. Demonstrating their intolerance of any political opposition, ZANU-PF supporters embarked on an orgy of violence against supporters of the opposition parties despite their party's overwhelming victory soon after the elections, beating up and terrorising all suspected political opponents. Thereafter, each of the three major opposition party leaders, Nkomo, Muzorewa and Sithole, was consecutively accused of plotting to overthrow the government and hounded into exile.

Meanwhile, constitutional changes in the 1980s strengthened the party's campaign for a one-party state. For example, the clause guaranteeing twenty reserved seat for the whites lapsed in 1987, while parliament scrapped the offices of the prime minister and ceremonial presidency inherited at independence and replaced them with a unitary executive presidency in October of the same year. Senate was abolished in November 1989, while parliament was enlarged from 100 to 150 seats; 120 of them would be filled through the ballot, while the president would appoint the other 30. By then, ZAPU had ceased to exist as a political party, having been swallowed up by ZANU-PF as a result of the peace negotiations leading to the 1987 Unity Accord which marked the end of the Matebeleland conflicts. As expected, the new united party pledged to work towards a one-party Marxist-Leninist state. All seemed set for the triumph of the one-party idea. Then the geopolitical climate changed at the same time that opposition to the one-party state was mounting within the country.

The end of the Cold War under Soviet President Mikhail Gorbachev's *perestroika* initiatives, followed by the collapse of the Soviet Union and the fall of the Berlin Wall, changed the geopolitical situation so much that it became very difficult for the Zimbabwe government to continue to push the Marxist-Leninist one-party agenda at a time when the leading socialist countries were not only opening up but also embracing multipartyism. The ideological carpet was thus proverbially pulled out from under the Mugabe regime's feet. In any case, domestic opposition to the project, both within and outside the party, had been mounting for some time. Within the party, there had been outspoken criticism of the one-party project at ZANU-PF's 1989 Congress, forcing Mugabe to actively persuade delegates to commit themselves to it at the meeting. One year later, in August 1990, the party's own politburo voted against the one-party state, putting paid to the project once and for all. Leading the opposition campaign within the party was ZANU-PF's Secretary General Edgar Tekere who had become increasingly disillusioned with his own party and was unhappy at what he regarded as Mugabe's excessive powers and growing dictatorial tendencies.[16] The Willowgate Scandal of the late 1980s involved prominent political figures who abused the state subsidy system for new car purchases by fraudulently acquiring cars from the state-owned Willowvale Car Assembly Plant at low subsidised prices and then reselling them at exorbitant prices in order to reap huge profits. The resultant public outcry led to the creation of a Commission of Enquiry which implicated several cabinet ministers and other high-ranking government personnel, some of whom were dismissed, while others were forced to resign.

Meanwhile, for publicly denouncing the corruption of the party leadership and dramatically proclaiming that under Mugabe's leadership, the country's democracy was now crippled and in 'intensive care', ZANU-PF's Secretary General Tekere was booted out of the party. He responded by forming his own political party, the Zimbabwe Unity Movement (ZUM) in 1989. ZUM was able to secure only two seats in the 1990 general elections which were marked by noticeable public apathy, and crumbled soon afterwards. Other equally short-lived political parties were the Democratic Party of Emmanuel Magoche in 1991, the Forum Party of Zimbabwe (FPZ) under retired Chief Justice Enoch Dumbutshena, the Popular Front for Zimbabwe (FPZ) under Austin Chakaodza and the

---

[16] For Tekere's political history, see Edgar Tekere, *Tekere: A Lifetime of Struggle* (Harare: Sapes Books, 2007).

Zimbabwe Union of Democrats (ZUD) under former liberation war fighter, Margaret Dongo. None of these parties were strong enough to meaningfully challenge the political hold of ZANU-PF which used its economic muscle, its considerable coercive power as lodged in the military, the police and the dreaded state intelligence organisation, the Central Intelligence Organisation (CIO), to intimidate opponents. Nevertheless, by the early 1990s, ZANU-PF's one-party state project had been abandoned because of mounting domestic opposition to the idea and to the changed geopolitical climate. It was also undermined by the country's weakening economic situation which forced the Zimbabwean government, its socialist rhetoric notwithstanding, increasingly into the embrace of the International Monetary Fund (IMF) and the World Bank for funding of its economic reform programme beginning in 1990, commonly known as the Economic Structural Adjustment Programme (ESAP).

While political opposition parties remained weak throughout the 1990s, several civil society organisations emerged and became increasingly vocal critics of ZANU-PF governance and its growing authoritarianism. These included advocacy groups ranging from human rights organisations, the Catholic Commission for Justice and Peace, Legal Resources Fund (LRF), ZimRights, the students movement and women's organisations to the Zimbabwe Congress of Trade Unions (ZCTU), which had found its own voice after the first decade of independence during which it acted, essentially, as a junior partner of ZANU-PF. The ZCTU's growing independence was evident in its opposition to the one-party state project, its 'refusal to endorse ZANU-PF in the 1990 election campaign' and in its 'solidarity with the student movement in its protests and demonstrations against corruption among the ruling elite in 1988'.[17] The organisation's change was partly the result of new leadership under Secretary General Morgan Tsvangirai, who brought a degree of militancy to the organisation that had been lacking earlier. Gradually, the ZCTU spoke for more than just its membership and about wider political concerns than simply bread-and-butter issues of a workers' organisation and became the de facto opposition voice. In the context of mounting economic discontent associated with the deleterious effects of ESAP and poor management by the ruling party, the ZCTU found itself having to provide leadership to a growing coalition of organisations and groupings that were demanding

[17] Lloyd Sachikonye, 'Between Authoritarianism and Democracy: Politics in Zimbabwe since 1990', in M. Lee and K. Colvard (eds.), *Unfinished Business: The Land Crisis in Southern Africa* (Cape Town: Africa Institute of South Africa, 2003), 97–132.

a new constitution to replace the 1980 Lancaster House Constitution which had been amended many times by the government to strengthen its hold on the nation. This led to the creation of the National Constitutional Assembly (NCA) in 1998, comprising more than 100 civil society organisations, all united in the need to press for a new constitution. Out of this coalition emerged the Movement for Democratic Change (MDC) in 1999.[18]

The Economy

At independence, Zimbabwe inherited a highly developed and diversified economy in which agricultural and mining were complemented by a well-developed manufacturing sector which produced a wide range of products that had been previously been imported before UDI. The country's economy had been developing in spite of, or perhaps because of, international sanctions, as policy makers and entrepreneurs had to resort to import substitution strategies in the face of international economic ostracism.

This economy was, however, based on gross inequalities on the basis of race, characterised by a highly skewed distribution of income and ownership of economic assets, including land, housing, businesses and other wealth, as well as unequal access to social services such as education and health,[19] in favour of the white minority and at the expense of the African majority who were largely marginalised and deprived. For example, while Africans accounted for nearly 97.6 per cent of the population, they commanded only 60 per cent share of wages and salaries, whereas whites received 37 per cent of the same although they comprised only 2 per cent of the population. The balance went to the country's Coloured and Indian people, as documented in Table 8.1.

Similarly, the ownership of land was largely skewed in favour of the minority white population – the result of a succession of discriminatory colonial land laws, such as the Land Apportionment Act of 1931, the Native Land Husbandry Act of 1951 and the Land Tenure Act of 1969. The whites, comprising only 4 per cent of the population, held the most productive land, whereas more than 80 per cent of the African majority were squeezed into overcrowded and unproductive African reserves that

---

[18] Sachikonye, 'Between Authoritarianism and Democracy'.
[19] Richard Saunders, 'Zimbabwe: ESAP's Fables II', *Southern Africa Report*, 11, 4 (July 1996), 1–30.

TABLE 8.1. *Distribution of Income by Race, 1981*

Group	Proportion of Population	Share of Wages and Salaries
African	97.6	60.0
European	2.0	37.0
Coloured	0.3	2.0
Indian	0.2	1.0

Source: Government of Zimbabwe 1981. National Manpower Survey, Vol. 1. Harare.

were fast deteriorating from soil erosion. Africans were also disadvantaged with regard to government-sponsored infrastructural development, with white areas receiving massive public financial support for the construction of dams, roads and railways in contrast to the assistance given to African areas.

In addition, white-owned companies controlled most of the country's mining, manufacturing and commercial industries. For example, by 1978, the following multinational conglomerates dominated the mining sector: Anglo-American, Rio Tinto, Messina Transvaal, Johannesburg Consolidated Investment, Union Carbide and Turner and Newall. The exclusion of Africans from the mining sector was the result of their inability to access capital because they were not legally permitted to own property in the country's urban centres. Moreover, Africans were severely under-represented in professional and managerial occupations, with Africans accounting for only 36 per cent of all professional and technical jobs and a mere 24 per cent in managerial and administrative positions.[20] Meanwhile, because they could not legally own land as individuals in the African reserves, Africans could not use land as collateral to raise bank loans and, therefore, could not undertake meaningful business ventures even if they had been allowed to own businesses in white areas, which they were not. Consequently, they participated in these economic sectors primarily as labourers. Commenting on the colonial system's economic discrimination against Africans, a 1996 Government of Zimbabwe publication argued:

[20] Government of Zimbabwe, *National Manpower Survey*, Vol. 1 (Harare: Government Printers, 1981), cited in Lucy Mazingi and Richard Kamhidza, 'Inequality in Zimbabwe', at http://www.osisa.org/sites/default/files/sup_files/chapter_5_-_zimbabwe.pdf (accessed 10 May 2013).

Development of the rural/peasant communal sector, which provides livelihood for
the majority of the population was generally neglected, while the modern money
economy, owned and controlled by a minority and heavily linked to international
capital, enjoyed all the benefits of development. The latter sector consists of the
industrial and commercial operations, primarily based in the major urban centres, and commercial agriculture. Its link with the peasant sector mainly consisted
of the latter acting as a reservoir for cheap labour and to some extent providing
a market for cheap quality goods.[21]

Race-based inequalities also dominated the social services sector, with
white urban centres enjoying first-class health, transport, communication, educational and housing services in contrast to non-existent or very
basic services in the African areas. To take education as an example, the
colonial regime had consistently under-funded African education while
pouring considerable resources into white education. For example, in the
1976–78 financial years, government spent twenty times more per capita
on white students than on African students.

   In addition, the educational fare fed to African pupils was designed
to undermine their history and identity through denigrating the past of
the 'Dark continent' or ignoring it altogether, while glorifying Western
history and achievements. Routinely, African precolonial societies and
their leaders were characterised as bloodthirsty savages who had nothing better to do than fight incessant and meaningless wars for the sheer
fun of it. Even the European conquest of Zimbabwe was glorified, as
African students were expected to celebrate the colonisation of the country during the Rhodes and Founders' holiday and to eulogise as heroes
the white soldiers who were killed in battles with Africans who were
resisting colonisation.[22]

   A major challenge facing the new independent government, therefore, was how to redress these inequalities of the past. Government's

[21] Ministry of Finance, Economic Planning and Development, *Socio-Economic Review,
   1980–1985* (Harare: The Ministry, 1986), 5.
[22] Two examples: history lessons included the adulation of the Allan Wilson Patrol, which
   was wiped out in a battle at the Shangani River, north of present-day Bulawayo, when
   they were overwhelmed by a superior Ndebele force in their pursuit of King Lobengula's
   retreat from his capital in Bulawayo after a military invasion by the white settlers; the
   emphasis being on how these 'heroes' were 'massacred' by the Africans. The other is a
   song that the author was required to sing as a member of the Boy Scouts Movement
   in honour of the founder of the Scouts Movement Baden Powell, which contained the
   following words: 'Let us thank Baden Powell for having come to Africa to help the children of Africa', even though he had ruthlessly suppressed the 1896 war of resistance
   in Matebeleland as one of the commanders of the colonial forces and was, at the time,
   under investigation for war crimes against the people of Matebeleland.

response was to adopt a development strategy enunciated in a series of policy documents, including *Growth with Equity, Transitional National Development Plan* and the *First Five Year National Development Plan*.[23] These strategies were designed to develop a mixed economy which would enable the government to realise its espoused socialist goals of redistributing wealth without necessarily destroying the inherited colonial capitalist institutions and practices.

Much was achieved in the first years of independence, particularly with respect to improving the quality of life of the majority. Government invested heavily in education and health. Under the slogans of 'Education for All by 2000' and 'Health for All by 2000', government registered notable achievements in the 'expansion of the education system and improved access to both preventative and curative health services'.[24] The number of primary and secondary schools had increased by 80 per cent, from 3,358 in 1980 to 6,042 in 1990, with primary school enrolment also rising from 1,235,994 to 2,119,865 in that period. Enrolment at the University of Zimbabwe, the only university then in the country, also increased fivefold between 1980 and 1990. Numerous teacher-training institutions were also established in the same period. Private colleges were encouraged so that by 1990, there were no less than 108 registered private colleges, graduating some 12,000 students annually. The introduction of free primary education at independence allowed more girls to get an education, unlike the past when parents favoured boys over girls when it came to education, because school fees were difficult to raise. By the end of the first independence decade, Zimbabwe had made impressive strides in promoting mass education, having educated, in the ten years, more Africans than had been educated by the colonial regimes in the previous ninety years. Such achievements led the United Nations Educational and Scientific Co-ordination Organisation (UNESCO) to commend Zimbabwe's educational system as a revolutionary system 'built on modern and enlightened principles of education that take

[23] Government of Zimbabwe, *Growth with Equity: An Economic Policy Statement*, (Harare: Ministry of Finance, Economic Planning and Development, 1982); Government of Zimbabwe, *Transitional National Development Plan, 1982/83 – 1984/85* (Harare: Government Printers, 1982); Government of Zimbabwe, *First Five-Year National Development Plan, 1986–1990*, 2 vols. (Harare: Ministry of Finance, Economic Planning and Development, 1986).

[24] Rob Davies, 'Memories of Underdevelopment: A Personal Interpretation of Zimbabwe's Economic Decline', at http://www.sarpn.org.za/documents/d0001154/P1273-davies_zimbabwe_2004.pdf (accessed 3 August 2012).

into account the country's particular circumstances, opportunities and constraints'.[25]

Government also expanded access to health facilities through the construction of hospitals and clinics throughout the country and the promotion of primary health care. Between 1980 and 1990, government restored 161 clinics that had been damaged during the war and also built 163 new health centres, legislated free medical care for the poor and decreed a minimum wage law to ensure that the workers had some disposable income. Meanwhile, the government's introduction of the Primary Health Care (PHC) system provided the majority with an affordable and easily accessible health service. At the same time, government ran child immunisation programmes to guard against preventable diseases, as well as nutrition and hygiene awareness campaigns and supplementary feeding and family planning schemes. By 1990, the country boasted the lowest child malnutrition rate in Africa and a child mortality rate that was way below the continent's average at 88 per 1,000, as well as a comparatively lower maternal mortality rate of 251 per 100,000 births.[26] The World Bank commented on Zimbabwe's achievements in health as 'truly impressive', citing the increase in the country's life expectancy from fifty-five to fifty-nine years, the country's highly successful child immunisation and contraception programmes and the notable decline in child mortality rates and maternal mortality, among other achievements.[27]

In addition, government introduced a number of reforms designed to improve the quality of life of the previously marginalised or downtrodden. These included the 1980 Minimum Wages Act, enabling government to periodically set minimum wages for workers, the Employment Act of 1980 and the Employment (Conditions of Service) Regulations of 1981, protecting workers from arbitrary dismissal by employers, as well as the 1985 Labour Relations Act which spelt out the rights of workers' unions. Government also decreed measures to protect and promote women and their interests. A Ministry of Women's Affairs, set up in 1980, oversaw the implementation of the 1982 Legal Age of Majority Act, giving both sexes majority status at the age of eighteen years. This was to correct the colonial dispensation under which women were regarded as minors who could not enter into a legal contract in their own right but always

[25] UNESCO, *Proceedings of the General Conference, Twenty Fourth Session, Paris, France* (Paris: UNESCO, 1987).

[26] World Bank, *Zimbabwe: Financing Health Services* (Washington, DC: World Bank, 1992), 7.

[27] World Bank, *Zimbabwe: Financing Health Services*, x.

needed the permission of a male guardian, even if, in some cases, the male guardian was their own child. The 1983 Maintenance Act legislated for financial support for children by their fathers until they reached the legal age of adulthood, while the 1985 Labour Relations Act prohibited discrimination against women in employment and recruitment. In 1987, the Deceased Persons Family Maintenance Act gave women inheritance rights. Finally, in 1991, government amended the Deeds Registry Act making it possible for women to buy immovable property without their husbands' consent.[28]

The independence government's enactment of otherwise seemingly progressive legislation with regard to women did not, however, mean that it had fully embraced gender equality, the rhetoric to this effect notwithstanding. Women continued to be short-changed, for instance, in law enforcement. For example, in 1983, under a police law enforcement 'clean-up' action code-named Operation Chinyavada [scorpion] conducted on the eve of the Harare Non-Aligned Movement meeting, police rounded up more than 3,000 women from the city's streets at night on allegations of prostitution and sent them to the Zambezi Valley to work on agricultural projects as a form of moral re-education. The message of this operation seemed to be that only males could legitimately go about their business in Zimbabwe's urban centres at night, thus perpetuating the colonial view of women as minors who could not be trusted to act responsibly on their own. This created a huge outcry among the women of Zimbabwe and gave birth to the Women's Action Group (WAG) in the same year – an organisation focusing on defending and promoting women's legal and other rights. Other women activist organisations soon followed, among them Women in Law and Development in Africa (WiLDAF), Women and Law in Southern Africa (WLSA), the Zimbabwe Women's Resource Centre and Network (ZWRCN) and the Federation of African Media Women Zimbabwe (FAMWZ).

Meanwhile, to help to fund the economic and infrastructural reconstruction of the country and its development projects, the new government held an international donor conference in Harare in March 1981. Known as the Zimbabwe Conference for Reconstruction and Development (ZIMCORD) Conference, the gathering was attended by delegates from forty-five countries, fifteen UN agencies and ten other international institutions. It pledged Z$1.29 billion, comprising 53 per cent in soft loans and the rest in grants. These impressive achievements

---

[28] Mazingi and Kamhidza, 'Inequality in Zimbabwe'.

were also made possible by the country's booming economy, especially in the first two years of independence, when the economy grew by 21 per cent in real terms, making the Zimbabwean economy the star performer in the region.[29]

Zimbabwe's economic boom at this time was the result of a set of unique circumstances including, inter alia, the removal of sanctions, which opened the country up for foreign investment and also enabled the country to market its products worldwide without the financial burden of sanctions busting of earlier years, and the achievement of peace which allowed the displaced thousands of peasants to return to their homes and resume agriculture. Also, the end of international economic sanctions allowed the country once again to participate freely in the international economy. Returning peasants received considerable government support in the form of agricultural extension services, agricultural inputs and help with the transportation of products to the markets. Good rainfalls combined with this support to produce bumper agricultural harvests in the 1980–81 crop year which had the highest yields on record.[30] Agricultural production, especially in the peasant sector, continued to increase so much thereafter that Zimbabwe was hailed as having achieved an agricultural miracle. For example, peasants and small-scale African farmers increased their production of maize, the staple food crop, from 41,000 tons in 1980–81 to 480,000 tons in 1985–86.[31]

By 1982, however, the country was facing an economic downturn, partly owing to the effects of a severe drought in that year, which incapacitated agriculture, the backbone of the country's economy, and partly because of a world recession which negatively affected the country's exports. Also, government's expenditures in the social sectors and the massive levels of investment in the provision of social services were not matched by increased productivity and income generation. Levels of inflation escalated and balance-of-payments problems worsened. To address this situation, government borrowed from the IMF in 1983 and found itself having to submit to that institution's 'conditionalities' the negative effects of which were such that the government ended the relationship quickly in 1984.[32] Thereafter, economic

[29] R. Riddell, 'Zimbabwe: The Economy Four Years after Independence', *African Affairs*, 83, 333 (October 1984), 463–76.

[30] Riddell, 'Zimbabwe: The Economy Four Years after Independence'.

[31] Rory Pilossof, *The Unbearable Whiteness of Being: Farmers' Voices in Zimbabwe* (Harare; Cape Town: Weaver Press; UCT Press , 2012), 27.

[32] Saunders, 'Economic Structural Adjustment Programme'.

performance improved, with real GDP growth averaging 5.3 per cent from 1985 to 1991.[33] But the South African apartheid regime's sabotage of Zimbabwe's institutions and economy as part of that country's destabilisation policy,[34] the high expenditure of maintaining armed forces in Mozambique to protect the country's oil pipeline and trade routes from the ravages of Mozambique's civil war,[35] and mismanagement and corruption in public enterprises (parastatals)[36] negatively impacted the country's economic performance. The situation was made worse by Zimbabwe's own fratricidal war of the 1980s, which saw government's Korean-trained Fifth Brigade killing an estimated 20,000 people in Matebeleland.[37] Thus, the country found itself confronted with a stagnating per capita income, as population growth outstripped job creation and the country had to contend with 'under and unemployment, [a] depressed state of investment, supply bottlenecks resulting from foreign exchange shortage and general deterioration in the standard of living of the people'.[38]

As Muzondidya has pointed out, 'the gains made in the first decade of independence were limited, unsustainable and ephemerally welfarist in nature,' with a series of challenges, including 'droughts, weakening terms of trade and high interest rates and oil prices', making it difficult for the government to finance all its programmes.[39] In addition, solutions to some old problems created new ones. For instance, the 'massification' of education led to the school system dumping approximately 100,000 school graduates onto the employment market in the late 1980s, when the economy was producing only 10,000 new jobs a year, thus creating a serious problem of a growing cohort of educated unemployed youths.

---

[33] M. Tekere, 'Trade Liberalisation under Structural Economic Adjustment – Impact on Social Welfare in Zimbabwe'. Paper for the Poverty Reduction Forum (PRF) Structural Adjustment Programme Review Initiative (SAPRI), April 2001.

[34] E. Mukonoweshuro, *Zimbabwe: Ten Years of Destabilisation, a Balance Sheet* (Stockholm: Bethany Books, 1992).

[35] N. Mlambo, 'The Costs of Reopening Zimbabwe's Trade Routes Through Mozambique', B.A. Honors dissertation, Department of Economic History, University of Zimbabwe, 1991.

[36] A. S. Mlambo, *The Economic Structural Adjustment Programme: The Case of Zimbabwe* (Harare: University of Zimbabwe Publications, 1997), 50–1.

[37] CCJP, Catholic Commission for Justice and Peace in Zimbabwe/Legal Resources Foundation, *Breaking the Silence*.

[38] G. Kanyenze, 'Trade Liberalisation', *Social Change and Development* (3rd Quarter, 1990), 12–13.

[39] J. Muzondidya, 'From Bouyancy to Crisis 1980 to 1997', in B. Raftopoulos and A. S. Mlambo (eds.), *Becoming Zimbabwe*, 168–9.

Moreover, the gains of the 1980s were uneven, with the new black middle class and white farmers benefitting more than the African majority did, while mounting inflation ate into workers wages as they faced growing challenges of housing and transportation, among others.[40] Generally, the surface appearance of economic transformation belied the lack of any fundamental structural changes in economy where white ownership and control of both land and the manufacturing sector persisted, while 'business participation by blacks in all sectors of the economy stood at only 2%' by 1993.[41]

For a variety of reasons, therefore, the country faced increasing economic challenges as the first independence decade ended. Moreover, it became increasingly clear that the gains made in the 1980s in the social sectors were unsustainable because they were 'based primarily on redistribution rather than growth, and the redistribution was of income rather than assets'.[42] Indeed, as early as 1986, government itself had acknowledged that:

The imbalance between material and non-material production, if continued, could have adverse effects on long-run growth performance of the economy and sustained development. The expansion of social services can only be sustained, in the medium and long term, through overall economic expansion at rates well above those attained in the previous five to six-year period.[43]

In a bid to revamp the economy, government resorted to the IMF/World Bank-sponsored Economic Structural Adjustment Programme (ESAP) in 1990. Government's decision to embrace the reform programme was hurtful to the working people. Despite growing evidence of the deleterious effects of Structural Adjustment Programmes (SAPs) in Latin America and across Africa, government decided to go ahead with the adoption of the austerity programme. The result was 'permanent joblessness, hopelessness and economic insecurity' for the majority and the mortgaging of Zimbabwe's economy to foreign capital.[44]

---

[40] Muzondidya, 'From Bouyancy to Crisis', 170–1.
[41] Muzondidya, 'From Bouyancy to Crisis', 170–1.
[42] Davies, 'Memories of Underdevelopment'.
[43] Government of Zimbabwe, *Zimbabwe: Socio-Economic Review of Zimbabwe, 1980–1985* (Harare: Ministry of Finance, Economic Planning and Development, 1986), 22.
[44] ZCTU, 'Strategy Document for the 1990 Congress', in B. Raftopoulos and Lloyd Sachikonye (eds.), *Striking Back: The Labour Movement and the Post-Colonial State in Zimbabwe, 1980–2000* (Harare: Weaver Press, 2001), 8.

The Economic Reform Era, 1990–2000

In 1990, the Zimbabwean government introduced the Economic Structural Adjustment Programme [ESAP]. The programme started with a trade liberalisation programme followed by the standard Structural Adjustment Programme (SAP) whose targets were spelt out in *Zimbabwe: A Framework for Economic Reform (1991–95)* as:

- reduction of the central government budget deficit to 5 per cent of GDP by 1994–95;
- achieving an annual growth rate of 5 per cent;
- reducing inflation from 20 per cent to 10 per cent by 1994;
- monetary policy and financial sector reform; civil service reform to reduce the number of civil servants by 25 per cent and thus reduce the public wage bill;
- domestic deregulation and investment promotion, to liberalise investment and deregulate prices; and
- protection of the poor and vulnerable groups through the social dimensions of adjustment programme.[45]

The targets were to be achieved through:

- removal of price controls;
- removal of exchange rate controls;
- public-sector reforms;
- privatisation of public enterprises;
- trade liberalisation;
- removal of the foreign currency allocation system; and
- financial sector liberalisation.[46]

The impact of ESAP on Zimbabwean society and economy was deleterious. The inherent weaknesses of the reform package itself,[47] poor implementation by government, and disruptions caused by exogenous factors were further complicated by the record drought of 1992–93. As Saunders points out,

---

[45] Government of Zimbabwe, *Budget Statement, 1991–1996* (Harare: Government Printers, 1990), 1–3.

[46] D. B. Ndhela, 'Zimbabwe's Economy since 1990', in Margaret C. Lee and Karen Colvard (eds.), *Unfinished Business: The Land Crisis in Southern Africa* (Pretoria: Africa Institute of South Africa, 2003), 134–5.

[47] For a detailed analysis and critique of the SAP package, see A. S. Mlambo, *The Economic Structural Adjustment Programme.*

ESAP's launch in the early 1990s hit the business sector and ordinary Zimbabweans very hard, and the impact ... was greatly exacerbated by the severe drought of the early 1990s. In 1992, after two consecutive poor rainy seasons, the economy contracted by at least 7.5%, with all sectors in Zimbabwe's agriculture-based productive sector affected. At the same time, price control relaxation saw inflation explode and consumer demand shrink, by as much as 30%.[48]

Rather than flourishing as expected, the manufacturing sector experienced de-industrialisation instead. Industries were forced either to downsize or to shut down because of the negative economic climate created by the ESAP regime. The textile industry, in particular, faced difficult times owing to the influx of cheap imports. As a result, 'following the introduction of ESAP, the share of the textiles sub-sector in manufacturing output declined from 11.3% in 1985 to 7.9% by 1995', while the 'share of the manufacturing sector in GDP declined from a high of 27% in 1992 to 19.2% by 1995'. According to Kanyenze,

The index of the volume of production for the textiles sub-sector plunged from 100 in 1990 to 59.3 by 1995 (due mainly to trade liberalisation).... The index for the clothing and footwear sub-sector fell from 100 in 1990 to 82.9 by 1995.... The manufacturing sector dropped from an index of 100 in 1990 to 96 by 1995. This indicates that the manufacturing sector suffered de-industrialisation following the liberalisation of trade since 1991, while the textiles sub-sector was the worst affected.[49]

In October 1994, for instance, it was reported that 87 out of the 280 companies in the textile sector in 1990 had closed down, while in the clothing sector 60 companies closed down between 1992 and 1994.[50] Unemployment escalated so that by 1992, about 25,000 employees had been retrenched. Nearly 300,000 school leavers were being thrown into the labour market annually at a time when only 10,000 or so jobs were being created and unemployment was high.

Some positive outcomes notwithstanding,[51] on the whole, ESAP failed to realise most of its targets and to increase economic growth and reduce

---

[48] Saunders, 'Zimbabwe: ESAP's Fables II'.

[49] G. Kanyenze, 'The Textile and Clothing Industry in Zimbabwe', in Herbert Jauch and Rudolph Traub (eds.), *The Future of the Textile and Clothing Industry in Sub-Saharan Africa* (Bonn: Friedrich-Ebert-Stiftung, 2006), 8. See also M. Tekere, 'Trade Liberalisation', 10.

[50] Reserve Bank of Zimbabwe, *Quarterly Economic and Statistical* Review, vol. 3, No. 6 (March 1994); vol. 3, No. 12 (December, 1994), 7–8.

[51] Such as the evident efficiency of some privatised parastatals like Dairibord Zimbabwe Limited, Cotton Company of Zimbabwe Limited, and the Commercial Bank of Zimbabwe and the emergence of several black-owned banks because of financial reforms

poverty. In fact, both the economy and the majority of the people of Zimbabwe were worse off at the end of the reform programme than they had been before it, as living standards were eroded through retrenchments and decline in per capita income. In the words of R. Saunders, whereas ESAP was 'meant to herald a new era of modernised, competitive, export-led industrialisation', the reality was that Zimbabwe's high-performing economy of the 1980s was so damaged by the reform programme that, after five years of ESAP reforms, the country found itself 'firmly lodged in a quagmire of mounting debt and erratic growth'.[52]

The burden of the now non-performing economy fell on the poor. For instance, studies of Kambuzuma, Tafara and Dzivaresekwa, Harare suburbs in the 1990s, revealed that many families were being forced by circumstances to reduce their food intake because their wages could not stretch far enough in the light of mounting inflation and escalating living costs.[53] By 1995, a Government of Zimbabwe Poverty Assessment Study was reporting that 62 per cent of the population were living below the Poverty Datum Line,[54] while in 1996 the Zimbabwe Congress of Trade Unions estimated that workers were 38 per cent poorer than in 1980.[55]

Public expenditure on health care declined by 39 per cent in 1994–95, while per capita annual spending declined from $58 in 1990–91 to $36 in 1995–96,[56] leading to what came to be known as 'ESAP deaths.' These were deaths of low-income people who could not afford to pay for treatment or for medicines because of cost recovery policies under ESAP. Even more significant was the fact that the country's rural clinics, which serviced approximately 80 per cent of the population, were receiving a dwindling portion of the country's public health budget, amounting to

undertaken under the programme and the reduction of the public wage bill through public service reforms. See Dan B. Ndhela, 'The Zimbabwean Economy since 1990', 136–7.
[52] Saunders, 'Zimbabwe: ESAP's Fables II'.
[53] P. Balleis, 'The Social Costs of ESAP in Zimbabwe and the Ethical Dimension of a Free-Market Based Economy', in Konrad-Adeneur-Stiftung and SAFER, *On the Road to a Market-Based Economy*, conference held in Harare, Zimbabwe, 3–5 November 1992; N. Matshalaga, *The Gender Dimensions of Urban Poverty: The Case of Dzivaresekwa* (Harare: Institute of Development Studies, 1993); N. Matshalaga, *The Gender Dimensions of Urban Poverty: The Case of Tafara* (Harare: Institute of Development Studies, 1993).
[54] Ministry of Public Service, Labour and Social Welfare, *1995 Poverty Assessment Study Survey Preliminary Report* (April 1996), 23.
[55] Zimbabwe Congress of Trade Unions, *Study of the Informal Sector in Zimbabwe* (Harare: ZCTU, 1993), 14.
[56] Saunders, 'Economic Structural Adjustment Programme'.

only 49 per cent in 1996.[57] Not surprisingly, the public health sector stagnated and even declined in some aspects, while there was a marked expansion of the private health sector which provided services that were largely unaffordable to the poor majority. The rapid liberalisation of the health sector in the 1990s opened the door to private capital to increase its share of the domestic market at a time of government cuts in public expenditure and fee payment for medical services, both of which initiated a process of decline in the public health sector that was eventually to result in the reversal of earlier gains of the 1980s, as 'the cost of both public and private health care soared, undermining access'[58]

Under the ESAP regime, government priorities in health provision shifted from the earlier people-oriented and egalitarian approach enunciated in 1984 to a more market-driven and liberalisation-based strategy. Thus, whereas the earlier policy position emphasised the need to redirect resources to the most needy, ending the inherited colonial rural/urban racial bias, greater accessibility for the poor majority and greater emphasis on preventive rather than curative medicine, the policy of the 1990s spoke a different language. Now the language was of decentralisation of health provision, outsourcing and privatisation, and the need to increase the role of the private sector in health provision.[59]

In education, most of the gains the country had made in the 1980s were under threat during ESAP. Cost recovery policies led to children dropping out of school because parents could not afford the school fees they were now required to pay. With the Education Act 1991, government introduced fees at primary school level, reversing the policy of free compulsory primary education introduced in 1987. The result was that some parents withdrew their children from school, while others withdrew only their female children when a choice had to be made between educating either boys or girls at a time of scarce resources. Traditional prejudices against educating girls were revived so that all the advances that had been made in promoting gender equality in education access were eroded. This was despite the fact that government established the National Plan of Action (NPA) for the 1994–96 period whose objectives included 'narrowing gender disparities in education, with particular reference to basic education' and 'provision of universal quality primary education by the year

---

[57] C. Thompson, 'Globalizing Land and Food in Zimbabwe: Implications for Southern Africa', *African Studies Quarterly*, 7, 2–3 (Fall 2003), 6.

[58] E. Munyuki and S. Jasi, 'Capital Flows in the Health Care Sector in Zimbabwe: Trends and Implications for the Health System', 4.

[59] GOZ, 'National Health Strategy (1997–2007).

2000'.[60] The school dropout rate increased even more when many parents lost their jobs as a result of ESAP-induced retrenchments. Reflecting the growing ESAP-induced hardships, the country experienced its first anti-IMF riots in reaction to a 30 per cent increase in bread prices in 1993, resulting in running street battles between the police and the people in the High Density Areas (former Townships).

With de-industrialisation and the shrinking economy came unemployment and the informalisation of the economy, as more and more workers lost their jobs in the formal economy and did whatever they could in the informal sector to survive. Informal economic activities had existed even under the harsh legislation and enforcement regime of the colonial regime. These included tin-smithing, *shebeens*[61] and tailoring which provided employment for segments of the urban population. After 1980, with the relaxation of legal controls over the urban African population, the informal sector expanded, with municipal authorities often encouraging such activities by setting up peoples' markets for the sale of vegetables, crafts and other items and designating home industry sites, where, in return for a small municipal levy, the self-employed could produce and sell their wares.

Because of ESAP, the informal economy came into its own in Zimbabwe in the 1990s. 'Back-yard industries' sprouted everywhere and more and more workers found their livelihood in this sector so that in the 1999–2000 fiscal year, the informal economy in Zimbabwe was estimated to be 59.4 per cent of GDP, the highest in Africa, whose average then was 42 per cent of GDP, and exceeded only by the transitional economy of Georgia at 67.3 per cent.[62] In November 2000, the Zimbabwe Confederation of Zimbabwean Industries (CZI) reported that approximately 1.7 million people were being supported by the informal sector.[63] By 2004, when unemployment was estimated at 70 per cent, the informal economy was providing approximately 40 per cent of the country's employment.[64]

[60] UNESCO, *Country Basic Information* (August 2006),
[61] Informal liquor-drinking places or, in American parlance of the 1920s, speakeasies.
[62] World Bank, 'The Informal Economy: Large and Growing in Most Developing Countries' (Moderated by Simeon Djankov), Online Discussions, Archived June 2003, cited in Sarbajit Chaudhuri and Ujjaini Mukhopadyay, *Revisiting the Informal Sector: A General Equilibrium Approach* (London: Springer, 2010), 228.
[63] *Financial Gazette*, Harare, Zimbabwe, 12 June 2002.
[64] A. K. Tibaijuka, *Report of the Fact-Finding Mission to Zimbabwe to Assess the Scope and Impact of Operation Murambatsvina by the UN Special Envoy on Human Settlements Issues in Zimbabwe* (New York: UNHCS-Habitat, 2005), 24. [Hereafter The Tibaijuka Report]

Compounding the country's economic problems in the late 1990s were two fateful government decisions. The first was the decision in November 1997 to award a lump sum of ZW$50,000 each to some 70,000 veterans of the liberation struggle in response to growing complaints by this pressure group about being neglected and sidelined. The impact on the economy was disastrous, as investor confidence was dented and the Zimbabwean currency crashed on November 14 of the same year. The second bad step was to deploy Zimbabwean soldiers into the Democratic Republic of the Congo (DRC) in August 1998 to defend the Laurent Kabila regime that was under attack from various rebel groups. Like the decision to pay large gratuities to war veterans, the decision to send soldiers into the Congo had not been budgeted for. The strain on the economy was evident in the country's slow economic growth, rising unemployment and declining living standards. The 1997 *Poverty Assessment Study Survey* revealed that 74 per cent (as compared to 65 per cent four years earlier) of Zimbabweans were poor and 45 per cent of Zimbabwean households were living below the food poverty line.[65] Not surprisingly, workers' unrest increased, with most sectors, including security companies, restaurants, hotels, banks, construction firms, cement companies and textile industries, experiencing workers strikes for better wages in 1997. Out of this workers' discontent and public unhappiness at the deteriorating standards of living emerged the opposition political party, the Movement for Democratic Change (MDC), in 1999, spearheaded by the Zimbabwe Congress of Trade Unions (ZCTU) and other groups.[66]

In an attempt to improve the deteriorating economy, government introduced a new austerity programme, the Zimbabwe Programme for Economic and Social Transformation (ZIMPREST), which sought to promote economic growth, job creation and good governance.[67] Like ESAP before it, however, ZIMPREST failed to deliver on all its targets.

Land

As noted earlier, one of the strongest motivations for African nationalists taking up arms was to win back the land that had been expropriated

---

[65] Ministry of Public Service, Labour and Social Welfare, *Poverty Assessment Study Survey: Main Report*, Social Dimension Fund (Harare: Government of Zimbabwe, 1997).

[66] B. Raftopoulos, 'The Labour Movement and the Emergence of Opposition Politics in Zimbabwe' in Brian Raftopoulos and Lloyd Sachikonye (eds.), *Striking Back*, 1–24.

[67] O. Sichone, 'Zimbabwe's Economic Policies 1980 to 2002', *DPMN Bulletin*, 10, 2 (April, 2005), online at http://www.dpmf.org/images/zimbabwe-economic-policy-sichone.html (accessed November 20, 2013).

by the colonial settlers. Because of this, independence was warmly welcomed as marking what the Africans hoped would be the beginning of a process to reverse the inequalities of the past and of restoring land to its rightful owners, namely the African people. Indeed, as indicated earlier, the Lancaster House negotiations of 1979 nearly foundered over disagreements on the way in which the land question would be dealt with and were only saved when the British indicated that they would mobilise resources to enable the independence government to acquire land for redistribution to the land-hungry African majority. At independence in 1980, 6,000 white farmers occupied 15.5 million hectares of land, while millions of Africans remained jammed in the Reserves, now euphemistically renamed Communal Areas (CAs).[68]

Moreover, while the African areas had no transport infrastructure and other services to talk about, the Large Scale Commercial Farming (LCSF) sector was well supported by the state. In the words of the Rukuni Land Commission established to investigate Zimbabwe's land ownership structure and usage soon after independence,

The LSCF are well served with physical and marketing infrastructure. Good roads and railway lines link large scale commercial farming to marketing outlets. This investment has been a result of colonial policies which favoured the development of this sector at the exclusion of other sectors which were occupied by black farmers.[69]

In view of this skewed ownership of land, the African majority hailed independence as the beginning of the process of redressing the inequities of the past and of restoring land to the African people.

The people's raised expectations over the possibilities of regaining alienated land were, unfortunately, not fulfilled, mostly because of the provisions of the Lancaster House Agreement of 1979 which had ended the fratricidal conflict in the country and ushered in Zimbabwe's independence in 1980. A number of reasons account for this, including the restrictions imposed by the Lancaster House Agreement on postcolonial land reform, the half-hearted way in which the Zimbabwe government addressed the land reform issue, and the resistance to land reform by white farmers. Under the provisions of the Lancaster House

---

[68] C. Palmer, 'Land Reform in Zimbabwe, 1980–1990', *African Affairs*, 89 (1990), 163–81; Zimbabwe, *Report of the Commission of Enquiry into Appropriate Agricultural Land Tenure Systems* (Rukuni Commission) (Harare: Government Printer, 1991) [Hereafter Rukuni Commission Report].

[69] Rukuni Commission Report, 94.

Constitution, the postcolonial government could only acquire land from white farmers for redistribution to the land-hungry African majority on the basis of the 'willing buyer, willing seller' principle, provided the government paid for such land at market prices and in foreign currency. This meant that if a farmer was not willing to sell his land or the government did not have the requisite foreign currency to pay the farmer at going market prices, the government had no other legal way of acquiring land for redistribution regardless of the clamour for such land from the African majority. This clearly ruled out any radical land reform and, thus, achieved what it was meant to achieve, namely 'protect the interests of the settlers ... by ensuring that their privileges in land ownership would not be abrogated unilaterally by the majority government', at least until 1990.[70]

Indeed, evidence suggests that commercial farmers offered mostly marginal land to government. It was reported, for instance, that by the end of the 1980s,

[o]ver 70% of land acquired for resettlement through the market has been agro-ecologically marginal and located mainly in the drier, more climatically erratic, southern regions of the country. The bulk of prime land in the three Mashonaland provinces (covering the central highlands) has largely been untouched. The land offered to the state has been geographically scattered, and thus moving settlers from communal areas to isolated farms in small groups was both expensive and logistically inefficient.[71]

Because they were conscious of being protected under the Lancaster House Constitution, most white farmers were not keen to give up the privileges they had enjoyed in the colonial period, including the monopoly of land. They were still rooted in what scholars have described as the 'settler culture', namely 'the great power exerted by settlers, their virtual monopoly over political and legal institutions, their coercive control over the labour and livelihoods of Africans, their manipulative methods for advancing the economic interests of themselves'.[72] Consequently, they neither tried very hard to be active participants in the postcolonial transformation process

---

[70] G. Mhone, 'Zimbabwe: A Country Overview', presented to the LEAD International Conference on Leadership for Environment and Development, Zimbabwe Session – Cohort 4, 21 April to May 1997.

[71] T. Lebert, 'An Introduction to Land and Agrarian Reform in Zimbabwe', at http://www.nlc.co.za/pubs2003/anintoto.pdf (accessed 5 August 2012).

[72] D. Kennedy, *Islands of White: Settler Society and Culture in Kenya and Southern Rhodesia, 1890 – 1939* (Durham, NC: Duke University Press, 1987), cited in Muzondidya, 'From Bouyancy to Crisis', 172.

nor demonstrated any inclination to reduce their 'pre-independence privi-leges' which most regarded as 'absolutely normal'.[73]

Indeed, this 'conundrum of race' remained unresolved in the imme-diate postcolonial period, creating a potentially explosive situation in the future. Commenting on this phenomenon, James Muzondidya has observed how a racial chasm existed in schools, sports and residences, with some whites responding to the entry of blacks into previously white-only residential suburbs by retreating into the safety of the exclusive sports club or home entertainment or by relocating to more expensive and exclusive suburbs. He adds:

In the educational sector, some white parents responded to the government's de-racialization of education and the admission of blacks into formerly white-only (Group A) schools by building new, independent schools whose fee structures were designed to exclude the majority of children from middle and low-income black families. Lack of social integration was similarly experienced in sport, espe-cially in the formerly white codes of rugby and cricket, where issues of transfor-mation continued to be a problem through to 2000 and beyond.[74]

As will become apparent later, the decision by Zimbabwean whites to with-draw into 'racial enclaves' and to distance themselves from the process of nation building and/or political participation was to make them easy tar-gets of charges of racism when, in 2000, a beleaguered ZANU-PF govern-ment needed scapegoats in order to bolster its waning popular support in the face of rising internal political opposition. This was more so because of the white community's evident affluence many years after independence.

Lack of sufficient funding also hampered meaningful land reform. As noted, the Lancaster House negotiations were only saved from collapse when Britain promised to provide adequate financial resources to enable the postcolonial government to acquire land for redistribution. In the event, the British only partially fulfilled their promise, providing some £44 million for the purpose but suspending the support thereafter over allegations of fiscal mismanagement and implementation delays.[75] It has been argued that more generous funding from the British government in

---

[73] L. Huyse, 'Zimbabwe: Why Reconciliation Failed', in D. Bloomfield et al. (eds.), *Reconciliation after Violent Conflict: A Handbook* (Stockholm: International Institute for Democracy and Electoral Assistance, 2003), 34–9.

[74] J. Muzondidya, 'The Zimbabwean Crisis and the Unresolved Conundrum of Race in the Post-Colonial Period', *Journal of Developing Societies*, 26, 1 (2010), 5–38.

[75] British High Commission, 'Britain in Zimbabwe: Background Briefing, March 2000', at http://www.britishembassy.gov.uk (accessed 15 August 2012).

line with its promise at Lancaster House would have led to greater success in land redistribution and averted future problems over land ownership. In one view,

[t]he 1979 Lancaster House agreement ... ensured that the Zimbabwean government could not use local currency only to buy land from farmers who were willing to sell. If it were to expropriate their property, it would have to compensate them with scarce and precious foreign exchange. The agreement bound the country to a programme of land reform whose implementation would have cost billions. Having hinted that we [the British] would pay for it, our government handed over only a fraction of the money required – £44 million – to make it happen. Had a sterner settlement been struck, or had Britain been more generous, there might not have been a land distribution problem. Our meanness, compounded perhaps by an unwillingness to undermine the white economic hegemony, perpetuated Zimbabwe's racial segregation.[76]

Meanwhile, the Zimbabwean government itself did not push the land reform programme as vigorously as it might have, content to make noises about the need for land reform during periodic general election campaigns but allowing the matter to lapse thereafter. Thus, despite the ruling party's rhetoric on the need to redress past land distribution inequities, not much was done to push for more radical land reform, giving substance to the reported claim by one white commercial farmer in the early 1980s that Mugabe's government was 'the best government for farmers that this country has seen'.[77] Not surprisingly, commercial farmers were doing extremely well in the first decade of independence, with crop sales from commercial farms increasing in value from Z$350 million (US$580 million) in 1980 to Z$1.65 billion (US$1.155 billion) at the end of the decade.[78]

Government's 'appeasement'[79] policy towards the farmers was mainly because government was reluctant to tamper with this very vibrant sector which was the backbone of the national economy, for, as Palmer observes, at the time, white commercial farmers were 'producing 90% of the country's marketed food requirements'.[80] The slow pace of land redistribution led to illegal farm invasions in the early 1980s by peasants who were

[76] G. Moinbot, 'We Share the Blame on Zimbabwe', *Guardian Unlimited* (UK), 20 April 2002.
[77] Palmer, 'Land Reform in Zimbabwe, 1980–1990', 163–81.
[78] Pilossof, *The Unbearable Whiteness of Being*, 27.
[79] Term borrowed from Pilossof, *The Unbearable Whiteness of Being*, 28.
[80] Palmer, 'Land Reform in Zimbabwe, 1980–1990'.

increasingly impatient of government inaction. Government responded by forcibly evicting the 'squatters' in defence of the status quo. Indeed, the then-Minister of Lands castigated the squatters, describing them as 'undisciplined and criminal elements' bent on disrupting the country's agricultural economy.[81] Because of these and other constraints, government was not able to meet its resettlement targets. Government's targets changed several times since independence, originally set in 1980 at 18,000 households over a five-year period and then increased in 1981 to 54,000 households and to 162,000 households in 1982. By June 1989, the government had settled only 52,000 families, out of the targeted 162,000 families.[82] This represented only 32 per cent of the original 1982 target. By the same date, only 2,713,725 hectares had been bought for resettlement, representing about 16 per cent of the area owned by the white commercial farmers at independence.[83]

After the lapse of the Lancaster House restrictions on land reform, the government enacted the 1992 Land Acquisition Act, removing the 'willing seller, willing buyer' clause and enabling government to acquire land for redistribution compulsorily in return for fair compensation. Land reform remained painfully slow, however, because of persistent resistance from white farmers[84] and the pressure brought to bear on the Zimbabwean government by international donors and Western governments at a time when it was highly dependent on them for support in the context of the debilitating Economic Structural Programme (ESAP) that Zimbabwe had begun to implement in 1990. By the end of the 1990s, two decades after the end of a war fought mainly over land, landholding patterns still remained highly skewed in favour of the minority white farming population, with 4,500 mainly white large-scale farmers continuing to monopolise the country's productive land.

Government's attempts to raise donor funding for land reform in the 1990s, including through hosting a donor's conference in 1998, failed. The Zimbabwean government was upset when the British government appeared to renege on its earlier responsibility to fund land reform in Zimbabwe, as the British Secretary of State for International Development in the New Labour government, Clare Short, wrote to the

---

[81] Cited in Pilossof, *The Unbearable Whiteness of Being*, 28.
[82] Palmer, 'Land Reform in Zimbabwe, 1980–1990'.
[83] Palmer, 'Land Reform in Zimbabwe, 1980–1990'.
[84] White farmers objected to the compulsory acquisition of 1,393 out of 1,471 farms designated by the government, of which 510 were upheld by the courts.

Zimbabwean Minister of Agriculture and Lands, Kumbirai Kangai, on 5
November 1997:

I should make it clear that we do not accept that Britain has a special responsibility to meet the costs of land purchase in Zimbabwe. We are a new Government
from diverse backgrounds without links to former colonial interests. My own
origins are Irish and, as you know, we were colonized not colonizers.[85]

By the end of the decade, therefore, the land issue remained unresolved,
creating an unhealthy climate which the ruling party could exploit to
whip up people's emotions in its favour should it ever face a serious challenge to its dominance, as did happen in 2000.

As has been shown, farm invasions in Zimbabwe that started in
February 2000 and marked the beginning of the fast-track land reform
programme, otherwise known as the Third Chimurenga,[86] came at the
tail end of a history of conflict and tension between whites and Africans
over land ownership. From the forcible expropriation of African land at
the turn of the twentieth century, through the years of the bitter armed
liberation struggle as Africans fought, among other things, to regain the
land, to the Lancaster House provisions and beyond, the land question
remained a central part of the country's political landscape and always
had the potential to cause conflict as long as it remained unresolved.

Zimbabwe's International Relations, 1980–2000

Zimbabwe's foreign policy after independence was influenced by a number of key geopolitical and economic considerations, including the need
for pragmatism with regard to apartheid South Africa next door in a context in which it had to maintain solidarity with the anti-apartheid struggle movements in its capacity as a member of the FLS and the SADCC,
later the Southern African Development community (SADC); the OAU;
and the Non-Aligned Movement (NAM), among other organisations.
With regard to the thorny problem of South Africa, Zimbabwe pursued
a pragmatic foreign policy approach in which it continued its trade and

---

[85] Letter from Clare Short to Hon. Kumbirai Kangai, MP, Minister of Agriculture and Land,
5 November 1997, reproduced in full in *New African*, February 2003. According to one
source, 'This letter was reportedly very badly received by the Zimbabwean government,
and apparently continues to be a source of discontent in the administration of President
Robert Mugabe.'

[86] This was regarded as the third in a series of struggles starting with the 1896 uprising,
followed by the armed struggle of the 1960s and beyond, both of which were mainly
political, while the current struggle focused on achieving economic freedom.

diplomatic relations with the country and avoided having its territory used for military attacks on its neighbour for both economic and security reasons, while publicly condemning the apartheid system and systematically calling for international sanctions against the South African regime. Its position was dictated by Zimbabwe's heavy economic dependence on South Africa, one of its major trading partners and an important international trade gateway. In addition, the military might of South Africa was such that the newly independent Zimbabwe could not afford to antagonise it to the extent of attracting military reprisals that would have devastated the country. Nevertheless, Zimbabwe consistently 'strongly argued against apartheid and frequently called for the imposition of economic sanctions against Pretoria' and provided moral support to the Namibian and South African liberation movements.[87]

Despite this caution on the part of the Zimbabwean government, South Africa did make efforts to destabilise Zimbabwe, most notably through support for the Super-ZAPU dissidents who went on a sabotage and guerrilla campaign in Matebeleland in the early 1980s and provoked the Zimbabwean government's Gukurahundi massacres. South Africa's policy of destabilisation was not limited only to Zimbabwe. At the time, a South African destabilisation campaign was mounted in Angola where South African Defence Forces supported Jonas Savimbi's UNITA and in Mozambique through its support of the National Resistance Movement (RENAMO) guerrillas led by Afonso Dhlakama, both of which were fighting against their national governments. The main purpose of South African destabilisation was to keep neighbouring black-ruled countries unstable so that they could not render meaningful support to anti-apartheid liberation movements, as well as to demonstrate to the South African black population that black rule did not work.

Also as part of the pragmatic approach to regional foreign policy, Zimbabwe became a member of the FLS at its independence in 1980, joining Tanzania, Zambia, Mozambique, Botswana and Angola as countries on the front line of the struggle against white rule and apartheid racism. The countries which it joined in 1980 had played a very supportive role in Zimbabwe's own struggle for independence by providing both logistical and moral support. Zimbabwe was, thus, duty-bound to do the same for the liberation movements of South Africa but, as noted, had

---

[87] Terrence M. Mashingaidze, 'The Zimbabwean Entrapment: An Analysis of the Nexus between Domestic and Foreign Policies in a "Collapsing" Militant State, 1990s–2006', *Alternatives*, 4 (Winter 2006), 57–76.

to be careful not to jeopardise its own economic and security interests by being too confrontational towards its neighbour. In this it followed the example of Botswana which also publicly condemned apartheid and gave support to the liberation movements while denying the movements usage of its soil for launching military attacks on South Africa. Perhaps even more so than Zimbabwe, Botswana was heavily dependent on South Africa economically – a factor that played a critical role in shaping Botswana's foreign policy towards its larger and more powerful southern neighbour.

The FLS established the SADCC in 1980. Zimbabwe became a member of the organisation. The organisation's main purpose was to lessen member countries' economic dependence on South Africa by promoting trade among themselves and sourcing foreign investment elsewhere. They were unhappy about their economic dependence on the apartheid regime to which they were so much opposed. There were, of course, many contradictions in the SADCC (later SADC) project, especially given the fact that the economies of the hostage states of Swaziland, Lesotho and, to an extent, Botswana were so intertwined with that of South Africa that it was not feasible to talk of any separation or economic independence of these states. Moreover, they all belonged to the South African Customs Union (SACU) that was administered by South Africa and from which they derived much revenue that they could not do without.

Soon after independence, Zimbabwe also became a member of NAM. This was a group of countries established at the Conference of Heads of State or Government of Non-Aligned Countries held in Belgrade, Yugoslavia, in 1961 where presidents Tito of Yugoslavia, Sukarno of Indonesia, Nasser of Egypt, Nkrumah of Ghana and Prime Minister Nehru of India took the lead in pushing for its formation. It grew to include almost all developing and socialist countries, or two-thirds of the members of the United Nations. The organisation pledged not to align itself with either of the two blocs in the Cold War. Its guiding five principles were:

- mutual respect for each other's territorial integrity and sovereignty;
- mutual non-aggression;
- mutual non-interference in domestic affairs;
- equality and mutual benefit; and
- peaceful coexistence.

The 1970 Lusaka NAM Conference added the aims of the peaceful resolution of disputes, abstaining from big-power military alliances and pacts, and opposing the stationing of military bases in foreign countries to the list. In 1986, Zimbabwe hosted the NAM Conference in Harare, and President Mugabe assumed chairmanship of the organisation at that meeting. Zimbabwe was also a member the Preferential Trade Area (PTA) – a regional economic organisation designed to promote regional trade. In addition to these international solidarity organisations, Zimbabwe also played its part in the United Nations, including participating in international peacekeeping efforts by sending its soldiers to Angola, Kosovo and Somalia, among other troubled countries. Zimbabwe also hosted the 1991 Commonwealth Heads of Government meeting (CHOGM) which adopted the Harare Declaration on good governance.

Zimbabwe was also a member of the OAU, first established in Addis Ababa in 1963 to promote pan-African solidarity and the liberation of the entire continent, among other objectives. Through its membership in the OAU and the UN, Zimbabwe played its role in helping to find resolutions to conflicts on the African continent, including in Mozambique where the FRELIMO government was under attack from RENAMO fighters. Zimbabwe deployed its military forces into Mozambique to protect the railway line linking it to the Indian Ocean from attacks by RENAMO until the end of the Mozambican civil war in the early 1990s. In summary, therefore,

[s]oon after independence in 1980, Harare quickly became Southern Africa's diplomatic hub and a key player in the Frontline States` efforts to dismantle apartheid and colonialism in Southern Africa. Zimbabwe adopted a policy of non-alignment in international affairs and its foreign policy trajectory was governed by sanctity of the right to life, self-determination, defense of national sovereignty, anti-imperialism, equality of sovereign states, and non-interference in the internal affairs of other states. Zimbabwe adhered to the positions of the Southern African Development Community, the Non-Aligned Movement (NAM), the Organization of African Unity (OAU), and the Commonwealth.[88]

With the end of apartheid in South Africa in 1994, the regional geopolitical circumstances changed, requiring appropriate adjustments in Zimbabwe's foreign policy. South Africa became a member of the OAU, SADCC and other regional organisations and, indeed, soon became dominant in them as the most powerful economy in the region and on the continent. In 2002, a new organisation, the African Union, replaced the OAU, with South Africa playing a central role both in its establishment and running. Two years before the democratic transition in South Africa,

[88] Mashingaidze, 'The Zimbabwean Entrapment'.

SADCC had been transformed into SADC, with the newly independent
Namibia as an additional member to the original SADCC line-up. SADC
was intended to promote socio-economic, political and security cooperation. With the end of apartheid, South Africa became a member of SADC.
With these political changes in the region, Zimbabwe's policy towards
South Africa also changed, as South Africa took over the region's leadership which Zimbabwe had enjoyed since the 1980s.

The most notable foreign policy issue in the 1990s for Zimbabwe was
its military intervention in the war in the Democratic Republic of the
Congo (DRC). What became known as the Second Congo War or the
Great War of Africa begun in August 1998 and lasted until July 2003.
Arguably the deadliest war in African history, the war involved eight
African nations and led to the deaths of millions of people. In the face of
mounting attacks on his government by Ugandan and Rwandan-backed
rebel groups, the DRC President Laurent Kabila appealed to SADC for
military assistance to save his government. Only three SADC countries –
Angola, Namibia and Zimbabwe – responded positively to this appeal.
Amidst great controversy at home about Zimbabwe's involvement in this
far-away war, the Zimbabwean government had sent in approximately
11,000 soldiers by the end of the conflict and had succeeded in saving
the Kabila regime.

In the wake of Zimbabwe's controversial land invasions of the early
2000s and the allegations of human rights abuses, Zimbabwe's relations
with the Western world became strained, as these governments imposed
travel and other restrictions on members of Zimbabwe's ruling elite. In
response, the Zimbabwe government cultivated stronger relations with
China as part of the 'Look East' policy propounded by President Mugabe.
This policy was based on the fact that China had supported ZANU-PF
during the anti-colonial struggle and had provided both military training and logistical support to its fighting arm, ZANLA. Because of these
long-established relations, the Zimbabwean government turned to China
when its links with the Western powers became stressed.

9

The Crisis Years, 2000–2008

Introduction

The first decade of the new millennium found Zimbabwe in the throes of a severe political, economic and social crisis that reversed the gains and achievements of the 1980s and deepened the problems and challenges facing the majority population, which had begun in the 1990s with ESAP. The crisis also turned the country into a pariah state, as human rights violations and political intolerance led to worldwide condemnations of the country's ruling elite, and a chaotic land reform programme turned the region's erstwhile breadbasket into a land dependent on food aid. This chapter examines the factors that led to the Zimbabwean crisis and its sociopolitical and economic manifestations throughout the first decade of the twenty-first century. It also analyses regional and international responses to the crisis, with a special focus on the SADC and the Western world.

Politics

The year 2000 marked the beginning of a turbulent time in Zimbabwean politics, one characterised by mounting political opposition to ZANU-PF rule and by increasing political repression of opposition forces, particularly the MDC which presented the strongest challenge to the ruling party. It witnessed a referendum, three controversial elections and growing use of violence and abuse of human rights by ZANU-PF structures. The decade ended with the formation of a Government of National Unity following the intervention of SADC, the regional organisation, first under the auspices of South African President Thabo Mbeki and then his successor, Jacob Zuma.

As noted, the deteriorating economic conditions and growing political discontent articulated by the various civic organisations in the late 1990s and the increasing desire for a new political dispensation led to the establishment of the Movement for Democratic Change (MDC) in 1999. Although led by the labour movement through the Zimbabwe Congress of Trade Unions (ZCTU), the MDC was more than a workers' organisation. It was a broad front of interest groups and organisations which included such disparate social classes as industrial and farm workers, business people, the intelligentsia and other groups of the country's middle class, students and commercial farmers, each of which had specific grievances against the prevailing dispensation and wanted a change of political leadership and culture. The potential weakness of this opposition movement was precisely the fact that is was such a broad church that accommodated unlikely allies such as farm workers and farm owners who had little to unite them except their determination to dislodge ZANU-PF rule, as well as its heavy dependence on funding by external donors, local businesses and commercial farmers, opening itself to charges that it was no more than a puppet organisation pandering to the whims of white and international neo-liberal interests.[1]

The birth of the MDC dates from February 1999 when the ZCTU held a meeting of more than 350 delegates from its structures and from other civic organisations across the country at a National Working People's Convention (NWPC) to discuss possible solutions to the country's economic challenges. The NWPC resolved, among other things, to unify the working people in a struggle to tackle such challenges. It also decried:

- the disempowerment of the people and breach of the rule of law through state-sponsored violence and abuse of human rights;
- the inability of the economy to address the basic needs of the majority of Zimbabweans;
- the severe decline in incomes, employment, health, food security and well-being of people;
- the unfair burden borne by working women and the persistence of gender discrimination;
- the decline and, in some cases, collapse of public services;

[1] Lloyd Sachikonye, 'Between Authoritarianism and Democracy', 112.

- the lack of progress in resolving land hunger and rural investment needs;
- the weak growth in industry and marginalisation of the vast majority of the nation's entrepreneurs; the absence of a national constitution framed by and for the people;
- the persistence of regionalism, racism, and other divisions undermining national integration; and
- widespread corruption and lack of public accountability in political and economic institutions.[2]

The NWPC recommended the establishment of a 'strong, democratic, popularly driven and organized movement of the people' to resolve the challenges facing the country. As a result, the MDC was born as

a united front of Zimbabweans representing various interests and constituent organisations coming together to pursue common objectives and principles that advance the interests of all people in Zimbabwe (workers, professionals, women, peasants, the disabled and the unemployed).

Its founders declared that the MDC would stand for 'social democratic, human centred development policies, pursued in an environment of political pluralism, participatory democracy, accountable and transparent governance' as well as non-racialism and non-sexism. The MDC was officially launched on 11 September 1999, under the leadership of Morgan Tsvangirai.[3]

The first major clash between the political opposition forces and the government was over a new constitution for the country. At its formation, the MDC had demanded 'a real people's constitution, written in a democratic, broad-based and participatory process involving all stakeholders, and accountable to a conference of elected representatives, civil and other social groups'. To this end, an organisation called the National Constitutional Assembly (NCA), a broad-based movement including civil society, human rights groups, churches and other groups, was established to push for a people-driven constitution. Responding to growing pressure for a new constitution from the NCA coalition, the government hijacked the project and proposed a constitution that included, among others,

[2] 'Prime Minister of Zimbabwe Morgan Richard Tsvangirai' at http://www.zimbabweprimeminister.org/index.php?option=com_content&view=article&id=43&Itemid=80 (accessed 26 October 2012).
[3] 'Prime Minister of Zimbabwe Morgan Richard Tsvangirai' at http://www.zimbabweprimeminister.org/index.php?option=com_content&view=article&id=43&Itemid=80 (accessed 26 October 2012).

provisions to increase presidential powers and to allow the government to confiscate white-owned land without compensation. The nation was invited to decide on the proposed constitution through a referendum in February 2000. The government suffered a humiliating blow when the people resoundingly rejected the constitutional draft following a well-orchestrated campaign by the MDC for its rejection. Then, in the general elections of June of the same year, the MDC unexpectedly won 57 of the 120 contested seats, sweeping most urban centres and sending shock-waves through the ruling party.

The MDC had achieved this result despite the ruling party's deployment of some liberation war veterans to prevent the opposition from campaigning in the rural areas by intimidating the rural population and virtually making most parts of the country 'no go areas' for MDC candidates. It was reported, for instance, that

[t]here was widespread violence in the pre-election period. Most of this violence was directed at candidates and supporters of political parties in opposition to ZANU (PF), and against commercial farmers and workers on commercial farms. Regrettably, violence against these persons has continued after the parliamentary elections on 24–25 June. In the cities and towns the army has been harassing and assaulting people in high density areas. There continue to be violent attacks and death threats against members and supporters of the MDC. People are still fleeing some rural areas to escape the violence. Commercial farmers and their workers continue to be attacked and threatened.[4]

In reprisal, starting in February 2000, the ruling party embarked on an all-out double campaign involving the vilification of the MDC as a puppet of the Western countries, on one hand, and a systematic attack on the white-dominated commercial agricultural sector, on the other. It took advantage of the fact that the land issue had never been satisfactorily resolved in order to mobilize public support against the country's white community which it accused of being the real force behind the MDC. These activities severely damaged the country's international reputation and earned it much criticism, especially from the Western countries.

Zimbabwe's international image was further dented by Operation Murambatsvina in May 2005. More than 700,000 were made homeless as a result of a swift and brutal government campaign to demolish temporary or unlicensed residential premises or shacks in the name of

---

[4] 'Post election violence', 18 November 2002, at www.hrforumzim.com/evmp/evmpreports/pevoo0807/pevio1000807.htm

urban renewal. Most of those affected were the urban poor suspected of constituting the MDC's urban base. The international outcry was deafening, with Western countries imposing economic and travel restrictions on targeted individuals closely associated with the violence and human rights abuse, as well as the withdrawal of development assistance and other forms of international support. These and other measures brought, in their wake, rapid economic decline and massive out-migration of Zimbabwean professionals, including doctors, nurses, pharmacists, educators, engineers and others.

Then, in March 2008, Zimbabwe held the so-called harmonised elections in which, for the first time since independence, voting for local government, parliament and the presidency was synchronized. The MDC won the parliamentary majority. Tsvangirai's MDC won 100 seats to ZANU-PF's 99, with the remaining 10 going to an MDC breakaway party. In the presidential race, Tsvangirai won 47.8 per cent of the vote, while Mugabe won 43.2 per cent, and the balance went to an independent candidate. The results were highly disputed, especially since it took thirty-four days for the country's electoral commission to release the election results, fuelling suspicion that the figures had been tampered with. Because there had been no outright winner, it was necessary for the country to hold a run-off election.

The unmitigated violence unleashed by ZANU-PF supporters against the opposition in a bid to intimidate them from voting in the June 2008 run-off elections was on a scale hitherto unknown except by people of Matebeleland in the 1980s. Tsvangirai withdrew from the race in protest and Mugabe was duly declared the winner. In a bid to resolve the political stalemate that the 2008 elections had created in Zimbabwe, President Mbeki of South Africa, on behalf of SADC, brokered an agreement in which ZANU-PF and the now two MDC formations (following a recent split in the party) signed a Global Political Agreement (GPA) agreeing to come together in a power-sharing arrangement as a transitional step, pending the implementation of various key political reforms, including a constitutional review, followed by credible elections that would, hopefully, resolve the Zimbabwean crisis once and for all. By the end of the decade, however, the political system remained unstable, while human rights violations, including violence against MDC supporters, continued, with the partisan national police force, which was headed by a former liberation combatant, applying the law selectively in favour of ZANU-PF. At the same time, the implementation of the agreed-upon political reforms proceeded at a very slow pace.

Farm Invasions and the Economy

The first land invasions occurred in June 1998, when peasants from the Svosve Communal Area east of the capital city of Harare occupied a white-owned farm and refused to move out until government resettled them. They complained of congestion and poor soils in their area and declared that they had grown tired of government's empty promises since independence that it would resettle them. Similar land invasions occurred in Matebeleland, Masvingo and Manicaland provinces at the same time. What seems to have started as spontaneous protests against government's failure to deliver on its promises regarding meaningful land reform was then hijacked by some veterans of Zimbabwe's liberation war and other government supporters in February 2000 when they began invading white farms and forcing farmers off the land across the country in what they called the Third Chimurenga. [5] That they had the approval of the government became clear when the police refused to either arrest or remove the farm occupiers, claiming that this was a political matter that was beyond their jurisdiction. Meanwhile, President Mugabe denounced white farmers as enemies of the state who deserved the treatment they were receiving. Thus began a period of mayhem that saw both white farmers and their farmworkers hounded off the land. This was soon followed by the government 'fast-track' land reform programme which targeted, initially, 2,076 white farms for compulsory acquisition by February 2001.

Farm invasions and the violence that accompanied them had far-reaching socio-economic and political consequences that ultimately made the country a pariah state in the international community. The invasions crippled the economy by disrupting normal agricultural activity and eventually ruining the agricultural sector. Given the fact that agriculture had always been the mainstay of the country's economy and the major foreign currency earner, apart from the heavy reliance of the local manufacturing sector on agriculture, the damage was immediate and far-reaching. Indeed, in November 2002, the Confederation of Zimbabwean Industries (CZI) was already reporting that, because of the disruption of the agriculture sector, no less than 540 engineering companies had had to reduce their working week in order to minimize their operational costs at a time of shrinking domestic demand for their

[5] Ostensibly, the third phase in the liberation struggle after the First Chimurenga of 1896 and the Second Chimurenga of the liberation war, both of which were mostly about political self-determination. The third phase was to be a struggle for economic independence.

products. In December of the same year, the CZI reported that 400 firms had shut down in 2000 resulting in the loss of 10,000 jobs. One hundred manufacturers had been liquidated in 2001, with a further loss of 3,500 jobs.[6] The decline of agricultural production at the time also hit hard the milling companies, bakeries, leather goods manufacturers, clothing and textile manufacturers and other industries that relied on agricultural products.

Moreover, the invasions displaced an estimated 450,000 farm labourers and their families who now became unemployed and destitute, with some drifting into the urban areas to join the ever-growing informal economy. As many of the farm labourers were of immigrant origin, descendants of migrant labourers from the neighbouring countries of Malawi, Zambia and Mozambique during the colonial period, they could not retire to the Communal Areas, as they had never had any land there. In any case, most of the people who were granted land under the programme were ill equipped to make it productive, either because of lack of farming experience or for lack of capital and other production inputs and supporting services. Compounding the problem was a severe drought in the 2001–2 season, which contributed to serious food shortages in the country. The result was that a country that was once the breadbasket of Southern Africa, responsible for the SADC food security portfolio, was no longer able to feed itself, let alone produce for export in order to earn much-needed foreign currency.[7] Indeed, in November 2002, it was reported that more than 6 million people were in need of food aid.

Meanwhile, tourism, another major income earner, suffered severe decline. In November 2002, the Zimbabwe Tourism Authority (ZTA) reported that tourist arrivals from the United Kingdom and Ireland had dropped by 51 per cent and those from the United States and Canada by 42 per cent since 2001. Arrivals from Australia and New Zealand had fallen by 36 per cent in the same period. Even more significant was the fact that arrivals from Zimbabwe's neighbouring countries of South Africa, Botswana and Zambia had dropped by a colossal 78 per cent in

[6] UN OCHA, 'Zimbabwe: Industry Hurt by Land Reform', November 2002, at http://www.reliefweb.int; *Financial Gazette* (Harare), 20 December 2002.
[7] 'Politically Motivated Violence in Zimbabwe, 2000–2001', at http://www.hrforumzim.com/evmp; Financial *Gazette* (Harare), 20 December 2002; UN OCHA, 'Zimbabwe: Industry Hurt by Land Reform', at http://www.reliefweb.int (accessed 16 November 2002).

the same period.[8] At the same time, the withdrawal or reduction of support by international funding agencies, such as the IMF and the World Bank, as well as from the European Union worsened the country's already precarious foreign currency situation.

By the end of 2002, therefore, Zimbabwe was in the throes of an economic meltdown of unprecedented proportions, described by the United Nations Economic Commission for Africa (UNECA) as the 'worst economic crisis of its history', with the economy confronting a complicated combination of 'domestic and external debt, crippling foreign exchange shortages, poor weather conditions, negative real interest rates and escalating inflation'.[9] Also by the same year, it was estimated that more than '200 000 jobs have been lost since the beginning of 2000, mostly in agriculture and manufacturing', that investment had shrunk by '80% between January and May' 2002, and that 'over 60% of the country's 12.5 million people' were living below the poverty line.[10] Other statistics told their own sad story of the extent of the country's economic meltdown. In 2004, inflation stood at 622.8 per cent, exports were a mere third of what they had been in 1977, the country's domestic and foreign debt was US$1.1 billion each,[11] while the Zimbabwean currency had lost 99 per cent of its value since 2001. This was, by all accounts, the worst peacetime decline of any economy.

At the lowest point in Zimbabwe's crisis decade, the country was suffering from 80 per cent unemployment, severe shortages of basic commodities, a cholera outbreak that killed no less than 4,000 people, a collapsing social services sector and hyperinflation of 231 million percent.

The situation was rescued only when the Unity Government decided to scrap the now totally worthless Zimbabwe currency and to adopt a multi-currency system based on the U.S. Dollar, the British Pound Sterling, the South African Rand and the Botswana Pula. This led to a noticeable recovery of the country's economy as inflation vanished and access to schools and hospitals once again became possible.

---

[8] 'Tourism Tumbles in Zimbabwe', *Business Day*, 22 November 2002.

[9] Economic Commission for Africa, 'Zimbabwe – A Crumbling Economy (Abstract)', in ECA, *Economic Report on Africa 2002: Tracking Performance and Progress* (Addis Ababa: ECA, 2002), 9.

[10] CIIR, 'Economy and Voters Lose Out: Post-Election Blues in Zimbabwe', at http://www.ciir.org/ciir.asp?section=news&page=story&id=90 (accessed 22 November 2002).

[11] IRIN News, February 2004; G. Mills, 'Agitator, Facilitator or Benefactor? Assessing South Africa's Zimbabwe Policy' Testimony given to the House Committee on International Relations, Sub-Committee on Africa, Global Human Rights and International Operations, Washington D.C., April 2005, 3.

Decline of Social Services

Health

Evidence of the disastrous impact of the economic meltdown on the country's public health sector is overwhelming. For instance, life expectancy declined from sixty-two to forty-four years between 1990 and 2008, while maternal mortality increased from 168 per 100,000 live births in 1990 to 880 per 100,000 live births in 2005.[12] Infant and under-five mortality rose, respectively, from 53 and 77 per 1,000 live births in 1995 to 60 and 80 per 1,000 live births in 2009. Stunting resulting from nutritional deficiency among children younger than five years old increased from 9.4 per cent in 1999 to 35 per cent in 2009.[13] The situation was arguably worse than this, as the very poor people no longer attended public health institutions where they were now required to pay fees, and so deaths in the rural areas may have gone unreported. Meanwhile, the HIV/AIDS epidemic was taking its toll on the Zimbabwean population.

AIDS was first reported in Zimbabwe in 1985 and quickly spread thereafter. By the end of the 1980s, approximately 10 per cent of the adult population was estimated to be infected with HIV, and by 1997 the figure had risen to 26.5 per cent.[14] The number of AIDS orphans increased rapidly from approximately 345 000 in 1988 to 1.4 million on 2003.[15] The Zimbabwean government was 'slow to acknowledge the problem and take appropriate action'. In 1987, it set up the National AIDS Co-ordination Programme (NACP) to address the pandemic on a rather ad hoc basis until 1999, when the country developed its first HIV and AIDS policy. A National AIDS Council (NAC) set up in the same year spearheaded the campaign against the pandemic thereafter. This effort was hampered by various socio-economic and political challenges of the new millennium, such as the mayhem associated with the farm invasions that began in 2000 and the displacement of farm workers, most of whom thus lost access to medical facilities. Operation Murambatsvina further worsened the situation by displacing even more people. By July 2005, an estimated 79,500 adults living with HIV had been displaced. Many of these people

---

[12] Cited in USAID, 'Zimbabwe Health System Assessment, 2010'.

[13] Anonymous, 'Health Services in Zimbabwe', at www.abaz.co.zw/pdf/Health%20 Services%20in%20Zimbabwe.pdf (accessed 26 April 2012).

[14] Avert, 'HIV and AIDS in Zimbabwe', at http://www.avert.org/aids-zimbabwe.htm (accessed 29 March 2013).

[15] Zimbabwe Government, Ministry of Health and Child Welfare, *The HIV and AIDS Epidemic in Zimbabwe* (Harare: Government of Zimbabwe, 2004), 49.

had previously been receiving antiretroviral drugs (ARVs) to delay the onset of AIDS, but now had no access to them as treatment centres and clinics had been demolished. Other HIV and AIDS-related services such as home-based care and prevention programmes were also disrupted.[16]

By 2006, AIDS was reportedly killing 2,500 individuals every week.[17] It was estimated that HIV prevalence among adults aged fifteen to forty-nine years was 15.6 per cent in 2007, while 1,320,739 adults and children were living with HIV and AIDS.[18] However, for a variety of reasons, including greater population awareness of the dangers of HIV/AIDS and the resultant change in lifestyles, Zimbabwe recorded a significant decline in HIV incidence, becoming one of 'the few countries where incidence has declined by more than 25 percent between 2001 and 2009'. This, notwithstanding, the country still had approximately 14 per cent of its population living with HIV in 2010, making it one of the countries with the highest HIV rates in the world.[19] Thus, the services of the country's health sector were in great demand in the face of the HIV/AIDS scourge at the very time that the sector was collapsing.

The clearest evidence of the collapse of the country's public health system was undoubtedly the cholera outbreak of 2008. In August of that year, the first cases were reported in Chitungwiza, a dormitory town outside the capital, Harare. Thereafter, the pandemic spread quickly across the country, while the numbers of those infected equally escalated so that by 9 December there were 16,141 suspected cases of cholera and 775 deaths in the country's 62 districts. By 26 December, the number of cases had risen to 26,497, while the numbers of the dead since the outbreak were reported by the Ministry of Health of Zimbabwe to have risen to 1,518, with outbreaks having spread to all of the country's 10 districts. The World Health Organisation (WHO) reported also that 'mortality outside of healthcare facilities remains very high' and, by implication, unrecorded. Cholera reportedly spread to Musina in South Africa, Palm Tree in Botswana and Guro District in Mozambique.[20]

Between August and December, the government downplayed the extent of the pandemic until it became impossible to pretend that there

---

[16] Avert, 'HIV and AIDS in Zimbabwe'.

[17] Hala Elhowersi and Gowri Parameswaran, 'AIDS in Zimbabwe', *Crosscurrents and Crosscutting Themes* (Charlotte: Information Age Publishing, 2006), 109.

[18] Cited in USAID, 'Zimbabwe Health System Assessment, 2010'.

[19] Avert, 'HIV and AIDS in Zimbabwe'.

[20] 'Mozambique: Cholera Spreads in Guro', at http://allafrica.com/stories/200811181021. html (accessed 20 October 2012).

was no crisis, especially given that the country's health care services were clearly unable to contain it. Rather than take full responsibility for the collapse of its health services, government resorted to a childish blame game in which Dr. Sikanyiso Ndlovu, then Minister of Higher Education, shamefacedly claimed that 'the cholera epidemic in Zimbabwe is a serious biological chemical war fare, a genocidal onslaught on the people of Zimbabwe by the British [and their] American and Western allies so that they invade the country'.[21]

The truth, of course, was that the cholera outbreak had been caused by poor sanitation and contaminated drinking water resulting from the total inability of the Zimbabwe National Water Authority (ZINWA) to provide purified water and maintain sanitation facilities. This parastatal had been established by the ruling party in 1999 in an attempt to wrest control of the country's urban centres following a recent sweeping victory by the MDC in the country's municipal elections which placed more than 80 per cent of local governments under opposition's control. ZINWA took over control of Harare's water supply in 2005 and failed to provide adequate water supplies from the very beginning, owing to a combination of incompetence and a severe shortage of purification chemicals, such as chlorine, because of inadequate financial resources in a collapsed economy. Commenting on the country's collapsing water supply system just before the cholera outbreak, UNICEF reported:

The proportion of people with access to safe drinking water has been declining since early 2000 and the situation is expected to worsen further during 2008 due to the current economic challenges and the crumbling infrastructure. Financial constraints, fuel shortages, lack of foreign currency for spare parts and treatment chemicals have resulted in decreased maintenance of current water systems. The situation is exacerbated by frequent electricity power cuts, which reduce the pumping time into the reticulation water systems.[22]

Furthermore, the country's sewage system was reportedly breaking down 'due to age, excessive load, pump breakdowns and poor maintenance', resulting in sewage discharges contaminating major water sources and supplies. As a result, Zimbabwe had suffered minor cholera and other diarrhoea outbreaks in 2007, resulting in more than 90 deaths.[23] Then

[21] H. G. Campbell, 'Zimbabwe: Where Is the Outrage? Mamdani, Mugabe and the African Scholarly Community', March 2009, at http://concernedafricascholars.org/bulletin/issue82/campbell/ (accessed 5 December 2012).
[22] UNICEF, 'UNICEF Humanitarian Action Zimbabwe 2008', at http://www.unicef.org/har08/files/har08_Zimbabwe_countrychapter.pdf (accessed 1 September 2012).
[23] UNICEF, 'UNICEF Humanitarian Action Zimbabwe 2008'.

on 1 December 2008, because of mounting economic and logistical challenges, ZINWA completely stopped pumping water to Harare, forcing the city's poor population, without access to boreholes, to use unprotected well water for household needs. A cholera outbreak was almost predictable under such conditions.

That the outbreak spread so quickly and took so many lives was also expected given the collapse of the health care delivery system in which four major hospitals had closed their doors for lack of staff and medicines, as the country's prevailing hyperinflation made it impossible for health institutions to purchase drugs and medicines. Thus, although the treatment of cholera basically focuses on 'replacing fluids and electrolytes at the same rate as their loss' and cholera deaths are entirely preventable, the ailing health delivery system simply could not cope. Hence, the government was forced to declare a national emergency on 3 December 2008, thus opening the doors to international assistance.

Indeed, by 2008, the country's public health system was in shambles. It was characterised in an Amnesty International country report as being 'on the verge of collapse'. The report further stated:

> The main referral hospitals in the country, including Harare Central, Parirenyatwa and United Bulawayo hospitals, are barely functioning and some wards have even been closed. Two government maternity hospitals in greater Harare have been closed. Many district hospitals and municipal clinics are either closed or operating at minimum capacity. The University of Zimbabwe Medical School closed indefinitely on 17 November. The system is paralysed by shortages of drugs and medical supplies, a dilapidated infrastructure, equipment failures and a brain drain. As a result, ordinary Zimbabweans are unable to access basic health care.[24]

Education

As in health care, following an impressive period of growth and expansion, the education sector went through a precipitous decline in the first decade of the new millennium. Hailed in the 1980s as a leader in Africa for access to education and already boasting a literacy rate of 93 per cent for males and 87 per cent for females by the end of the twentieth century, Zimbabwe had come very close to achieving its goals of 'education for all by 2000' that had been set at independence.[25] These notable achievements

---

[24] Amnesty International USA, 'Zimbabwe's health system in chaos', 21 November 2008', at http://www.amnesty.org/en/news-and-updates/news/zimbabwes-health-system-chaos-20081121 (accessed 30 April 2012).

[25] D. Tonini, 'The Breadbasket Goes Empty: Zimbabwe – A Country in Crisis', in D. Burde (ed.), *Education in Emergencies and Post-Conflict Situations: Problems, Responses and Possibilities*, Vol. 2 (Fall 2005), 95.

were reversed in the new millennium as the country's declining economic situation and falling living standards and the chaotic land reform exercise displaced thousands of farm workers, forcing children out of school and to work in order to support their families or to seek refuge in the cities where they became street kids, engaging in prostitution, begging and crime. Meanwhile, the children of those who 'invaded' former commercial farms without any educational infrastructure could no longer attend school or had to contend with schools without adequate infrastructure or staff.[26]

Commenting on the deteriorating state of Zimbabwe's education system, UNICEF noted how the poor economic situation was negatively influencing school attendance, and the education system was increasingly characterised by 'low enrolment rates, declining attendance and completion rates, low transition rate to secondary and insufficient learning spaces, teachers and learning materials'. For these and other reasons, pupils' 'performance rates have been declining – only 30% of pupils pass their grade 7 exams'.[27] By 2009, the Zimbabwe Teachers' Association (ZIMTA) was warning that the education system was on the verge of collapse because of a 'critical shortage of teachers, teaching and learning materials, poor remuneration and low morale' and reported that teachers were either leaving the country or 'simply stay away from their schools' as they 'are some of the lowest paid professionals in the country'.[28]

Problems also bedevilled the higher education sector where deterioration of standards, a serious brain drain – as senior and experienced academics voted with their feet in search of greener pastures abroad, escaping low salaries and growing political intolerance – and government interference in university matters and curtailment of academic freedom reduced the once acclaimed higher education system to a sorry state. As expected, the result was a severe decline in educational standards, as less qualified and inexperienced teaching staff was employed at the country's universities and colleges. Thus, increasingly, students were condemned to study at progressively dysfunctional institutions with rapidly dwindling manpower and other resources. A prominent example of an increasingly dysfunctional institution was the flagship of the country's higher education sector, the University of Zimbabwe, where manpower and other

---

[26] Tonini, 'The Breadbasket Goes Empty', 96.
[27] UNICEF, 'UNICEF Humanitarian Action Zimbabwe in 2008'.
[28] Sokwanele, 'Zimta warns of collapse of education sector', at http://www.sokwanele.com/thisiszimbabwe/archives/2066 (accessed 04 April 2013).

shortages and poor leadership resulted in a rapid decline of what had
previously been regarded as a world-class university.[29] It is not possible to
give an accurate figure of the number of Zimbabweans who had become
part of the brain drain by 2010, but it is clear that the total was considerable and was variously estimated at between 3 million and 4 million people. The majority of these went to South Africa, the United Kingdom, the
United States and Australia. Because of this and other aforementioned
factors, both the education and health sectors were in dire straits by the
end of the first decade of the twenty-first century.

Chimurenga Music in the Post-Colony

Chimurenga protest music which had surfaced in the 1970s as part of the
African anti-colonial struggles did not die with the attainment of independence.[30] The genre continued well into the independence era 'as a vehicle
for criticizing corruption, poor governance by new leaders, and delays in
redistributing land to the African masses',[31] and was now targeting postcolonial ruling elites who were increasingly seen as uncaring, inept and
corrupt. Chimurenga music was not all critical of government and the
ruling elites; it was sometimes employed by the ruling elites themselves to
buttress their own position and mobilize support for their policies. The
music of one Dickson Chingaira, a.k.a. Comrade Chinx, long-time leader
of the ZANLA Choir during the liberation war, was supported by the
state because it praised the fast-track land reform that took land away
from the whites and evoked the anti-colonial mood of the struggle years.
Thus, his well-known struggle song 'Maruza Imi vapambipfumi' [You
have lost, you exploiters], which 'recount(ed) the history of Zimbabwe,
beginning with the colonization of the country in 1890, and the countless
acts of white arrogance that culminated in Africans taking up arms', was
revived and sung together with other songs that glorified the land invasions as the intensification of the war of African liberation.[32]

---

[29] Alois S. Mlambo, 'Postcolonial Higher Education in Zimbabwe: The University of
Zimbabwe as a Case Study 1980–2004', *African Historical Review*, 37, 1 (2005), 107–
30 provides an analysis of the decline in Zimbabwe's higher education with a focus on
the University of Zimbabwe.
[30] This section is heavily dependent on M. T. Vambe, 'Versions and Sub-Versions: Trends
in Chimurenga Musical Discourses of Post Independence Zimbabwe', *African Study
Monographs*, 25, 4 (2004), 167–93.
[31] Vambe, 'Versions and Sub-Versions'.
[32] Vambe, 'Versions and Sub-Versions'.

On the other side of the political divide and continuing the tradition of critiquing the ruling elites that had began under colonial rule, veteran Chimurenga singers like Mapfumo and Mutukudzi sang songs that were highly critical of the new dispensation. For instance, Mapfumo's 1988 song entitled 'Corruption' denounced the growing public corruption characterised by demands for bribes by those in power for any services to be rendered to the public. In mockery of the fast-track land reform which was touted by the ruling elites as designed to 'empower' the black Zimbabweans, but which ushered in a period of rapid agricultural decline and food shortages, Mapfumo sang 'Maiti Kurima Hamubvire' [You used to claim that you were excellent farmers], the obvious message being that the land reform was a disaster. A more explicit criticism of ZANU-PF's land policy came in his 2001 song entitled 'Marima Nzara' [You have cultivated hunger], instead of food. Other songs openly critical of the failures of the postcolonial ruling elites had titles such as 'Disaster' (implying that the country had turned into a disaster) and 'Mamvemve', namely 'the country is in tatters', sang in 1997 and 1998, respectively.[33] Thereafter, Mapfumo went into self-imposed exile in the United States, vowing not to return until there was a change of government in the country.

On his part, Mutukudzi remained in the country but continued to sing songs that were critical of the establishment, although not in as overt a manner as Mapfumo. A good example is his song 'Wenge Mambo' [You behave like a king], in which he 'satirises new black politicians who view themselves as kings'. In this song, the new leader is depicted as a tyrant 'who acquires enormous powers, becomes uncontrollable, rejects overtures toward peace and good-neighbourliness ... promotes the culture of war, and metes out violence not only on the weak, but also on his own people, who have put him in a position of power'.[34]

In the postcolonial period, therefore, Chimurenga music has served sometimes contradictory purposes of legitimizing the ruling elite's policies and of criticizing the failures and excesses of the same elite. Thus, the different forms of Chimurenga music have reflected the complicated and sometimes conflicting interests that are characteristic of postcolonial Zimbabwean society.

---

[33] Vambe, 'Versions and Sub-Versions'.
[34] Vambe, 'Versions and Sub-Versions'.

International Responses to the Crisis

International reactions to the Zimbabwean crisis throughout the first decade of the twenty-first century were mixed. Western countries reacted with a mixture of public condemnation and a wide range of sanctions against identified individuals in the Zimbabwe government, whereas African countries either publicly supported Mugabe's policies or remained largely silent.

Western Countries

Western countries in general initially responded to the unfolding crisis in Zimbabwe by making largely ineffectual public denunciations of the Mugabe regime, imposition of international sanctions and calls for regime change.[35] British policy towards Zimbabwe, in particular, was as ineffective as its earlier reaction to Ian Smith's UDI in 1965. There too, the British government had been indecisive, opting to denounce UDI from a distance, to impose international economic sanctions rather than acting more robustly to put down the rebellion as African nationalist leaders and many African heads of state advocated, and to engage Ian Smith in endless negotiations which resolved little.[36]

In May 2000, Britain imposed an arms embargo on Zimbabwe, stopped the provision of 450 British Land Rovers destined for the Zimbabwe Republic Police as part of a standing Britain-Zimbabwe agreement and later, together with the European Union, imposed 'smart' or targeted sanctions: financial sanctions, travel bans, arms embargoes and commodity boycotts. General sanctions as those that had been imposed at UDI were rejected because they would worsen the suffering of the ordinary Zimbabweans. On its part, the United States passed the Zimbabwe Democracy and Economic Recovery Act (ZDERA) in 2001, laying down the criteria allowing Washington to put severe economic pressure on Zimbabwe. ZDERA instructed its representatives on international financial institutions to oppose any extension of loans or financial guarantees to the Zimbabwe government and any proposal to cancel the Zimbabwe government's debts owed to either the United States or any international financial institutions. These and other sanctions were to remain in place

---

[35] I. Taylor and P. Williams, 'The Limits of Engagement: British Foreign Policy and the Crisis in Zimbabwe', *International Affairs*, 78, 3 (2002), 547–65.

[36] K. Young, *Rhodesia and Independence: A Study in British Colonial Policy* (London: J. M. Dent and Sons, 1969); F. R. Metrowitch, *Rhodesia: Birth of a Nation* (Pretoria: Africa Institute of South Africa, 1969).

until the Zimbabwe government demonstrated 'a commitment to an equitable, legal and transparent land reform program which should respect existing ownership of, and title to, property by providing fair, market-based compensation to sellers'. It supported the Zimbabwe political opposition to Mugabe and his party's leadership and provided for American aid to a post-Mugabe government in Zimbabwe.[37] Then in March 2003, the American government under President George W. Bush imposed sanctions on President Mugabe and seventy-six members of his government, prohibiting any U.S. corporation from making business deals with Zimbabwe and also freezing any assets these Zimbabwean officials had in U.S. banking institutions.[38] Meanwhile, under pressure from Britain, an organisation comprising its former colonies, the Commonwealth, suspended Zimbabwe's membership, prompting Mugabe to pull the country out of the organisation.

Western policy towards Zimbabwe in general and British policy in particular failed to resonate with African and indeed developing-world perspectives, which were suspicious of Western motives and regarded the Western attitude as arrogant, while admiring Mugabe's ability to stand up to the West and to dare to correct colonial inequities. Moreover, African leaders were deeply suspicious of Western countries' motives, particularly because the latter continued to champion neo-liberal economic strategies that had come to be associated with the economic havoc caused by IMF and World Bank Structural Adjustment Programmes in Africa in the previous three-plus decades. Mugabe took advantage of this by using a strongly Pan-African and anti-Western rhetoric that appealed to some African heads of state.

Africa/South African Reactions

An interesting contrast was how African countries responded to the Zimbabwean crisis as compared to their responses to UDI. Whereas African heads of state reacted to UDI with considerable outrage and calls for Britain, the responsible colonial power, to intervene militarily to end Ian Smith's rebellion, in contrast, African leaders remained largely silent about reported human rights abuses perpetrated by the Zimbabwe

---

[37] U. S. The Zimbabwe Democracy and Economic Recovery Act of 2001 (Public Law 107–99, 115 Stat. 962–965).

[38] M. Moorehead, 'Bush Attacks Zimbabwe with Sanctions', 13 March 2003, at http://ww.iacenter.org (accessed 3 February 2012).

government and its supporters since 2000. Indeed, at various meetings of the African Union (successor to the OAU), some leaders openly supported the Zimbabwean government's policies, despite widespread documentation of the political and economic crisis occurring in Zimbabwe. While they were keen to participate in sanctions against the Ian Smith regime in the 1960s, they were now very reluctant to participate in sanctions against the Zimbabwe ruling elite, for example those imposed by the European Union and the American government.

Particularly controversial was neighbouring South Africa's reaction to the Zimbabwean crisis. Well placed to influence policies in Zimbabwe because of its considerable economic clout as Zimbabwe's biggest trading partner in the region and controlling its neighbour's most important rail and road trade routes, it was expected, by those opposed to ongoing political developments in Zimbabwe, to use its muscle to compel the Zimbabwe ruling elites to reform. Yet, as in the past when apartheid South Africa refused to enforce international sanctions against Rhodesia during the UDI period, the South African government also refused to apply sanctions against Zimbabwe, preferring instead to use non-coercive diplomatic measures in what came to be known as quiet diplomacy. An interim solution was eventually crafted by the regional organisation, the SADC, when it facilitated the formation of the Government of National Unity (GNU) in Zimbabwe, bringing ZANU-PF and the MDC into a temporary coalition government that was tasked with paving the way for free and fair elections that would usher in an undisputed and legitimate government.

10

Conclusion: Zimbabwe Past, Present and Future Prospects

As shown throughout this book, the country that became Rhodesia in 1890 and Zimbabwe at independence in 1980 had a long history of indigenous civilisations before British colonisation. The coming of British colonialism spearheaded by Cecil John Rhodes and his British South Africa Company (BSAC) in 1890 transformed the country's social, political and economic landscape and introduced Western systems of government and a modern economy. The two mainstays of the economy of the country, now renamed Southern Rhodesia, in the early years were mining and agriculture, but gradually secondary manufacturing took root and then rapidly expanded during and after the Second World War, partly as a result of import-substitution industrialisation strategies actively pursued by the colonial government and investors. In the meantime, the country became progressively industrialised as the African population moved into the emerging urban centres to work in the expanding secondary manufacturing sector. Economic growth continued in the Federation period from 1953 to 1963, but suffered a brief setback following the Rhodesian government's UDI in 1965, which resulted in international economic sanctions in reprisal. Thereafter, the economy grew rapidly, again, because of import-substitution industrialisation strategies adopted by the beleaguered country, only to go into decline in the late 1970s owing to a combination of factors that included more effective implementation of sanctions and the intensification of the liberation war by African nationalist fighters.

White domination of the country caused much resentment among the African majority, especially in the very early years when they lost their independence and self-determination and became second-class citizens in their own land. Not surprisingly, most African communities across the country rose against colonial rule in the Chimurenga/Umvukela wars of 1896 and 1897, but were defeated. Thereafter Africans mobilised themselves, first in support or solidarity groups and, gradually, in political organisations and workers movements in the 1930s and after, until the flowering of militant mass African nationalism in the 1950s. From petitioning the white rulers for good governance in the interwar years, Africans now demanded the right to rule themselves under the principle of 'one man one vote' or 'majority rule'. When the colonial authority, Britain, refused to grant independence to Southern Rhodesia under white minority rule, the white government under Rhodesian-born Ian Douglass Smith declared unilateral independence in 1965.

UDI opened the floodgates for bloody military confrontation between colonial forces and African guerrillas fighting for independence. For a variety of complicated reasons, including economic need, prestige and notions of masculinity, among others, many Africans fought in the colonial army in defence of a system which marginalised them. The fighting only ended with the Lancaster House Agreement in 1979 which paved the way for general elections which ushered in the country's first independence government in 1980 under Robert Gabriel Mugabe. Before then, an unsuccessful attempt to establish a moderate 'independence' government under Bishop Abel Muzorewa had been made. Voted into power in the 1979 national elections, Muzorewa served as prime minister in the renamed Zimbabwe-Rhodesia government from June to November 1979 before he lost power to Robert Mugabe in the 1980 general elections.

Since independence, Zimbabwe has had a chequered political and economic history which has complicated and sometimes negated efforts to build the country as a united and prosperous nation. Mention has already been made of the Gukurahundi massacres in Matebeleland in the early 1980s and how they soured relations between the Ndebele people and the government. Since the formation of the Movement for Democratic Change (MDC) in 1999, Zimbabwean society was polarised between supporters of ZANU-PF, the party that had ruled the country since independence, and members of the opposition parties, the most prominent of which was the MDC. In addition, farm seizures that started in 2000, which saw the country's white commercial farmers being violently thrown off the land by government supporters, poisoned relations between the white Zimbabwean community and the government, further making the realisation of the national project more difficult.

A major challenge facing Zimbabwe's ongoing nation-building project is how to mould a national identity in the light of the country's complicated and contested precolonial, colonial and postcolonial history stemming partly from the fact that, like most African countries, its present configuration is essentially a product of the colonialism and the nationalist imagination. After all, there was no country known as Rhodesia until the 1890s. Thus, both the name and the boundaries that demarcate the territory were European creations. What developed as Southern Rhodesia, Rhodesia, and then Zimbabwe was, therefore, an amalgam of various factors and influences that were not necessarily rooted in a common historical past or a shared language, religion or culture of the country's inhabitants. In Zimbabwean historian Sabelo Ndlovu-Gatsheni's words, Zimbabwe is, thus

a construction not only moulded out of pre-colonial, colonial and nationalist pasts, but also out of global values of sovereignty, self determination and territorial integrity. It is an idea born out of continuing synthesis of multilayered, overlapping and cross-pollinating historical genealogies, and contending nationalisms, as well as suppressed local and regional sovereignties.[1]

Moreover, the country has to deal with the complications of its ethnic diversity and the challenges arising from the colonial legacy of racism, autocratic intolerance of political dissent and a racialised unequal socioeconomic regime, the armed conflict that tore the fabric of Zimbabwe's society for almost two decades and left the races divided, the policy of reconciliation after independence notwithstanding, as well as the fallout from the vexatious question of land ownership that remained dangerously unresolved for twenty years and was acrimoniously addressed in the new millennium. These issues are discussed in this chapter.

While it is customary, in recounting the colonial history of Zimbabwe and the indigenous people's struggle for freedom and independence, to speak generically of 'the Africans', it is necessary to acknowledge the fact

---

[1] This section is based on the author's inaugural lecture entitled 'Becoming Zimbabwe or Becoming Zimbabwean: Identity, Nationalism and State Building in the Historical Context of Southern Africa' presented to at the University of Pretoria on 30 October 2012 and later published as Alois S. Mlambo, 'Becoming Zimbabwe or Becoming Zimbabwean: Identity, Nationalism and State-building', *Africa Spectrum* 1 (2013), 49–70 and as A. S. Mlambo, 'Becoming Zimbabwean: Nation and State-Building in the Context of Southern Africa', in Sabelo J. Ndlovu-Gatsheni and Finex Ndhlovu (eds.), *Nationalism and National Projects in Southern Africa: New Critical Reflections* (Pretoria: Africa Institute of South Africa, 2013), 235–50. Bhebe and Ranger, *Historical Dimensions*, 20.

that this population group was by no means culturally or linguistically homogenous, nor did they all share a common precolonial history, language or culture. While the Shona-speaking people are the majority of the country's population – currently comprising approximately 80 per cent of the population – and have been there longer than most other groups that claim Zimbabwe as their home, they are by no means the only ethnic, racial or cultural group; neither are they, themselves, a monolithic entity, as competing subethnic forces exist within the seemingly united Shona grouping. As shown in Chapter 2, the country has witnessed a number of in-migrations, beginning with the Bantu-speaking groups, the ancestors of the Shona, thousands of years ago, followed by the Nguni groups and ending with the arrival of the whites and immigrant workers from surrounding territories in the late nineteenth and early twentieth centuries, respectively. The result is that, apart from the major ethno-linguistic groups already mentioned, presently there are also other minor groups, such as the Nyanja/Chewa, Tonga, Shangani, Barwe, Sotho, Venda, Chikunda, Xhosa, Sena, Hwesa and Nambya communities.

As argued, while there was a succession of precolonial political entities, such as Mapungubwe, Great Zimbabwe, Munhumutapa and Rozvi Kingdoms, which were dominated by ancestors of the present Shona-speaking groups, not everyone in the area lived under, was governed by, or subscribed to the political authority of these dominant political units.[2] Moreover, the arrival of different ethnic and cultural groups in the form of Nguni warriors from the south in the mid-nineteenth century, including the Jere of Zwangendava and the Gaza-Nguni of Soshangane and, finally, the Ndebele of Mzilikazi Khumalo, further complicated the country's ethnic makeup and nation-building efforts. On the eve of European colonisation, therefore, what was to become Rhodesia (Zimbabwe) was a territory composed of variegated ethnic/cultural groupings comprising the 'Shona' cluster and its various subgroups, small autochthonous communities, the Ndau, now incorporating the Gaza-Nguni, and the Ndebele Nguni who were themselves multiethnic, as they comprised the original Nguni groups from Zululand (*Abezansi*), Sotho and others groups incorporated by Mzilikazi en route to Matebeleland (*abenhla*), and the conquered Rozvi groups (*Amahole*) who were also made part of the Ndebele state.[3]

[2] G. C. Mazarire, 'Reflections on Pre-Colonial Zimbabwe, c.850–1880', in B. Raftopoulos and A. S. Mlambo (eds.), *Becoming Zimbabwe*, 1–38.

[3] Sabelo J. Ndlovu-Gatsheni, *The Ndebele Nation: Hegemony, Memory, Historiography* (Amsterdam; Pretoria: Rozenberg; UNISA, 2009).

Then the whites colonized the country in 1890. They, too, were not a homogenous group, as colonizing parties and early white settlers were a mixture of people of British and Afrikaans stock, soon to be joined by Poles, European Jews, Italians, Greeks and other shades of whiteness that made it equally impossible to speak of a homogenous culture even among whites. Indeed, tensions soon developed in the white community, as settlers of British stock fought hard to ensure that Rhodesia remained a British colony and regarded themselves as being 'more white than others'.[4]

Meanwhile, the rate at which white immigrants left for greener pastures soon after entering the country was so high that white Rhodesia was truly a nation of immigrants rather than a society rooted in the Pioneers of the early colonial period. It is interesting, for instance, that 'most of the 1965 UDI rebels who appealed to the free and proud spirit of their Pioneer ancestors to mobilize domestic support for their defiance of the world were, in fact, not descendants of the Pioneers at all', as only 27 per cent of the Rhodesian Front Party leadership were Rhodesian born.[5] Thus, even among the dominant white population, there was no real sense of nationhood or even a shared vision of what constituted 'Rhodesian-ness'. Add to this already complex mix the Asian and Coloured communities, with their own distinct cultures, and Zimbabwe's racial, cultural and ethnic complexity becomes more evident.

As if this ethnic and racial diversity was not enough, the Rhodesian and South African economies, based mainly on mining and plantation agriculture, spawned migrant labour systems that drew African labourers from as far afield as Nyasaland (Malawi), Northern Rhodesia (Zambia) and Mozambique. This labour system, well studied by historian Charles van Onselen in his seminal book *Chibharo*,[6] saw thousands of non-indigenous African workers pouring into Rhodesia to take up mining and agricultural jobs that the local Africans shunned as beneath their dignity. At the end of the contracts, many migrant labourers settled in the country with local women and raised families. By the time of independence,

---

[4] A. S. Mlambo, 'Building a White Man's Country: Trends in White Immigration into Rhodesia, 1890 to 1945', *Zambezia*, 25, 2 (1998), 123–46; A. S. Mlambo, '"Some Are More White Than Others": Racial Chauvinism as a Factor in Rhodesian Immigration Policy, 1890 to 1963', *Zambezia*, 2 (2000), 139–60; Mlambo, *White Immigration into Rhodesia*.

[5] Barry M. Schultz, 'Homeward Bound? A Survey Study of the Limits of White Rhodesian Nationalism and Permanence', *Ufahamu* 3, 3 (1975), 605.

[6] C. van Onselen, *Chibharo: African Mine Labour in Southern Rhodesia, 1900–1933* (Johannesburg: Ravan Press, 1976).

therefore, Zimbabwe was a complex mixture of various ethno-linguistic and racial groups and cultures that had to be moulded into one nation.

Colonial Rule and Its Legacy

While European colonialism brought several benefits to the country, its racist policies, which manifested themselves in a variety of ways, did not make for good race relations and the development of a common national identity between whites and the majority African population. Among the most obvious racist policies were a colour bar legislated by Southern Rhodesian Prime Minister Godfrey Huggins in his well-known 'two-pyramid policy', which was a milder version of what later became the apartheid policy of separate development in South Africa; a job reservation policy that kept certain jobs and professions exclusively for whites; the petty racial policies that were designed to humiliate Africans at every turn; and the exclusion of Africans from meaningful political and economic participation, reducing them to second-class citizens.

Under colonial rule, there were, in fact, two Rhodesias made up of, to borrow from Mahmood Mamdani, Citizens (White Rhodesians – politically and economically powerful, and enjoying full rights of citizenship) and Subjects, namely those derogatively known as the 'Natives' (the African majority who were subject to a special type of jurisprudence known as 'customary law' which was not applicable to the whites).[7] Often, when colonial administrators spoke of Rhodesians, they did not, as a rule, include Africans as full-fledged members of that group, regarding them merely as wards under the whites' paternalist care.

It was, indeed, grievances about these and other policies which contributed to the armed struggle of the 1960s and 1970s, when Africans, under the banner of two nationalist liberation movements, the Zimbabwe African People's Union (ZAPU) and the Zimbabwe African National Union (ZANU), took up arms to overthrow white rule. The armed struggle pitted African liberation forces against those fighting to defend the status quo, both whites and blacks, in the Rhodesian police, armed forces, the notorious Selous Scouts, and the Rhodesian intelligence agencies.[8]

---

[7] For this concept, see Mahmood Mamdani, *Citizen and Subject: Contemporary Africa and the Legacy of Late Colonialism* (Princeton, NJ: Princeton University Press, 1996).

[8] For an insightful discussion of the role of Africans in the defence of the Rhodesian government, see T. Stapleton, *African Police and Soldiers in Colonial Zimbabwe, 1923–80* (Rochester, NY: University of Rochester Press, 2011).

What is important here is that the armed conflict sowed deep seeds of racial hostility that would prove almost impossible to overcome after independence. As Rory Pilossof documented in his recent book,[9] when white farmers came under siege during the farm invasions of the 2000s, the terms they used to describe Africans in general and those who were invading their farms in particular were a disturbing throwback to the racist labels of liberation war period. Similarly, those who were invading white farms sang liberation war songs and chanted liberation war slogans that denounced white people. Thus, deeply embedded in the Zimbabwean psyche is the mutual hostility born of the armed conflict days – something that has militated against meaningful reconciliation which is a necessary prerequisite for true nation-building.

Further complicating the issue were the divisions among the Africans fighting colonial rule, which entrenched ethnic/political tensions rather than promoting unity and cooperation among the African people. As noted, while the two Zimbabwean liberation movements were not entirely ethnically based, as each continued to have some leaders from each of the two major ethnic groups, the movements were, however, essentially ethnically based in terms of general membership. Thus, ZAPU, under Joshua Nkomo, was mainly a Ndebele party, whereas ZANU, under Ndabaningi Sithole and, subsequently, under Robert Mugabe, was associated mostly with the Shona majority. ZANU had broken away from ZAPU in 1963, followed by bitter clashes between rival supporters of the parties until the two parties were banned by the colonial administration in 1964. The bitter rivalry between the two parties never really disappeared. It is telling, for instance, that some of the bitterest armed clashes during the years of the liberation struggle were between ZANLA (ZANU) and ZIPRA (ZAPU) fighters when they met in the field, testifying to the deepening hostility between the two groups.

The two parties did come together towards the end of the liberation struggle as the Patriotic Front (PF) in order to negotiate the handover of power to the African majority, but the partnership unravelled soon after the 1979 Lancaster House Agreement, when Mugabe's ZANU-PF decided to contest the independence general elections separately from ZAPU-PF. The old rivalry soon resurfaced when the ruling party under Mugabe's leadership accused ZAPU of being in league with bandits who had begun to attack government properties and installations in Matebeleland in protest against the manner in which their party had been sidelined after

[9] Pilossof, *The Unbearable Whiteness of Being.*

independence. Consequently, the government launched a savage military campaign in Matebeleland that ended only when ZAPU-PF agreed to merge with ZANU-PF in the 1987 Unity Agreement that virtually saw the former being swallowed up by the latter.

On the surface, the Unity Agreement appeared to have resolved the ethnic conflict of the dissident war, but the massacre of the Ndebele citizens by the Fifth Brigade had sown seeds of deep resentment among some Ndebeles, not just against the ruling ZANU-PF government but, as it was to turn out, against the Shona people in general. The result was the emergence in later years of a Ndebele ethno-nationalist movement calling itself the Mthwakazi Liberation Front (MLF), which was advocating for the secession of Matebeleland and the establishment of an independent Ndebele state.

Meanwhile, as noted, despite the announcement of reconciliation at independence, the bad blood between whites and Africans had not entirely dissipated. The 'elephant in the room' of postcolonial Zimbabwe, to paraphrase Zimbabwean historian James Muzondidya, was the unresolved question of race.[10] African resentment against the whites arose, in part, from memories of the colonial past but also from the perceived continued economic privileges enjoyed by the white population into the independence period, especially their continued domination of the economy. It was also fed by the tendency of Zimbabwean whites, for a variety of reasons, to withdraw from public political life and to retire into exclusive social spaces, such as private sport clubs with high membership fees and expensive private schools for their children. This was read by some Africans as the white people's refusal to identify with the new nation and evidence of a continuation of the social segregation of yesteryear.

As noted in Chapter 8, African hostility was particularly fuelled by the persistently skewed land distribution that left a small white farming population with most of the arable land, while Africans remained crowded in the former Native Reserves. Radical land reform by the incoming independence government had been forestalled by the 1979 Lancaster House Agreement which ruled that land could only be acquired from white farmers on a willing-buyer-willing-seller basis, and that compensation for any acquired land could only be in hard currency. In any case, the independence government had not really pushed the land reform issue for the

---

[10] J. Muzondidya, 'The Elephant in the Room: A Critical Reflection on Race in Zimbabwe's Protracted Crisis', *Zimbabwe Review* (October 2010), at http://www.solidaritypeacetrust.org (accessed 10 October 2012).

first two decades, fearing to upset the applecart and ruin the agricultural industry which was the country's proverbial cash cow. Meanwhile, it was charged at the time that, because of corruption and nepotism, acquired land for resettlement did not always go to the needy poor majority but to members of the powerful ruling elite.

Thus, by 2000, two decades after independence, land distribution remained highly skewed against the African majority. This was potentially dangerous if some demagogues of the ruling party should ever need a cause with which to inflame anti-white sentiments, for selfish party gains, as did occur after 2000 when, facing declining political popularity, the ruling party used white farmers as scapegoats for Zimbabwe's economic and political problems as a way of reviving popular support.

Meanwhile the autocratic nature of colonial rule which had not allowed African people space to voice their grievances freely or to challenge the political status quo came back to haunt the postcolonial efforts at nation-building. Just as in the colonial period, Zimbabwe's new rulers, themselves direct victims of this autocracy, were quick to resort to the use the various instruments of state repression to silence political dissent. After all, many of those who formed Zimbabwe's independence government in 1980 were members of what anti-colonial struggle activists had come to identify, proudly, as 'prison graduates'. In fact, the first independent cabinet comprised the who's who of Rhodesia's political prisoners. Among these were Joshua Nkomo and Robert Mugabe who spent no less than ten years in detention each for advocating political rights for the African majority.

Thus the programmed default position for many of the postcolonial leaders was, unfortunately, repression and the use of violence when they felt threatened by alternative political imaginations. It seems the lesson had been well learnt that political dissent was best handled by the police, prisons and the security intelligence services rather than through dialogue and negotiation. In fact, the culture of intolerance for political opponents seems to have been inherited lock stock and barrel by the new ruling elites and deployed effectively against political opponents.

In his work on postcolonial governments emerging from former liberation movements in Southern Africa, Henning Melber has pointed out the irony of the fact that those who had fought so hard to end colonial injustices tended to exhibit the very negative and repressive characteristics of the systems they fought so hard to overthrow when they became rulers of their countries. It is as if, in fighting against colonial domination and racial discrimination, liberation movements inadvertently became the very thing they were fighting against.[11] This would seem to be the case here.

Meanwhile, matters came to a head in 2000, when the ruling party, ZANU-PF, was confronted for the first time since independence in 1980 by the strongest political opposition to its rule ever in the form of the MDC. In the wake of the government's defeat in the constitutional referendum of 2000, the ruling party lashed out at those it considered its enemies, namely white farmers whom it accused of being the funders and brains behind the formation of the MDC and farm workers, many of whom it suspected of voting against the government in the referendum and at white farmers' instigation. It also attacked MDC supporters who posed such a strong challenge to ZANU-PF's hitherto unchallenged dominance. The result was commercial white farm invasions characterised by widespread violence across the land. The international outcry that accompanied these activities and the violations of human rights they entailed led to the country's ostracism by most Western governments and the subsequent economic meltdown that started the Zimbabwean crisis of the first decade of the new millennium.

In this heated atmosphere, the national project quickly unravelled, as reverse racism against whites peaked, while black-on-black violence was widespread as members of the opposition MDC were targeted by the ZANU-PF militia and some ex-fighters of the liberation war. All this mayhem occurred under the slogan of 'Zimbabwe will never be a colony again', because it was charged by the ruling party that the reaction by Western powers of ostracizing their government and imposing travel restrictions on some of them were attempts to recolonise the country by Britain and its Western allies. Thus, supporters of the ruling party now divided Zimbabweans into patriots (those in support of government policies and farm invasions) and 'sell-outs', 'traitors' or 'puppets of the West', which included anyone critical of any aspect of ZANU-PF's policies and practices.

As discussed in Chapter 9, the lowest point in the postcolonial era came with the acrimonious 2008 presidential elections which were marred by unprecedented political violence that saw one of the contestants, Tsvangirai of the MDC, withdrawing from the race in protest,

---

[11] H. Melber, 'Limits to Liberation', in H. Melber (ed.), *Re-Examining Liberation in Namibia: Political Culture since Independence* (Stockholm: Nordiska Afrikainistitutet, 2003), 9–24; H. Melber (ed.), *Limits to Liberation: The Unfinished Business of Democratic Consolidation* (Pretoria: HSRC Press, 2003); Henning Melber, 'Post-independence authoritarianism', *Development & Cooperation*, 49, 10 (2008), 378–81.

with victory being claimed by President Mugabe under very questionable circumstances. The political stalemate that resulted from these developments was partially solved only when the main Zimbabwean political parties agreed to enter into a transitional power-sharing arrangement under the Global Political Agreement (GPA) brokered by the SADC in 2009.

Zimbabwe's contested precolonial and colonial history thus did not provide a favourable and solid foundation for postcolonial nation-building or the development of a common national identity. Colonial rule and the anti-colonial armed struggle that it provoked had polarized the population along mainly racial lines, while African struggle movements were divided along largely ethnic lines in what Zimbabwean Political Scientist Masipula Sithole characterised as 'struggles within the struggle'. Meanwhile, postcolonial government policies and practices did little to unify the country.[12] At 2012, therefore, Zimbabwe was a very divided country that was characterised by tensions between some Ndebeles and the state, arising from the 1980s Gukurahundi massacres; between the state and its supporters on the one hand and whites on the other, particularly former white farmers, over the controversial land reform programme that displaced them from the land; and within the African population in general over political differences in which ZANU-PF supporters stood antagonistic to opposition movements such as the MDC and other smaller parties with regard to issues of governance and human rights. There were also divisions within ZANU-PF itself.

These challenges make the quest for a shared national identity difficult but not necessarily insurmountable. Indeed, the previous and present struggles of the Zimbabwean people for a just and democratic dispensation, which is characterised by respect for human rights and fairness and by the development of a socio-economic climate in which they can realise their full potential, are positive signs for the country's future. Given the Zimbabwean people's record of working together in the face of adversity and for a common purpose, regardless of their ethnic, cultural and political backgrounds – a trait which enabled them to successfully challenge colonial rule – there is every reason to hope that, the considerable challenges outlined above notwithstanding, Zimbabwe will succeed in becoming a united, democratic and prosperous country.

---

[12] Masipula Sithole, *Zimbabwe Struggles within the Struggle* (Harare: Rujeko Publishers, 1979).

Select Bibliography

Alexander, J. 'Dissident Perspectives of Zimbabwe's Post-Independence War', *Africa: Journal of International African Institute*, 68, 2 (1998).
The Unsettled Land: State-Making and the Politics of Land in Zimbabwe, 1893– 2003. Harare: Weaver Press, 2006.
Alexander, J. J. et al., *Violence and Memory: One Hundred Years in the 'Dark Forests' of Matebeleland*. Harare: Weaver Press, 2000.
Arrighi, G. *The Political Economy of Rhodesia*. The Hague: Mouton and Co., 1967.
'Labour Supplies in Historical Perspective: A Study of the Proletarianisation of the African Peasantry in Rhodesia', *Journal of Development Studies*, 6, 3 (1970).
Astrow, A. *Zimbabwe: A Revolution That Lost Its Way*. London: Zed Books, 1983.
Atkinson, D. N. 'The Missionary Contributions to Early Education in Rhodesia', in Dachs, J. A. (ed.), *Christianity South of the Zambezi*. Gwelo: Mambo Press, 1973.
Auret, D. *A Decade of Development, Zimbabwe 1980–1990*. Gweru: Mambo Press, 1990.
Banana, C. *Turmoil and Tenacity*. Harare: College Press, 1989.
The Politics of Repression and Resistance. Gweru: Mambo Press, 1996.
Barnes, T. A. 'The Fight for Control of African Women's Mobility in Colonial Zimbabwe, 1900–1939', *Signs: Journal of Women in Culture and Society*, 17, 3 (1992).
'"So that a labourer could live with his family": Overlooked Factors in Social and Economic Strife in Urban Colonial Zimbabwe, 1945–52', *Journal of Southern African Studies*, 21, 1 (1995).
We Women Worked So Hard: Gender, Urbanization and Social Reproduction in Colonial Harare, Zimbabwe, 1930–1956. Portsmouth: Heinemann, 1999.
Barnes, T. A. and E. Win. *To Live a Better Life: An Oral History of Women in the City of Harare 1930–70*. Harare: Baobab Books, 1992.

Beach, D. N. '"Chimurenga": The Shona Rising of 1897–1897', *Journal of African History*, 20, 3 (1979).

The Shona and Zimbabwe, 900–1850. Gweru: Mambo Press, 1980.

War and Politics in Zimbabwe, 1840–1900. Gweru: Mambo Press, 1986.

Mapondera: Heroism and History in Northern Zimbabwe, 1840–1904. Gweru: Mambo Press, 1989.

Bhebe, N. *Benjamin Burombo: African Politics in Colonial Zimbabwe, 1945–1958.* Harare: College Press, 1989.

ZAPU and ZANU Guerrilla Warfare and the Evangelical Lutheran Church in Zimbabwe. Gweru: Mambo Press, 1999.

Simon Vengesayi Muzenda and the Struggle for and Liberation of Zimbabwe. Gweru: Mambo Press, 2004.

Bhebe, N. and T. O. Ranger. *Soldiers in Zimbabwe's Liberation War.* Harare: University of Zimbabwe Publications, 1995.

Society in Zimbabwe's Liberation War. Harare: University of Zimbabwe Publications, 1996.

The Historical Dimensions of Democracy and Human Rights in Zimbabwe: Pre-Colonial and Colonial Legacies, Vol. 1. Harare: Zimbabwe University, 2001.

Bhila, H. H. K. *Trade and Politics in a Shona Kingdom: The Manyika and Their African and Portuguese Neighbours, 1575–1902.* Harlow: Longman, 1982.

Bond, P. *Uneven Zimbabwe: A Study of Finance, Development and Underdevelopment.* Trenton, NJ: Africa World Press, 1998.

Bond, P. and Masimba M. *Zimbabwe's Plunge: Exhausted Nationalism, Neo-Liberalism, and the Search for Social Justice.* Harare: Weaver Press, 2003.

Bruwer, A. J. *Zimbabwe: Rhodesia's Ancient Greatness.* Johannesburg: Hugh Keartland Publishers, 1965.

Burke, T. *Lifebouy Men, Lux Women: Commodification, Consumption and Cleanliness in Modern Zimbabwe.* Durham, NC: Duke University Press, 1996.

Cairns, H. *Prelude to Imperialism: British Reactions to Central African Society, 1840–1890.* London: Routledge and Kegan Paul, 1965.

Carver, R. and D. Saunders. 'Zimbabwe's Biased Health Service', *New African* (August 1980).

Catholic Commission for Justice and Peace in Zimbabwe and Legal Resources Foundation. *Breaking the Silence, Building True Peace: Report on the Disturbances in Matebeleland and the Midlands, 1980–1989.* Harare: CCJPZ and LRF, 1997.

Catholic Commission for Justice and Peace and the Legal Resources Foundation. *Gukurahundi in Zimbabwe: A Report on the Disturbances in Matebeleland and the Midlands, 1980–1988* (2008).

Caute, D. *Under the Skin: The Death of White Rhodesia.* Evanston, IL: Northwestern University Press, 1983.

Chan, S. *Robert Mugabe: A Life of Power and Violence.* Ann Arbor: University of Michigan Press, 2003.

Chanaiwa, D. 'Politics and Long Distance Trade in the Mwene Mutapa Empire during the Sixteenth Century', *The International Journal of African Historical Studies*, 5, 3 (1972).

The Zimbabwe Controversy: A Case of Colonial Historiography. New York: Maxwell School of Citizenship and Public Affairs, 1973.

Chaza, G. A. *Bhurakuwacha: Black Policeman in Rhodesia*. Harare: College Press, 1998.

Cheater, A. P. 'The Role and Position of Women on Pre-Colonial and Colonial Zimbabwe', *Zambezia*, 13, 2 (1986).

Chikanda, A. 'The Migration of Health Professionals from Zimbabwe', in J. Connell (ed.), *The International Migration of Health Workers*. London: Routledge, 2008.

Chikowero, M. '"Our People Father, They Haven't Learned Yet": Music and Postcolonial Identities in Zimbabwe, 1980–2000', *Journal of Southern African Studies*, 34, 1 (2008).

Chimhundu, H. 'Early Missionaries and the Ethnolinguistic Factor during the "Invention of Tribalism" in Zimbabwe', *Journal of African History*, 33, 1 (1992).

Chung, F. *Re-Living the Second Chimurenga: Memories from Zimbabwe's Liberation Struggle* Harare: Weaver Press, 2005.

Clarke, D. G. *Agricultural and Plantation Workers in Rhodesia: A Report on the Conditions of Labour and Subsistence*. Gwelo: Mambo Press, 1971.

Contract Workers and Underdevelopment in Rhodesia. Gwelo: Mambo Press, 1974.

Clements, F. *Rhodesia: The Course to Collision*. London: Pall Mall, 1969.

Cobbing. J. 'The Absent Priesthood: Another Look at the Rhodesian Risings of 1896–1897', *Journal of African History*, 18, 1 (1977).

'The Mfecane as Alibi: Thoughts on Dithakong and Mbolomo', *Journal of African History*, 29 (1988).

Cooper, F. *Africa since 1940: The Past of the Present*. Cambridge: Cambridge University Press, 2002.

Creighton, T. R. M. *The Anatomy of Partnership: Southern Rhodesia and the Central African Federation*. London: Faber, 1960.

Crush, J. and D. Tevera (eds.). *Zimbabwe's Exodus: Crisis, Migration, Survival*. Kingston; Cape Town: SAMP, 2010.

Curtin, P. *The Image of Africa: British Ideas and Action 1780–1850*. Madison: University of Wisconsin Press, 1973.

Darnolf, S. and L. Laasko (eds.). *Twenty Years of Independence in Zimbabwe: From Liberation to Authoritarianism*. London: Routledge, 1967.

De Roche, A. *Black, White and Chrome: The United States and Zimbabwe, 1953–1998*. Trenton, NJ: Africa World Press, 2001.

Dube, C. 'The Changing Context of African Music Performance in Zimbabwe', *Zambezia*, 23, 2 (1996).

Dumbutshena, E. *Zimbabwe Tragedy*. Nairobi: East African Publication House, 1975.

Dzimba, J. *South Africa's Destabilisation of Zimbabwe, 1980–89*. London: Palgrave Macmillan, 1998.

Economist Intelligence Unit. *Zimbabwe's First Five Years: Economic Prospects Following Independence*. London: The Unit, Special Report 11, 1981.

Ellert, H. *The Rhodesian Front War: Counter-Insurgency and Guerrilla Warfare, 1962–1980*. Gweru: Mambo Press, 1989.

Flower, K. *Serving Secretly: Rhodesia to Zimbabwe 1964–1981*. London: John Murray, 1987.

Frederikse, J. *None but Ourselves: Masses vs. Media in the Making of Zimbabwe*. Harare: Zimbabwe Publishing House, 1982.

Gaidzanwa, R. *Voting with Their Feet: Migrant Zimbabwean Nurses and Doctors in the Era of Structural Adjustment*. Uppsala: Nordiska Afrikainstitutet, 1999.

Gale, W. *The Years between, 1923–1973: Half a Century of Responsible Government in Rhodesia*. Salisbury: H. C. P. Andersen, 1973.

Gann, L. *A History of Southern Rhodesia*. London: Chatto & Windus, 1965.

Garlake, P. S. *Great Zimbabwe Described and Explained*. London: Thames and Hudson, 1973.

The Painted Caves: An Introduction to the Prehistoric Art of Zimbabwe. Harare: Modus Publications, 1987.

Gelfand, M. (ed.). *Godfrey Huggins: Viscount Malvern, 1883–1971 – His Life and Work*. Salisbury: Central African Journal of Medicine, n.d.

Gilmurray, J., R. Riddell and D. Sanders. *From Rhodesia to Zimbabwe: The Struggle for Health*. London: Catholic Institute for International Relations, 1979.

Godwin, P. and I. Hancock. *Rhodesians Never Die: The Impact of War and Political Change on White Rhodesia c.1970–1980*. Oxford: Oxford University Press, 1993; Harare: Baobab Books, 1995.

Gray, R. *The Two Nations*. London: Oxford University Press, 1960.

Hachipola, A. J. *A Survey of the Minority Languages in Zimbabwe*. Harare: University of Zimbabwe Publications, 1998.

Hallencreutz, C. and A. Moyo (eds.). *Church and State in Zimbabwe*, Gweru: Mambo Press, 1988.

Hamilton, Carolyn (ed.). *The Mfecane Aftermath: Reconstructive Debates in Southern African History*. Johannesburg: Witwatersrand University Press, 1995.

Hammar, A., B. Raftopoulos and S. Jensen (eds.). *Zimbabwe's Unfinished Business: Rethinking Land, State and Nation in the Context of the Crisis*. Harare: Weaver Press, 2003.

Handford, J. *A Portrait of an Economy under Sanctions, 1965–1975*. Salisbury: Mercury Press, 1976.

Hanlon, J. *Beggar Your Neighbours: Apartheid Power in Southern Africa*. London: Catholic Institute for International Relations, 1986.

Hanna, A. J. *The Story of the Rhodesias and Nyasaland*. London: Oxford University Press, 1960.

Herbst, J. *State Politics in Zimbabwe*. Harare: University of Zimbabwe Publications, 1990.

Hobson, J. A. *Imperialism: A Study*. London: Allen and Unwin, 1948.

Hodder-Williams, R. *White Farmers in Rhodesia, 1890–1965*. London: Macmillan Press, 1983.

Hofstadter, R. *Social Darwinism in American Thought.* Boston: Bacon Press, 1944.

Holderness, H. *Lost Chance: Southern Rhodesia 1945–58.* Harare: Zimbabwe Publishing House, 1985.

Horne, G. *From the Barrel of a Gun: The United States and the War against Zimbabwe, 1965–1980.* Chapel Hill: The University of North Carolina Press, 2001.

Huffman, T. N. *The Leopard Kopje Tradition.* Salisbury: Trustees of the National Museums and Monuments of Rhodesia, 1974.

Hyam, R. 'The Geographical Origins of the Central African Federation: Britain, Rhodesia and South Africa, 1948–1953', *Historical Journal*, 30, 1 (1987).

Isaac, J. *British Post-War Migration.* Cambridge: Cambridge University Press, 1954.

Itote, W. *'Mau Mau' General.* Nairobi: East African Publishing House, 1967.

Jardim, J. *Sanctions Double Cross: Oil to Rhodesia.* Bulawayo: Books of Rhodesia, 1979.

Jeater, D. *Marriage, Perversion and Power: The Construction of Moral discourse in Southern Rhodesia 1894–1930.* Oxford: Oxford University Press, 1993.

Kapungu, L. *The United Nations and Economic Sanctions against Rhodesia.* Lexington: Lexington Press, 1973.

Katiyo, W. *A Son of the Soil.* London: Rex Collings, 1976.

Kennedy, D. *Islands of White: Settler Society and Culture in Kenya and Southern Rhodesia, 1890–1939.* Durhan, NC: Duke University Press, 1987.

Keppel-Jones, A. *Rhodes and Rhodesia: The White Conquest of Zimbabwe, 1884–1902.* Montreal and Kingston: McGill-Queen's University Press, 1983.

Kramer, E. 'A Clash of Economies: Early Centralisation Efforts in Colonial Zimbabwe, 1929–1935', *Zambezia*, 25, 1 (1998).

Kriger, N. *Zimbabwe's Guerrilla War: Peasant Voices.* Cambridge: Cambridge University Press, 1992.

  Guerrilla Veterans in Post-War Zimbabwe: Symbolic and Violent Politics, 1980–1987. Cambridge and New York: Cambridge University Press, 2003.

Kwaramba, A. D. *Popular Music and Society: The Language of Chimurenga Music. The Case of Thomas Mapfumo in Zimbabwe.* Oslo: University of Oslo, 1997.

Lan, D. *Guns and Rain: Guerrillas & Spirit Mediums in Zimbabwe.* Harare: Zimbabwe Publishing House, 1985.

Lee, M. C. and K. Colvard (eds.). *Unfinished Business: The Land Crisis in Southern Africa.* Pretoria: Africa Institute of South Africa, 2003.

Leisegang, G. J. 'Nguni Migrations between Delagoa Bay and the Zambezi, 1821–1939', *African Historical Studies*, 3, 2 (1970).

  'Aspects of Gaza Nguni History', *Rhodesian History*, 6 (1975).

Lenin, V. I. *Imperialism: The Highest State of Capitalism.* Petrograd: Progressive Publishers, 1917.

Lessing, D. *The Grass Is Singing.* London: Heinemann, 1950.

Loney, M. *Rhodesia: White Racism and Imperial Response.* Harmondsworth: Penguin, 1975.

Lunn, J. 'The Political Economy of Primary Railway Construction in the Rhodesias, 1890–1911', *Journal of African History*, 33, 2 (1992).

Lyons, T. *Guns and Guerrilla Girls: Women in Zimbabwe's Liberation Struggle.* Trenton, NJ: Africa World Press, 2004.

MacGonagle, E. *Crafting Identity in Zimbabwe and Mozambique.* Rochester, NY: University of Rochester Press, 2007.

Machingaidze, V. E. M. 'Agrarian Change from Above: The Southern Rhodesia native Land Husbandry Act and African Response', *International Journal of African Historical Studies*, 24, 3 (1991).

Machingura, D. *Dzino: Memories of a Freedom Fighter.* Harare: Weaver Press, 2011.

Makwenda, J. J. *Zimbabwe Township Music.* Harare: Storytime Promotions, 2005.

Mamdani, M. *Citizen and Subject: Contemporary Africa and the Legacy of Late Colonialism.* Princeton, NJ: Princeton University Press, 1996.

Mandaza, I. (ed.). *Zimbabwe: The Political Economy of Transition 1980–1986.* Dakar: Codesria, 1986.

Mandaza, I. and L. Sachikonye (eds.). *The One-Party State and Democracy: The Zimbabwe Debate.* Harare: SAPES Trust, 1991.

Manungo. K. D. *The Role the Peasants Played in the Zimbabwe War of Liberation, with Special Emphasis on Chiweshe District* D.Phil. thesis, Ohio University, 1991.

Manyanga, M. *Resilient Landscapes: Socio-Environmental Dynamics in the Shashi-Limpopo Basin Southern Zimbabwe c. AD 800 to the Present.* Uppsala: Department of Archaeology and Ancient History 2007.

Marechera, D. *The House of Hunger: Short Stories.* London: Heinemann, 1978; Harare: Zimbabwe Publishing House, 1982.

Martin, D. and P. Johnson. *The Struggle for Zimbabwe.* Harare: ZPH, 1981; Bloomington and Indianapolis: Indiana State University Press, 2000.

McGregor, J. 'The Politics of Disruption: War Veterans and the Local State in Zimbabwe', *African Affairs*, 101 (2002).

McLaughlin, J. *On the Frontline: Catholic Missions in Zimbabwe's Liberation War.* Harare: Baobab Books, 1996.

Melber, H. (ed.). *Limits to Liberation in Southern Africa: The Unfinished Business of Democratic Consolidation.* Cape Town: HSRC Press, 2003.

Meredith, M. *The Past is Another Country: Rhodesia, UDI to Zimbabwe.* London: Pan Books, 1980.

Minter, M. and E. Schmidt, 'When Sanctions Worked: The Case of Rhodesia Re-Examined', *African Affairs*, 87, 347 (1988).

Mlambo, A. S. 'Civil Aviation in Colonial Zimbabwe, 1912–1980', *Zambezia*, 19, 2 (1992).

'From Dirt Tracks to Modern Highways: Towards a History of Roads and Road Transportation in Colonial Zimbabwe, 1890 to World War II', *Zambezia*, 21, 2 (1994).

'A Decade of Civil Aviation in Zimbabwe: Towards a History of Air Zimbabwe Corporation, 1980–19190', *Zambezia*, 22, 1 (1995).

'The Cold Storage Commission: A Colonial Parastatal, 1938–1963', *Zambezia*, 23, 1 (1996).

The Economic Structural Adjustment Programme: The Zimbabwean Case, 1990–1995. Harare: University of Zimbabwe Publications, 1997.

'"Some Are More White Than Others": Racial Chauvinism as a Factor in Rhodesian Migration Policy, 1890 to 1963', *Zambezia*, 27, 2 (2000).

White Immigration into Rhodesia: From Occupation to Federation. Harare: University of Zimbabwe Publications, 2003.

'Land Grab or Taking Back Stolen Land: The Fast Track Land Reform Process in Zimbabwe in Historical Perspective', *Compass* (July 2005a).

'Postcolonial Higher Education in Zimbabwe: The University of Zimbabwe as a Case Study, 1980–2004', *Kleio*, 37 (2005b).

'Prelude to the 1979 Lancaster House Constitutional Conference on Rhodesia: The Role of International Sanctions Reconsidered', *Historia*, 50, 1 (2005c).

'We Have Blood Relations Over the Border: South Africa and Rhodesian Sanctions, 1965–1975', *African Historical Review*, 40, 1 (July 2008).

'A History of Zimbabwean Migration to 1990', in Crush, J. and S. Tevera (eds.), *Zimbabwe Exodus: Crisis, Migration, Survival.* Cape Town: IDRC, 2010a.

'"This Is Our Land": The Racialization of Land in the Context of the Current Zimbabwe Crisis', *Journal of Developing Societies*, 26 (2010b).

Mlambo, A. S. and E. S. Pangeti, *The Political Economy of the Zimbabwean Sugar Industry, 1920–1990.* Harare: University of Zimbabwe Publications, 1996.

Mlambo, A. S., E. S. Pangeti, and I. Phimister, *Zimbabwe: A History of Manufacturing, 1890–1995.* Harare: University of Zimbabwe Publications, 2000.

Mlambo, A. S. and I. Phimister, 'Partly Protected: The Origins and Growth of Colonial Zimbabwe's Textile Industry', *Historia*, 51, 2 (2006).

Mlambo, E. *Rhodesia: The Struggle for a Birthright.* London: Hurst, 1972.

Moore, D. 'Democracy, Violence and Identity in the Zimbabwean War of National Liberation: Reflections from Realms of Dissent', *Canadian Journal of African Studies*, 29, 3 (1995).

Morris, W. H. and D. Austin (eds.). *From Rhodesia to Zimbabwe.* London: Cass, 1980.

Morris-Jones, W. H. *From Rhodesia to Zimbabwe: Behind and beyond Lancaster House.* London: Frank Cass, 1980.

Mosley, P. *The Settler Economies: Studies in the Economic History of Kenya and Southern Rhodesia 1900–1963.* Cambridge: Cambridge University Press, 1903.

Mothibe, T. H. 'Zimbabwe: African Working Class Nationalism 1957–1963', *Zambezia*, 23, 2 (1996).

Moyana, H. V. *The Political Economy of Land in Zimbabwe.* Gweru: Mambo Press, 2002.

Moyo, S. *The Land Question in Zimbabwe.* Harare: SAPES Books, 1995.

'The Political Economy of land Acquisition and Redistribution in Zimbabwe, 1990–1999', *Journal of Southern African Studies*, 26, 1 (2000).

'The Land Occupation Movement and Democratisation in Zimbabwe: Contradictions of Neo-Liberalism', *Millennium: Journal of International Studies*, 30, 2 (2001).

Moyo, S. and P. Yeros. *Reclaiming Land: The Resurgence of Rural Movements in Africa, Asia and Latin America*. Cape Town: David Phillip, 2005.

Msindo, E. 'Ethnicity and Nationalism in Urban Colonial Zimbabwe: Bulawayo, 1950–1963', *Journal of African History*, 48 (2007).

Mudenge, S. I. G. *A Political History of Munhumutapa c. 1400–1902*. Harare: Zimbabwe Publishing House, 1988.

Mugabe, R. G. *Inside the Third Chimurenga: Our Land in Our Prosperity*. Harare: Government of Zimbabwe, 2001.

Mungoshi, C. L. *Coming of the Dry Season*. Oxford: Oxford University Press, 1972; Salisbury: Zimbabwe Publishing House, 1981a.

Waiting for the Rain. London: Heinemann, 1975; Salisbury: Zimbabwe Publishing House, 1981b.

Musemwa, M. 'The Ambiguities of Democracy: The Demobilisation of the Zimbabwean Ex-Combatants and the Ordeal of Rehabilitation, 1980–1993', *Transformation*, 26 (1995).

Mutswairo, S. *Chaminuka: Prophet of Zimbabwe*. Washington, DC: Three Continents Press, 1983a.

Mapondera: Soldier of Zimbabwe. Harare: Longman Zimbabwe, 1983b.

Muzondidya, J. *Walking a Tightrope: Towards a Social History of Coloured People of Zimbabwe*, Asmara: Africa World Press, 2004.

'Echoing Silences: Ethnicity in Post-Colonial Zimbabwe, 1980–2007', *African Journal of Conflict Resolution*, 27, 2 (2007a).

'*Jambanja*: Ideological Ambiguities in the Politics of land and Resource Ownership in Zimbabwe', *Journal of Southern African History*, 33, 2 (2007b).

'The Zimbabwean Crisis and the Unresolved Conundrum of Race in the Post-Colonial Period', *Journal of Developing Societies*, 26, 1 (2010).

Muzondidya, J. and S. Ndlovu-Gatsheni. 'Echoing Silences: Ethnicity in Post-colonial Zimbabwe, 1980–2007', *African Journal of Conflict Resolution*, 27, 2 (2007).

Muzorewa, A. T. *Rise Up and Walk: An Autobiography*. London: Evans, 1979.

Ndlovu-Gatsheni, S. 'Re-Thinking the Colonial Encounter in Zimbabwe in the Early Twentieth Century', *Journal of Southern African Studies*, 33, 1 (2007).

Do 'Zimbabweans' Exist: Trajectories of Nationalism, National Identity Formation and Crisis in a Postcolonial State. Oxford: Peter Land, 2009a.

The Ndebele Nation: Hegemony, Memory, Historiography. Pretoria: UNISA Press, 2009b.

Nhongo-Simbanegavi, J. *For Better or For Worse? Women and ZANLA in Zimbabwe's Liberation Struggle*. Harare: Weaver Press, 2000.

Nkomo, J. *The Story of My Life*. London: Methuen, 1984.

Nyagumbo, M. *With the People*. Salisbury: Graham Publishing, 1980.

Nyambara, P. S. 'The Politics of Land Acquisition and Struggles over Land in the "Communal" Areas of Zimbabwe: The Gokwe Region in the 1980s and 1990s', *Africa*, 71, 2 (2001).

'Madheruka and Shangwe: Ethnic Identities and the Culture of Modernity in Gokwe, Northwestern Zimbabwe, 1963', *Journal of African History*, 42 (2002).

Okoth, A. *A History of Africa: African Societies and the Establishment of Colonial Rule 1899–1915, Volume 1.* Nairobi: East African Educational Publishers, 2006.

Omer-Cooper, J. D. *The Zulu Aftermath: Revolution in Bantu Africa.* London: Longman, 1966.

Palley, C. *The Constitutional History and Law of Southern Rhodesia, 1898–1965.* Oxford: Oxford University Press, 1966.

Palmer, C. 'Land Reform in Zimbabwe, 1980–1990', *African Affairs*, 89 (1990).

Palmer, R. 'Red Soils in Rhodesia', *African Social Research*, 10 (December 1970).

Land and Racial Domination. London: Heinemann, 1977.

Palmer, R. and I. Birch. *Zimbabwe: A Land Divided.* Oxford: Oxfam, 1992.

Palmer R. and N. Parsons (eds.). *The Roots of Rural Poverty in Central and Southern Africa.* London: Heinemann, 1977.

Pangeti, E. S. *The State and the Manufacturing Industry: A Study of the State as Regulator and Entrepreneur in Zimbabwe, 1930–1990*, D.Phil. thesis, University of Zimbabwe, 1995.

Pape, J. 'Black and White: The "Perils of Sex" in Colonial Zimbabwe', *Journal of Southern African Studies*, 16, 4 (1990).

Phimister, I. 'Peasant Production and Underdevelopment in Southern Rhodesia, 1890–1914', *African Affairs*, 73, 291 (1974).

'Meat Monopolies: Beef Cattle in Southern Rhodesia, 1890–1938', *Journal of African History*, 19, 3 (1978).

'Accommodating Imperialism: The Compromise of the Settler State in Southern Rhodesia, 1923–1929', *Journal of African History*, 25, 3 (1984).

An Economic and Social History of Zimbabwe, 1890–1948: Capital Accumulation and Class Struggle. London: Longman, 1988.

'Rethinking the Reserves: Southern Rhodesia's Land Husbandry Act Reviewed', *Journal of Southern African Studies*, 19, 2 (1993).

'The Origins and Development of Manufacturing in Southern Rhodesia, 1894–1939', in A. S. Mlambo, E. S. Pangeti, and I. Phimister (eds.), *Zimbabwe: A History of Manufacturing 1890–1995.* Harare: University of Zimbabwe Publications, 2000.

'Speculation and Exploitation: The Southern Rhodesian Mining Industry in the Company Era', *Zambezia*, 30, 2 (2003).

Phimister, I. and B. Raftopoulos. '"Kana Sora Ratsva Ngaritsve": African Nationalists and Black Workers: The 1948 General Strike in Colonial Zimbabwe', *Journal of Historical Sociology*, 13, 3 (2000).

Pikirayi, I. *The Zimbabwe Culture: Origins and Decline of Southern Zambezian States.* Walnut Creek, CA: Altamira Press, 2001.

Pilosoff, R. *The Unbearable Whiteness of Being: Farmers' Voices in Zimbabwe.* Harare: Weaver Press, 2012.

Pongweni, A. J. C. *Songs that Won the Liberation War.* Harare: College Press, 1982.

Punt, E. *The Development of African Agriculture in Southern Rhodesia with particular Reference to the Inter-War Years.* M.A. thesis, University of Natal, 1997.

Pwiti, G. 'Trade and Economies in Southern Africa: The Archaeological Evidence', *Zambezia*, 18 (1991).

Continuity and Change: An Archaeological Study of Farming Communities in Northern Zimbabwe, AD 500–1700. Uppsala: Department of Archaeology, 1996.

Caves, Monuments and Texts: Zimbabwean Archaeology Today. Uppsala: Department of Archaeology and Ancient History, 1997.

Raeburn, M. *Black Fire! Accounts of the Guerrilla War in Zimbabwe*. Harare: Mambo Press, 1986.

Raftopoulos, B. *Zimbabwe: Race and Nationalism in a Post-Colonial State*. Harare: SAPES Books, 1996.

'Problematising Nationalism in Zimbabwe: A Historiographical Review', *Zambezia*, 26, 2 (1999).

(ed.). *The Hard Road to Reform: The Politics of Zimbabwe's Global Political Agreement*. Harare: Weaver Press, 2013.

Raftopoulos, B. and A. Mlambo (eds.). *Becoming Zimbabwe: A History from the Pre-Colonial Period to 2008*. Harare: Weaver Press, 2009.

Raftopoulos, B. and I. Phimister. *Keep on Knocking: History of the Labour Movement in Zimbabwe 1900–97*. Harare: Baobab Books, 1997.

Raftopoulos, B. and L. Sachikonye (eds.). *Striking Back: The Labour Movement and the Post-Colonial State in Zimbabwe, 1980–2000*. Harare: Weaver Press, 2001.

Raftopoulos, B. and T. Savage (eds.). *Zimbabwe: Injustice and Political Reconciliation*. Cape Town: Institute for Justice and Reconciliation, 2004.

Raftopoulos, B. and T. Yoshikuni, *Sites of Struggle*. Harare: Weaver Press, 1999.

Ranger, T. 'The Role of Shona and Ndebele Religious Authorities in the Rebellions of 1896 and 1897', in E. Stokes and R. Brown (eds.), *The Zambezi Past: Studies in Central African History*. Manchester: Manchester University Press, 1966.

Revolt in Southern Rhodesia, 1986–97: A Study in African Resistance. Evanston: Northwestern University Press, 1967.

The African Voice in Southern Rhodesia, 1898–1930. London: Heinemann, 1970.

Peasant Consciousness & Guerrilla War in Zimbabwe. London: James Currey, 1985.

Peasant Consciousness and Guerrilla War in Zimbabwe: A Comparative Study. London: James Currey, 1985.

Are We Not Also Men? The Samkange Family and African Politics in Zimbabwe. Harare: Baobab Books, 1995.

Voices from the Rocks: Nature, Culture, and History in the Matopos Hills of Zimbabwe. Harare: Baobab Books, 1999.

'Nationalist Historiography, Patriotic History and the History of the Nation: The Struggle Over the Past in Zimbabwe', *Journal of Southern African Studies*, 30, 2 (2004).

Bulawayo Burning: The Social History of a Southern African City, 1893–1960, Oxford: James Currey, 2010.

Ranger, T. and N. Bhebe (eds.). *Society in Zimbabwe's Liberation War*. Harare: University of Zimbabwe Publications, 1996.

Rasmussen, R. K. *Migrant Kingdom: Mzilikazi's Ndebele in South Africa*. Cape Town: Rex Collings, 1978.

Riddell, R. 'Zimbabwe's Land Problem: The Central Issue', in W. H. Morris-Jones (ed.), *From Rhodesia to Zimbabwe: Behind and Beyond Lancaster House*. London: Frank Cass, 1980.

Rupiya, M. 'Demobilisation and Integration: "Operation Merger" and the Zimbabwe National Defence Forces, 1980–1987', *Africa Security Review*, 4, 3 (1995).

Rutherford, B. *Working on the Margins: Black Workers, White Farmers in Postcolonial Zimbabwe*. Harare: Weaver Press, 2001.

Sachikonye, L. 'Between Authoritarianism and Democracy: Politics in Zimbabwe since 1990', in M. Lee and K. Colvard (eds.), *Unfinished Business: The Land Crisis in Southern Africa* Pretoria: Africa Institute of South Africa, 2003.

  When a State Turns on Its Citizens: Institutionalised Violence and Political Culture. Johannesburg: Jacana Media, 2011.

Sadomba, Z. W. *War Veterans in Zimbabwe's Revolution: Challenging Neo-Colonialism, Settler and International Capital*. Harare: Weaver Press, 2011.

Samkange, S. *On Trial for My Country*. London: Heinemann, 1966.

  The Origins of Rhodesia. London: Heinemann, 1968.

  The Mourned One. London: Heinemann, 1975.

  Year of the Uprising. London, Heinemann, 1978.

Saunders, R. 'Economic Structural Adjustment Programme (ESAP)'s Fables', *Southern Africa Report Archive*, 11, 4 (1996).

Scarnecchia, T. 'Poor Women and Nationalist Politics: Alliances and Fissures in the Formation of a Nationalist Political Movement in Salisbury, Rhodesia, 1950–56', *Journal of African History*, 37, 3 (1996).

  The Urban Roots of Democracy and Political Violence in Zimbabwe: Harare and Highfield, 1940–1964. Rochester, NY: University of Rochester Press, 2008.

Schmidt, E. 'Farmers, Hunters and Gold Washers: A Re-Evaluation of Women's Roles in Pre-Colonial and Colonial Zimbabwe', *African Economic History*, 17 (1988).

  'Negotiated Spaces and contested Terrain: Men, Women and the Law in Colonial Zimbabwe, 1890–1939', *Journal of Southern African Studies*, 16, 4 (1990).

  'Patriarchy, Capitalism and the Colonial State in Zimbabwe', *Signs: Journal of Women in Culture and Society*, 16, 4 (1991).

  Peasants, Traders, & Wives: Shona. Harare: Baobab, 1992.

Schmidt, H. I. *Colonialism and Violence in Zimbabwe: A History of Suffering*. Suffolk: James Currey, 2013.

Schultz, B. 'European Population Patterns, cultural Resistance and Political Change in Rhodesia', *Canadian Journal of African Studies*, 7, 1 (1973).

  'Homeward Bound? A Survey Study of the Limits of White Rhodesian Nationalism and Permanence', *Ufahamu*, 5, 3 (1975).

Scoones, I. et al. *Zimbabwe's Land Reform: Myths and Realities*. Oxford: James Currey, 2010.

Selby, A. *Commercial Farmers and the State: Interest Group Politics and Land Reform in Zimbabwe*. D.Phil. thesis, Oxford University, 1965.

Shamuyarira, N. *Crisis in Rhodesia*. London: Deutsch, 1965.

Shillington, K. *History of Africa*, 2nd ed. New York: Macmillan, 2005.

Shutt, A. 'The Natives Are Getting Out of Hand: Legislating Manners, Insolence and Contemptuous Behaviour in Southern Rhodesia c. 1910–1963', *Journal of Southern African Studies*, 33, 2 (2007).

Sibanda, E. *The Zimbabwe African People's Union, 1961–87: A Political History of Insurgency in Southern Rhodesia*. Trento, NJ: Africa World Press, 2005.

Sithole, M. *Zimbabwe Struggles within the Struggles*. Harare: Rujeko Publishers, 1979.

  'Ethnicity and Factionalism in Zimbabwean Nationalist Politics, 1957–79', *Ethnic and Racial Studies*, 3, 1 (1980).

Sithole, N. *African Nationalism*. London: Oxford University Press, 1968.

Smith, I. D. *The Great Betrayal: The Memoirs of Ian Douglas Smith*. London: Blake, 1997.

Stapleton, T. J. *African Police and Soldiers in Colonial Zimbabwe, 1923–80*. New York: Rochester Press, 2011.

Stoneman, C. (ed.). *Zimbabwe's Inheritance*. London: Macmillan, 1981.

  (ed.). *Zimbabwe's Prospects: Issues of Race, Class, State and Capital in Southern Africa*. London: Macmillan, 1988.

Strack, H. R. *Sanctions: The Case of Rhodesia*. Syracuse, NY: Syracuse University Press, 1978.

Sutcliffe, P. 'The Political Economy of Rhodesian Sanctions', *Journal of Commonwealth Political Studies*, 7 (1979).

Sylvester, C. *Zimbabwe: A Terrain of Contradictory Development*. Boulder, CO: Westview Press, 1991.

Tekere, E. *Edgar '2-Boy' Zivanayi Tekere: A Lifetime of Struggle*. Harare: Sapes Books, 2007.

Tendi, M. B. *Making History in Mugabe's Zimbabwe*. Oxford: Peter Land, 2010.

Tevera, D. and J. Crush. *The New Brain Drain from Zimbabwe*. Cape Town: SAMP Migration Series, No. 29, 2003.

Tibaijuka, A. K. *Report of the Fact-Finding Mission to Zimbabwe to Assess the Scope and Impact of Operation Murambatsvina by the UN Special Envoy on human Settlements Issues in Zimbabwe*. New York: UNHCS-Habitat, 2005.

Thompson, C. B. *Challenge to Imperialism: The Frontline States in the Liberation of Zimbabwe*. Harare: Zimbabwe Publishing House, 1986.

Todd, J. *The Right to Say No*. London: Sidgwick and Jackson, 1972.

  Through the Darkness: A Life in Zimbabwe. Cape Town: Zebra Press, 2007.

Tsvangirai, M. *At the Deep End*. Johannesburg: Penguin Group, 2011.

Vambe, L. *An Ill-Fated People*. London: Heinemann, 1972.

  From Rhodesia to Zimbabwe. London: Heinemann, 1976.

Vambe, M. T. 'Versions and Sub-Versions: Trends in Chimurenga Musical Discourses of Post-Independence Zimbabwe', *African Study Monographs*, 25, 4 (2004).

Van Onselen, C. *Chibaro: African Mine Labour in Southern Rhodesia, 1900–1933*. Johannesburg: Ravan Press, 1976.

Vickery, K. P. 'The Rhodesian Railways African Strike of 1945, Part I: A Narrative Account', *Journal of Southern African Studies*, 24, 3 (1998).

'The Rhodesian Railways African Strike of 1945, Part II: Cause, Consequence, Significance', *Journal of Southern African Studies*, 25, 1 (1999).

Weitzer, R. J. *Transforming Settler States: Communal Conflict and Internal Security in Northern Ireland and Zimbabwe*. Berkeley and Los Angeles: University of California Press, 1990.

Welensky, R. *Welensky's 400 Days: The Life and Death of the Federation of Rhodesia and Nyasaland*. London: Collins, 1964.

West, M. O. *The Rise of an African Middle Class: Colonial Zimbabwe, 1898–1965*. Bloomington: Indiana University Press, 2002.

'The Seeds are Sown: The Impact of Garveyism in Zimbabwe in the Interwar Years', *International Journal of African Historical Studies*, 35, 2–3 (2002).

White, L. *The Assassination of Herbert Chitepo: Texts and Politics in Zimbabwe*. Bloomington: Indiana University Press, 2003.

Yoshikuni, T. 'Strike Action and Self-Help Associations: Zimbabwean Worker Protest and Culture after World War I', *Journal of Southern African Studies*, 15, 3 (1989).

'African Harare, 1890–1925: Labor Migrancy and an Emerging Urban Community', *African Study Monographs*, 12, 3 (1990).

African Urban Experiences in Colonial Zimbabwe: A Social History of Harare before 1925. Harare: Weaver Press, 2007.

Yudelman, M. *Africans on the Land*. London: Oxford University Press, 1964.

Zacchrisson, P. *An African Area in Change: Belingwe 1894–1946*. Gothenburg: University of Gothenburg, 1978.

Zimbabwe Women Writers (eds.). *Women of Resilience: The Voices of Women Ex-Combatants*. Harare: Zimbabwe Women Writers, 2000.

Zimudzi, T. 'Spies and Informers on Campus: Vetting, Surveillance and Deportation of Expatriate University Lecturers in Colonial Zimbabwe, 1954–1963', *Journal of Southern African Studies*, 33, 1 (2007).

Zimunya, M. B. 'Music in Zimbabwean History: Music as Historical Communication', in M. B. Zimunya (ed.), *Media, Culture and Development*. Oslo: Department of Media and Communication, 1993.

Zinyama, L. M. D., D. S. Tevera and S. D. Cumming (eds.). *Harare: The Growth and Problems of the City*. Harare: University of Zimbabwe Publications, 1993.

Zvobgo, C. J. M. 'Christian Missionaries and the Establishment of Colonial Rule in Zimbabwe, 1888–1898', *Journal of Southern African Affairs*, 2, 1 (1977).

'Medical Missions: A Neglected Theme in Zimbabwe's History, 1893–1957', *Zambezia*, 13, ii (1986).

A History of Christian Missions in Zimbabwe, 1890–1939. Gweru: Mambo Press, 1996.

Index